MAKING GLOBALIZATION GOOD

The Moral Challenges of
Global Capitalism

'This book explores one of most fundamental questions of our time—the relationship between business and society and its moral underpinning. The arguments made are powerful and important for policy makers, business people, and scholars alike. Clearly, the book fills an important void in discussions about globalization and gives valuable perspectives and practical solutions towards a more responsible global capitalism.'

Georg Kell, Executive Head of Global Compact, United Nations

'In the opinion of the majority of the world's population global capitalism is under judgement. This timely and very important book addresses the moral questions that demand answers, and should be required reading for all business leaders, politicians, and all who long for a better world.'

Lord George Carey, Former Archbishop of Canterbury

'These essays are essential reading for those who wonder whether global capitalism can become a force for good in the world. The different religious and secular perspectives brought to bear on the question reveal an extraordinarily wide area of common concerns and values. If the shared values can indeed inform the structures and relationships through which globalization is managed, there is hope for cooperation rather than conflict between cultures, and for some closure of the divide between those who have all the choices and those who have none.'

Dr Farhan Ahmad Nizami, Director, Oxford Centre for Islamic Studies

Making Globalization Good

The Moral Challenges of Global Capitalism

Edited by

JOHN H. DUNNING

with a Foreword by

HRH The Prince of Wales

OXFORD

UNIVERSITY PRESS

OXFORD

UNIVERSITY PRESS

Great Clarendon Street, Oxford OX2 6DP

Oxford University Press is a department of the University of Oxford.
It furthers the University's objective of excellence in research, scholarship,
and education by publishing worldwide in

Oxford New York

Auckland Bangkok Buenos Aires Cape Town Chennai
Dar es Salaam Delhi Hong Kong Istanbul Karachi Kolkata
Kuala Lumpur Madrid Melbourne Mexico City Mumbai Nairobi
São Paulo Taipei Tokyo Toronto

Oxford is a registered trade mark of Oxford University Press
in the UK and in certain other countries

Published in the United States
by Oxford University Press Inc., New York

© Oxford University Press, 2003

British Library Cataloguing in Publication Data

Data available

Library of Congress Cataloging in Publication Data
The moral imperatives of global capitalism / edited by John H. Dunning.
p. cm.
Includes index.
1. Capitalism—Moral and ethical aspects. 2. Globalization—Moral and ethical aspects.
3. Economics—Moral and ethical aspects. 4. Business ethics.
HB501 .M72144 2003   174—dc21   2002192556

ISBN 0-19-925701-9 (hbk)
ISBN 0-19-927522-X (pbk)

1 3 5 7 9 10 8 6 4 2

Typeset by Newgen Imaging Systems (P) Ltd., Chennai, India
Printed in Great Britain
on acid-free paper by
Biddles Ltd., King's Lynn, Norfolk

Acknowledgements

My first word of appreciation must be to the Templeton and Carnegie Bosch Foundations. Without their generous financial support and their faith in my determination and capability to translate an idea into a worthwhile product, this volume would not have been possible.

Second, I am conscious of an enormous debt I owe to the writers of the chapters of this monograph, each of whom has given generously of his or her time and has made a unique and very personal contribution to this project. In particular, I am most encouraged that each shares some of my own views and anxieties about the current challenges and opportunities of global capitalism as it is now emerging, and feels that a re-energizing and upgrading of the moral values and ethical mores underpinning its constituent institutions is imperative if global capitalism is to fulfil its wealth-creating functions in a geographically inclusive and democratically acceptable way.

Third, I wish to warmly thank Mrs Jill Turner, Executive Assistant in the School of Business at the University of Reading, who has been tireless in her efforts not only in helping me prepare my own chapters, but also in my correspondence with the authors and putting the whole volume together for publication.

This project has been a major team effort, and I believe an eminently rewarding one. Many friends and colleagues helpfully offered their views and advice as the book proceeded; and I am most grateful to them for this. But most of all, I would like to acknowledge the love and support of my wife Christine, who, for the last eighteen months, has had to suffer from a husband with his head even more in the clouds than usual!

J. H. D.

Reading and Rutgers Universities
September 2002

*Dedicated to the memory
of my parents*

Foreword

by HRH The Prince of Wales

I am delighted to have the opportunity to write a foreword to this timely collection of essays by some of the world's leading thinkers on economic and social issues, judiciously edited by Professor Dunning, looking at some of the problems and moral dangers associated with the growth of market capitalism and globalization.

It has seemed to me from the start of the process, following the collapse of Communism and opening-up of many economies to so-called free markets in the early 1990s, that there were some real risks associated with the rapid and headlong race of countries towards market economics. When I addressed the World Economic Forum at Davos in February 1992, I said: 'It is one thing … to have brought the cold war to an end. It is quite another to bring about the adjustments necessary to convert that success into a better life for all the people concerned.' Above all, I was concerned that there were, in my view, inherent dangers in the potential for inhumane application of market principles in countries and communities without the developed institutions and checks and balances needed to protect people and whole communities from the harsh and untoward effects of unfettered market capitalism.

The last ten years, during which global business has expanded to proportions unimaginable during the cold war, have at the same time seen all too many examples of the negative impacts of the development of a global market. The rapid drift of people en masse from the land to urban slums, rising youth unemployment, environmental degradation, and the apparent willingness of some big corporations to 'gamble with Nature' are all fundamental issues that beg for business and political leaders with longer-term views and an understanding of both value and values. The global economic system in which companies operate, and in which many people and communities appear powerless to stop the pace of change, cannot exist in a moral vacuum devoid of consideration for the effects of corporate actions, respect for people, concern for long-term sustainability, and even, dare I say it, a sense of the intangible, spiritual dimension so important to human lives.

For example, in many rural economics in the developing world—often the product of centuries of social development, sustainable husbandry, and organic community—the growing involvement of multinational food concerns and the consequent commercially driven pressure for growing yields and intensification of production are threatening to create a dangerous imbalance in society and its delicate interaction with Nature. Even such an apparently innocuous process as cultivating warm-water prawns for developed world markets is causing widespread environmental problems. The large areas of mangrove swamp that have to be cleared to make way for this new sort of farming provide an important buffer between the sea and the land, and provide a habitat that is important for many wild species. More generally, there are plenty of examples across the developing world of farmers' being encouraged to enter into contracts with biotech and other 'agribusiness' companies which, in return for assisting with inputs and technical advice, will provide an assured market. But who controls the market and the new technologies? How appropriate will the new technologies be to local needs? And what happens if the crop fails? There may well be no intention to coerce farmers into participating in a certain model of production, but the combination of commercial and financial muscle, state incentives, and a policy framework designed to increase production would, almost inevitably, mean that this was the result. 'Corporate enslavement' of whole communities becomes a reality.

And yet there is another way. The UNDP *Poverty Report 2000* made clear that 'The poor are often excluded from poverty assessments—as they are from poverty programmes. Whether expensive or cheap, rapid or slow, surveys that fail to incorporate the views of the poor are likely to miss the essence of the problem. After all, they are the people most directly affected—keenly aware of the problems they face and probably the most knowledgeable about solutions'. When seeking economic solutions to the problems of hunger, overcrowding, or the drift to the cities from the land, why not start by examining the livelihoods of resource-poor farmers and seek to build on their existing knowledge, skills, and resources, nurtured and refined over centuries, applying technologies appropriate to their circumstances and tradition? The answers they provide may well be surprisingly effective—and would certainly be rooted in local traditions and methods.

Over the last decade, I have also found myself increasingly concerned that the promotion of global economic opportunities without a well-developed sense of corporate responsibility might bring new dangers and forms of corruption alongside the undoubted new economic and social freedoms stifled by the former regimes. One form of brutalism could all too easily be replaced by another. This is just one of many reasons that, through organizations with which I have been associated—such as my International Business Leaders Forum, which I founded in 1990—I have tried to promote what might be called a 'middle course' which stressed business social responsibility and sustainability as vital and necessary components of an open market. Apart from anything else, it had become clear to me that, while producing a generation of excellent corporate managers, business schools were failing to inculcate in their students a values-based system through the teaching of history—a value system that placed balance and sustainability at the heart of economic development.

After all, values and a moral compass are surely essential if the extension of free markets is not to result in a short-term race to the bottom? In what might be called an earlier phase of 'globalization', the British Empire was often characterized—and certainly has been since—as a machine created for the commercial exploitation of its peoples for the benefit of Britain. And yet it could be argued that the existence of the Commonwealth today—an organization that, more than any other, exists on the basis of a shared set of values—suggests that the Empire must have been about more than simple exploitation. For all its many imperfections, justice, fairness, and incorruptibility lay at the heart of Imperial administration. The District Officer, at the coalface of Empire, found himself involved—like Leonard Woolf in Hambauto District in Ceylon in the early 1900s—in customs, collecting revenue, authorizing expenditure, police, prisons, local government, roads, irrigation, Crown lands, welfare, law and order, fisheries, wildlife, and court cases. He ought in many ways to be the ideal model for the businessman of today. Woolf wrote: 'I worked all day from the moment I got up in the morning until I went to bed at night, for I rarely thought of anything else except the District and the people, to increase their prosperity, diminish poverty and disease, start irrigation works, open schools … I did not idealise or romanticise the people or the country; I just like them aesthetically and humanly and socially.' Yet Woolf was also a cog in an efficient, lucrative, and often risk-taking commercial enterprise.

It is, therefore, perhaps appropriate for us to be reminded of the timeless principles and ethics that must be the foundation of sound and humane market economies, as well as the part that religions play in the workplace and marketplace. A wider debate is long overdue, providing the opportunity for serious thinking about the terrible results in terms of opportunities for future generations if we get this wrong. No reader will agree with everything written in this book (and several of the contributors would probably come to blows!), but Professor Dunning has done us all a service in providing us with a starting-point for a debate that is essential for the future development of our planet.

Contents

Part III

List of Contributors

Khurshid Ahmad, Professor and Chairman, Islamic Foundation, Markfield, Leicestershire

Jack Behrman, Luther Hodges Distinguished Professor of International Business and Ethics (Emeritus), University of North Carolina

Gordon Brown, UK Chancellor of the Exchequer, and member of the House of Commons

Robert Davies, Chief Executive, Prince of Wales International Business Leaders' Forum

John H. Dunning, Emeritus Professor of International Business Universities of Reading, UK and Rutgers, USA

Richard Falk, Albert G. Milbank Emeritus Professor of International Law and Practice, and Emeritus Professor of Politics and International Affairs, Princeton University, Woodrow Wilson School of Public and International Affairs

Brian Griffiths, Vice Chairman, Goldman Sachs International and Member of the House of Lords

Alan Hamlin, Professor of Economics and Dean of Social Sciences, University of Southampton

Hans Küng, Emeritus Professor of Ecumenical Theology and President of the Global Ethics Foundation in Tübingen, Germany

Deepak Lal, James S. Coleman Professor of International Development Studies, UCLA, California

David Loy, Professor, Faculty of International Studies, Bunkyo University, Chigasaki, Japan

Michael Novak, Director of Social and Political Studies, American Enterprise Institute, Washington, DC, and George Frederick Jewett Professor of Religion and Public Policy

Jonathan Sacks, Chief Rabbi of the United Hebrew Congregations of the Commonwealth

Joseph Stiglitz, Professor of Economics, Columbia University, New York, Nobel Laureate in Economics 2001

Baroness Shirley Williams, Leader of the Liberal Democrats in the House of Lords, Emeritus Professor at the John F. Kennedy School of Government, Harvard University

Introduction

JOHN H. DUNNING

This volume assembles the views and opinions of a prestigious group of religious leaders, politicians, businessmen, and academic scholars on a topic which is at the forefront of the debate on the merits and demerits of *global capitalism* (GC). It takes the view that if GC—arguably the most efficient wealth creating system currently known to man—is to be both economically viable and socially acceptable, then each of its four constituent institutions (*viz.* markets, governments, supra-national agencies, and civil society) must be not only entrepreneurial and technically competent, but buttressed and challenged by a strong and appropriate moral ecology.

The volume is divided into three main parts. Part One presents the analytical framework underlying the volume's main themes. Chapter 1 by *John Dunning* sets the background and attempts to guide the reader through the main contents of the book. Among the issues it identifies are:

- The unique characteristics of GC (and, indeed, questions how far, and in what respects, such a phenomenon actually does exist); and how GC relates to its sister concepts of the *global market place* and *globalization*.
- The reasons why the (inter-related) functions of GC's four constituent institutions (identified above), is presently sub-optimal; and the challenges and opportunities offered by the globalizing economy.
- A discussion of 'technical' and 'moral' institutional failures. To what extent can one conceive of 'absolute' or 'fundamental' cf. 'relative', or 'context specific' moral standards in a world which comprises countries and/or regions at various stages of development, and whose inhabitants practise different religious beliefs, political ideologies, and cultural norms.
- What must be done to upgrade moral standards? What role should incentive structures, formal and informal rules, and enforcement instruments play in the twenty-first century (cf. in previous times)? What is the influence of religious thought and practice? What action might be taken by the institutions of GC to sustain and advance the moral imperatives demanded by the system of which they are part?

In Chapter 2, *Deepak Lal* traces the changing interface between *societal and cultural values and capitalism* as each has evolved since the later Middle Ages. To what extent can the past successes or failures of capitalism (in its various guises) be attributed to the moral ecology of the institutions underpinning and shaping it? What indeed, have been the ethical foundations of the great civilizations of the past? What part have social customs, cosmological beliefs, and religious authority played in this evolution? What lessons can be drawn from the experiences of our forefathers? The chapter concludes with a brief discussion of the role of post-Westphalian states in influencing the moral content and structure of capitalism. In so doing, Professor Lal offers some comparisons and contrasts between the actions taken by the liberal minded (Western) governments of the nineteenth century, and their more paternalistic modern counterparts.

In Chapter 3, *Alan Hamlin* revisits some of his earlier work on *the moral basis, scope, and evaluation of markets*, and extends his analysis to a global setting by considering both the international market place and its institutional foundations. His key questions are 'How does the changing form and extended geographical radius of the market (for goods, services, information, and capital) affect the morality of the market and other institutions of GC?' and 'How should these considerations influence the debate on the design of the political landscape?' Professor Hamlin believes that an evolutionary, bottom-up, and multicultural approach towards achieving more responsible and sustainable global capitalism offers the best promise; and that an upgrading of virtues such as trust, forbearance, and reciprocity, and a more meaningful dissemination and exchange of these virtues across national boundaries, is an essential prerequisite to building a more integrated global society.

In Chapter 4, *Joseph Stiglitz* considers some of the ethical issues associated with the *economic transformation of societies* (both developed and developing), which globalization and technological advances are bringing about. Building on his 1998 Prebisch lecture, presented at UNCTAD in Geneva, he zeroes down to considering how both national and international institutions need to be reconfigured to cope with the structural adaptations arising from the economic and political challenges of the new global economy: and the kind of moral imperatives (specific to global capitalism) which must be addressed if these institutions are to achieve their objectives in an uncertain and volatile world, and to do so in a holistic and socially responsible manner. Professor Stiglitz also calls for a new consensus in tackling the issue of sustainable development, for more openness, partnership, and moral responsibility by it constituents; and for a better recognition of the role which social capital can play in this process.

In Chapter 5, *Jack Behrman* looks beyond *the transformation of economic priorities to those of society (or societies)* at large. What are the challenges and opportunities of GC for wider societal aspirations and goals; and what are the implications for the attitudes and behaviour of individuals and communities? In his analysis, Professor Behrman pays especial attention to those goals of society, such as good health, and the absence of violent behaviour, which are not normally captured in the standard measures of economic welfare. He identifies and discusses seven criteria of acceptability of a new global order; and outlines the contribution of the different elements of society in promoting these in an equitable and sustainable way. Professor Behrman believes that the extended geographical radius of capitalism demands a careful reappraisal of its moral foundations; and offers a blueprint of how such a transformation may be accomplished by a reconfiguration of values and responsibilities.

Part Two of the volume concentrates on the challenges, opportunities, and dilemmas posed by GC. It begins in Chapter 6 with a contribution by the eminent theologian *Hans Küng*, who looks at the various attempts to formulate an acceptable global ethic, which might be used, both as an end in itself, and a basis for the motives and conduct of the institutions which fashion GC. Such an ethic (notably that proposed by Professor Küng himself and the Parliament of the World's Religions) is designed to identify and promote an agreed set of core human values and behavioural standards as agreed by the leading faith traditions, but which might also be endorsed by non-religious persons and institutions. Professor Küng is well aware of the difficulties in identifying and practising a universally acceptable moral code; but he considers that, not only is the idea of such a code gaining increasing support, but it is undergirding and guiding the strategies and policies of many global institutions, particularly global businesses.

The following four chapters (Chapters 7–10) take a specifically religious approach to the moral imperatives of GC. Once again, the underlying assumptions of each of the contributors are (*a*) that global capitalism is, (or has the ability to be), the most efficient economic system for wealth creation, but (*b*) that without a firm and socially inclusive moral foundation, its institutions will not be motivated or conduct themselves in a way which is both democratically acceptable and sustainable over time. Clearly a distinction needs to be made between a specific Christian, Islam, Jewish, etc. ethic towards the different basis, characteristics, and effects of GC, and the theology and revelation underpinning that ethic. It is, for example, one thing to accept Christian behavioural mores: it is another to believe in Christianity as a necessary prerequisite for promoting and practising those mores. However, it is one of the purposes of this volume to seek to identify both the unique and common features of the different faith persuasions, to discuss alternative approaches for action, and to promote a more effective and influential ecumenical dialogue.

In Chapter 7, *Brian Griffiths* sets out his interpretation of the *Christian attitude and response to GC*. After identifying the foundations of a Christian perspective *viz.* the nature of the world God created, the covenants, the moral law of the Old Testament and the Incarnation, Lord Griffiths identifies six distinctive components of an acceptable global economy. He then goes on to distinguish between the Christian viewpoint and that of liberal economists who tend to regard the market (as one of the critical institutions of capitalism) as an autonomous entity and independent of any reference to morality. He also has little sympathy with those theologians who view capitalism 'as powered by the unremitting stimulation of covetousness' (Newbigin 1986, quoted p. 168). Indeed—as a Christian—he strongly defends the moral legitimacy of the concept of private ownership, and the freedom of individuals and firms to do business in the market place. At the same time, Lord Griffiths is in no doubt that, without a vigorous and clearly enunciated moral framework which embraces Christian values, the risks of extreme poverty, social injustice and exclusivity, and the threat to the environment—three downsides of the present state of capitalism discussed in the chapter—will remain.

Finally, he avers that individual Christians and the Christian church bear a major responsibility for advocating and promulgating their beliefs and opinions, and also for co-operating with other religious persuasions to identify ways of upgrading the moral ecology of the constituent institution of GC.

In Chapter 8, *Khurshid Ahmad* presents the *Islamic approach to GC.* He takes a rather more critical view of the endemic qualities of global capitalism; which, he argues, even if it were to become more socially responsible and inclusive, would not be comfortably embraced by the Muslim world, because of its underpinning moral ethos and hegemonic character. This, he explains, is partly because it contains and expresses values and behavioural norms which are specific to its historical and cultural context, and partly because it does not sufficiently endorse the ethical virtues which the Islamic religion believes are essential to the well-being of mankind. At the same time, Professor Ahmad believes that, with tolerance and understanding, it is possible for Western and Islamic-style economic systems to exist side by side, with each retaining its own unique characteristics. In his words, 'this would make the global society a matrix where different cultures and systems can co-exist' (p. 200) and again 'what inspires persons like myself is the vision of a world where all participants have the confidence that they can live according to their own values and yet be partners in a global enterprise' (p. 200).

In Chapter 9, *Jonathan Sacks*, in presenting a *Jewish perspective on global capitalism* argues the case for a more covenantal (rather than contractual) approach towards its governance, which should take, as its starting point, the belief in the moral equality of each and every human being. He traces this idea back to the prophets of ancient Israel who conceived God as 'transcending place and national boundaries and humanity as a single moral community linked by a covenant of mutual responsibility' (p. 212); and then develops and reframes this theme in the light of the dramatic and far-reaching changes in information and communications technology in economic and institutional structures, and in social mores which have occurred over the intervening centuries. Professor Sacks avers that, if nothing else, the current age of global capitalism is underpinning the need for the upgrading and reprioritization of many virtues which have always been especially valued by Judaism. To those of *creativity, co-operation,* and *compassion* identified by John Dunning in Chapter 1, Dr Sacks adds four more, *viz. control* (over one's destiny under the guidance and authority of God), *conservation* (environmental sustainability), *coexistence* (the dignity, and acceptance of, cultural and religious diversity), and *covenant.* He, like several other contributors to this volume, argues for a multicultural ethical approach to tackling many of the current ills of GC, and is at pains to stress that Judaism embodies a dual morality—one based on a universal code applying to all persons (thus emphasizing our shared humanity), and the other on a particular way of life 'demanded of the heirs of those who followed Moses into the wilderness' (p. 227).

Chapter 10 by *David Loy* looks at the moral ecology of global capitalism *from an Eastern religious—and particularly a Buddhist—perspective.* He first points out that Buddhism does not depend on a theistic revelation of values and behavioural norms in the way Abrahamic religions do. Rather it should be thought of as a philosophy which reveals the path each of us must walk in order 'to obtain a wisdom that realizes the true nature of the world, including the true nature of oneself' (p. 233). Such a credo is translated into a pragmatic and undogmatic attitude towards wealth creation, property, and social justice, and to global capitalism as an economic system. Buddhists judge the 'religion of the market'—as Professor Loy puts it—by the individual and social values it promotes. In this respect, in his view, it is found wanting, as, all too often it endorses, and even encourages, self aggrandisement, merit-seeking, and materialism—all unwholesome traits according to Buddhist teaching. To achieve a more morally acceptable economic system, Dr Loy recommends that greater emphasis should be placed on the value of such virtues as social responsibility, compassion, generosity, and wisdom—each of which, far from undermining the benefits of GC, would help to ensure a better quality of life for people and a healthier society. To achieve some of these goals, Professor Loy accepts the necessity for *top-down* regulatory measures and incentive systems by Governments, but believes that, in the long run, only a wider acceptance and spontaneous upgrading by individuals and institutions of the values which Buddhists hold dear will help raise the moral profile of GC.

In Part Three of the volume we turn to considering 'how' the global society might better organize itself, and its constituent institutions, to respond to the challenges of GC, and to do so in a way which helps embrace an agreed set of 'core' moral values, while accepting the need for a degree of cultural diversity and tolerance in respect of the interpretation of these and the identification and practice of the non-core values.

In Chapter 11, *Michael Novak* addresses some broad issues relating *to culture, basic human values, and globalization*; and how these affect both individuals and institutions as societies are transforming themselves within the framework of GC. In identifying the political, economic, and cultural attributes of GC, he argues that its success and acceptability no less depend on a supportive moral ecology, the ingredients of which he describes at some length. Professor Novak believes we are currently experiencing a crisis in moral ecology both at an individual and societal level. He cites, as evidence, the cult of excessive self-interest in the market place, the emphasis of power and vested interests in politics, and the widespread expression of relativism and subjectivity in culture. He then discusses four cardinal virtues which he believes must be embraced by individuals and institutions engaged in, or influencing, the character of global economic activity *viz.* cultural humility, truth, respect for human dignity, and solidarity. At the same time, he believes that to reach a socially acceptable global vision, it is not necessary, nor indeed desirable, to work for univocal moral principles. To quote directly from Professor Novak 'It is not necessary to find a single formulation that does justice to all virtues. For practical co-operation in moral conduct family resemblances may be quite sufficient' (p. 273).

Professor Novak concludes his chapter by referring to the Earthly City described by St Augustine in *The City of God*. St Augustine observed that, in his time, the world was in conflict, racked by injustice and scarred by unacceptable moral practices; and the best its inhabitants could do to combat these was to reach a tentative balance of power—often based on fear—and to work for some measure of cross-cultural tolerance. Professor Novak believes such measures, though necessary, are not sufficient, to ensure the sustainability of global capitalism—and one of its most valued components—freedom of choice. He argues that only by our respecting each other's views and values—or as he puts it to 'pay one another the honour of taking each other seriously'—can one make a start towards an Earthly City which resembles that which he terms *Caritapolis*—the city of friendship and communion.

In Chapter 12, *Richard Falk* zeroes down to consider the *(changing) role of civil society as an institution influencing the form and content of GC*—and particularly its goals and values. This is a critical chapter, which, after placing the whole range of NGO functions within a historical context, acknowledges that, as values and aspirations change, new demands are made on the organizations comprising these institutions. Once again, the implications of GC are given especial attention. How far, and in what respects, are NGOs (including global NGOs) our twenty-first century moral guardians (cf. governments and markets); and/or to what extent do they need to be injected with a new or reconfigured code of behaviour suitable to the particular needs of the global economy? Professor Falk clearly believes that global civil society has an important role to play in influencing the course and content of global capitalism—and its underlying ethical ethos. He particularly favours a *globalization-from-below* approach, which he believes provides a useful counter-force to the *globalization-from-above* approach practised by large firms and governments. In elaborating this view, he makes the case for a *normative democracy*—which in his words 'reconnects politicians with moral purpose and values' (p. 293). He then goes on to identify the components of normative democracy, and argues that most of these can best be served not by *globalization-from-above* mechanisms but rather by those of civil society as it 'redefines its role as mediating between the logic of capitalism and the priorities of peoples' (p. 297).

Chapter 13 by *Robert Davies* turns to the *ethical ingredients, strategies, and conduct of business institutions.* This is also an important chapter, as a great deal of criticism has been, and is being, levelled against the social responsibilities and moral conduct of large enterprises (and particularly multinational enterprises (MNEs). Some of this (Mr Davies readily acknowledges) is justified in respect of some firms; some is not. This chapter attempts to set the record straight by acknowledging that MNEs do have a responsibility to all their stakeholders and to the community at large; and at the end of the day judicial or 'proper' selfishness pays off. He also addresses the social-cum-altruistic role of businesses and the business community. Mr Davies pulls no punches and gives several examples of recent businesses, both in the US and the UK, which, by their actions portray the unacceptable face of global capitalism. This is a refreshing look at the demands being made on the business community by the various stakeholders in global capitalism. As the Executive Director of the Prince of Wales' International

Business Forum, he is the first to acknowledge that business leaders need to play a more proactive and progressive role in fashioning corporate values and social responsibility, and upgrading these from the realm of business philanthropy. As he colourfully puts it 'why wait for the Barbarians to arrive at their gate?' (p. 317).

Chapters 14 and 15 turn to consider the responsibilities of governments both as overseers and monitors of domestic economic systems, and as active participators in global capitalism. In Chapter 14, the *UK Chancellor of the Exchequer, Gordon Brown*, makes a strong plea for a greater sense of *economic and moral responsibility of the wealthier nations towards their poorer counterparts*. It is also his conviction that for global prosperity to be sustained, it has to be fairly shared, and, as a success story, cites the institutional innovations of the early post-war era to create an international architecture to advance this goal. However, the contemporary global economic and political scenario is very different, and Mr Brown is now advocating a reconfiguration of the role of supra-national institutions both to meet the specific needs of global capitalism and drastically reduce poverty. More particularly, he is proposing a new global consensus which will (1) better enable the poorer countries to fully participate in the global economy and benefit from it; (2) encourage the international business community to adopt high corporate standards for their participation as reliable and consistent partners in the development process; (3) lead to improved trade regimes designed to improve the participation of developing countries in decision taking; and (4) substantially increase development aid to nations most in need and willing to focus on the fight against poverty. Mr Brown concludes his contribution by stressing the responsibilities of each of the various institutions of GC and, most notably, those of the business community, civil society, and governments of both the richer and poorer countries, and individuals throughout the world. To quote his own words 'Unless all participants fully embrace this message there is a real danger that the very real benefits of global capitalism as they are now emerging will be swallowed up in political "turmoil and social unrest"' (p. 331).

Baroness Shirley Williams takes up Mr Brown's theme in Chapter 15, and looks more specifically at the moral issues surrounding the global distribution of resources, capabilities, and incomes. She is highly critical of some of the economic policies and political regimes of some of the rich countries, and demonstrates, from Indonesian and Russian examples, how Western governments and international agencies failed to recognize and give support to the institutional reforms necessary to ensure that their transition to a market-based economic system would be successful. She emphasizes, as does Professor Stiglitz in Chapter 4, the need for a new and more holistic approach to economic development; indeed, she avers that global social justice demands it. Lady Williams concludes by observing that the moral conscience of society is very much alive, and reminds us of the role of the churches and private individuals that helped initiate the Jubilee 2000 movement, geared towards lifting the burden of debt from some of the poorest countries in the world. But she is clearly not satisfied that either national governments or supra-national agencies are doing enough to ensure that global capitalism works to the benefit of all the peoples of the world—and particularly to those in the greatest need.

In the final chapter *John Dunning* attempts to draw together the main themes and thoughts of the contributors to this volume, and to summarize his own views on what might be done to upgrade the economic and moral ecology of global capitalism—in other words, to make globalization good. In doing so, he pays especial attention to the role which the globally oriented and promulgated values and behavioural norms of the various religious persuasions can play in advancing this goal.

We would offer one final observation. The contributions in this volume should best be regarded as exploratory ventures into relatively new territory. True, issues of morality in economic affairs have been with us since the time of Aristotle—or before then—but they have never been discussed in the context of the globalizing, knowledge-intensive, and alliance-based economy of the late twentieth and early twenty-first century. We hope that, at the very least, the essays in this volume will not only stimulate further debate on the subject, but also trigger action of both a *bottom-up* and *top-down* kind, and, in so doing, help our global village work towards a responsible global economic system that acknowledges the cultural richness of its diverse institutions, and, at the same time, is more efficient, socially inclusive, and morally acceptable than the one which is currently on offer.

PART I

1

The Moral Imperatives Of Global Capitalism: An Overview

JOHN H. DUNNING

1.1 INTRODUCTION

It is just over a decade since the fall of the Berlin Wall, and the burgeoning of the Internet and e-commerce. These events, the one political and the other technological, coupled with the extensive liberalization of cross-border markets, and the advent of several new players on the world economic stage, heralded a new era for the global community. Since the late 1980s, a plethora of scholarly and popular monographs and articles have explored the implications of this phenomenon—popularly referred to as globalization. In the beginning, there was nothing but praise for it; then, in the mid-1990s, its downsides began to be highlighted. More recently, there has been a 'backlash' against the 'backlash'—fuelled in part, by the events of 11 September 2001 and their aftermath. My reading of the latest contributions on the subject by such analysts as George Soros (1998, 2002), Thomas Friedman (2000), Paul Streeten (2001), and Joseph Stiglitz (2002) is that they are showing a much more realistic and balanced understanding of the limits and challenges of globalization; and I sense that there is a growing feeling that if we can 'get it right' (and 'right' includes the right *way* to globalize) global capitalism, as it is now emerging, can help achieve many of the economic and social goals and aspirations which most people hold dear, better than any other alternative *currently* on offer (Dunning 2000; Friedman 2000; Fukuyama 1999; Sen 1999).

If we get it right. *If* is clearly the critical word. What, then, needs to be done to devise and monitor a global economic architecture which is efficient, morally acceptable, geographically inclusive, and sustainable over time?[1] In this introductory chapter, I will try and identify a few of the more important conditions which, I believe, need to be put in place if this is to be accomplished. Several of these—particularly the economic prerequisites—have already been well aired elsewhere.[2] Because of this my thoughts, and those of the other contributors to this volume, will focus on (what each of us, in our different ways perceive to be) the essential ethical foundations of the global architecture if it is to meet the demands likely to be made of it.

More particularly, in this chapter I propose to explore and base my comments on three propositions. These are:

1. Responsible global capitalism (RGC) (and I will explain what I mean by this later) should be considered not as an end in itself, but as a means of providing

a richer, healthier and more meaningful life style for individuals and their families; and of advancing the economic objectives and social transformation of societies (Stiglitz 1998, and Chapter 4 of this volume).

2. In order to move towards a more acceptable global capitalism, the organizational structures and managerial strategies of each of its participating institutions, *viz.* markets, governments, civil society, and supranational entities, need to be reconfigured and strengthened.

3. RGC can only be achieved and sustained if there is a strong and generally acceptable moral ecology underpinning the attitudes, motives, and behaviour of its constituent individuals and institutions; and that, in a transforming global society, this basis needs continual reappraisal and careful nurturing by the appropriate suasion, incentives, and regulatory mechanisms.

1.2 GLOBALIZATION, GLOBAL MARKETS, AND RESPONSIBLE GLOBAL CAPITALISM

Let me now briefly define the main global concepts I shall deal with in this chapter. These are *globalization* itself, *the global market place*, and *global capitalism*. Each has its own distinctive meaning, although, all too often—and erroneously—they are treated as if they were one and the same. By *globalization*, I mean the *connectivity of individuals and institutions across the globe, or at least, over most of it*. Such connectivity may be shallow or deep; short or long lasting. It may be geared to advancing personal or institutional interests; and economic, cultural, or political goals. There are many channels of cross-border connectivity; but the Internet is the quintessential vehicle of contemporary and interpersonal and inter-corporate communication. Globalization is a morally neutral concept. In itself, it is neither good nor bad, but it may be motivated for good or bad reasons, and used to bring about more or less good or bad results.

The *global market place* refers more specifically to the flow of goods, services, and assets across national boundaries, which are mediated through the market, the price, quantity, and quality of which are determined by the participants in the market. All of us, directly, or indirectly, participate in global markets; look, if you will, at the labels of origin on the goods each of us buys at our local supermarkets. As workers too, many of us are helping to supply goods and services for sale in export markets—or are employed by a foreign owned firm. In our leisure pursuits, we may travel abroad, look at foreign TV, and purchase the services of foreign airlines, hotels, and ethnic restaurants. All of us, be we individuals or enterprises, like to get the best deal we can out of the market; indeed the market system is designed on the premise that the self seeking of its participants may yield socially beneficial results.

The concept of *global capitalism* (GC) is more difficult to get a handle on. There is really no such thing as a global capitalist system today in the same way as there is a global firm. For this to be so there would have to be a single and centralized system of global governance. Instead, what we have is a large number of distinctive national (or regional) capitalist systems which are connected through a network of cross-border relationships, but particularly through the free or relatively free movement of goods, services, capital, and information across the globe (Hall and Soskice 2001). I use the word system advisedly. *RGC embraces much more than global markets. It includes the set of non-market institutions within which the market is embedded and which, together, characterize a global society* (Hamlin 1995). *Inter alia* it is the task of these institutions to set the rules and monitor the behaviour of markets; to engage in a variety of market facilitating and/or regulatory activities; and to produce such socially desirable products, which, left unaided, the market is unable or unwilling to produce.[3]

RGC then is a system made up of individuals, private commercial corporations, non-governmental organizations (NGOs), governments, and supranational agencies. Each has a unique and critical role to play in advancing and sustaining its goals. *Inter alia* (and this applies particularly in the case of developing countries), this includes the transformation and upgrading of the economic structure and social fabric of societies (Stiglitz 1998).

The inability (or unwillingness) of many commentators to distinguish between these three concepts often leads to unnecessary obfuscation. In my judgement, few people (except for those who are completely xenophobic), are against globalization as I have defined it. Indeed those individuals and institutions most critical of globalization are those most likely to use its products to advance their own ends. Most, instead, target their criticisms in two directions. First, to the perceived failure of global markets to deliver the kind of goods and services society considers desirable, at a fair and affordable price; and also to ensure an equitable distribution of the benefits of wealth-creating activities. Second, and quite differently, the charge is made that GC, as an economic and social system, all too frequently allows unfettered markets—and particularly the actions of large multinational enterprises (MNEs) engaging in these markets to override the rights of democratically elected non-market institutions and those of civil society; and that, in some cases, such institutions e.g. governments, are in cahoots with the market to instigate actions which may rebound to the latter's advantage, rather than to that of the constituents they represent (Hertz 2000).

For the rest of this chapter, I shall direct my attention primarily to *global capitalism* rather than *globalization* or the *global market place*, or more particularly what I shall choose to call responsible global capitalism (RGC)[5]—elsewhere referred to as societal or democratic capitalism.

Let me then turn to the particular focus of this volume—*viz.* the moral imperatives of global capitalism. It is my contention that if RGC is to achieve its goals (and I will describe these more fully a little later) there has to be a set of ethical standards—both general and specific to RGC—to which all its participants must adhere. It is not enough for the institutions of RGC to perform *efficiently*. They have to do so in a way which conforms to certain *moral standards*. For, at the end of the day, the answers to the questions of 'what goods and services should be produced', 'how, and where best to produce them', and 'how should the benefits be distributed' (the three tasks which RGC must seek to address), critically depend on the values and priorities of the individuals and institutions participating in the system. Unless these values and priorities, including those which are not easily translated into a monetary value, are factored into the workings of RGC, then *economic* benefits are unlikely to be either fully realized or sustainable.

The interaction between the moral obligations of the participants in the RGC system—be they individuals or institutions—is a complex and changing one. It has long been acknowledged that if the market system is to be both efficient and equitable, the transacting participants must behave in an ethically responsible manner. But some commentators[6] take this a step further and assert that there are certain endogenous features of the market which generate the required standards of honesty, truth, reciprocity, and integrity for this to be ensured.[7] However, this claim may be questioned whenever markets are imperfect, uncertain, or volatile or where its participants behave in a non-competitive way. And it is these features of global markets on which those who are the most critical of them tend to focus.[8]

Similarly, it is generally accepted that good government does not just mean that governments should perform their tasks efficiently, but that they should do so without corruption, dishonesty, or nepotism, and with a commitment to transparency, accountability, and the pursuit of social justice. History, indeed, is replete with examples of private enterprises, labour unions, governments, and NGOs eroding the benefits of societal capitalism by their unacceptable moral codes and behaviour.

At the same time, the moral dimension of RGC must also reflect the wider social and cultural mores of society, and these are likely to be highly contextual over time and space. Thus societies with a Confucian tradition are likely to interpret the ideal conduct of their capitalistic institutions differently from those steeped in a Christian or Jewish tradition; while the strong emphasis currently being placed on individual freedom by contemporary Western economies is likely to generate mind-sets and behaviour, for example, towards education, innovation, and entrepreneurship, and to the idea of social safety nets, very differently than the erstwhile Communist countries or Islamic societies. The questions then arise 'Should contemporary RGC be modified to reflect these different attitudes and virtues?' and 'Does its emergence demand that, as, when, and where appropriate, these mores, or their prioritization, be harmonized?'

1.3 THE TASKS OF RGC

I have suggested that the success of RGC is best judged by its ability to deliver economically efficient and socially acceptable answers to three questions—'what to produce', 'how to produce', and 'how to distribute' the benefits arising from global economic activity. I have further averred that each answer must rest on both the capabilities and the intentions of each of the participating institutions, and the moral outcomes of their actions. Let me now explain what I mean by evaluating the current status of RGC.

1.3.1 The Goals of RGC:
The 'what should be produced' Question

Until quite recently, the efficiency of alternative economic systems has been largely assessed by the value of the individual goods and services produced, *and* that the price attached to these by the market was deemed to represent their true value to society. The aggregate of these individual values was the gross national (or domestic) product *per capita*. Not surprisingly, then, the goal of capitalism was perceived to be that of increasing GNP (or GDP) per head.

Such a measure is increasingly viewed as only a partial reflection of economic and social well-being, though sages of yesteryear were no less critical of the benefits of wealth *per se*.[9] This is partly because it is recognized that money prices, even when markets work well, do not accurately reflect real economic welfare of society (a dollar allocated to reducing such 'bads' as AIDS, mental stress, or crime is counted the same as that spent on housing, food, and clothing). Moreover such an index excludes those goods and services which are not transacted in the market place, e.g. the output of subsistence farming, 'do it yourself' handiwork, and those to which it is difficult to attach a price tag, e.g. the protection of the environment, road safety, a fair judicial system, reduced hospital waiting lists, and such intangible benefits as reputation, status, sovereignty, and, most of all, freedom of choice (Sen 1999). Several attempts have been made to devise more acceptable measures of living standards. The United Nations Development Program, for example, has compiled a human development index (HDI) which adds to GNP per head such variables as life expectancy and educational attainment (UNDP 2000).[10]

However, the point I wish to emphasize here is that, in evaluating the efficacy of RGC *we need to first decide on the criteria by which we are to judge it*. Exactly what *are* the objectives and aspirations of society which, if they are to be met, involve the use of scarce resources? Moreover, such goals and aspirations are not static; new goods and services are continually entering the salad bowl of economic welfare, and many of these are either not marketed, or take the form of public goods i.e. goods we share with other people. At the same time, consumer preferences are often highly contextual. Compare, for example, the contents of a desirable standard of living of a contemporary English or Canadian family with those of its counterpart a century ago; or those of an average Japanese with an average Nigerian family today.

What of the specific impact of *global* capitalism on societal objectives? The main impact is surely twofold. First, thanks to modern travel, TV, and information channels, there is an increasing *awareness* of the needs, preferences, and aspirations of people throughout the world. This is leading both to a convergence and a divergence of consumer *et al* wants—convergence in the demand for such global products as Nike shoes, Gucci handbags, mass-produced cars, musical and sporting events, five-star hotels, some TV programmes and financial services. But there is also divergence to cater for localized needs and tastes: ethnic food, location-bound tourist attractions, and intangible assets such as indigenous culture, are examples. Second, I sense that part of the awareness is a growing recognition that 'man does not live by bread alone', and that values such as reputation, personal security, adequate health provision, minimum labour standards, environmental protection and economic and social stability must be reprioritized and targeted by the institutions of RGC; and that these values—some of which have a high moral content—are germane to our discussion whenever and wherever their attainment involves the use of the world's scarce resources.

1.3.2   Production and RGC:
The 'how and where best to produce' Question

The second task of RGC is to produce the type, quantity, and quality of goods and services that global society wants in the most efficient and socially acceptable way. Again, most economists accept there are some goods and services best provided by the market; and others by non-market institutions; e.g. by governments or NGOs, and some jointly by the private and public sector. The costs and benefits of production are also likely to vary according to the location of that production. In the textbook case of perfect competition, the market is fully up to meeting these objectives. But increasingly, in an uncertain, unstable, and innovation-driven global economy—and one in which international public goods are being increasingly valued—this ideal state of affairs is far from reality.

More often than not, markets—be they product, finance, technology, or labour markets—are structurally or intrinsically imperfect; and in many, but not all, instances, globalization has exacerbated these imperfections. Cross-border movements of corporate and financial capital do tend to be more volatile than their domestic equivalents. An innovation-led economy is, almost by definition, an uncertain and unstable economy. Global markets today are frequently dominated by a few large firms or interest groups, which, because of their size and geographical scope, can exploit such market failures as information asymmetries, monopoly power, and privileged access to markets; and, where it is perceived to be in their interests, engage in unacceptable social or moral behaviour.[11] Some factor inputs, e.g. unskilled or semi-skilled labour, and some kinds of activity, are location bound, and cannot easily respond to global market signals. Attempts to regulate the conduct of market participants (e.g. by way of anti-trust and fair trading legislation) and to facilitate the response of producers and workers to changing market needs have been around since the late nineteenth century. But the twin impact of recent technological advances and globalization have added a new, and more urgent, dimension to the debate. At the same time, demands by consumers for more transparency and accountability, and a closer monitoring of the behaviour of producers in sensitive markets, e.g. the provision of health products and educational services, are becoming more vocal.

Such concerns, both for 'proper' selfish[12] and genuine philanthropic reasons apply no less to non-market value-added activities, especially where quality-of-life issues are at stake. Much of the *raison d'être* for the current trend towards the privatization of public services (often, let it be said, at the initiative of left-of-centre governments) is geared towards injecting more competition and professional management into the delivery process, while offering both 'sticks' and 'carrots' for the privatized firms to behave in a socially acceptable way.

In short, the standards expected from the value-adding activities of the institutions of RGC are being upgraded, while the ethical underpinnings of these activities are becoming a more integral part of their success. This is particularly seen in two directions. The first is in the dramatic increase in the number of co-operative ventures concluded between firms—including many across national boundaries—which, themselves, are reactions to the imperatives of the global market place and knowledge-based economy. It is here where the virtues of interpersonal relationships such as trust, reciprocity, and forbearance—moral qualities, which cannot easily be built into a purely contractual transaction—are the *sine qua non* of business success.[13]

The second direction relates to the growing ease with which companies can tap global markets for their inputs, either by trade or by foreign direct investment (fdi). The ability to engage in both the horizontal and vertical division of labour by MNEs has dramatically increased as transport costs and tariff barriers have declined. But one ethical challenge arising from the shifts in the 'where' of production, demanded on efficiency grounds, has been the growth of sweatshops in several poorer developing countries, notably in East Asia. As we shall demonstrate later in this chapter, the worst of such sweatshops may be likened to the 'dark satanic mills' of nineteenth-century Britain so vividly portrayed by William Blake.

1.3.3 RGC and the Distribution of Income: The 'who gets what' Question

It is often said that capitalism is a better instrument for the creation of wealth than it is for the equitable distribution of its benefits. Indeed, some would go as far as to say that this latter task is the responsibility of governments rather than that of markets. Certainly, it is widely accepted that capitalism, and especially the market economy, is likely to result in an uneven distribution of income. Economists usually explain this in terms of the differential productivity of the factors of production, and the ability of some individuals and institutions to command large economic rents for goods and services which are absolutely scarce, or where they have the power to prevent or eradicate competition. Whatever one's conception of a fair wage or salary, it is a fact of life that there is only one Bill Gates, one Michael Jordan, and one Madonna; while it is also human nature to charge what the market will bear for one's labour. At the same time, it seems to me somewhat incongruous that while deploring huge income differentials between individuals and the huge profits of some firms, we—as consumers—are often all too ready to pay large sums of money to buy the goods or services they provide.

Again, there is nothing new in this attribute of free markets. Markets have always rewarded success (as judged by its own criteria) and penalized failure. However it is worth remembering that success can be both short lived (e.g. as in the sporting world), unpredictable (as in the world of business), and fickle (as in the world of entertainment); and that high rewards may have taken much investment in time and money to achieve. And I repeat, it has always been accepted by capitalist societies that it is the responsibility of voluntarism and governments to put right any perceived injustices of the market place.

So why is this issue of equity and social justice such a central part of the agenda of those critical of GC; and why are so many of us schizophrenic in our attitudes to wealth creation and wealth distribution? I would suggest three reasons. First globalization—and all the features associated with it—has exposed us as never before to the huge income gaps both between countries and within countries. Thus, for example, it is estimated that 90 per cent of the world's innovatory capacity resides in the Triad nations which account for only 10 per cent of the world's population (UNDP 2000). However, of greater moral concern, perhaps, is the fact that over a billion people, or one-quarter of the world's population live on less than $1 a day (World Bank 2001), while the 100 or so richest *individuals* in the world (some of whom, incidentally, live in some of the poorer countries) have amassed fortunes worth more than this combined income, seems the height of inequity, and to be morally indefensible.

Second, I perceive there is a heightened sense of cognizance by citizens in the richer nations about the extreme economic deprivation of those in the poorest regions of the world. However, when this comes to taking action which might redound to their own disadvantage, there is a good deal of hesitancy;[14] while, at a governmental level (as seen by the reaction to appeals to millennium debt cancellation and to the boosting of aid), there is both an anxiousness not to upset the workings of the free market, nor to offend future voters by an unacceptable reprioritizing of objectives. Once again, I believe the moral conscience of both individuals and nation states is central to this issue; but let me also emphasize that the reconciliation of the demands of global social justice with the economic interests of individual nation states—not to mention firms and individuals—is a highly complex issue. Yet it is one which the institutions—and particularly governments and international agencies—of RGC will need to address more seriously in the coming years.

Third, and, perhaps, most importantly, there is currently no supranational form of governance which can correct or lessen *inter-country* social injustices arising from the global market place, in the same way as national governments can, and do, help to mitigate the effects of *intra-country* injustices. Nor is it clear that there could be a universally agreed consensus of the contents of global social justice. Because of this, I do not foresee any easy or comprehensive answer to this particular moral dilemma of RGC—and it worries me a great deal when the words and actions of well-meaning individuals and NGOs often give the impression that this is so. I shall take up this point again later in this chapter.

1.4 CAN WE LEARN FROM HISTORY?

I have already alluded to the fact that much of the debate over the content and performance of RGC is but a rehearsal—albeit an extended and more complex rehearsal—of that which was sparked off by the emergence of industrial capitalism two centuries ago. I think it may be instructive to pause for a moment and consider how our Victorian forefathers dealt with the challenges of this new phenomenon at the time, and what, if any, lessons we can draw from their actions. For, either deliberately or unintentionally (and over the past two centuries there have been many unintended consequences of capitalism and the reactions to it (Lal 1998; Soros 1998; Friedman 2000)), the fact remains that the face of capitalism, which embraces the conduct of each of the institutions influencing its shape, character, and effects, was very different at the peak of its success in the first decade of the twentieth century, and even more so in its retrenchment during the interwar years, and later in the 1970s, than it is today.

While the economic benefits of the ideas and technologies which fuelled the industrial revolution, and those of the new market economy which fashioned the organization of production and exchange, were quickly evident, their less welcome social and moral consequences, took longer to reveal themselves, and even longer to deal with. Nevertheless, the Victorian era in Britain was as well known for its moral and social regeneration as for its material progress. For, by the time of the Queen's death in 1901, both the institutional and social fabric underpinning the UK's economic system was fundamentally different from when she ascended the throne in 1827; and, according to some historians, the way in which it was reconfigured saved Britain from suffering the more turbulent response to capitalism of her Continental neighbours, and in particular, that of Russia in 1917 (Searle 1998; Landes 1998).

A recitation of the challenges posed by nineteenth-century capitalism would contain almost all those posed by its contemporary counterpart, except that the former's geographical ambit rarely extended beyond national boundaries. Such social downsides as child labour, prostitution, the absence of safety nets, the lack of an appropriate legal and social infrastructure, limited property rights, poor hygiene or safety regulations, harsh working conditions, financial fraud, inadequate consumer protection, unemployment, widespread poverty, an increase in serious crime, all ran alongside the unparalleled increases in material welfare (Searle 1998).

Of course, not all these social ills could, or should, be attributed to *laissez-faire* capitalism. Indeed, many were inherited from the libertarianism of the pre-Victorian era, and the results of the Napoleonic wars: but certainly, most were exacerbated by the new industrial age. What then were the responses to these challenges? They were many and varied—but I will pinpoint just one or two which are of particular relevance to our present interests.

First, successive governments stepped in by enacting a variety of laws and regulations—starting with the Factory Act of 1833—to improve working conditions, and initiating major reforms with respect to health, sanitation, and housing (Himmelfarb 1995). In addition, they introduced a series of social provisions—including the New Poor Law of 1834—which were intended both to provide safety nets for those most desperately disadvantaged, but at the same time to discourage moral indigence. No less important, they widened the franchise of the electorate—the 1832 Reform Act saw the true beginnings of inclusive democracy—and pioneered compulsory and free education. The introduction of limited liability and improved legislation to protect property rights followed. Both local and central governments helped provide and finance public utilities and new means of transport. Successive administrations, not to mention the Queen herself, did much to set and support (but not to enforce by legislation) a moral framework for Victorian society[15] by stressing the importance of family life, self discipline, thrift, and social responsibility; virtues which Max Weber (1930) so much admired in his study of the Protestant ethic and the spirit of capitalism.

Secondly, the nineteenth century saw a spectacular rise in the role of civil society—in the guise of religious organizations, friendly societies, and philanthropic agencies. These early NGOs took upon themselves the task of ameliorating the worst social effects of a new industrial age—including that of unrestrained urbanization—as they affected individuals and their families. There was a strong humanitarian motive behind this movement, which was as much in evidence in the US as in the UK (De Tocqueville 1981). It is no accident that, in these two countries, the burgeoning of civil society did much to stave off more drastic reactions to early industrial capitalism which occurred on the European Continent.

The third response—and this occurred more abruptly across the English Channel—was to partly or wholly replace capitalism by socialism or social democracy. Here the argument was that, however much capitalism may have pushed out the boundaries of material wealth, it had failed dismally to ensure the social well-being of the majority of people. It was *de facto* an exclusive economic system; and governments were either unable or unwilling to intervene in the workings of the market to foster more inclusiveness. Those espousing a socialist economic cause believed it to be a morally superior system, as it was based on 'to each according to his needs, from each according to his ability' philosophy. While these ideals were applauded by some Christian moralists at the time—notably Frederick Maurice (and as recently as 1971 the eminent theologian Paul Tillich was portraying democratic capitalism as 'demonic'), others, led by Thomas Chalmers and Harriet Martineau preferred to tackle the downsides of capitalism by fostering more morally acceptable patterns of behaviour by its constituents (Searle 1998; Dunning 2001). In this, they re-echoed the sentiments of the eighteenth-century philosopher Edmund Burke that civil liberty can only flourish if individuals put moral chains on their appetites (Himmelfarb 1995). In any event, the socialist challenge was held at bay in the UK (and US), until the interwar depression of the 1920s and 1930s, and the writings of the economists J. M. Keynes and William Beveridge began to take root. But, perhaps most of all, it was the post-1945 disillusionment of ordinary men and women with the perceived exclusiveness and social divisiveness of pre-war capitalism that led to the maturation of socialist economic policies in the UK. In spite of alternating conservative administrations, the tide towards reducing the influence, or ameliorating the adverse affects, of these policies, did not turn until the arrival of Mrs Thatcher at 10 Downing Street in 1979.

Fourth, and interacting with each of these three responses, there was a concerted and vigorous effort by Victorian writers such as Charles Dickens and Charles Kingsley, and reformers and commentators such as Elizabeth Fry, Herbert Spencer, and Arthur Hassall, to expose some of the social and moral downsides of industrial capitalism; and to encourage more humane, prudent, and responsible behaviour on the part of both firms and the UK government. At the same time, the preaching of the Protestant ethic by such Christian advocates as Frederick Maurice and Thomas Chalmers, the moralizing by such writers as Samuel Smiles, and the example set by Queen Victoria and her household, not only helped inculcate in large swathes of the population such virtues as honesty, thrift, temperance, self-discipline, duty, character, and a sense of social responsibility, but also strengthened the hand of the non-market institutions of capitalism. Prominent examples include the emergence of a clutch of charitable enterprises and socially responsible firms, such as Rowntrees and Cadburys; and of several philanthropic, civic, and educational institutions, such as Toynbee Hall.[16]

So what now of the contemporary stage of capitalism? Well, like its predecessor, it is now heralding a new phase of economic organization. Like its predecessor, it is being fuelled by a succession of new ideas, dramatic technological breakthroughs, and a widening and deepening of cross-border commerce. Such events are challenging established values, economic structures, organizational modes, and life-styles by their speed, scope, and intensity; and, in so doing, are creating a host of social disruptions and moral challenges. But, also, they are occurring at a time when the cult of the individual liberty of action and self expression is reaching new heights, and the value and legitimacy of such concepts as solidarity and community are being severely questioned. Robert Putnam (1995), Amitai Etzioni (1996, 1998), and Francis Fukuyama (2000) are just three of several observers who have catalogued the growing social dysfunction and rise of moral relativism of Western societies between 1960 and the early 1990s—they believe this may have been reversed in the mid to late 1990s[17]—in terms of the depletion of the relational and ethical assets of each of the institutions of capitalism. This, it is worth noting, has occurred just at the time when such assets are becoming a more critical component of RGC. I shall explain what I mean by this a little later.

At the same time, there are some unique features of the globalizing economy that offer their own particular challenges. First and most obvious, the geographical radius of the market place, through such means as commerce, travel, and the Internet, is now embracing institutions from more diverse ideologies, social structures, and cultural mores than ever before. Secondly, the critical engine of wealth in today's global economy is human capital. Such an asset is not only the main source of innovation, entrepreneurship, and the upgrading of managerial and organizational expertise, but also of ideals and moral values.[18] *Inter alia*, this demands that employers should accord more attention and respect to the aspirations, behaviour, and participation of their work forces in the wealth-creating process than has previously been the case.

Thirdly, we are entering an age of global alliance capitalism, where, to better advance their own economic objectives, individuals, enterprises, governments, and other non-market institutions need to co-operate with each other in a wide variety of ways. As evidence of this, we have seen a huge growth in all forms of inter-firm coalitions and inter-government agreements over the past two decades (UNCTAD 2000). Fourthly, today we live in a multicultural society, and one in which (not withstanding the burgeoning of fundamentalism) the religious source and underpinning of values—at least in Western societies—plays a much less potent role than a century or more ago. This, as I shall explain later, has considerable implications for the extent to which, and the ways in which, society's stock of moral capital can be upgraded.

These four aspects of contemporary global society then pose both problems and opportunities to the institutions of RGC. On the one hand, we have far more knowledge and experience than we had in the past on how to deal with the challenges and imperfections of the global market place; and, there are far more non-government agencies seeking solutions to these challenges and imperfections than ever before. In particular, in the future, I foresee a more active role being played by NGOs (including transnational NGOs) not only as philanthropic, cultural, and educational institutions, but as pressure groups to influence the other institutions of RGC to promote (what they perceive to be) more socially acceptable and inclusive strategies and policies.

On the other hand, contemporary capitalism comprises more uncertain and volatile characteristics than that of its predecessors; while some of the reactions to its less desirable effects adopted in the nineteenth century are not as readily available today. In particular (for the moment at least) religious revelation as a mentor to moral behaviour is not as strong or pervasive as it once was. At the same time, even some of the most vocal critics of RGC concede that socialism—at least that of the nineteenth-and twentieth-century variety—is not currently a feasible alternative economic system.[19] Neither is a return to the traditional society of the pre-industrial age. But, as I shall suggest later, there remain important elements of both forms of organization, which, if redesigned and updated, can (and indeed must) be a critical component of sustainable RGC of the twenty-first century—and, not least, of the moral and ethical norms underpinning it.

1.5 THE MORAL DIMENSION

In taking my thoughts a step further, I want now to examine, in more depth, the particular role of the four institutions comprising global capitalism; and see how far, and in which direction, they can influence, and be influenced by, the moral ecology of the societies of which they are part. However, before doing so, I think it appropriate to take a look at the concept of morality itself. Here, I am going to eschew any philosophical debate, and take a pragmatic approach. In this context, I interpret *moral behaviour*, first, in a negative sense, as the absence of *immoral* behaviour (which is generally more easily identifiable); second, that it is behaviour which is perceived to be 'right', not just by the persons or institutions engaging it, but by the wider community of which they are part. In this sense, moral behaviour is a step removed from amoral behaviour. I shall also define *moral capital* as the accumulated stock of virtues and values which determines or influences moral behaviour.

Now, of course, this begs the question what is 'right' and takes us to the heart of the debate between *absolute* and *relative* moral values: to what extent, and in what circumstances, is the 'right' moral behaviour transcendent of persons or institutions, and of time and space; and to what extent is it culturally contextual. This latter view—the 'when in Rome do as the Romans do' view—is currently the dominant one of the libertarian ideology of much of Western society. Moral relativism *appears* to reign supreme—but not, I might add, among Eastern societies and particular interest groups. Yet, in practice, in all societies, there are 'no-go' areas, and there are patterns of behaviour which, except in extreme cases, or by minority groups (e.g. terrorists), are thought to be fundamentally wrong.

For myself, I am fully taken with the idea of a pyramid of morals. At its apex there are a limited number of universally accepted moral absolutes; and there is an overlapping consensus between different societies as to the interpretation of these. The philosophy behind these cardinal values is a 'do as you would be done by' philosophy[20] which the Dalai Lama (1999) has chosen to embrace under the twin universal desires of 'happiness' and 'avoidance of suffering'. Tom Donaldson (1996) identifies three of these absolutes, namely respect for human dignity, respect for basic rights, and good citizenship, the latter being defined as 'the need of members of a community to work together to support and improve the institutions on which the community depends' (Donaldson, p. 54).

Further down the pyramid we can identify other values which, to a greater or lesser extent, and depending on how near to the top of the pyramid they are, veer towards the absolute or the relative. Thus, near the top of the pyramid (and some cultures would regard these as absolute) are such virtues as truthfulness, reciprocity, honesty, and justice (although the interpretation of this latter virtue varies greatly across and between societies). At a slightly lower level are such virtues as trust, solidarity, reliability, and loyalty; while most culturally relative of all are likely to be such virtues as duty, prudence, forbearance, diligence, and a sense of guilt or shame.

So, let us accept—as all great sages in history have accepted—that it is possible to identify a set of universally—or near universally—accepted moral values, while at the same time, there are others which are specific to particular societies, institutions and individuals—although the degree of this specificity should not be regarded as being static or unchangeable.

What now of the implications of RGC for moral standards? Capitalism has always set a high premium on certain virtues; although it has also brought to the fore (I am careful not to use the word 'caused!') some un-virtuous characteristics, e.g. greed, acquisitiveness, corruption, and insensitivity. But today's RGC—if it is to be sustained—has its own unique moral imperatives. Not only do some virtues need to be upgraded, and be more generally practised in a global community; but globalization itself is a compelling reappraisal of the content and significance of particular virtues. In one of my earlier contributions (Dunning 2000) I identified three of these, which I named the three Cs: *creativity, co-operation*, and *compassion*.

First consider *creativity*. In today's knowledge-based economy, it is critical to foster the moral virtues which promote human resource development, innovation, initiative, and entrepreneurship. These include, at an individual level, the desire for self-betterment, diligence, and perseverance; and, at a societal level, the recognition and desire to promote the intellectual, emotional, and spiritual potential of all its citizens (the opposite of the 'cog in the wheel' syndrome.)

Secondly, *co-operation*. For reasons I alluded to earlier, we are moving out of an age of hierarchical capitalism and into an age of alliance capitalism. This is placing a premium on the virtues needed for fruitful and sustainable coalitions and partnerships (be they within or between institutions), such as trust, reciprocity, and due diligence—not to mention mutually acceptable moral standards. In addition to their self-generated stock of technical and organizational competence, firms will increasingly need to draw upon the entrepreneurship and capabilities of other institutions. And, to do this successfully, they need to build up their *relational assets*, which comprise the motivation and capability of both managers and workers to get the most out of collaborative agreements (Dunning 2002).

Such alliance capitalism, then, demands a reordering and reprioritization of moral values, and an attitude of mind which Michael Novak has called solidarity, and which in Chapter 11 he suggests 'points simultaneously to personal responsibility and initiative of the human subject and to communion with others'. Although *contractual*, i.e. legally binding relationships, still dominate cross-border business transactions, I suspect that, at the critical points along the value chain, as corporations juggle to balance the advantages of globalization with those of meeting the special needs of local communities, the *covenantal* relationship (which is essentially a trust-intensive relationship) is likely to become more important. (This point is taken up in more detail by Jonathan Sacks in Chapter 9.) The question now arises—do the institutions of RGC currently have the necessary moral expertise and equipment to make this work? Will trust be upgraded as a moral virtue—and will its radius be extended to distant places?

Of course, the unique nature of RGC is precisely that it exposes cross-border economic and social activity to a mosaic of cultural mores. Some of these relate to different religious and other ideologies, some reflect different stages of economic development, the competence of non-market institutions, and the inheritance of traditional behavioural values. Here the question arises as to whether there is—or should be—an ideal, or dominant, moral culture to which individuals and institutions throughout the globe might ascribe (e.g. with respect to honesty, accountability, transparency, and the absence of bribery), which, at the same time, acknowledges and respects the more sensitive differences in cultural mores.

This surely is an area where the combination of the virtues of moral suasion and emotional intelligence needs to be fostered.

In short, I believe, that if RGC is to be upgraded and sustained, the scope and intent of universally accepted moral standards—as they appertain to economic transactions—will have to be both widened and reconfigured; and that a high priority needs to be placed on promoting these standards. At the same time, I also foresee a continuing trend towards the strengthening of local customs and traditions, and the moral values which undergird these (Thomas Friedman has called the balancing of these two forces the 'glocalization' of culture (Friedman 1999)). Here the virtues of tolerance, understanding, and flexibility will be at a premium, but, once again, except in the case of religious fundamentalism, I see the interpretation of these virtues more likely to converge than diverge as globalization progresses.

The *moral absolutes* vs. *moral relatives* debate is not the only one relevant to our current interest. One other worth mentioning, although I do not have the space to dwell on it at length, is the distinction between the kind of socially responsible behaviour, which in the end benefits the individual or institution practising it (what Charles Handy (1998) has called 'proper selfishness'); and that which has no expectation of gain—what we might call pure unselfish behaviour. The latter kind of behaviour is, in fact, quite widespread. It is obviously practised within families; but, also among many NGOs, such as the Red Cross (founded in 1864), philanthropic and religious organizations, and disaster relief agencies. And, both in the past and currently, many firms and wealthy business tycoons have donated large sums of money to educational, cultural, or charitable causes and to the particular needs of developing countries.[21]

What are the implications of RGC for the virtues earlier described? Here, as an example, I come to the third of my C virtues, *compassion*. Compassion I take to incorporate such virtues as benevolence, fairness, justice, and empathy towards others' suffering—be it material or social. One of the attributes of RGC is that it challenges us to widen the 'radius of compassion'. But, to what extent is this a necessary ingredient for its sustainability? Let me put the question another way around. What are the likely consequences of the *absence* of compassionate behaviour—namely, indifference or even hostility towards those who, through no fault of their own, are ill-served by GC or are excluded from its benefits? I think, in the long run at least—as history has demonstrated time and time again—they could be extremely serious, and cut at the very heart of Western civilization as we know it today.

This, then, suggests the need for the richer countries (and particularly those which have benefited from globalization), as a matter of 'proper' selfishness if nothing else, to help upgrade the economic capabilities of their poorer neighbours; and give priority to lowering or removing any import barriers on their products. In addition, à propos the plight of the least developed countries, it is surely incumbent on governments of the wealthier nations, and international agencies to help reduce absolute poverty, by such means as relief debt and/or providing financial and other assistance to help foster the early stages of development (HMSO 2000).[22] This, of course, is not to deny that even the poorer developing countries can do much to help themselves. It is an unpalatable fact that no less than twenty-eight of the forty poorest nations of the world are currently in the midst of armed conflict or have recently emerged from it (HMSO 2000: para. 78). Moreover, in many developing and some transition economies, a considerable part of private savings (40 per cent in the case of sub-Saharan Africa), is held abroad rather than being directed to domestic economic development,[23] and if nothing else, the East Asian economic crisis of the late 1990s, exposed the imperfections and fragility of the financial and institutional architecture of several countries in the region.

1.6   THE INSTITUTIONS OF RGC

But let me now return to look at the role of the institutions of RGC—and those of society in general—in fashioning moral standards. Earlier, while I acknowledged the pre-eminence of the market as an instrument for wealth creation in the new global economy, I argued that governments, supranational agencies, and NGOs had a no less critical role to play. It is, after all, the responsibility of national governments to set up a workable economic system, to supervise its functioning, and to counteract, or compensate for, its deficiencies. It is the responsibility of governments to provide the necessary legal and commercial infrastructure to ensure that the markets within their jurisdiction operate efficiently and fairly. It is supranational agencies which are frequently responsible for setting the terms under which international trade and investment take place. It is NGOs that frequently perform functions which markets and government cannot do or choose not to do, and to act as activist groups to persuade the other institutions of capitalism to reconfigure or reprioritize their objectives, or to tackle them in a different way.

To what extent is RGC leading to a convergence across countries in the way their institutions view their role in the wealth-creating and distributing process? At the one extreme, there are those governments which continue to believe that, subject to minimum safeguards, markets should be left as unencumbered as possible to undertake these tasks. At the other, there are those who doubt the willingness or capability of markets to function in a socially acceptable manner, and believe that only by the positive intervention and co-ordinated policies of extra-market institutions can this be achieved.[24] At the same time, as the power and influence of NGOs is growing, moral issues are coming increasingly to the fore.

I think it is likely that cultural and ideological differences between countries will continue to ensure the active presence of several brands of capitalism for the foreseeable future; though I *do* anticipate that the demands of globalization will tend to lead to a convergence in the respective roles of the four institutions; and that those of intermediate associations, governments, and supranational agencies will become *more* rather than *less* important.[25] I anticipate this, partly because of the changing characteristics of capitalism, as I described earlier, and because it is becoming more widely accepted that RGC should be regarded as a means of advancing human well-being rather than as an end in itself. And, in so far as the unique ingredients of RGC, and the goals by which its success is judged, contain a high moral component, it follows that more attention needs to be given to that content, and how it affects, or is affected by, its institutions.

A great deal has been recently written on the failure of markets to perform in an optimum socially acceptable way; and rather less on their success as wealth-creating institutions. But it is often perceptions, rather than reality and achievements, that influence the judgements and actions of decision takers and those of the general public. It is, after all, human nature to seek the best out of any institution, and to criticize it when it fails to live up to the best. That markets—and for that matter non-market institutions—are imperfect is first, and foremost, a function of the failure of the participants to behave in a way which is conducive to their success. This, in turn, may reflect their incapacity to do so; or because there is insufficient motivation to perform successfully; or, that there is some abuse of economic power by one group of market participants over another; or that the former behave in an unscrupulous or dishonest way. In its turn, such power may arise from the possession of financial or technical strength, or from privileged access to markets of one kind or another. All of these possible deficiencies have a moral content to some extent or other, and each is reflected in the way that the three societal tasks of RGC are tackled. And it is my contention that, although the way these *are* tackled will inevitably reflect country-specific differences in capabilities and social mores, actions of the individuals and institutions must be contained within a set of universally endorsed and practical moral ground rules. There must, in other words, be a common currency of morally acceptable behaviour which guides the attitudes, strategies, and actions of the institutions of RGC.

1.7 HOW BEST TO PROMOTE AND UPGRADE MORAL BEHAVIOUR

We now come to the central (and final) part of this chapter. In the belief that improving the moral standards of the institutions of RGC, and those of their participants, is necessary to broaden and deepen its inclusiveness, and to sustain it in a socially acceptable way, how can this best be achieved in a world made up of countries with many distinctive cultures, ideologies, and types of government regimes; and at different stages of economic development?

I want to suggest we should adopt a dual approach to answering this question. One is a *top-down* approach and the other is a *bottom-up* approach.[26] The *top-down* approach is one in which moral attitudes and standards are coerced (e.g. by means of laws and regulations), or encouraged (e.g. by means of incentives or moral suasion), on one group of individuals and institutions, by another group of individuals or institutions, at a higher level of governance. Examples include, at a macro level, the legal prohibition of the possession of hard drugs, and anti-monopoly legislation; and at a micro level, school authorities disallowing or discouraging anti-social behaviour among their students. The *bottom-up* approach implies the spontaneous or internalized upgrading of moral values and conduct by individuals firms or interest groups which might act as a ground-swell affecting the values and conduct of higher governance institutions. We have seen that many of the nineteenth-century social, educational, and health reforms arose in this way. Today, individuals and NGOs are among the most vocal activist groups, pleading, for example, for the abolition of social discrimination, human rights abuses, and the employment of child labour; and more positively, for upgrading health, safety and labour standards, and environmental protection.

Again, one can use this approach to see how each of the three tasks of RGC may be upgraded, and also how the particular institutions involved may prefer to adopt, or be influenced, by one or other approach. Let me give just a couple of examples of what I mean.

Take first societal goals and the means of better achieving these goals by a *bottom-up* approach. Where the present system is perceived to be deficient in delivering these, consumers, both individually and collectively, can use their purchasing power, to exert a powerful influence both on supermarkets not to stock certain products, and on corporations not to engage in, or buy from, suppliers that engage in unacceptable business practices.[27] Consumer activism is, indeed, very much alive. A Gallup poll in Britain in 1995 found that three out of five UK consumers were prepared to boycott stores or products because they were concerned with the ethical standards of the suppliers. A survey in the US at the same time, revealed that 75 per cent of Americans would not buy from stores selling goods produced in sweatshops; while, a more recent UK poll showed that three quarters of respondents made their choice of products on a green or ethical basis (Hertz 2000: 119–20). Corporations too, like The Body Shop, have quite spontaneously tried to incorporate these values into their product and production profiles.[28] Though this frequently takes the form of 'proper' selfishness, it can still exert a positive influence on the goals and quality of RGC.

These are examples of a *bottom-up* approach, which is now being further abetted by the Internet. Though not without its downsides, I believe that e-commerce could well inject a further element of my third C—compassion—into the value chain. This, I believe, adds to the sustainability of RGC. I also like the idea of shareholder activism, which has been, at least partly, responsible for the launch of a series of ethical funds in several stock markets, and in London, of an ethical share index (FTSE 4 GOOD) comprising 283 publicly quoted companies (each of which has to meet certain environmental, human rights and social standards to merit inclusion.)

I cannot, at this point, resist a comment about the role of NGOs in the global economy.[29] NGOs, as a twenty-first-century version of civil society of the nineteenth century, can perform an essential and valuable function. They can and do prick the social conscience of the other institutions of RGC; and they can, and do, engage in a variety of value-adding activities which neither markets nor governments are able or willing to undertake.

NGOs are, of course, a highly heterogeneous group of institutions ranging from philanthropic societies through religious, educational, and arts-based institutions to political activists and consumer pressure groups. Each has its own particular agenda. Sometimes this is central to the issues addressed by RGC, and sometimes not at all. But certainly there is little doubt that as a result of their activism, issues such as debt relief, human rights, the environment, and safety standards (to name but a few) accorded more serious attention by world leaders and international fora than they would otherwise have been.

Where I think the NGO movement goes awry, or is in danger of going awry, is first in associating itself with the kind of violent (and anti-democratic) demonstrations we have seen in Seattle and Genoa; but secondly, and more importantly, in targeting global capitalism *in toto*, rather than focussing on the inability and unwillingness of particular institutions of GC to properly get to grips with their concerns. It is rarely that globalization *per se* is the cause of such concerns. As much as anything, it is technological advance, and the concentration of economic power, and the inability or unwillingness of some (but not all) of the institutions of capitalism to deal adequately with the phenomena of global connectivity.[30] I also believe that NGOs tend to underestimate the progress which is being made towards RGC (both by MNEs and governments) and of the role RGC itself could play to meet their own needs and aspirations. Indeed, I believe that the smart civil activists are those who recognise that RGC can help them to achieve their objectives, and know how to use it, rather than destroy it.

Thirdly, whatever the justification for their causes, NGOs are rarely in the position to fully comprehend the long-term, or spill-over, effects of their demands. *Inter alia* this is because most NGOs are micro-issue oriented; and, in some cases, their goals are inconsistent with each other. Exactly who and by what means are these conflicts to be resolved? Finally, NGOs are neither the main creators of wealth nor the ultimate guardians of societal interests. They represent part of civil society and of the democratic process, but no more than the other participants in the global market place, do they have the right to dictate societal goals, or the means by which they are achieved. Indeed, a raising of the moral standards of NGOs is itself to be encouraged as part of the upgrading of RGC.

What of the *top-down* approach? This is essentially to do with law making, regulatory, and other coercive mechanisms. Let me concentrate on the role of national governments. While (as I have already said) I do not believe that governments should determine the ethical mores of society, it *is* their job to provide an infrastructure and a safety net, which encourages the kind of virtues which make up acceptable moral behaviour. This is exactly what corporate, civil, and criminal law, backed by appropriate incentives, example, and suasion seeks to do. And it is the quality of these ingredients of capitalism which separates the thriving economies in the world from the rest—and sustains the former in times of social upheaval better than the latter.

A case in point is the reintroduction of capitalism into the Russian Federation in the early 1990s.[31] When the erstwhile communist country was opened up, the

IMF and World Bank stepped in to aid its transition to a market-based economy. But almost the entire focus of the guidance given by these two institutions was directed to removing the technical barriers to free markets—and, to do so, according to the principles of the Washington Consensus. Yet what was no less needed from the West was its help to establish a modern, transparent and corruption-free political, legal, and banking system, and to provide the moral underpinnings for free markets, the like of which had been absent in Russia for the past three generations.

As a result, the aftermath of the Cold War saw little effort being made (as it was in the case of Marshall Aid directed to Europe after 1945) to reform the Federation's institutional framework, or to encourage the renaissance of civic societies which had been dormant for so long. To this extent, the West failed the erstwhile Soviet Union; it offered a new materialism without the social capital and moral values necessary to support and sustain it. As a result, over the last decade, there has been a huge increase in crime and kleptocracy,[32] and in income inequality, while the real economy has shrunk by up to a third (Stiglitz 1998). Should we not be surprised then that, in a recent poll, four out of five Russians indicated they would support a reinstatement of the old Soviet Union? All too late, the protagonists of free global markets have begun to realize that, without the right institutional and moral infrastructure, the profit motive—combined with full capital market liberalization—rather than offering the right incentives for wealth creation is likely to 'spark off a drive to strip assets and ship wealth abroad' (Stiglitz 1998).

1.8   THE DRIVING FORCE OF MORAL BEHAVIOUR

What then drives (or should drive) the individuals and institutions shaping RGC to behave as they do? What is the source of their moral standards; and what influences them to upgrade these standards? I shall eschew the 'nature' versus 'nurture' debate, and, instead, draw upon Brian Griffiths' threefold categorization of the sources of moral values influencing business conduct, which he made in a perceptive contribution three years ago (Griffiths 1999).

The first source, is one to which we have already referred, and what Griffiths terms *enlightened self interest*. This philosophy acknowledges few moral absolutes and is fully consistent with the current cult of self-centred and secular individualism. But, because of its particularity, its subjectivity, and its instability, both Griffiths and I would aver it is too insecure a foundation on which to build RGC; though, as I have already acknowledged, a 'when in Rome' type cultural relativism may be appropriate at the lower end of the moral pyramid.

The second source is adherence to *global ethic* based upon a universal consensus on 'particular human values, criteria and basic attitudes' (Küng 1998). This ethic is particularly associated with the German theologian, Professor Hans Küng (although other analysts such as Amitai Etzioni, George Soros, and Francis Fukuyama come near to endorsing it) and is described by him in Chapter 6 of this volume. It was first promulgated at an inaugural meeting of the Council of the Parliament of the World's Religions in Chicago in 1993. It is based very much on a 'do as you would be done by' credo which emphasizes the need for a broad consensus among the different institutions of global capitalism. At the top of its moral pyramid, it identifies such basic values as humanity and reciprocity; and, at the next layer, the core values of respect for life, non-violence, solidarity, justice, truthfulness, and partnership. It then relates these to a series of overlapping circles which embrace the main institutions of global capitalism.

The strength of this particular approach, as Lord Griffiths observes, is in its acceptance of both religious pluralism and secularism, its inclusive geographical coverage, and the fact that it 'carries with it no baggage from the past'. At the same time, it recognizes that the quality of global society cannot be enhanced without, 'the consciousness of individuals'—and that is the rub. Exactly how is this done? If there is a concern I have with this concept, it is that it tends to be 'all things to all men', and it is left to each individual to find his or her moral salvation. Nevertheless, it is a huge advance in helping us to formulate and better understand the moral prerequisites for sustainable RGC.

The third source of moral standards identified by Griffiths is the *revealed monotheistic faiths* of Christianity, Islam, and Judaism—though I would extend these to embrace at least some of the Eastern religions.[33] It is my interpretation that the difference between this approach and that of a global ethic is that the former believes it to be an absolute necessity for there to be some kind of external (= beyond self) revelation or inspiration which prompts and guides spontaneous moral behaviour. In other words, it is not enough to identify a number of virtues as set out, for example, by the Parliament of the World's Religions which must be embraced by any new global morality. What is also required is a belief in a supreme being (or the principles enumerated by the disciples of a supreme being), which guides and inspires one's conduct,[34] and adds to one's inclination to behave in a moral fashion.

Now clearly, in this post-modern age, for the time being at least, a morality based on religious *belief*—as opposed to religious *teachings*—is unlikely to appeal to the majority of individuals, especially in the West; and certainly Professor Küng's eclectic approach seems to offer more realistic promise. Yet the impact of this third way should not be underestimated, in so far as those men and women who cling to the belief that there is a force beyond themselves influencing their actions, may well provide an inspirational catalyst for those who accept the behavioural principles of particular religions without having any religious faith themselves.

It is this combination of revelation, example, and education, and of a '*bottom-up*' and '*top-down*' approach to instilling general agreed ethical standards, that I believe is likely to prove the best approach to providing the moral capital necessary to upgrade and sustain RGC.[35] And I further believe that there is sufficient in common among the teachings of the revealed religions, and particularly the three monotheistic faiths, to suggest that their leaders have an enormous responsibility to both clearly identify these and promote them among their followers.

However, I also believe—with Jonathan Sacks (1997*a*, *b*)—that just as economists and business strategists should take care not to extrapolate their ideas and measuring techniques into domains which value goods and services other than by the measuring rod of money,[36] religious leaders, and others interested in promoting *extra*-market virtues, should be cautious in proselytizing their beliefs with respect to the economic management of capitalist institutions. Extending the views of Sacks, the task of the mainstream religions should be less to cast aspersions on the integrity and workings of the institutions of RGC, and more to 'shape the way its participants function with a serious moral commitment to values not reducible to the market' (Sacks 1999*b*: 54). Coming from a different perspective, this view is endorsed by George Soros who argues that a purely transactional approach to economic activity (or what he calls market fundamentalism) governed by the principle of self interest, is in danger of undermining social values and loosening moral constraints (Soros 1998: 75).

1.9 SUMMARY AND CONCLUSIONS

The time has come to sum up the main points of this introductory chapter. I started with the proposition that, at its best, global capitalism (as I defined it) is, in our present state of knowledge, the most efficient economic system for creating and sustaining wealth. But I quickly went on to say that its efficacy must be judged in relation to its willingness and capabilities to meet the broader economic and social goals of society. In this, as things stand today, it is currently found wanting for three reasons. The first is its institutions—and particularly the market—are less well designed for the production and exchange of *public* or social goods and services than *private* goods and services; and that the former are becoming a rising component of our daily welfare. The second is that there are a series of 'technical' failures in each of its institutions judged by their ability to meet the demands of democratic capitalism *per se*. The third is that the moral underpinning of these same institutions needs reconfiguring and upgrading.

I suggested that, up to now, the attention of scholars has been primarily directed at reducing these imperfections which range from specific distortions, e.g. monopoly power, to the instability of international financial markets at a time of volatility, uncertainty, and the ease at which capital can move across national boundaries. Rather differently, however, my focus has been to identify and evaluate the kind of current moral failures of the institutions of global capitalism, which not only constrain the willingness and capability of the system to operate efficiently and equitably, but also the quality of societal values as a whole.

I then went on to distinguish between absolute and relative moral values, and argued that globalization was leading to a convergence of the former, but a divergence of the latter. This, in and of itself, called for the virtues of tolerance and patience. I also distinguished between virtuous self-interest and pure unselfishness, and indicated how both had a role to play in making for a more compassionate global society. In identifying the virtues especially needed to upgrade and sustain RGC, I focused on those embodied in the 3 Cs—*creativity, co-operation,* and *compassion.* I then went on to indicate how both a *top-down* (an externally imposed or influenced) approach, and a *bottom-up* (a spontaneous or internally generated) approach to upgrading moral attitudes and values were complementary routes of achieving this goal; although, I suggested the balance of choice between these two options was likely to vary between interest groups and societies over time, and according to the particular aspect of RGC being considered.

I finally tackled (albeit somewhat tentatively) two related questions. From whence do our moral values come and what must be done to promote those most relevant to RGC? I explored three possibilities. The first was a nurturing of such values primarily through the stick (punishment of bad behaviour) and carrot (praise of good behaviour), in order to steer self interest in the right direction. Here, I would also like to see a renaissance of relatively unfamiliar and generally disliked concepts of shame and guilt.[37] Second, I examined the value of a global ethic, and third I looked at the role of the religious revelation, which might guide both *top-down* and *bottom-up* approaches. Here I suggested that, in addition to a reasoned acceptance of the need for upgraded ethical mores, there was an additional *viz.* an external, source of authority, and that all monotheistic faiths believed in this—although, they differ in their valuation or prioritization of particular virtues.[38] I argued that this put a huge responsibility on the part of the religious leaders to present a concerted vociferous, reasoned, but conciliatory, voice on this issue—without, I might add, straying too much into the methodological territory of economics and politics. Might we not conceive of a group of five, six, or seven (or whatever number) of religious leaders to perform a similar task in the *moral* domain to that of the group of eight in the economic and political domain? Is this such a pipe dream?

Finally, I would like to think my colleagues engaged in the teaching and research of international business (IB) will grasp the cudgel in exploring the relevance of morally related issues to the functioning of global capitalism and the global market place. It is too important a subject to be neglected. Of course, for a long time, IB scholars have identified the importance of culture in influencing the success of firms and countries; and some economists, notably the Nobel Prize winner Amartya Sen, have argued for moral issues to be more widely embraced by economists. Sen's recent book on *Development as Freedom* is a brilliant exposition of how the transformation of societies through economic development cannot be successfully achieved without a simultaneous reconfiguration and upgrading of moral standards. My plea is for mainstream IB scholars to integrate the moral dimension, in their analysis and thinking as they seek to explain how global capitalism might both benefit and be made more acceptable to a much larger number of people across the planet, than it is at present; and for each of its institutions to work in a holistic and co-operative manner to achieve this goal.

NOTES

I am indebted to Jack Behrman, Peter Buckley, Mark Casson, Tony Corley, Peter Hart, Robert Heillsronner and Steve Kobrin for the helpful comments they made on an earlier draft of this chapter.

1. See especially Friedman (2000), Gray (1998), Hertz (2000), HMSO (2000), Soros (1998), Stiglitz (1998), and the World Bank (2001).

2. As reviewed and identified, for example, in Dunning (2000), Dicken (2000), Hirst and Thompson (1999), HMSO (2000), and Svetlicic (2000).

3. Amartya Sen (1995) reminds us that the production of public and/or not for profit goods and services are part of the capitalist economic system; and that non-market institutions are frequently in a better position to supply these goods and services. Many years earlier, Fred Hirsch (1976) argued that in post-industrial economies, social goods and services (e.g. health, safety, pollution control, parks, etc.) were assuming an increasing role in the GDP of countries.

4. In 1991, the Pope gave his definition of responsible capitalism as 'an economic system which recognizes the fundamental and positive role of business, the market and private property and the resulting responsibility for the means of production, as well as the free human creativity in the economic sector' (as quoted by Sirocco 1994: 18).

5. Thus emphasizing that capitalism should be an inclusive economic system and directed to meeting the needs of society as a whole rather than simply those participating in market transactions.

6. See e.g. the writings of Smith (1776), Hirschman (1982), Gray (1992), Barry (1995).

7. Albert Hirschman has called this the 'doux-commerce' or civilizing force of markets (Hirschman 1982).

8. Much of the defence of the market as a moral system rests on the assumption that markets are ideally competitive (or perfect in the economists' sense). But as Soros (1998: 197) has pointed out, if this is so, such markets *de facto* exempt its participants from a moral choice *as long as they abide by its rules*. Only when markets are less than perfect (as indeed is usually the case), does the issue of choice enter the picture. And, in such a situation, there is absolutely no reason to suppose that there is something inherent in the market which will compel each of its participants to behave in a morally responsible way.

9. To quote from Aristotle, for example. He wrote: 'Wealth obviously is not the good we seek, for the sole purpose it serves is to provide the means of getting something else. So far as it goes the ends we have already mentioned (pleasure, virtue, and honour) would have a better title to be considered the good, for they are to be desired for their own account.' Quoted by Handy 1998: 15.

10. More generally, several studies have questioned the idea that economic welfare (as normally measured) buys happiness. A report compiled by Robert Worcester in 1998 for Demos found that there was little correlation between GNP per head and people's 'perception' of their own contentment or happiness; while another more recent study (Cooper, Garcia-Penolosa, and Funk 2001) has shown that while real incomes and consumption have more than trebled in the UK, Italy, and Germany over the past thirty years, reported happiness levels in the those countries have declined. By contrast, other surveys have suggested there is quite a significant correlation between economic freedom and economic prosperity (Johnson, Holmes, and Kirkpatrick 1999).

11. Such behaviour includes corruption, the by-passing of safety or hygiene regulations, and questionable labour practices (as in the case of some sweatshops and child labour). Of course, these are not new concerns; nor are they specific to globalization. But they have been exacerbated and brought to the public awareness as a result of globalization.

12. A concept spelled out by Charles Handy (Handy 1997).

13. As set out in some detail in Buckley and Casson (1988), Dunning (2002).

14. There are, however, outstanding exceptions to this statement. For a discussion of the contribution of leading US business-related trusts and foundations the betterment of living standards in developing countries, see Cowley (2002).

15. Victorian moralists believed in a strictly limited role of the state. T. H. Green, for example, was opposed to paternal government. He wrote 'The State should promote morality by strengthening the moral disposition of the individual, not by subjecting the individual to any kind of moral tutelage' Green (1941) quoted in Himmelfarb 1995. Wise words; and highly relevant to todays's debate!

16. Set up as a microcosm of civil society in 1884 by the Revd. Samuel Barnett, Vicar of St Jude's in London, Toynbee Hall was not a charitable institution. Instead of providing economic relief, it dispensed learning, culture, and social amenities, and it did so in Whitechapel, the poorest district of London. The Hall was dedicated in memory of Arnold Toynbee, who believed the Victorian middle classes had a duty both to set an example and to educate the working classes in the concept of citizenship (Himmelfarb 1995).

17. The terrorist attacks in New York and Washington in September 2001 may well add impetus to a reappraisal of social values.

18. To quote from Michael Novak 'Human capital includes moral labels, such as hard work, co-operativeness, social trust, alertness, honesty and social habits such as respect for the rule of law' (Novak 1999).

19. At the same time, as one observer (Rothkopf 2002: 2) has put it 'Somewhere in the world today walks the next Marx . . . we may not know from which region he will hail or his particular approach. But we can be sure that someone, somewhere will offer an alternative vision.'

20. From time immemorial, most, if not all, major faiths and moral philosophies accept this as one of—if not *the*—universal moral values. Each religion and philosophy has its particular manner of expressing it. In the Christian faith for example, it is essentially contained in Christ's injunction 'Thou shalt love thy neighbour as thyself'.

21. The Bill and Melinda Gates Foundation, for example, has an asset base of $24.2 billion for promoting healthcare in the developing world (Cowley 2002).

22. This issue is taken up in some detail, by Gordon Brown in Chapter 14 and Shirley Williams in Chapter 15.

23. Such a flight of sorely needed capital can be reversed. In Uganda, for example, following domestic economic reform, and a crackdown on corruption, net private capital more than doubled as a percentage of GNP in the 1990s (HMSO 2000: para. 153).

24. In Hall and Soskice (2001) a distinction is made between the policies pursued by governments of *liberal market* economies (where firms 'coordinate their activities primarily via hierarchies and competitive market arrangements') and *co-ordinated market* economies (where firms 'depend more heavily on non-market relationships to coordinate their endeavours with other actors, and to construct their core competencies')

(2001: 8). Examples of the former economies are the US, the UK, Taiwan, and until recently Hong Kong; and of the latter, Germany, South Korea, and China.

25. See also the views of Paul Streeten (2001) on this subject.

26. See also the incisive comments made on an earlier contribution of mine (Dunning 2000) by Buckley and Casson (2001).

27. Noreen Hertz, in her discussion of this issue, quotes the words of two CEOs of leading brand name corporations. The one told her 'What we fear most is not legislation', and another 'If people think corporations are powerful they haven't been in a corporation...Consumer choice does not allow us to have unfettered power' (Hertz 2000: 126).

28. In 1999, following a series of exposures of the use of child labour and sweatshops by some of the leading US apparel manufacturers and clothing retailers, a group of these corporations joined with human rights and labour representatives to establish a Fair Labour Association. *Inter alia* the Association would formally accredit auditors to certify companies as complying with an agreed code of conduct relating to minimum wages and working conditions including restrictions on child labour and working hours. This was followed by a Workers Rights Consortium, a body comprising university students and officials and labour and human rights campaigners. (Friedman 2000: 206, Hertz 2000: 138). At the same time, as mainstream economists frequently point out, in the past, the first stage of economic development of industrializing countries has always taken the form of something akin to sweatshops. The question which moralists and others have to address is not so much 'whether' but 'what kind' of sweatshops.

29. For a more extensive discussion of the role of global civil society as it is now emerging, see Chapter 12, by Richard Falk.

30. For a recent examination of the panoply of NGOs and popular transnational movements see e.g. Sinnar (1995/6), Scholtz et al. (1999), Ostry (1998), Vakil (1997), and Wilson and Whitmore (1998).

31. As discussed further by Joseph Stiglitz in Chapter 4 and Shirley Williams in Chapter 15.

32. Thomas Friedman (2000: 146) defines kleptocracy as a situation in which many, or all, of the functions of state system—from tax collection to customs, to privatization to regulation—have become so infected by corruption that legal transactions become the exception rather than the norm.

33. See especially Chapters 7–10 of this volume; and also the observations of Jack Behrman (Chapter 5) and Michael Novak (Chapter 11).

34. The ultimate is the Christian belief that the spirit of a living Christ may motivate and guide a person's attitudes and behaviour. See also Brian Griffith's views in Chapter 7.

35. A view also shared by other contributors to this volume, and particularly by Khurshid Ahmad in Chapter 8.

36. Beyond, that is, of the moral scope of the transactional economics. For a discussion on the commensurability of non-market values and the concept of value pluralism by which it may be possible to compare values which themselves require different measurement techniques, see Hamlin (1995) and Chapter 3 of this volume.

37. As set out in Lal (1998) and Chapter 2 in this volume.

38. For example, Islam places great stress on social justice as a primary virtue; Judaism lays particular emphasis on duty and tradition; while Christianity places love and compassion at the top of the pyramid of its virtues. (See Chapters 7–9 of this volume.)

REFERENCES

Barry, N. (1995), 'What Moral Constraints for Business?' In S. Brittan and A. Hamlin (eds.), *Market Capitalism and Moral Values* (Aldershot: Edward Elgar), 57–78.

Buckley, P. J., and Casson, M. (1988), 'A Theory of Cooperation in International Business.' In F. J. Contractor and P. Lorange, (eds.), *Cooperative Strategies in International Business* (Lexington: D. C. Heath and Co.), 31–53.

—— (2001), 'The Moral Basis of Global Capitalism: Beyond the Eclectic Theory', *International Journal of the Economics of Business* 8(2): 303–27.

Church of England (2000), *Faith in a Global Economy* (London: General Synod of the Church of England), GS Misc. 538.

Cooper, B., Garcia-Penolosa, C., and Funk, P. (2001), 'Status Effects and Negative Utility Growth', *Economic Journal* 111(473): 642–65.

Cowley, G., (2002), 'Bill's biggest bet yet', *Newsweek*, 4 February, 45–52.

Dahrendorf, R. (2000), *Politics and Society*. Lecture presented at Reading University, Nov. (mimeo).

Dalai Lama (1999), *Ethics for the New Millenium* (New York: Riverhead Books).

Davies, J. (ed.) (1995), *God and the Market Place* (London: Institute of Economic Affairs, Health and Welfare Unit), Choice in Welfare, No. 14.

De Tocqueville (1981), *Democracy in America*, abbreviated. with an introduction by Thomas Bender (New York: The Modern Library).

Dicken, P. (2000), *Global Shift*, 4th edn. (New York: The Guilford Press).

Donaldson, T. (1996), 'Values in Tension: Ethics Away from Home', *Harvard Business Review*, Sept/Oct.: 48–62.

Dunning, J. H. (2000), *Global Capitalism at Bay?* (London and New York: Routledge).

—— (2002), 'Relational Assets, Networks and International Business'. In F. Contractor and P. Lorange (eds.), *Cooperative Strategies and Alliances* (Oxford: Elsevier Science), 570–93.

Elazar, D. (1989), *People and Polity: The Organizational Dynamics of World Jewry* (Detroit: Wayne State University Press).

Etzioni, A. (1996), *The New Golden Rule: Community and Morality in a Democratic Society* (New York: Basic Books).

—— (1998), *The Moral Dimension: Towards a New Economics* (New York: Free Press).

Falk, R. (1998), 'Global Civil Society: Perspectives, Initiatives, Movements', *Oxford Development Studies* 26(1): 99–110.

Flemming, J. S. (1995), 'The Ethics of Unemployment and Mafia Capitalism.' In S. Brittan and A. Hamlin (eds.), *Market Capitalism and Moral Values* (Aldershot: Edward Elgar).

Friedman, T. L. (2000), *The Lexus and the Olive Tree* (New York: Anchor Books).

Fukuyama, F. (1999), *The Great Disruption* (London: Profile Books).

Gray, J. (1992), *The Moral Foundations of Market Institutions* (London: Institute of Economic Affairs, Health and Welfare Unit), Choice in Welfare Series No. 10.

—— (1998), *False Dawn* (New York: The New Press).

Green, D. (1993), *Reinventing Civil Society* (London: Institute of Economic Affairs, Health and Welfare Unit), Choice in Welfare, No. 17.

Green, T. H. (1941/1882), *Lectures on the Principles of Political Obligation* (London).

Griffiths, B. (1996), *The Business of Values*. Inaugural Hansen-Wessner Memorial Lecture (US Service Master Company).

—— (1999), *The Role of the Business Corporation as a Moral Community* (Oxford: The Hansen-Wessner Memorial Lecture 1999).

Hall, P., and Soskice, D. (2001), *Varieties of Capitalism* (Oxford: Oxford University Press).

Hamlin, A. (1995), 'The Morality of the Market.' In S. Brittan and A. Hamlin (eds.), *Market Capitalism and Moral Values* (Aldershot: Edward Elgar), 137–50.

——Giersch, H., and Norton, A. (1996), *Markets, Morals and Community* (St. Leonards, Australia: Centre for Independent Studies).

Handy, C. (1998), *The Hungry Spirit* (London: Arrow Books).

Harrison, L. E., and Huntington, S. P. (eds.) (2000), *Culture Matters: How Values Shape Human Progress* (New York: Basic Books).

Heilbroner, R. (1992), *21st Century Capitalism* (London: University College Press).

Henderson, D. (1998), *The Changing Fortunes of Economic Liberalism* (London: Institute of Economic Affairs).

Hertz, N. (2000), *The Silent Takeover: Global Capitalism and the Death of Democracy* (London: William Heinemann).

Himmelfarb, G. (1995), *The Demoralization of Society: From Victorian Virtues to Modern Values* (London: Institute of Economic Affairs, Health and Welfare Unit).

Hirsch, F. (1976), *Social Limits to Growth* (Cambridge, Mass.: Harvard University Press).

Hirschman, A. (1977), *The Passions and the Interests: Political Arguments for Capitalism before its Triumph* (Princeton: Princeton University Press).

——(1982), 'Rival Interpretations of Market Society: Civilizing, Destructive or Feeble', *Journal of Economic Literature* 20 (Dec.): 1463–84.

Hirst, P., and Thompson, G. (1999), *Globalisation in Question?* 2nd edn. (Cambridge: Polity Press).

HMSO (2000), *Eliminating World Poverty: Making Globalisation Work for the Poor* (London: HMSO. Cmd. 5006).

Johnson, B. R., Holmes, K. R., and Kirkpatrick, M. (1999), *The 1999 Index of Economic Freedom* (New York: The Heritage Foundation/*Wall Street Journal*).

Kennedy, P. (1993), *Preparing for the Twenty First Century* (New York: Vintage Books).

Küng, H. (1998), *A Global Ethic for Global Politics and Economics* (Oxford: Oxford University Press).

——(2001), *Globale Markwirtschaft und Ethische Rahmenordnu* (Tübingen: mimeo).

Lal, D. (1998), *Unintended Consequences* (Cambridge, Mass.: MIT Press).

Landes, D. (1998), *The Wealth and Poverty of Nations* (New York: W. W. Norton & Co.).

Lewis, C. S. (1978), *The Abolition of Man* (London: Collins).

Mandeville, B. (1924/1729), *The Fable of the Bees*, ed. F. B. Kaye (Oxford: Clarendon Press). *Newsweek* (2002).

North, D. C. (1999), *Understanding the Process of Economic Change* (London: Institute of Economic Affairs, The 1998 Wincott Lecture).

Novak, M. (1991), *The Spirit of Democratic Capitalism* (Lanham, Md.: Madison Books).

——(1999), *Solidarity in a Time of Globalization* (Notre Dame: University of Notre Dame, mimeo).

——and Preston, R. (1994), *Christian Capitalism or Christian Socialism?* (London: Institute of Economic Affairs, Health and Welfare Unit).

Olson, M. (1982), *The Rise and Fall of Nation* (New Haven and London: Yale University Press).

Ostry, S. (1998), *Convergence between Sovereignty and Policy Scope for Compromise* (Ottawa: Carleton University, mimeo).

Presbyterian Church (1984), *Christian Faith and Economic Justice* (Atlanta, Ga.: Office of the General Assembly).

Preston, R. H. (1993), *Religion and the Ambiguities of Capitalism* (Cleveland, Oh.: The Pilgrim Press).

Putnam, R. D. (1995), 'Bowling Alone: America's Declining Social Capital', *Journal of Democracy* 6: 65–78.

Rawls, J. (1972), *A Theory of Justice* (Oxford: Clarendon Press).

Reed., C. (ed.) (2001), *Development Matters. Christian Perspectives on Globalization* (London: Church House Publishing).

Rifkin, J. (2000), *The Age of Access* (London: Penguin Books).

Rothkopth, D. J. (2002), 'The Failures of Capitalism', *Washington Post National*, weekly edn., 28 Jan.–3 Feb.: 2.

Russell, B. (1962), *A History of Western Philosophy* (London: George Allen & Unwin).

Sacks, J. (1997*a*), 'New Members Please Apply', *Time*, 7 July: 11–12.

—— (1997*b*), *The Politics of Hope* (London: Jonathan Cape).

—— (1999), *Morals and Markets* (London: Institute of Economic Affairs).

Salamon, L. M. (1994), 'The Rise of the Non-Profit Sector', *Foreign Affairs* 73(4): 109–22.

Scholtz, J.A., O'Brien, R., and Williams, M. (1999), 'The WTO and Civil Society', *Journal of World Trade* 33(1): 107–23.

Searle, G. R. (1998), *Morality and the Market in Victorian Britain* (Oxford: Clarendon Press).

Sen. A. (1995), 'Moral Codes and Economic Success.' In S. Brittan and A. Hamlin (eds.), *Market Capitalism and Moral Values* (Aldershot: Edward Elgar).

—— (1999), *Development as Freedom* (Oxford: Oxford University Press).

Sinnar, S. (1995/6), 'Mixed Blessing: The Growing Influence of NGOs', *Harvard International Review* 18(1): 54–7, 79, 80.

Sirocco, R. A. (1994), *A Moral Basis for Liberty* (London: Institute for Economic Affairs, Health and Welfare Unit), Religion and Liberty Series, No. 2.

Smith, A. (1937/1776), *An Inquiry into the Nature and Causes of the Wealth of Nations*, ed. Edwin Cannon (London: Modern Library).

Soros, G. (1998), *The Crisis of Global Capitalism* (London: Little, Brown and Company).

—— (2002), *On Globalization* (Oxford: Public Affairs).

Stiglitz, J. (1998), *Towards a New Paradigm for Development* (Geneva: UNCTAD), 9th Raul Prebisch Lecture, 1998.

—— (2002), *Globalization and its Discontents* (London: Allen Lane).

Streeten, P. (2001), *Globalization: Threat or Opportunity* (Copenhagen: Copenhagen Business Press).

Svetlicic, M. (2000), 'Globalisation: Neither Hell nor Paradise', *Journal of International Relations and Development* 3(4): 369–94.

Tawney, R. (1926), *Religion and the Rise of Capitalism* (London: John Murray).

Tillich, P. (1971), 'Political Expectations.' In J. L. Adams (ed.), (New York: Harper & Row), 51.

UNCTAD (2000), *World Investment Report 2000: Cross Border Mergers and Acquisition* (New York and Geneva: UN).

UNDP (2000), *Human Development Report 2000* (Oxford: Oxford University Press).

Vakil, A. C. (1997), 'Confronting the Classification Problem; Towards a Taxonomy of NGOs', *World Development* 25(12): 2057–70.

Weber, M. (1930), *The Protestant Ethic and the Spirit of Capitalism* (London: George Allen & Unwin).

Wilson, M. G., and Whitmore, E. (1998), 'The Transnationalization of Popular Movements: Social Policy Making from Below', *Canadian Journal of Development Studies* 19(1): 7–36.

Worcester, R. (1998), 'More than Money.' In I. Christie and L. Nash (eds.), *The Good Life* (London: Demos).

World Bank (1999), *Attacking Poverty: World Development Report 2000–2001* (Oxford: Oxford University Press).

2

Private Morality and Capitalism:
Learning from the Past

DEEPAK LAL

2.1 INTRODUCTION

In thinking about the role of morality in economic life I propose to use an analytical framework I developed in my *Unintended Consequences* (Lal 1998*a*), which is somewhat different from the one presented by John Dunning in the first chapter. At the same time it will seek to pose and answer some of the questions he has raised concerning the role of morality and global capitalism. This framework is presented in Section 2.2. From this, I provide a highly condensed account of the role of morality in economic life from the Stone Age to the present. In particular I shall emphasize the Great Divergence that took place among the leading Eurasian civilizations in the high Middle Ages as a result of two Papal revolutions which replaced a *communalist* ethic, common to most of the agrarian Eurasian civilizations, by an *individualist* ethic of Western Christendom. This is the theme of Section 2.3.

These two theories provide an obvious point of departure for the discussion in Section 2.4 of the differences in the ethics of the great civilizations down to our own day, and the strange course that Western individualism has taken over the last two hundred years. In doing so, I hope it will be possible to examine whether or not a global or universally agreed morality is needed for global capitalism to thrive, and, if it is, what form it should take. Section 2.5 relates my conclusions to the role of three of the four institutions of global capitalism identified by Dunning—viz. markets, governments, and civil society—in fostering global capitalism. In doing so, while I accept Dunning's distinctions between globalization, the global market place, and global capitalism, I intend to use a somewhat narrower definition of the latter—which roughly corresponds to what has been called (sometimes derisively) the Anglo-Saxon model of capitalism.

2.2 ANALYTICAL FRAMEWORK

From an economist's perspective, morality is best looked upon as part of the institutional infrastructure of a society. This institutional infrastructure, broadly defined, consists of informal constraints like cultural norms (which encompass morality) and the more formal ones which are embodied in particular and more purposeful organizational structures. *Inter alia* such formal rules embrace the Common Law, which form a spontaneous order in Fredrich Hayek's sense (Hayek 1960, 1979) as having evolved without any conscious design, and which constrain human behaviour.

But as soon as we talk about constraining human behaviour, we are implicitly acknowledging that there is some basic 'human nature' to be constrained. While we take up this question in greater detail below, as a first cut we can accept the economist's model of '*Homo Economicus*' which assumes that human beings are both rational and motivated purely by self interest: maximizing utility as consumers and (long term) profits (or some other goal) as producers. So, as a start, the function of the rules constraining human nature which comprise institutions must be to limit such self-seeking behaviour.

This immediately points to another significant feature and reason for the existence of institutions. If Robinson Crusoe was alone on his island he would have no reason to constrain his basic human nature. It is only with the appearance of Man Friday that some constraints on both him and Crusoe might be necessary if each co-operates so as to increase their mutual gains: and to do so by specializing in tasks in which each has a comparative advantage. This, then immediately leads us to the notion of 'transactions costs'—a concept which is even more slippery to deal with than that of institutions.

The reason why there is a close relation between institutions and transactions costs is that, as Robin Matthews pointed out several years ago, 'to a large extent transactions costs are costs of relations between people' (Matthews 1986: 906); and that institutions are *par excellence* ways of controlling or influencing the form, content, and outcome of these interactions.

Culture is the informal aspect of institutions which influence and constrain human behaviour. But if 'institutions' are a murky concept, 'culture' is even more so. From my perspective, I have found an interpretation adopted by ecologists particularly useful (see e.g. Colinvaux 1983). They emphasize that, unlike other animals, the human being is unique because of its intelligence and motivation to change its environment by learning. It does not have to mutate into a new species to adapt to the changed environment. It learns new ways of surviving in the new environment, and then fixes them by social custom. These social customs form the culture of the relevant group, which is then transmitted to new members of the group (mainly children) who do not have to invent these 'new' ways *de novo* for themselves.

This definition of culture fits in well with the economists' notion of equilibrium. Frank Hahn has described an equilibrium state as one where self-seeking agents learn nothing new so that their behaviour is routinized (Hahn 1973). It represents an adaptation by agents to the economic environment in which the economy 'generates messages which do not cause agents to change the theories which they hold or the policies which they pursue' (Hahn 1973: 28). This routinized behaviour is clearly close to the ecologist's notion of social custom which fixes a particular human niche. On this view, the equilibrium will only be disturbed if the environment changes, and so, in the subsequent process of adjustment, the human agents will have to abandon their past theories, which would now have been falsified. To survive, they must learn to adapt to their new environment through a process of trial and error. There will then be a new social equilibrium, which relates to a state of society and economy in which 'agents have adapted themselves to their economic environment and where their expectations in the widest sense are in the proper meaning not falsified' (Hahn, ibid.).

This equilibrium need not be unique nor optimal, given the environmental parameters. But once a particular socio-economic order is established, and is proved to be an adequate adaptation to the new environment, it is likely to be stable, as there is no reason for the human agents to alter it in any fundamental manner, unless and until the environmental parameters are altered. Nor is this social order likely to be the result of a deliberate rationalist plan. We have known since Adam Smith that it is possible for an unplanned, but coherent and seemingly planned, social system to emerge from the independent actions of many individuals pursuing their different ends, which may lead to final outcomes very different from those intended.

Here it may be useful to distinguish between two major sorts of beliefs relating to different aspects of the environment. These are the *material* and *cosmological* beliefs of a particular culture. The former relate to ways of making a living, and beliefs about the material world—in particular about the economy. The latter relate to our understanding of the world around us and mankind's place in it; which, in turn, will determine how people view the purpose and meaning of their lives, and their interpersonal relationships. There is considerable cross-cultural evidence that material beliefs are more malleable than cosmological ones. The former can and do respond rapidly to changes in the material environment. There is greater hysterisis in cosmological beliefs—on how, in Plato's words, 'one should live'. Moreover the cross-cultural evidence shows that, rather than the environment, it is the language group to which people belong that influences these world-views (Hallpike 1986).

This distinction between material and cosmological beliefs is important for economic performance because it translates into two distinct types of transactions costs which are important in explaining not only market but also government (or bureaucratic) failure. Broadly speaking, transactions costs can usefully be distinguished between those associated with the efficiency of *exchange*, and those associated with *policing* opportunistic behaviour by economic agents. The former relate to the costs of finding potential trading partners and determining their supply–demand offers, and the latter to monitoring or enforcing the execution of promises and agreements.

These two types of transactions costs need to be kept distinct from each other. The economic historian Douglass North (1990) and the institutionalist theorist Oliver Williamson (1985) have both evoked the notion of transactions costs, and used them to explain various organizational arrangements relevant for economic performance. While both are primarily concerned with the costs of opportunistic behaviour, for North these arise as a result of the more idiosyncratic and non-repeated transactions accompanying the widening of the market, while for

Williamson they stem from the asymmetries in information facing principals and agents in cases where the critical performance related characteristics of the agent can be concealed from the principal. Both these are cases where it is the policing aspects of transactions costs which are at issue, not those concerning exchange.

To see the relevance of the distinction between beliefs and transactions costs for economic performance, it may be useful to briefly delineate how material and cosmological beliefs have altered since the Stone Age in Eurasia.

2.3 CHANGING MATERIAL AND COSMOLOGICAL BELIEFS

2.3.1 On Human Nature

Evolutionary anthropologists and psychologists maintain that human nature was set during the period of evolution ending with the Stone Age. Since then, there has not been sufficient time for any further evolution. This concept of human nature appears darker than Rousseau's and brighter than Hobbes' characterizations of it. It is closer to Hume's view that 'there is some benevolence, however small... some particle of the dove kneaded into our frame, along with the elements of the wolf and serpent' (Hume 1740/1985). For even the hunter-gatherer of the Stone Age would have found some form of what evolutionary biologists term 'reciprocal altruism' to his own benefit. He would have discovered that, in the various tasks he had to pursue, co-operation with his fellows yielded gains which might be further increased if he could cheat and be a free rider. In the repeated interactions between the selfish humans comprising the tribe, such cheating could be mitigated by playing the game of 'tit for tat'. Evolutionary biologists claim that the resulting 'reciprocal altruism' was part of our basic human nature in the Stone Age.

Archaeologists have also established that the instinct to 'truck and barter'—the trading instinct based on what John Hicks used to call the 'economic principle' (Hicks 1979)[1]—is also of Stone Age vintage. It is also part of our basic human nature.

2.3.2 Agrarian Civilizations

With the rise of settled agriculture and the civilizations that evolved around them, however, and the stratification this involved between three classes of individuals—those wielding respectively the sword, the pen, and the plough—most of the basic instincts which comprised our human nature in the Stone Age were to become dysfunctional. Thus with the multiplication of interactions between human beings in agrarian civilizations, many of the transactions would have been with anonymous strangers who might never be seen again. The 'reciprocal altruism' of the Stone Age which depended upon a repetition of transactions would not be sufficient to curtail opportunistic behaviour.

Putting it differently, the 'tit for tat' strategy of the repeated Prisoners Dilemma (PD) game among a band of hunter-gatherers in the Stone Age, would not suffice with the increased number of one-shot games consequential upon the arrival of settled agriculture, and the widening of the market for its output. To prevent the resulting dissipation of the mutual gains from co-operation, agrarian civilizations internalized restraints on such 'anti-social' action through moral codes which were part of their religions. But these religions were more ways of life, and did not necessarily depend upon a belief in God.

Throughout much of history, the moral emotions of shame and guilt have been the predominant means by which moral codes embodied in cultural traditions are internalized in the socialization process during infancy. Shame was the major instrument of this internalization in the great agrarian civilizations. Their resulting cosmological beliefs can fairly be described as being 'communalist'.

The basic human instinct to trade would also be disruptive for settled agriculture. For traders are motivated by instrumental rationality which maximizes economic advantage. This would threaten the communal bonds that all agrarian civilizations tried to foster. Not surprisingly, most of them have looked upon merchants and markets as a necessary evil, and sought to suppress them and the market which is their institutional embodiment. The material beliefs of the agrarian civilizations were thus not conducive to modern economic growth, the major institutions of which can be summed up as capitalism.

2.3.3　The Rise of the West

As I have argued elsewhere (Lal 1998*b*), the great divergence of Western Europe from the other Eurasian civilizations occurred because of a change in the cosmological and material beliefs, mediated by the Catholic Church in the sixth to eleventh centuries. These it promoted through encouraging the cult of individualism, first in family affairs and later in material relationships. The first were a series of pronouncements by Pope Gregory I in the sixth century on family matters (Goody 1983), and the second those by Gregory VII in the eleventh century on property and institutionally related issues (Berman 1983). This latter pronouncement was particularly important, in that it set down all the legal and institutional requirements of a market economy, the adoption of which was to put the West on a different economic trajectory than its Eurasian peers.

These twin Papal revolutions arose because of the unintended consequences of the church's search for bequests—a trait that goes back to its earliest days. From its inception it had grown as a temporal power through gifts and donations—particularly from rich widows. So much so that, in July 370 the Emperor Valentinian had addressed a ruling to the Pope that male clerics and unmarried ascetics should not 'hang around' the houses of women and widows trying to worm themselves and their churches into their bequests, at the expense of the women's families and blood relations. From its very beginnings then, the church was in the race for inheritances. In this respect, the early church's extolling of virginity and preventing second marriages helped it in creating more single women who would leave bequests to the church.

This process of inhibiting a family from retaining its property and promoting its alienation, accelerated with the answers that Pope Gregory I gave to some nine questions that the first Archbishop of Canterbury, Augustine, had sent in 597 concerning his new charges. Four of these nine questions concerned issues related to sex and marriage. Gregory's answers overturned the traditional Mediterranean and Middle Eastern patterns of legal and customary practices in the domestic domain. The traditional system was concerned with the provision of an heir to inherit family property. It allowed marriages between close kin, close affines, or widows of close kin; it also permitted the transfer of children by adoption, and finally concubinage, which is a form of secondary union. Gregory banned all four practices. There was for instance, no adoption of children allowed in England until the nineteenth century. There was no basis for these injunctions rather in Scripture, Roman law, or the existing customs in the areas that were Christianized (Goody 1983).

This Papal family revolution made the church unbelievably rich. Demographers have estimated that the net effect of the prohibitions on traditional methods to deal with childlessness was to leave 40 per cent of families with no immediate male heirs. The church became the chief beneficiary of the resulting bequests. Its accumulation was phenomenal. In France, for instance, it is estimated that one-third of productive land was in ecclesiastical hands by the end of the seventh century! (Goody 1983).

But this accumulation also drew predators from within and outside the church to deprive it of its acquired property. It was to deal with this denudation that Pope Gregory VII instigated his Papal revolution in 1075. In this, he put the power of God—through the spiritual weapon of excommunication—above that of Caesar's. With the church then entering into the realm of the world, the new church-state also created an extensive administrative and legal paraphernalia which, in many respects, was the forerunner of our modern polity. This provided the essential institutional infrastructure for the Western dynamic that, in time, was to lead to Promethean growth.[2] Thus Pope Gregory VII's Papal revolution lifted the lid on the basic human instinct to 'truck and barter', and this triggered a change in the traditional Eurasian pattern of material beliefs with their suspicion of markets and merchants. This eventually led to modern economic growth.

But the first Papal revolution of Gregory the Great also led to a change in the traditional Eurasian family patterns which were based on various forms of 'joint families' and family values. This essentially removed the lid placed on the other opportunistic basic instincts by the shame-based moral codes of Eurasia. To counter the potential threat this posed to its way of making a living by way of settled agriculture, the church created a fierce guilt culture in which the concept of Original Sin was paramount, and morality was underwritten by the belief in the Christian God (Delumeau 1990).

2.4 COMMUNALISM VERSUS INDIVIDUALISM

Of the major Eurasian civilizations, the ethic of the Sinic (and its derivatives in Japan and Korea) and the Hindu, has remained distinctly 'communalist' rather than individualist for millennia. But there were important differences in the cosmological beliefs of these two ancient civilizations.

2.4.1 Hindu Civilization

The ancient Hindu, unlike the Sinic, civilization did have a role for a form of individualism, which was reminiscent of that found among the Greek Stoics. The anthropologist Louis Dumont has labelled this as 'out-worldly' individualism as contrasted with the 'in-worldly' individualism, which is the hallmark of the 'modern' individual. Hinduism allows the person who renounces the world and becomes an ascetic to pursue his own personal salvation without any concern for the social world. Like the Greek Stoic, this Hindu 'renouncer is self-sufficient, concerned only with himself. His thought is similar to that of the modern Western individual, but with one basic difference: we live in the social world, he lives outside it' (Dumont 1986: 26).

For a Hindu who had not renounced the social world Western individualism is impossible. Ernest Gellner explains why, by imagining a Hindu Robinson Crusoe, a polyglot called Robinson Chatterjee. 'A Hindu Crusoe', he notes, 'would be a contradiction. He would be destined for perpetual pollution: if a priest, then his isolation and forced self-sufficiency would oblige him to perform demeaning and polluting acts. If not a priest, he would be doomed through his inability to perform the obligatory rituals' (Gellner 1988: 121).

2.4.2 Sinic Civilization

The ancient Sinic civilization did not even have the 'out-worldly' individualism of the Hindus and the Greeks. Its central cosmological beliefs may be summarized as its optimism, its familialism and its bureaucratic authoritarianism (Hallpike 1986; Jenner 1992). Interacting and influencing these characteristics were the embedded customs of 'ancestor worship and its social and political correlates involving hierarchy, ritual deference, obedience and reciprocity' (Keightely 1990: 45). There is little room for even the 'out-worldly' individualism of the Hindus or Greeks in these cosmological views which became labelled as Confucianism. This is in spite of the continuing controversy over whether the ancient sage should be lumbered with whatever were (and are) seen to be the distinctive features of Chinese civilization.

In our own day and age, partly provoked by the events surrounding Tianenmen Square in 1992, there has been an attempt to reconcile Confucianism with Western notions of 'human rights' (de Bary 1998; de Bary and Tu Weiming 1998). But apart from the murkiness surrounding the notion of 'rights', even within the Western philosophical tradition, as Henry Rosemont rightly notes, within the Confucian framework

rights-talk was not spoken, and within which I am not a free, autonomous individual. I am a son, husband, father, grandfather, neighbour, colleague, student, teacher, citizen, friend. I have a very large number of relational obligations and responsibilities, which severely constrain what I do. These responsibilities occasionally frustrate or annoy, they more often are satisfying and they are always binding...And my individuality, if anyone wishes to keep the concept, will come from the specific actions I take in meeting my relational responsibilities. (Rosemont 1998: 63)

As he rightly notes, the attempt to reconcile a different 'way to live' with the universal claims of Christianity has been a constant factor in the West's encounter with China. Throughout history, views have differed between those who thought the Chinese way was incompatible with universal Christian beliefs seeking conversion, and others—of a less imperialist bent—who have sought ways of making Chinese beliefs fit the universal Christian ethic.

2.4.3 Christianity

In this context, it is worth noting the important difference between the cosmological beliefs of what became the Christian West and the ancient agrarian civilizations of Eurasia. Christianity has a number of distinctive features which it shares with its Semitic cousin Islam, and, in part, with its parent Judaism, but which are not to be found in any of the other great Eurasian religions. First and most important is its universality. Neither the Jews, nor the Hindu or Sinic civilizations had religions claiming to be universal. You could not choose to be a Hindu, Chinese, or Jew; you were born as one. Second, this also meant that, unlike Christianity and Islam, these religions did not proselytize. Third, only the Semitic-based monotheistic religions have been egalitarian. Nearly all the other Eurasian religions believed in some form of hierarchical social order. By contrast, alone among the Eurasian civilizations, the Semitic ones (though least so the Jewish) emphasized the equality of men's souls. Dumont (1970) has rightly characterized the resulting and profound divide between the societies of *Homo Aequalis* which believe all men are born equal (as the *philosophes,* and the American Constitution proclaim) and those of *Homo Hierarchicus* which believe no such thing.

Thus Christianity, as we shall see, is and remains at the nub of the West's beliefs, and at the heart of the 'clash of civilizations' posited by Samuel Huntington (Huntington 1997). There can be little doubt that neither the Hindu nor the Sinic civilizations have adhered to the Western notions of liberty and equality based on individualism.

But, neither did the West, for a long time. For though Christianity came inadvertently to promote the 'in-worldly' individualism which is a hallmark of Western civilization, in its basic teachings it did not differ greatly from the communalism found in the other great ethical beliefs systems of the Ancient world. Like Stoicism and the Hindu religion, it provided a place for 'out-worldly' individualism. As Dumont notes: 'there is no doubt about the fundamental conception of man that flowed from the teaching of Christ...man is an individual in-relation-to God...this means that man is in essence an out-worldly individual' (Dumont 1986: 27).

It was St Augustine who, in his *City of God*, by substituting the absolute submission of the state to the church for the previous endorsement of sacral kingship, analogous to the Hindus, brought the church 'into the world' with Gregory VII's proclamation: 'Let the terrestrial kingdom serve—or be the slave of—the celestial.'

2.4.4 The Course of Western Individualism

But the course of individualism has not been simple in the West. It would take us too far afield to go into this in detail, but the importance of St Augustine's *City of God* must be noted. Throughout the last millennium, the West has been haunted by its cosmology. From the Enlightenment to Marxism, Freudianism, and Eco-fundamentalism, Augustine's vision of the Heavenly City has maintained a tenacious hold on the Western mind. The same narrative, with a Garden of Eden, a Fall leading to Original Sin and a Day of Judgement, keeps recurring. Thus the eighteenth-century philosophers of the Enlightenment, in their refurbishment of Augustine, displaced the Garden of Eden by classical Greece and Rome, and God became an abstract cause—the Divine Watchmaker. The Christian centuries were now taken to be the Fall, with the Christian revelations perceived to be a fraud as the 'enlightened' deity expressed his purpose through his laws recorded in the Great Book of Nature. The Enlightened were the elect and the Christian paradise was replaced by Posterity. By this reconfiguration of the Christian narrative, the Enlightenment philosophers thought they had been able to salvage a basis for morality and social order in the world of the Divine Watchmaker. But as soon as Darwin perceived that 'God was blind', and later Nietzsche proclaimed from the housetops 'God was Dead', the moral foundations of the West took on a completely new trajectory.

The subsequent attempts to found a morality based on reason are open to Friederich Nietzsche's fatal objection in his aphorism about utilitarianism. He wrote: 'moral sensibilities are nowadays at such cross purposes that to one man a morality is proved by its utility, while to another its utility refutes it' (Nietzsche 1881/1982: 220).[3]

Nietzsche's main contribution lies in his clear recognition of the moral abyss that the death of its God had created for the West. Kant's attempt to ground a rational morality on the principle of universality—harking back to the biblical injunction 'therefore all things whatsoever ye would that men should do to you, do even so to them'—founders on Hegel's two objections. First it is merely a principle of logical consistency without any specific moral content, and second as a result of this, it is powerless to prevent any immoral conduct that takes our fancy. The subsequent ink spilt by moral philosophers has merely clothed their particular prejudices in rational form.

The perceived death of the Christian God did not, however, end variations on the theme of Augustine's 'City'. It was to go through two further mutations in the form of Marxism and Freudianism (Gellner 1993; Webster 1995), and a more recent and bizarre mutation in the form of Ecofundamentalism.[4]

Marxism, like the Christian faith, looks to the past and the future. There is a counterpart to the Garden of Eden, i.e. the time before 'property' relations corrupted 'natural man'. The following Fall is best regarded as 'commodification', which leads to a class society and a continuing but impersonal conflict of material forces. This, in turn, Marxism perceived would lead to the Day of Judgement with the Revolution and the Millennial Paradise of Communism. Marx also claimed that this movement towards earthly salvation was mediated, not, as the Enlightenment sages had claimed, through enlightenment and the preaching of goodwill, but by the inexorable forces of historical materialism. Another secular 'City of God' has been created.

Ecofundamentalism is the latest of these secular mutations of Augustine's 'City of God' (Lal 1995). It carries the Christian notion of *contemptus mundi* to its logical conclusion. Humankind is evil, it claims, and only by living in harmony with a deified Nature can it be saved.

The West's current cosmological beliefs, inadequately summarized by the word 'liberty' are thus, at present, incoherent. As the philosopher Alasdair Macintyre has powerfully argued (Macintyre 1990), the contemporary Western notion of self has three contradictory elements. The first derives from the Enlightenment. It views individuals as being able to stand apart from exogenous social influences and constraints, and allows them to mould themselves in accordance with their own preferences. The second component concerns the evaluation of oneself by others. Here the standards are increasingly those of acquisitive and competitive success, as nurtured (so some would believe) by a bureaucratized and individualistic market economy. The third element derives from its remaining religious and moral norms, and is open to various 'invocations of values as various as those which inform the public rhetoric of politics on the one hand and the success of Habits of the Heart on the other' (Macintyre 1990: 492). This aspect of the self harks back to the Christian conception of the soul, and its transcendental salvation.

We believe that these three elements comprising the Western conception of self are not only mutually incompatible, they are incommensurable. They also lead to incoherence as there are no shared standards by which the inevitable conflicts between them can be resolved. So as Macintyre puts it

rights based claims, utility-based claims, contractarian claims, and claims based upon this or that ideal conception of the good will be advanced in different contexts, with relatively little discomfort at the incoherence involved. For unacknowledged incoherence is the hallmark of this contemporary developing American self, a self whose public voice oscillates between phases not merely of toleration, but admiration for ruthlessly self-serving behaviour and phases of high moral dudgeon and indignation at exactly the same behaviour. (Macintyre 1990: 492)

Many in the West can be seen as going back to the worship of the multiplicity of 'gods' and personal moral codes (particularly in the realm of sexuality) which are reminiscent of the pre-Christian Graeco-Roman world. The growing number of non-Christian 'New Age' religions, which is occurring at a time the traditional churches continue to lose followers, is a testament to the growing 'neo-paganism' in the West. In the ensuing plethora of moral beliefs—particularly in a cross-cultural context—it is a brave soul who would be able to find any basis for a universal ethic. But if reason or a universally acceptable God cannot provide us with a common basis for morality, and if—as we have seen—morality is needed to reduce the 'policing' type of transactions costs for economic efficiency, on what basis are we to found this morality?

Here it is interesting to re-examine David Hume's views of two and a half centuries ago. In his *Treatise of Human Nature* (1740/1985), he begins by recognizing that morality is essential to control man's self-aggrandizing instincts to garner the gains from co-operation. However, he does not try to ground morality in a belief in God or in reason, but rather in tradition. As he observes: 'the sense of justice and injustice is not derived from nature, but arises artificially, tho' necessarily from education and human conventions' (p. 535). Once they are in place 'a sympathy with public interest is the source of moral approbation, which attends that virtue [justice]' (p. 551). This leads parents 'to inculcate in their children from the earliest infancy, the principles of probity, and teach them to regard the observance of those rules by which society is maintained as worthy and honorable, and their violation as base and infamous' (p. 271). Hume, then, while clearly accepting the role of morality in maintaining the social cement of society, believes that its contents are primarily dependent on a society's traditions and forms of socialization. Neither God nor reason needs to be evoked to justify these conditioned and necessary habits. This is very much the view of ethics taken by the older Eurasian civilizations with their moral ecology based on shame.

Given the multiplicity of ethical traditions, does it matter for our contemporary economy if there is no common agreement about the content of morality, as long as each society has its own morality to constrain immoral behaviour? As we have argued elsewhere (Lal 1998*b*), although in the rise of the West the change in cosmological and material beliefs were conjoined, this is no longer necessary once the legal and other infrastructure for a market and commercial society (e.g. as created by Gregory VII's eleventh-century Papal revolution) is in place. Today, the rest of the world has the option—as is dramatically illustrated by the Japanese example—of adopting the West's material beliefs, which are necessary for prosperity, without adopting the West's cosmological belief's and surrendering its own moral ecology. In short, it is possible to modernize without Westernizing.

Nor, as Adam Smith demonstrated so effectively in *The Wealth of Nations* (Smith 1776/1991), does a market economy have to depend upon the scarce virtues—like benevolence (which for Smith in *The Theory of Moral Sentiments* was the highest virtue)—for its efficient functioning. It only requires a vast number of people to deal and live together, even if they have no personal relationships, as long as they do not violate the 'laws of justice'. The resulting commercial society promotes some virtues (what Shirley Letwin (1992) has labelled the 'vigorous virtues')—such as hard work, prudence, thrift, and self-reliance.

As these virtues directly benefit the economic agents in commercial society, and only indirectly benefit others, they are inferior to altruism. But by promoting general prosperity, these lower level virtues (what John Dunning calls 'proper selfishness') do unintentionally help others. Hence, it may be argued, the resulting commercial or capitalist society is neither immoral or amoral.

2.5 IMPLICATIONS FOR GLOBAL CAPITALISM

What implications does all this have for global capitalism? A major implication, as I see it, is that, in a global context many of the ethical complaints against capitalism are misdirected. In many cases they are atavistic, harking back to the material beliefs of the old agrarian civilizations. In the following section we shall examine this contention from the viewpoint of three of the critical institutions of capitalism, *viz.* markets, the state, and NGOs.

2.5.1 Markets

Because of space limitations, I shall confine my discussion to some common complaints about the global capital market—but from a historical perspective economic historians consider the creation of the national public debt and the Bank of England in the late seventeenth century, as an essential element in the rise in economic power and social status of the merchant and financier in the subsequent years. This rise, however, posed severe problems for the prevailing Aristotelian ethical beliefs of these societies, which as we have seen questioned the virtue of acquiring wealth by the lending of money. More especially a ban on interest was common to all the ethical systems of the pre-modern world. It was based on Aristotle's unequivocal statement:

Usury is detested above all and for the best of reasons. It makes profit out of money itself, not for money's natural object . . . Money was intended as a means of exchange, not to increase at interest. (Aristotle n.d.: 20–1)

This prohibition on interest was gradually lifted in the West. But, ethical worries about the 'unreality' of credit and of the socially unproductive nature of interest resurfaced with a vengeance following the Financial Revolution of 1694–6, which created a vastly expanded credit mechanism, leading to the rise of the *rentier*. In J. G. A. Pocock's words:

The stocks which were his title to a return upon the loans he had made became themselves a commodity, and their value was manipulated by a new class of stockjobbers. (Pocock 1975: 72)

In the ensuing Augustan debates, this posed a severe problem for the traditional value system shared by both opponents and friends of the new goddess Credit. In this system, the moral foundation for civic virtue and moral personality was taken to be independence and real property. Property in the form of land was the most real asset, and though the wealth of the trader and the merchant was moveable, and hence not as reliable in inducing civic virtue as that owned by the landlord, it did at least consist of real things. By contrast, the wealth of the stockholder and the stock jobber, as created by the new system of public credit, was thought to be unreal and fantastical: Again as Pocock puts it:

When the commodities to be bought and sold were paper tokens of men's confidence in their rulers and one another, the concept of fantasy could be more properly applied, and could bear the meaning not only of illusion and imagination, but of men's opinions of others' opinions of them. (Pocock 1995*b*: 76)

This is a view of commerce, and the speculation it necessarily engenders, which survives to our day in the outpourings of the various critics of global financial and capital markets. Lest it be thought to be the untutored prejudice of economic illiterates, one only has to remember Keynes' peroration on the stock market in his General Theory (Keynes 1936: 155), which clearly echoes the Augustan critique of commerce.

2.5.2   The State

The atavistic material belief just described, which was relevant in pre-modern agrarian economies has no place in the set of material beliefs which form our modern market economy. Equally atavistic are many of the other critiques of global capitalism by Western critics. To appreciate this, it is useful to outline the story that the English political philosopher Michael Oakeshott tells about the impact of the evolution of Western thought on the functions of the post-Westphalian state (Oakeshott 1993). He makes a crucial distinction between the state viewed as a *civil association*, and as an *enterprise association*.

Oakeshott notes that the view of the state as a civil association dates back to ancient Greece. At that time, the state was seen as the custodian of laws which did not seek to impose any preferred content of societal goals (including abstractions such as the general (social) welfare, and fundamental human rights), but which merely facilitated individuals to pursue their own ends. This view has been challenged by the rival conception of the state as an enterprise association, which has its roots in the Judaeo-Christian tradition. In this tradition, the state is seen as the manager of an enterprise seeking to use the law for its own substantive purposes, and, in particular, for the legislation of morality. The classical liberalism of Smith and Hume embraces the former view of the state, while the socialists viewed it as an enterprise association, with a moral aim of equalizing the worth of, and opportunities for, people.

Oakeshott also notes that, as in many other pre-industrial societies, modern Europe inherited a 'morality of communal ties' from the Middle Ages. From the sixteenth century onwards, this was gradually superseded by a morality of individuality, whereby individuals came to value making their own choices concerning activities, occupations, beliefs, opinions, duties, and responsibilities (Oakshott 1993) and to approve of this self-determined conduct in others. This individualist morality was fostered by the gradual breakdown of the medieval order which allowed a growing number of people to escape from the corporate and communal organizational structure of medieval life.

But this dissolution of communal ties also bred a set of ideas and values, which Oakeshott terms the 'anti-individual'. These ideas and values were promulgated by a group of individuals who were unwilling or unable to make their own choices. Of this group, some were resigned to their fate, but in others it provoked envy, jealousy and resentment. And, in these emotions, a new disposition was generated: viz. the impulse to escape from the predicament by imposing it upon all mankind' (Oakshott 1993: 24). This attempt to revert to the pre-industrial communalist world by the anti-individual took two forms. The first was to look to some kind of authority to 'protect him from the necessity of being an individual' (p. 25) A large number of government activities in the UK from the introduction of the Elizabethan Poor Laws in the sixteenth century were devoted in Oakshott's words 'to the protection of those who, by circumstance or temperament, were unable to look after themselves in this world of crumbling communal ties' (p. 25).

The anti-individual, secondly, sought to escape his 'feeling of guilt and inadequacy which his inability to embrace the morality of individuality provoked' (p. 25). By calling forth a 'morality of collectivism', where ' "security" is preferred to "liberty", "solidarity" to "enterprise" and "equality" to "self determination"' (p. 27). This trend became particularly important with the various socialist and collectivist movements of the nineteenth century. Both the individualist and collectivist moralities were different modifications of the earlier communal morality, but with the collectivist morality also being a reaction to the morality of individualism.

This collectivist morality inevitably supported the concept of the state as an enterprise association. While this view dates back to antiquity, few, if any, pre-modern states were able to be 'enterprising', as their resources were barely sufficient to undertake the basic tasks of government, *viz.* law and order and external defence. This changed with the creation of centralized 'nation states' by the Renaissance princes and the subsequent 'Administrative' revolution of the sixteenth century—a term which Hicks (1969: 99) used to denote the gradual expansion of the tax base and increased span of control of the government over its subjects' lives. Governments now had the power to look upon their activities as an enterprise.

Oakeshott (1993) identifies three versions of the collectivist morality which such governments have since sought to enforce. Since the truce declared in the eighteenth century in the European wars of religion, the major substantive purposes sought by states seen as enterprise associations are 'nation building' and 'the promotion of some form of egalitarianism'. These correspond to what Oakeshott calls the productivist and distributionist versions of the modern embodiments of the enterprise association, whose religious version was epitomized by Calvinist Geneva, and in, our own times, is provided by Khomeini's Iran. Each of these collective forms conjures up some notion of perfection, believed to be 'the common good'.[5]

In my view, this Oakeshottian taxonomy allows us to think clearly about the links between ethics, economics, and politics. The fog created by distinctions like negative and positive liberty and continuing attempts to reconcile these irreconcilables,[6] can be readily dispelled by keeping Oakeshott's distinction between these two interpretations of the state in mind. The state seen as a civil association does not seek to legislate morality. The state seen as an enterprise association does. The main difference between the first liberal international economic order (LIEO) established under British leadership in the nineteenth century and the contemporary LIEO fostered by most Western governments is that, while the former embodied the classical liberal view of the state—*viz.* it did not seek to legislate morality[7]—the latter is infected by the enterprise view in both the domestic concerns for social welfare and the desire to export Western values like 'human rights' and 'democracy' to the rest of the world.

This allows us to see that the desire by many current critics of globalization to use the state to legislate their preferred ethics is antithetical to the Western classical liberal tradition. It would take us too far afield to show why this view of the world which seeks to combine the market with various social demands is likely to be counterproductive. These socialist impulses—however well intentioned—as the above discussion should make clear are atavistic. The state should—and it can if it chooses—restrict itself to providing the public goods which are an essential part of the infrastructure for efficient globalization, and the support of a moral ecology as decided by individuals, families, and other institutions of civil society.

2.5.3 NGOs

This brings us to the NGOs. It is not sufficiently appreciated that most are really pressure groups (see Lal 1999). As Mancur Olson (1965) has shown, rather than regard these as benign constituents of civil society *à la* de Tocqueville and the American pluralist political science model, they are better seen as engaged in a redistributive political game to garner a larger share for sectional interests. They are now part of Oakeshott's enterprise associations. Thus whereas in Victorian England, for instance, civil society mainly comprised charitable, religious- and art-based associations—and helped to provide the social cement of society (Himmelfarb 1995), today many NGOs are promoting their own, often political, ends. The international NGOs, it maybe argued, are altruistic as they are not seeking benefits for themselves but for mankind. They are promoting an international moral order and thence an international civil society. But in the three areas in which they are most active, namely issues relating to labour standards, human rights, and the environment, their attempts to enforce universal global standards are more likely than not to do great harm, particularly to the constituency in whose name they claim to speak—the world's poorest people—as we have argued on many an occasion (Lal 1998*a*, 2000*a*). Moreover, as I have earlier suggested in this chapter, since there is currently no universal moral code, the morality that these 'global salvationists', as David Henderson (2001) has labelled them, is nothing else but the culture-specific, proselytizing, universal and egalitarian ethic of what remains at heart Western Christendom. Apart from the disorder this can cause as the rest of the world resists this Western ethical imperialism, it will also damage the prospects of the world's most needy citizens.

Thus the environmental NGOs are in the vanguard in attempting to in effect stop growth (and the poverty alleviation it entails) in the third world by seeking to limit their carbon emissions (Lal 1999). The consumer NGOs are seeking to prevent imports of goods from developing countries produced by means which do not meet their moral standards, in the name of ethical trading (Lal 1998*b*). The human rights NGOs are attempting to legislate a new extra-territorial principle based on Western moral values categorized as 'human rights' (Lal 2000). The health NGOs have taken on a crusade against genetically modified (GM) foods, which promise the same hope for the hungry of the world that the Green Revolution (which too was based on the genetic modification of plants) delivered in the last three decades (Lal 2000*a*).

This attempt by the self-appointed to do good, as they see it, of course has its historical parallels (Lal 1988). With the establishment of the British Raj and its policy of free trade, imports of cheap Lancashire textiles destroyed the Indian export trade in cotton textiles, and undoubtedly led to a reduction in employment in the domestic handloom industry, though not—as many nationalists and Marxists maintained—its total destruction. But, by 1850, a modern cotton textile industry was established with Indian entrepreneurship and capital, and in a few decades it had turned the tables on Lancashire. This led to repeated representations by the cotton textile interests of Manchester to the Secretary of State for India 'to apply British factory legislation en bloc to India so as to neutralize the "unfair" advantages which the Indian mill industry was enjoying because of its large scale employment of child labor and long hours of work' (Bhattacharya 1979: 171).

In these appeals, they were supported by various well-meaning pressure groups. This led to the institution of the first of the Factory Acts of 1881, which subsequently had disastrous effects on the fortunes of the Indian textile industry and labour. By raising the effective price of labour they led to lower employment levels than would otherwise have occurred and, by hobbling the industry, made it inevitable that it, too, would ask for protection from Japanese imports. This was granted and the outcome led to growing inefficiency in this pioneering industry in the Third World. So much so that, for the last fifty years it has been one of India's sickest industries. Until today, these nineteenth-century labour laws continue to harm both Indian industrial employment levels and efficiency. They have rightly been described by one historian as the result of agitation by 'ignorant English philanthropists and grasping English manufacturers' (Bhattacharya 1979: 171). But that is precisely the kind of alliance we witnessed on the streets of Seattle at the 1999 WTO meeting—with the Americans replacing the English!

Today these global salvationists are, first, attempting to engender what they call corporate social responsibility among multinational enterprises (MNEs).

David Henderson (2001) provides a devastating critique of this millennial collectivism, and its claims that globalization has marginalized poor peoples and poor countries, increased the power of MNEs, and reduced those of states.

While its claim for a new tripartism between businesses, governments, and selected NGOs—which has unfortunately been embraced by some businesses—'confers on businesses and NGO's alike a status which they have no rightful claim to, since they are neither elected nor politically accountable'.

The second tack taken by the global salvationists is an old trick, previously resorted to by Communist Parties which could not win power through elections, entryism. Having failed by and large (outside of Germany and the Scandinavian countries) to win enough public support for their agenda in elections, the Greens are seeking to legislate it through the unelected bureaucracies of the transnational institutions like UNEP, the World Bank, WHO, and—they hope—through the WTO. Their aim is to push through international treaties and conventions sponsored by these organizations to regulate various aspects of the economies, particularly of the Third World. These supra-national institutions, apart from the WTO, are thus now becoming party to the ethical imperialism being promoted by the global salvationists (Lal 2000a). So, unlike many of the other authors in this book, I believe that, even though in the past many of these supra-national institutions were in the vanguard of promoting the LIEO, today many of them, rather than aiding globalization are increasingly having the reverse effect by promoting a global collectivism, which embodies the 'ethical' enterprise association view of the state adumbrated by Oakeshott.[8]

2.6 CONCLUSIONS

My conclusions can be brief. To allow the gains from trade to be reaped and to reduce the 'policing' type of transactions costs, morality is needed to reign in opportunistic behaviour. But given that, as Hume saw so clearly, it is not necessary to invoke either God or Reason to justify any particular morality, its only source must surely be local traditions which socialize children through the moral emotions of shame and guilt to 'be good'. Capitalism *does* require moral behaviour. But this cannot be enforced—although it can be influenced by the behaviour of governments, NGOs, or supra-national institutions. If one does want to strengthen morality it is important not to undermine its traditional mainsprings in the non-Western part of the world in the name of a mistaken belief in a universal Western ethic. For it is possible for countries to modernize (i.e. embrace capitalism) without Westernizing (i.e. accepting the West's morality—its cosmological beliefs). In fact, if one looks at the non-Western world, the moral foundations of most—though by no means all—have remained remarkably intact over the years. It is in the West that there is growing doubt about its fractured and incoherent morality. Writing as a Hindu, it is not for me to preach about the ways in which the morality which is required for capitalism to function with minimal transactions costs can be engendered in the West.

NOTES

1. In his words 'people would act economically; when an opportunity of an advantage was presented to them they would take it' (Hicks 1979: 43).
2. Elsewhere (Lal 1998b), I have distinguished between two types of intensive growth, *viz.* Smithian and Promethean. Intensive growth is a sustained rise in *per capita* income as contrasted with extensive growth where output keeps pace with population so that *per capita* income is constant. In traditional agrarian economies, intensive growth occurred normally when a new empire linked previously autarkic regions into a common economic space, giving rise to the gains from trade and specialization and consequently a rise in *per capita* income as emphasized by Adam Smith. With the advent of the Industrial Revolution, based as it was on utilizing the limitless supply of fossil fuels, sustained intensive growth, which I call Promethean, occurred.
3. A point which is reiterated by several of the contributions to Sen and Williams (1982).
4. That Freudianism follows the same Augustinian narrative is shown in Gellner (1993) and Webster (1995).
5. Roger Sugden in a review of Sen's work makes much the same distinction between the two divergent views of public policy embodied in the technocratic 'market failure' school and those of the neo-Austrian and Virginia public choice model.
6. That these two divergent views of the state cannot be reconciled by arguing as Sen (1992) does that classical liberals are also egalitarians as they are concerned with the equality of liberty, is cogently refuted by Sugden (1993).
7. Though, as Dunning points out in Chapter 1, the state did play an important role in fashioning and supporting the moral ecology of Victorian England. But more often than not it was the church, charitable associations, individuals, and families that were the real instigators of the changes in morality in this era described by Searle (1998) and Himmelfarb (1995) among others.
8. The argument that these supra-national institutions are required to provide global public goods is discussed in Lal 2000b.

REFERENCES

Aristotle (1959), *Politics* translation by John Warrington for Everyman's Library (London: Dent and Sons).

Becker, C. L. (1932), *The Heavenly City of the Eighteenth Century Philosophers.* (New Haven: Yale University Press).

Bhattacharya, D. A. (1979), *A Concise History of the Indian Economy 1750–1950,* 2nd edn. (New Delhi: Prentice Hall).

Berman, H. J. (1983), *Law and Revolution* (Cambridge, Mass.: Harvard).

Colinvaux, P. (1983), *The Fates of Nations* (London: Penguin).

De Bary, W. T. (1998), *Asian Values and Human Rights* (Cambridge, Mass.: Harvard University Press).

——and Tu Weiming (eds.) (1998), *Confucianism and Human Rights* (New York: Columbia University Press).

Delumeau, J. (1990), *Sin and Fear: The Emergence of a Western Guilt Culture 13–18th Centuries* (New York: St. Martin's Press).

Dumont, L. (1970), *Homo Hierarchicus* (London: Weidenfeld & Nicolson).

——(1986), *Essays on Individualism* (Chicago: University of Chicago Press).

Gellner, E. (1988), *Plough, Book and Sword: The Structure of Human History* (London: Collins Harvill).

—— (1993), *The Psychoanalytic Movement: the Cunning of Unreason.* (Evanston, Ill.: Northwestern University Press).

Goody, J. (1983), *The Development of the Family and Marriage in Europe* (New York: Cambridge University Press).

Hahn, F. (1973), *On the Notion of Equilibrium in Economics* (Cambridge: Cambridge University Press).

Hallpike, C. R. (1986), *The Principles of Social Evolution* (Oxford: Clarendon Press).

Hayek, F. (1960), *The Constitution of Liberty* (London: Routledge & Kegan Paul).

—— (1979), *Law, Legislation and Liberty* (Chicago: University of Chicago Press).

Henderson, P. D. (2001), *Misguided Virtue* (London: Institute of Economic Affairs).

Hicks, R. J. (1969), *The Theory of Economic History* (Oxford: Oxford University Press).

—— (1979), *Causality in Economics* (Oxford: Blackwell).

Himmelfarb, G. (1994), *The Demoralisation of Society* (New York: Knopf).

Hume, D. (1740/1985), *A Treatise on Human Nature* (London: Penguin Classics).

Huntington, S. P. (1997), *The Clash of Civilizations* (New York: Touchstone Books).

Jenner, W. J. F. (1992), *The Tyranny of History* (London: Penguin).

Keightley, D. N. (1990), 'Early Civilization in China: Reflections on How it Became Chinese.' In P. S. Ropp (ed.), *Heritage of China* (Berkeley: University of California Press).

Keynes, J. M. (1936), *The General Theory of Employment, Interest and Money* (Basingstoke: Macmillan).

Lal, D. (1983, 1997, 2001), *The Poverty of Development Economics* (London: Institute of Economic Affairs).

—— (1985), 'Nationalism, Socialism and Planning—Influential Ideas in the South.' *World Development* 13(3): 749–59; reprinted in Lal (1993).

—— (1988), *The Hindu Equilibrium* (Oxford: Clarendon Press).

—— (1993), *The Repressed Economy: Economists of the 20th Century Series* (Aldershot: Edward Elgar).

—— (1994), *Against Dirigisme* (San Francisco: ICS Press).

—— (1995), 'Eco-fundamentalism', *International Affairs*, 71: 515–28.

—— (1998*a*), *Unintended Consequences: The Impact of Factor Endowments, Culture and Politics on Economic Performance in the Long Run.* The Ohlin Lectures (Cambridge, Mass.: MIT Press).

—— (1998*b*), 'Social Standards and Social Dumping.' In H. Giersch (ed.), *The Merits of Markets* (Berlin: Springer).

—— (1999), *Unfinished Business* (New Delhi: Oxford University Press).

—— (2000*a*), 'Does Modernization Require Westernisation?' *The Independent Review* 5(1): 5–24.

—— (2000*b*), 'The New Cultural Imperialism: The Greens and Economic Development.' *The inaugural Julian Simon Memorial Lecture* (New Delhi: Liberty Institute).

—— (2000*c*), 'Globalization, Imperialism and Regulation', *Cambridge Review of International Affairs* 14(1): 107–21.

Letwin, S. (1992), *The Anatomy of Thatcherism* (London: Fontana).

Macintyre, A. (1990), 'Individual and Social Morality in Japan and the United States: Rival Conceptions of the Self', *Philosophy East and West* 40(4): 489–97.

Matthews, R. C. O. (1986), 'The Economics of Institutions and the Sources of Growth', *Economic Journal* 96: 903–18.

Nietzsche, F. (1881/1982), *Daybreak: Thoughts on the Prejudices of Morality* (Cambridge: Cambridge University Press).

North, D. C. (1990), *Institutions, Institutional Change and Economic Performance* (Cambridge: Cambridge University Press).

Oakeshott, M. (1993), *Morality and Politics in Modern Europe* (New Haven: Yale University Press).

Olson, M. (1965), *The Logic of Collective Action* (Cambridge, Mass.: Harvard University Press).

Pocock, J. G. A. (1975a), *The Machiavellian Moment* (Princeton: Princeton University Press).

—— (1975b), 'Early Modern Capitalism: The Augustan Perception', in E. Kamenka and R. S. Neale (eds.), *Feudalism, Capitalism and Beyond* (London: Arnold).

Rosemont, H., Jr. (1998), 'Human Rights: A Bill of Worries.' In De Bary and Tu Weiming (eds.), *Confucianism and Human Rights* (New York: Cambridge University Press), 54–66.

Searle, G. R. (1998), *Morality and the Market in Victorian Britain* (Oxford: Clarendon Press).

Sen, A. K. (1992), *Inequality Re-examined* (Oxford: Clarendon Press).

—— and Williams, B. (eds.) (1982), *Utilitarianism, For and Against* (Cambridge: Cambridge University Press).

Smith, A. (1776/1991), *The Wealth of Nations* (Indianapolis: Liberty Fund).

Sugden, R. (1986), *The Economics of Rights, Cooperation and Welfare* (Oxford: Blackwell).

—— (1993), 'A Review of "Inequality Re-examined" by Amartya Sen', *Journal of Economic Literature* 31(4): 1947–86.

Webster, R. (1995), *Why Freud Was Wrong* (London: HarperCollins).

Williamson, O. E. (1985), *The Economic Institutions of Capitalism* (New York: Free Press).

3

Institutions and Morality: An Economist's Appraisal

ALAN HAMLIN

3.1 INTRODUCTION

To what extent should the shift from local or national markets to global markets, or from local or national capitalism to global capitalism, influence our analysis of the morality of the market? In attempting to address this issue I will build on an earlier discussion of the morality of the market that focused on the case of what might be termed 'capitalism in one country'. That discussion[1] started from the presumption that there exists a single 'society' defined in terms of a broadly shared set of institutions, conventions, and norms, and proceeded to define and discuss three aspects of the relationship between morality and the market within that society—the moral *basis* of the market, the moral *scope* of the market, and the moral *evaluation* of the market. At the global level, however, it is by no means clear that we have (or will have in the foreseeable future) anything like a single society. Rather, we might describe the situation in terms of a number of inter-connected societies which differ in many ways in terms of their internal institutions, conventions, and norms (including those relating directly to the market), and which support a limited range of international (or transnational) institutions that often fall short of being fully global in their reach. The substantive question that opened this paragraph might then be rephrased to ask whether our understanding of the morality of the market should alter when the market is conceived as operating between and across societies rather than within a society.

To caricature the range of positions available, we might think of a continuum depicting the variety of outcomes that might arise as capitalism becomes more global in its scope. The pessimistic extreme of this continuum might be labelled 'new medieval brutalism', with the optimistic extreme labelled 'post-nationalist utopia'.[2] A common theme across this continuum relates to the reduction in the role, power, and sovereignty of the nation state. Put crudely, the basic question that separates the pessimists from the optimists is whether the regulatory role that has been played by the nation state in respect of national and local markets will be lost as the global economy 'descends' to a form of anarchy in which global corporations fill the roles associated with medieval barons and warlords; or whether this regulatory role will be reconstructed at the global level as the global economy 'rises' to a utopian state in which a network of co-operative and innovative post-national institutions emerge to effectively transform the world into a single society. Clearly, the pessimists tend to include those who take a rather negative view of the market as an institution, emphasizing the pursuit of private interests, greed, and a sort of imperialist materialism; while the optimists tend to include those who take a more positive view of the market, emphasizing efficiency, consumer sovereignty, and co-operation.

At the pessimistic extreme, the market is seen as a sort of necessary evil—an effective but potentially dangerous institution that must be kept confined to a restricted domain and regulated by a strong authoritative body, supplemented by a range of other institutions, and which threatens to escape effective regulation by moving to the global level. At the optimistic extreme, the market is seen as a vital and progressive force that can liberate individuals and provide an engine for the growth of prosperity. As usual, neither extreme position is particularly attractive—but finding an appropriate position in the interior of the continuum requires the careful consideration of a large number of issues that cannot be reduced to a single academic specialism. In this chapter I intend to outline just some of these issues from the perspective of an economist.

I should, however, make it clear from the outset that, although I will offer a point of view that I describe as 'an economist's appraisal', I have no wish to pretend that the views that I outline are typical of those held by economists—they are not. Nevertheless, I think that it is an important part of the position I outline that it can be developed within the resources of the broadly economic approach to social analysis—an approach that emphasizes individually rational action within institutional contexts.

The main body of this chapter is presented in two further sections, each made up of three subsections. In order to build on the foundations provided by the earlier discussion of the morality of the market to address the substantial question posed in the opening paragraph, I must first strengthen those foundations somewhat, both by developing some of the general lines of argument sketched in the earlier discussion, and by adding some new points specifically relating to key issues raised by the recognition of more than one society. This will be the task of the next section (3.2) which includes both a review of the distinctions between the moral basis, scope, and evaluation of markets, and some of the further groundwork necessary for the extension of the argument to the global context. Section 3.3 then turns to the substantive question already posed and divides the issue into the moral analysis of the current international order, and the discussion of the prospects for superficial or basic improvements in that order.

3.2 FOUNDATIONS: BASIS, SCOPE, AND EVALUATION

It will be useful to begin by revisiting the original statements defining three aspects of the relationship between market capitalism and morality[3] before considering each aspect in a little more detail:

- Market capitalism might itself depend upon the satisfaction of moral background conditions and, in particular, on the moral beliefs and views of individual agents. We might term this the moral *basis* of markets. The potential problems here include the possibility of incompatibility between the moral character of individual agents required to satisfy the background conditions for markets to exist, and the character of agents required to operate efficient markets. A second potential problem derives from the possibility that the operation of market capitalism might causally influence the moral beliefs and views of individual agents, so that the moral background conditions may be eroded over time.

- Moral considerations might also arise in determining the range of application of market capitalism—that is, in determining which aspects of society should, and should not, be allocated to the 'market sphere'.[4] We might term this the moral *scope* of markets. Problems arising in this area include the substantive questions of whether this or that activity should be mediated through the market, and the more formal question of how the moral limits of the market sphere might be determined in principle.

- Even within the market sphere, a further set of moral questions arises concerning the normative assessment of market processes and outcomes themselves. We might term this the moral *evaluation* of markets. Problems arising in this area include the normative questions associated with inequality and poverty in market economies, and the moral arguments for intervention in market processes or outcomes.

3.2.1 The Moral Basis of the Market

As normally analysed by economists, the market mechanism operates as an 'invisible hand' mechanism—that is to say that, under ideal conditions, competitive markets achieve a socially efficient outcome *despite* the fact that social efficiency plays no part in the motivation of the participating agents. We might say that such mechanisms 'economize on virtue'[5] in the sense that they do not rely on virtuous individuals to achieve desirable outcomes, but rather use institutional means to substitute for virtue. Indeed, in the standard demonstration of the efficiency of perfectly competitive markets, economizing on virtue is complete, since individuals are simply assumed to be completely lacking in virtue and motivated only by their self-interest.

Clearly, economizing on virtue is the only institutional strategy available if we insist that individuals are completely lacking in virtue in their motivational structure. However, once we recognize that at least some individuals may be directly motivated by moral considerations in at least some circumstances, other institutional strategies, and other forms of analysis, become relevant. Of course, economists are typically (and rightly) very cautious about arguments that depend upon re-specifying the motivations of the agents involved. If one allows oneself the power to specify motivations in any manner at all, it is trivial to 'explain' any form of behaviour at all. 'Explanation' here means little more than saying 'they do it because they are motivated to do it' and, since there is no real distance between the motivational assumption and the behavioural conclusion, there is no real explanation. This caution in the matter of motivational variety is, however, also a severe limitation when the object of the exercise is not only explanation but also some form of normative discussion. If I (the analyst) am to assert that Pareto efficiency (for example) is an appropriate normative criterion to use in the context of a particular model, how am I to defend the fact that none of the agents in my model are actually motivated by a concern for Pareto efficiency? If Pareto efficiency is claimed to matter, it must surely matter for someone, and for someone inside the model.

In many traditional economic models there were agents who were directly motivated by efficiency consideration: the Government, for example, was frequently modelled in this way—effectively as a benevolent dictator. But more modern and more thoroughgoing economic approaches have sought to endogenize the democratic political process in such a way that policy is seen to emerge as the result of the interactions among rational individuals in the context of political institutions, such as voting, lobbying, and coalition formation.[6] Clearly, if the assumption of amoral, self-interested, and mutually disinterested agents is maintained, the only strategy available for the analysis or design of economic, political, or social institutions will be the strategy of the invisible hand or of economizing on virtue. But in this more ambitious world where political and social institutions, as well as market institutions, are to be analysed and evaluated, the problem of recognizing the link between the normative criterion employed and the motivations of the agents modelled is even more apparent.

If we are to admit the possibility of moral motivation, we need to be clear what we are doing. I will make several brief points in this context. First, it would be inappropriate to assume that there are just two types of individual—the moral angels and the selfish knaves. Rather it should be assumed that moral considerations play some role in the motivations of all agents, but that the weight and extent of this role may vary—so that we see a full continuum of behaviour. Second, we must maintain a sharp differentiation between motivation and behaviour: just because an agent includes moral arguments in her motivational structure does not imply that she will act as morality requires. Moral considerations will sit alongside other considerations and will often be overwhelmed. Different situations—including different institutional structures—may emphasize or render salient particular aspects of the agent's motivational structure, so that some decision settings may 'encourage' self-interested behaviour, while others may 'encourage' more moral behaviour. Third, we should be aware that what counts as a moral argument for one individual, may not count in that way for another individual. This third point has an immediate implication: that the introduction of moral motivation may have no impact on overall social outcomes, even if it does have some impact on the behaviour of individuals. If morality is so person-specific that it has no significant systematic effect on behaviour, self-interest may still be the best guide to overall social outcomes. It would be as if moral motivations simply add some statistical noise to individual behaviour, with individuals departing from self-interested behaviour in essentially random ways that might be expected to cancel out in their aggregate effects. So, moral motivations must be at least somewhat correlated across the relevant population if we are to believe that they are likely to have a significant effect on social outcomes. And this point will be important in what follows. If only commonly held, or widely shared, moral views will be likely to have any significant impact we might ask whether it is appropriate to define 'societies' in terms of a shared moral code. For only in such 'societies' will institutions that operate by building on the moral motivations of individuals, rather than by economizing on virtue, stand a real chance of operating successfully.

If we have at least some degree of moral motivation in a given society, and the relevant morality is sufficiently shared to make this a potentially effective force, how will this influence the institutional structure and normative performance of the society? The most obvious point is that institutional structures that might perform badly under some motivational assumptions may perform well under others—and that the optimal mix of institutional structures may shift in recognition of variations in the underlying motivations of individuals. Institutions may deploy strategies very different from 'economizing on virtue'. They may attempt to amplify whatever virtue is available, they may attempt to select individuals with particular motivations into particular roles (in line with the basic economic idea of comparative advantage), they may attempt to increase the stock of virtue in society, and so on.

As a simple illustration of the issues at stake, imagine that we were charged with the task of designing a university system, on the assumption that all individuals— all academics—were entirely venal in their motivations, so that no one could be relied on to act in the interests of students, or their discipline, university, or society in general unless they had a private motivation to do so. Of course, such a task is possible—indeed it is the sort of task that economists often set themselves. But the resultant institutional structure would inevitably rely heavily on financial incentive schemes and various forms of monitoring (institutional structures that economize on virtue). Although recent reforms (in the UK at least) have pushed universities in this direction, it is still clear that universities are not actually organized on this basis. Rather they are organized on a basis that assumes that academics and others are at least partly motivated by commitments to their students, their disciplines, and so on. Academics, and others, are given more freedom, and are subject to less control than would be optimal under the assumption of venal self-interest. In a world of venal self-interest, freedom from institutional constraint is always exploited by the individual, in a world of more mixed motivations, freedom may allow the individuals greater space for genuine innovation and contribution.

As with universities, so with societies. Once we admit of mixed motivations in which normative considerations have directly motivational force for at least some individuals, so our preferred institutional structures can be expected to shift away from a pattern dominated by narrowly focused incentives and attempts to economize on virtue, and towards a pattern that allows rather greater discretion and relies rather more on individual fidelity. Of course, this will only be a tendency—there is no assumption that such a shift will be dramatic. Even in a world that recognizes the existence and potential importance of virtue, it is still likely that virtue will be scarce, and that the strategy of economizing on virtue will be appropriate in many cases.

3.2.2 The Moral Scope of the Market

This leads naturally to a point concerning the scope of the market. If the market is seen as an example—perhaps the leading example—of an institutional mechanism that economizes on virtue, it seems to follow from the discussion of the last subsection that the market sphere might be expected to be greater in settings where there is no commonly accepted moral code, or where, for other reasons, we cannot rely on personal motivations. To put the logic in an extreme form, in a compact and homogeneous group such as a family or clan we would not expect the market (or market-like mechanisms) to play a significant role. As the size of the group increases, and the connectedness of the group and the extent of a shared moral code decreases, we might expect market-like mechanisms to become more and more important until we reach the opposite extreme of a large group of mutually disinterested and atomistic individuals who have no basis for relying on each other. In this final setting the market, or a similarly structured institution, provides the only feasible means of co-ordination and co-operation. It is no accident that this final extreme setting looks rather like a textbook case of a perfectly competitive market.

At least, this logic *seems* to follow. But there is an offsetting argument. The initial point of the discussion of the moral basis of the market was to suggest that, in fact, the market could not really be seen as operating in isolation from other institutions, and in particular that the market might only work well when set within a society which balanced the market sphere with a non-market sphere. When this point is included, we might argue that although as we move along the spectrum from the family to the large impersonal group we move in a direction that will rely more and more heavily on market-like mechanisms, it may also be expected that as we move along this continuum so market-like mechanisms will become less effective in their own terms. That is to say, market-like institutions will become less effective as mechanisms for securing normative ends, exactly as they become the only type of mechanisms available. This is very different from saying that market-like mechanisms will be bad or counterproductive in these settings. It is simply to point out that market-like institutions that economize on virtue will perform systematically better when embedded within a 'society' which displays a shared moral code and a variety of institutional strategies which support markets and compensate for their relative failings, than when they are operating in a much sparser social landscape and without the support of alternative institutional structures.

There is a superficially paradoxical feel about this conclusion. On the one hand, in a setting of mutual disinterest and narrow self-interest the market-like institution is the only institution available that can hope to support mutually beneficial outcomes. In that sense, it is precisely in this setting that the market as an institution is most valuable—it offers access to benefits that other institutional mechanisms cannot reach. On the other hand, the market itself would work better still in a rather richer motivational and institutional context. In this sense, the market offers less good outcomes in the setting of mutual disinterest and narrow self-interest than it does in other settings. Taking these two points together, the market is most valuable where it works least effectively! But there is no real paradox here: it is the robustness of the market to the lack of moral motivations that is key—the market-like institution keeps working reasonably well when others institutions that rely on virtue in individuals fail.

3.2.3 The Moral Evaluation of Markets

A primary concern under this heading relates to the evaluation of the inequality that may arise in market systems, and the potential for either regulating markets to avoid undesired inequality (for example through minimum wage laws) or putting in place other institutional structures of social insurance to compensate for inequality. Clearly these issues are still more significant as we move from national to global capitalism. This is precisely an example of the sort of issue stressed in the last subsection—where the market will work less well (in relation to some normative criterion) as we move from a more closely defined society with many other compensating institutional structures to a more widely defined setting with fewer institutional safeguards.

A foundational question is whether the geographic and/or political extension of the market carries any deep moral significance in itself. That is, should the moral weight that we attach to inequality differ depending on the geographic or political distance between the individuals concerned? In more immediately practical terms—if we believe that a minimum wage (associated with a particular standard of living identified as 'acceptable', perhaps) is morally justified within a society like the UK, should that imply a commitment to a global minimum wage (set by reference to the local cost of some minimum 'acceptable' standard of living, perhaps)?

This is one of the points at which the distinction between one society and the interaction among societies may carry real and direct moral consequences. Even within the broadly liberal and egalitarian tradition, there is real debate on the applicability of egalitarian principles across societies. For example, Rawls' (1971) classic analysis of justice that identifies the 'difference principle' (the principle that social and economic inequalities should be arranged so as to be to the greatest benefit of the least advantaged—so that an equal distribution of primary goods is just unless an unequal distribution can be shown to be to the advantage of all) is explicitly limited in scope to a single society, and his extension to a multi-society world (Rawls 1999) specifically rejects an international equivalent of the difference principle—or any similar commitment to the reduction of interpersonal inequality in the global domain. In its place, Rawls argues for a very limited 'principle of assistance' under which wealthy countries owe some support to poor countries in order that they might develop appropriate institutional structures. By contrast, more cosmopolitan egalitarian writers, such as Beitz (1999) and Pogge (2000, 2001), have argued that since the developing institutional structure of the world forms an important part of the basic structure of all societies, there is a corresponding obligation to ensure that international structures, no less than national or local structures are acceptable to all who live under them. This then creates the circumstances in which the conditions of the original Rawlsian analysis apply directly, so that something like the difference principle interpreted as a principle of egalitarianism at the individual level would follow. What is at stake in this debate between the 'cosmopolitan egalitarians' and the more 'parochial egalitarians' is essentially the question of whether the global community is (or should be) sufficiently integrated in terms of its basic political culture to allow it to be treated as a single society. The cosmopolitans answer this question in the affirmative—and point to the fact that global political and economic activity are major determinants of the well-being of individuals in the poorest countries of the world to support their claim; while Rawls and others answer the question in the negative—and point to the lack of determinative political institutions at the global level, and the clear contrasts between political and economic regimes within the countries of the world as evidence of the lack of a common or widely shared political culture.

3.3 SUBSTANCE: GLOBAL CAPITALISM

It is now time to gather together some of the resources outlined above and apply them more directly to the substantive question of the moral analysis of global capitalism, or at least of something that is almost global capitalism. I begin from John Dunning's point[7] that global capitalism refers not simply to an international market place, but rather to a complete politico-economic system. Dunning suggests that this requires a truly global structure of governance which we currently lack. This suggestion is clearly in line with the view that *if* the world could be seen as an integrated society, then all the standard discussion of the morality of the market, and the need for supervision, regulation, and intervention would follow (what Dunning refers to as 'responsible global capitalism'). I agree, but I also take it that a real question of current practical interest is concerned with the moral analysis of an international market system that falls some way short of full global capitalism, a system that falls short of the standard of a single society. The specific questions that must be addressed include: how should we evaluate the current system of 'almost global capitalism'; what institutional, political or other steps can be taken to improve the performance of the current system; and is there any dynamic that moves the system from the current state of 'almost global capitalism' toward 'responsible global capitalism'? I will take these three questions in turn.

3.3.1 Evaluating 'almost global capitalism'

One of the characteristics of the economic approach to evaluation is that it emphasizes the importance of issues of feasibility alongside issues of desirability. This may seem obvious, but it is both more important and more misunderstood than it might seem. For an economist to claim that a particular institutional arrangement or policy is 'optimal' (or close to optimal) relative to a particular normative criterion is not to say that that arrangement or policy is particularly good—certainly not to say that it is in any sense ideal. Rather it is simply to say that it is the best that can be achieved in the given circumstances. And this may be saying rather little. For example, in the context of a lottery, where you have no information on the likely winning combination of numbers, the optimal strategy (assuming you play at all) is to pick your selection randomly. This is not to say that this is a 'good' strategy in any real sense, it is rather a demonstration that in these circumstances there are no 'good' strategies. In this case, the constraints of feasibility are extremely tight—there is literally nothing you can do, given the lack of information; so that the question of the precise meaning of desirability in this context has no real impact on the analysis of optimality.

In the context of the international social order, we also need to be clear about the distinction between feasibility and desirability, and, in particular, to recognize the sad truth that thinking something desirable does not render it feasible. In this context, four points emerge from the earlier discussion. First, that a shared moral code—and perhaps a shared political culture—is a necessary prerequisite for the existence of a 'society' that can support a full range of institutions. Second, that market-like mechanisms are able to operate without such shared moral and political codes. Third, that without the support of such codes and the non-market institutions that they support, markets will tend to produce less favourable outcomes than might be expected within a 'society'. Fourth, that the criteria of desirability that we employ in evaluating outcomes may themselves need to reflect the prevailing political and cultural circumstances.

The first three of these points address the issue of feasibility. If we accept, for the moment, that the current world is one in which there is no shared moral code, and no shared political culture, and we also take the extant moral and political environment as given—that is, as constraints on what is feasible—then it may be that we are forced to accept that the set of feasible institutional structures at the international or global level is severely limited. In particular, we may have to admit that an international market operating without the support of a wider set of truly global institutions may be the best that is currently available. Of course, some further international institutions exist, but these fall some way short of the model of global institutions that reflect a truly integrated society. Rather they might be understood either as organizations that operate as means of enabling debate and policy co-ordination among states (or, at least, subsets of states) or as agencies set up to promote a particular set of policies promoted by some sponsoring states. In each case, there are clear reasons for viewing most of these institutions as operating as intermediaries between states, or as the representatives of states, rather than as truly global institutions.

The fourth point mentioned above addresses the issue of desirability directly. Here the point is that we should not judge international institutions, including international markets, by the same criteria that we use in evaluating institutions within a society. And this not because of any simple form of ethical relativism, but because of a specifically liberal notion of the tolerance of alternative moral codes and political cultures. Of course this view is contentious, but the issue on which the debate hangs is the extent to which the required background assumptions of a global society are met. The cosmopolitan egalitarians base much of their argument on the claim that the extant set of international and transnational institutions—including the practice of international trade—have profound effects on individuals throughout the world, and particularly on those in the poorer parts of the world. Indeed, they suggest that these individuals may be much more strongly affected by these institutions than they are by the more local or national institutions that they live under. Since these individuals are profoundly affected by these institutions, the argument goes, these institutions should be morally accountable to those individuals to at least some extent—so that the individuals have at least some rights relative to the set of social institutions that they live under. Note that this line of argument starts from a (surely plausible) claim about the effects of extant institutions, and attempts to argue this into a moral claim about those institutions. By contrast, the more parochial egalitarian may be interpreted as arguing that institutions have to be grounded in some overarching political consensus before those institutions can be evaluated in this way. It is not sufficient to show that some institution has a particular effect; it has also to be argued that this institution is part of a 'comprehensive social structure' that includes the individuals of concern.

Whatever the merits of these alternative positions, it seems very likely that, as a matter of descriptive fact, the range of moral motivations that individuals actually display in their behaviour are subject to distance and border effects, so that the concerns that individuals show for each other fade with distance and decline sharply as borders are crossed. This is not to say that moral motivations do not have global reach, but merely to suggest that they are attenuated by distance and national boundaries. So, for example, while individuals in countries like the UK, acting alone or through collective representative agencies (governmental or charitable), are clearly willing to engage in some redistribution on a global scale, it is not comparable to the extent of domestic social insurance despite the obvious increased scale of inequality on the global scale. And if we are to take seriously the motivations of individuals in assessing the institutions and policies in the world, this fact must be relevant.

This brings us back to the initial assumption that the world is characterized by the lack of both a shared moral code and a shared political culture. The argument that the moral analysis of 'almost global capitalism' differs sharply from the moral analysis of capitalism within an integrated society sketched here clearly depends upon this assumption, and it should be questioned directly. It seems obvious enough that the world lacks a shared political culture—even granted the developments in the post-communist countries of Eastern Europe. The world is still a remarkably heterogeneous place with stable democracies by no means the only political game in town. But perhaps it is commonality of moral code, rather than political culture that is really important, and here it might seem that there is a greater convergence—at least in principle. But I would suggest that such convergence of moral codes as actually exists is at a level that carries rather little in the way of implications for the operation of the institutions that constitute a single society. On this matter I am somewhat more sceptical than John Dunning. In terms of his 'pyramid of moral virtue' I agree that there are some 'high level' moral values that are widely (if not universally) shared, but these values may be more formal than real. Take, for example, the case of 'good citizenship' mentioned by Dunning following Donaldson[8] and defined as 'the need of members of a community to work together to support and improve the institutions on which the community depends'. Even if it were the case that each and every community in the world subscribed to this value, it would clearly not imply a single society. Indeed, if each community sees itself as a separate community, and supports internal norms and institutions that promote this distinctive identity, this universally shared value might be a strong force against the emergence of an integrated global society. Only if the substantive contents of moral values—rather than their formal structures—are widely shared, and only then if all (or most) agree that the substantive values apply universally and not just within their own communities, would we have the basis for a single society.

While I agree with John Dunning that many sages and ethical theorists have argued for universal moral values, and even that they often argue for a similar set of universal moral values, this is some considerable distance from providing strong evidence for the practical existence of shared moral codes at the level of the motivations of real people. So, in terms of an evaluation of the current state of 'almost global capitalism' I can summon at most two cheers. From my economic perspective, the international market operates in an environment in which relatively few other institutions could survive, and it is the fact that few other institutions do operate at the truly global level that limits the ability to harness and control the power of the market. On this view, the major limiting factors are not essentially economic, but are rather moral and political; just as they are not to do with the failures of the international market but rather to do with the failure (or absence of) a range of other institutions, norms, and conventions.

3.3.2 Improving 'almost global capitalism'

Improvement here may come in at least two forms, that I will term superficial and basic. By a superficial improvement I mean one that operates at the level of detail in terms of the operation of international markets, or the behaviour of other international and transnational institutions, without changing the underlying constraints imposed by the lack of a moral or political society. A basic improvement, then, is one that operates by relaxing these underlying constraints so as to move the situation towards responsible global capitalism. I shall return to these more basic improvements in the next subsection.

At the superficial, but nevertheless important, level there are clearly a range of possibilities that might improve the operation of international markets and serve to supplement market institutions to some extent. These might involve such things as the fine tuning of the principles and policies of institutions such as the IMF and World Bank, the further development of international trade agreements, the adoption of internationally enforced policies that restrict the ability of despots and dictators to enrich themselves at the expense of their subjects—often leaving their subjects with international debts that they have no prospect of repaying. A common feature of many of these possibilities is that they are '*top down*' interventions that depend on nation states exercising power. However, herein lies a basic problem since it is clear that it may not always be in the interests of individual states, or coalitions of states, to act in a manner that would generate a global improvement. Prisoner's dilemmas and other forms of strategic interaction that may provide incentives to act in ways that are not appropriate from a normative perspective are as common in the field of international negotiations as they are in other areas.

I will not dwell on this issue, but it is no less important for that. I will make just one countervailing comment that relates to the recognition of potentially virtuous motivations. Recall the point (made in subsection 3.2.1 above) that within a society, institutions may operate to build on and reinforce virtue rather than to economize on virtue. Elsewhere I have argued[9] that representative democracy, as an institutional structure, may operate in this way, so that an appropriately elected government might be expected to be 'more moral' than the population it represents. This is not necessarily to say that the individuals who occupy high office in a representative democracy are more moral than other members of the society (although they may be), but rather to point out that even amoral politicians will find it systematically in their own interests to offer policies that appeal to the moral motivations of voters. Electoral politics, in short, is an institutional structure that tends to amplify moral motivations. And this will apply in the context of global political issues as well as domestic issues, so that there may be reasons to believe that democratic nations will select policies with respect to the design and support of international and transnational institutions, and to the arrangements for international trade, that are more moral, and less narrowly focused on national self-interest than might be predicted by the standard economic analysis. This argument may then provide some basis for believing that the policy actions of at least democratic states will tend to improve the operation of the global economy, rather than merely exploit the international domain in the national interest.

Not all superficial improvements are of this '*top down*' variety, dependent on the actions of nation states or other major players in the international domain. One clear example of a '*bottom up*' improvement might arise from the directly moral behaviour of individual market participants. Thus, for example, the idea of 'fair trade' consumer groups, or 'ethical investment' funds offer direct mechanisms by which the power of the market may be harnessed to directly moral ends. And notice that these examples do not depend on extreme specifications of moral motivations. It is relatively simple to show that an ethical investment strategy can be pursued at very little cost in terms of any reduction in the rate of return earned. It is precisely in this sort of context where a moral view may be acted upon at little cost, that we would expect morally motivated action to be most evident, and such action may have very real effects through the market despite its low initial cost.

Whatever the extent of these superficial improvements—whether '*top down*' or '*bottom up*'—it will still be the case that the basic problem of the lack of an integrated global society will place severe limitations on the realization of the full potential of global co-operation.

3.3.3   Towards Responsible Global Capitalism?

What then of more basic improvements—that is, changes in the background conditions of moral and political culture that might radically improve the prospects for truly global institutions? Is there any evidence of real and substantive convergence to a shared moral and political culture, and what, if anything can be done to improve the prospects for such convergence? These are surely the big questions. And like most big questions, they are the most difficult to address. Here it would seem that the prime movement must be '*bottom up*'—real shifts in the moral and political landscape must grow out of individual beliefs and commitments, rather than be imposed on them. But this is not to suggest that there is not an important social and institutional endogeneity in the formation of beliefs and commitments.

If beliefs and commitments and their associated moral dispositions evolve over time, especially across generations, we might expect them to evolve in a manner that responds to experience and correlates positively with relative success. And the pattern of evolution may be influenced by existing institutional structures. Thus, for example, the mere fact of living within a democratic society governed by norms and conventions of social insurance, collective provision of basic public goods, and so on, may encourage one to adopt particular beliefs and attitudes toward others that recognize the potential for co-operation and mutual benefit, even when the relevant others live outside of the society. By contrast, if the only interpersonal interactions that one encounters are of an arms-length, non-co-operative and untrusting kind, it will surely pay to adopt a more disinterested and suspicious mind-set. Equally, improved communications between societies (not least through the process of international trade) open up at least the possibility that individuals will see alternative models of society, and even this limited experience may influence their beliefs and attitudes.

Of course, evolutionary models are capable of supporting many equilibria—we might easily imagine a convergent outcome in which the world evolves into a single integrated society, but we might equally easily imagine divergent equilibria in which multiple societies continue to exist even in the long run. There is nothing in the idea of the evolution of norms, or of normative dispositions, that guarantees a happy ending. But neither should one suggest that a happy ending requires some sort of total convergence that dissolves all cultural, ethnic, or religious variation. All that is required for a globally integrated society is a rough sort of convergence to a set of norms and political cultures that are sufficiently shared and sufficiently deeply embedded to sustain common institutions. It will be sufficient that most of the people, most of the time, recognize and identify with these norms and political customs, even if the norms and cultures play rather different roles in the lives of different individuals and groups within the overarching society. Society here is not a dull vision of uniform homogeneity, but is capable of recognizing very considerable heterogeneity provided that there are certain key threads that hold the society together—and chief among these threads is the idea that most of the members of the society must indeed conceive of themselves as members of that society, where membership carries both certain rights and certain responsibilities.

However, we do not have to rely solely on evolutionary pressures to move us towards such a global society. We can, to at least some extent, take purposive action—action relating to social and moral education for example—that we have good reason to believe will improve the prospects of a more integrated global society. And it is an appropriate point on which to end that the engagement with the task of such social and moral education is itself likely to be an act that would be rather difficult to explain under the standard economic model of motivation. When we recognize our own motivations with respect to such concerns, and generalize them to the individuals that populate our models, we begin to see the prospects for improvement, as well as the risks involved, more clearly.

NOTES

1. See Hamlin (1995).
2. Since these are caricatures, I would stress that I do not associate such extreme views with particular authors. A more moderate range of views may be found in Bull (1977), Reinicke (1989), and Gilpin (2001).
3. Hamlin (1995: 137–8). This categorization was presented as a more detailed view of one part of the categorization of the relationship between ethics and economics offered by Hausman and McPherson (1993).
4. This usage of 'market sphere' echoes the usage of Walzer (1983) and Anderson (1990, 1993).
5. For more detailed analysis of the idea of economizing on virtue see Brennan and Hamlin (1995, 2000).
6. See Brennan and Hamlin (2000), Persson and Tabellini (2000).
7. Dunning (above, Ch. 1), see Section 2.2.
8. See Dunning (above, Ch. 1, p. 23).
9. See Brennan and Hamlin (1999) for details.

REFERENCES

Anderson, E. (1990), 'The Ethical Limitations of the Market', *Economics and Philosophy* 6: 179–205.

——(1993), *Value in Ethics and Economics* (Cambridge: Harvard University Press).

Beitz, C. (1999), 'Cosmopolitan Ideas and National Sentiment', *Journal of Philosophy* 80: 591–600.

Brennan, G., and Hamlin, A. (1995), 'Economizing on Virtue', *Constitutional Political Economy* 6: 35–56.

——— (1999), 'On Political Representation', *British Journal of Political Science* 29: 109–27.

——— (2000), *Democratic Devices and Desires* (Cambridge: Cambridge University Press).

Bull, H. (1977), *The Anarchical Society: A Study of Order in World Politics* (London: Macmillan).

Gilpin, R. (2001), *Global Political Economy: Understanding the International Economic Order* (Princeton: Princeton University Press).

Hamlin, A. (1995), 'The Morality of the Market', In S. Brittan and A. Hamlin (eds.), *Market Capitalism and Moral Values* (Aldershot: Edward Elgar).

Hausman, D., and McPherson, M. (1993), 'Taking Ethics Seriously: Economics and Contemporary Moral Philosophy', *Journal of Economic Literature* 31: 671–731.

Persson, T., and Tabellini, G. (2000), *Political Economics: Explaining Economic Policy* (Cambridge, Mass.: MIT Press).

Pogge, T. (2001), 'Priorities of Global Justice', *Metaphilosophy* 32(1–2): 6–24.

—— (2000), 'The Moral Demands of Global Justice', *Dissent* 47(4): 37–43.

Rawls, J. (1971), *A Theory of Justice* (Cambridge, Mass.: Harvard University Press).

—— (1999), *The Law of Peoples* (Cambridge Mass.: Harvard University Press).

Reinicke, W. H. (1989), *Global Public Policy: Governing without Government?* (Washington, DC: Brookings Institution).

Walzer, M. (1983), *Spheres of Justice* (New York: Basic Books).

4

Towards a New Paradigm of Development*

JOSEPH STIGLITZ

4.1 INTRODUCTION

The purpose of this chapter is to explore the relationship between the trend towards the globalization of the world economy and the transformation of societies through the process of development. More specifically, its task is to question the traditional notion of 'development', as construed, for example by the Washington Consensus;[1] and to argue that, if global capitalism is to be made more democratically inclusive and economically sustainable, a more holistic approach to development is needed. Such an approach should embrace a social, moral and environmental dimension as well as an economic one. Although we shall primarily focus on issues of concern to developing countries, much of what we have to say also applies to advanced industrial economies. For the essence of development in the twenty-first century is *change* and *transformation*, and the individual and societal challenges and opportunities such change and transformation bring with them. Later chapters in this volume will address in more detail the specifically moral responsibilities of the organizations of the global economy, as they seek to reduce poverty and empower the less developed and transitional economies of the world with the resources, capabilities, entrepreneurship, and the legal or institutional infrastructure they need to transform their societies in a way acceptable to their constituents.

This being so, this chapter will focus on the form and content of a new (i.e. post Washington Consensus) paradigm of development; the role of national governments, civil society, and international agencies in helping to promote such development; and the ways in which the appropriate strategies, policies, and processes may best be conceived and delivered.

The chapter will be divided into five main parts. First, we shall describe our broader vision for the future course of development. Second, we shall explain that not only the Washington Consensus but also earlier development paradigms failed, because they viewed development too narrowly. In doing so, we shall outline briefly some of the key factors—including recent events in East Asia and the

---

*A revised version of the 9th Rául Prebisch lecture delivered at UNCTAD in Geneva on 19th October 1998.

Russian Federation—that have helped us realize the inadequacies of the old approaches. Third, we shall outline what we would regard to be key principles of a development strategy based on a holistic concept of development. Fourth, we shall identify the major components of such a development strategy. And fifth, we shall conclude with some general observations, focusing on the importance of a full and fair participation in the global economy in furthering development based on this new paradigm.

4.2 DEVELOPMENT AS A TRANSFORMATION OF SOCIETY

The essential feature of development is that it represents a transformation of society. In particular it embraces a movement from traditional relations, traditional cultures and social mores, traditional ways of dealing with health and education, and traditional methods of production to more 'modern' ways. For instance, a characteristic of traditional societies was (and is) the acceptance of the world as it is. By contrast, most modern knowledge-based economies recognize change as an inherent feature of economic and social life. *Inter alia*, it is acknowledged that we, as individuals and societies, can take actions that, for instance, reduce infant mortality, extend life spans, and increase productivity. Key to these changes is the movement to 'scientific' ways of thinking—the identification of critical variables that affect outcomes and attempting to make inferences based on available data—recognizing what we know and what we do not know.

All societies are a blend of the old and the new. Even in more 'advanced' societies there are sectors and regions that remain wedded to traditional modes of operation, and people wedded to traditional moral values and ways of thinking. But while in more advanced societies, these constitute a relatively small proportion, in less advanced societies they may predominate. Indeed, one characteristic of many of the less developed countries in the world is the failure of the more advanced sectors to penetrate deeply into society. This results in what many have called the phenomenon of the 'dual' economy, in which more advanced production methods among the more educated and wealthier sections of society may coexist with very primitive technologies among the less educated and poorer sections of society.

Change is not an end in itself, but a means to other objectives. The changes that are associated with development provide individuals and societies with more control and influences over their own destiny. Development enriches the lives of individuals by widening their horizons of choice and freedom and reducing their sense of isolation. It reduces the afflictions brought on by disease and poverty and environmental degradation, not only increasing life spans, but improving the quality and vitality of life.

Given this definition of development, it is clear that a development strategy must be aimed at facilitating the transformation of society, in identifying the barriers to, as well as potential catalysts of, change. In the following pages, we outline some of the ingredients of such a new development strategy. Approaching development from the perspective of transforming society has profound implications not only for what national governments and international agencies do, but also for the way in which they proceed—how they engage, for instance, in participation and partnership, particularly with market-related institutions and civil society. Thus, this chapter may be seen as providing an analytic framework for much of the rethinking that has been occurring in the last few years about how best to promote development.

4.3   THE NEED FOR A NEW DEVELOPMENT STRATEGY

The experience of the past fifty years has demonstrated that development is possible, but not inevitable. While a few countries have succeeded in making rapid economic growth, and have narrowed the gap between themselves and the more advanced countries, and bringing millions of their citizens out of poverty, many more have actually seen that gap grow and poverty increase. Today the number of people living in poverty—even measured by the minimal standard of a dollar a day—is about 1.3 billion.[2] Strategies of the past, even when they have been assiduously followed, have not guaranteed success. Furthermore, many of the most successful countries (representing the largest part of growth within the low income countries) have not actually followed the 'recommended' strategies, but have carved out paths of their own.

What Development is Not: A Critique of Previous Conceptions

Many previous development strategies have focused on pieces of this transformation, but because they have failed to see the broader context, they have failed, and often miserably. Most of these have focused narrowly on economics. Economics is important: after all, one of the features that distinguishes more developed from less developed countries is their higher GDP per capita. But, as John Dunning has pointed out in Chapter 1, the focus on economics has confused not only means with ends, but also cause with effect. It has confused means with ends, because higher GDP is not an end in itself, but a means to improved living standards and a better society, with less poverty, better health, less crime, improved education, and less environmental pollution. Contrary to Kuznets's contention, by and large, increases in GDP per capita are accompanied by reductions in poverty.[3] It has confused cause with effect, because to some extent, the changes in society, which may be called modernization, are as much a cause of the increases in GDP as a result.

For more than four decades, development was seen (at least by mainstream economists) as mainly a matter of economics—increasing the capital stock (either through transfers from abroad or through higher savings rates at home) and improving the allocation of resources. These changes would lead to higher incomes and hopefully higher sustained growth rates. Less developed countries were portrayed as being identical to more developed countries—except, perhaps, in the extent of the inefficiencies in resource allocation (which, in turn, were related to the greater incidence of missing or malfunctioning markets).

However, economists differed in their views of how best to improve resource allocation, and what role governments should play. Those of the left attributed the underlying problems to market failures. The thrust of the development programming models that were popular in the 1960s was for governments, using these models, to replace the absent and imperfect markets, and to guide the economy towards a more efficient allocation of resources. By contrast, economists of the right assumed that governments were the problem and left to themselves, markets would lead to efficient resource allocation. This view was buttressed by the perception that governments not only lacked the capabilities to undertake a major role in resource allocation, but, all too often, were prone to use whatever capabilities they had not for increasing national production, but for diverting rents to the politically powerful. The solution, in this perspective, was increased reliance on markets, and in particular, the elimination of government-imposed distortions associated with protectionism, government subsidies, and government ownership.

In the 1980s, the strategic focus on development shifted from micro management policies to macroeconomic policies, and, in particular, to the adjustment of fiscal imbalances and monetary policies. Given the macroeconomic imbalances, it was impossible for markets to function, or at least to function well.

Now the critical feature of each of these development strategies was that they saw development as a technical problem requiring technical solutions: better planning algorithms; better trade, FDI, and pricing policies; and better macroeconomic frameworks. They did not reach deep down into society, nor did they believe such a participatory approach (e.g. of civil society) in the decision taking process was necessary. The laws of economics were assumed to be universal: demand and supply curves and the fundamental theorems of welfare economies were expected to apply as well to Africa and Asia as they did to Europe and North America. These scientific laws were not bound by time or space. Little attention was paid to institutional constraints or cross-cultural value differences.

4.3.1 The Lessons of History

As remarkable as the narrow focus of these approaches was, they lacked historic context. In particular, they failed to recognize that: (*a*) in their early stages, successful development efforts in the United States as well as many other countries had involved an active role for government; (*b*) many societies in the decades before active government involvement—or interference, as these doctrines would put it—failed to develop; indeed, development was the exception around the world, not the rule; and (*c*) worse still, capitalist economies before the era of greater government involvement, were characterized not only by high levels of economic instability, but also by widespread social/economic problems; large groups, such as the aged and the unskilled, were often left out of any progress and were left destitute in the economic crashes that occurred with such regularity.

Indeed, one of the puzzles is how these narrow approaches ignored the failure of certain regions within seemingly developed countries to develop, such as South Italy for most of the past century. No trade barriers separated North from

South Italy; the overall macroeconomic framework in both regions was the same; and the South even benefited from economic policies specifically designed to encourage it. Yet while the North boomed, the South stagnated. This, by itself, should have suggested that there was more to development than is acknowledged by the technical approaches; for instance, trade liberalization, as valuable as it might be, would not solve the problem of Italy's South.

Three events of the past quarter-century have played a central role in helping to shape views concerning development strategies.

Collapse of the Socialist/Communist Economies and the End of the Cold War

The first event is the collapse of the socialist/communist economies and the end of the Cold War. Some have focused on a single lesson that emerges—the inefficacy (and dangers) of a large government role in the economy. From this, some jump to the opposite conclusion; that more reliance should be placed on markets.

But the failure of the communist system was as much a failure of the political, social, and moral order, on which it was based, as of the economic system itself. The economic models that showed the equivalence between market socialism and capitalist economies were fundamentally misguided, partly because they did not properly acknowledge the role of institutions (particularly those designed to facilitate efficiency and socially acceptable resource deployment), but partly, also, because they did not grasp the importance of the interface between the economic transactions, narrowly defined, and the broader goals and values of society.[4]

The Limitations of the Washington Consensus

The second defining event was that many countries followed the dictums of liberalization, stabilization, and privatization, the central premises of the so-called Washington Consensus, and still did not grow. The technical solutions—the prescriptions of the Washington Consensus—were evidently not enough. This should not have come as a surprise; as we have already observed, history was not encouraging. Moreover, developments in theoretical economics, many of which emphasized the limitations of the market, should have served to provide insights into both the historical as well as the more recent, institutional and moral market failures of the Russian Federation and East Asian economies.

In many ways, the problems in the Russian Federation seem to be of a very different nature than those in East Asia. In the Russian Federation, for example, we see an economy in transition facing huge government deficits, severe political problems, and social unrest. Yet there are some common threads. In both cases, the Washington Consensus failed, and for similar reasons. A failure to understand the subtleties of the market economy, to appreciate that private property and 'getting prices right' (that is, liberalization) are not sufficient to make a market economy work. An economy needs an institutional infrastructure and an underpinning moral ecology. To be fair, the failures in the Russian Federation were considerably greater than those of East Asia, as the latter had remarkable growth, stability, and reductions in poverty over the previous quarter-century.

While the banks in East Asia lacked adequate supervision, those in the Russian Federation not only lacked that supervision, but did not even perform their core function of providing capital to new and growing enterprises. We all know that the standard theorems of economics emphasize that an economy needs both private property, competition, and appropriate legal infrastructure within which markets could perform their proper functions.

The Washington Consensus, while occasionally paying lip service to the first and third necessity, placed its emphasis on the second, in the belief that with private property, at least owners would have an incentive to increase efficiency. Worries about distribution and competition—or even concerns about democratic processes being undermined by excessive concentration of wealth—could be addressed later! The Russian Federation succeeded in turning ordinary economic laws on their head, in that it managed to reverse the usual trade-offs between equity and efficiency. Reforms such as moving from inefficient central planning to decentralized pricing mechanism, from inefficient state ownership to private property and the profit motive, should have increased output, even if perhaps at the price of a slight increase in inequality. Instead, the Russian Federation achieved huge increases in inequality, while, at the same time, it managed to shrink the economy, by up to a third according to some estimates. Living standards collapsed with GDP statistics, as life spans were shortened and the quality of health worsened. Bribery and corruption mushroomed. All too late, it was recognized that, without the right institutional infrastructure and moral ecology, the profit motive, combined with full capital market liberalization, rather than providing the incentives for wealth creation, could only spark off a drive to strip assets and ship wealth abroad.

The East Asian Miracle

The third defining event was the East Asian miracle: the rapid growth of most of the East Asian economies showed that development was possible, and that successful development could be accompanied by a reduction of poverty, widespread improvements in living standards, and even a process of democratization. But for those advocating the technical solutions, the East Asian miracle countries were deeply disturbing. For these countries did not follow the standard prescriptions. In most cases, national governments played a large role. They followed some of the accepted technical prescriptions, such as (by and large) stable macroeconomic policies, but ignored others. For example, rather than privatizing, governments actually started some highly productive steel mills, and more generally pursued industrial policies to promote particular sectors. Governments intervened in trade, though more to promote exports than to inhibit particular imports. Governments regulated financial markets, engaged in mild financial restraint, by lowering interest rates and increasing profitability of banks and firms. Governments adopted a conservative and co-ordinated approach to market-related decision taking. And both the actions of the governments and the other institutions in most East Asian economies were strongly buttressed by Confucian-based social and ethical mores.

Many of the policies on which these governments focused were simply areas that had been assigned a low priority by Western governments in the past. These included, for example, the heavy emphasis on education and technology, on closing the knowledge gap between them and the more advanced countries. While the impact of individual policies remains a subject of dispute, the mix of policies clearly worked well. Perhaps had these countries followed all of the dictums of liberalization and privatization, they would have grown even faster, but there is little evidence for that proposition. In some cases, such as financial restraint, there is some evidence—as well as a considerable body of theory—that suggests that these policies did enhance growth.

But perhaps the most important lesson of East Asia was that, to a large extent, they succeeded in a transformation of their societies, a fact that is evident to any visitor to the region. To be sure, the transformation is still far from complete: witness the sectors in several of these countries that exhibit rigidities and have failed to adopt modern technologies and modes of business. And while the crisis, which overtook the East Asian economies in the mid-1990s, has raised questions in many circles concerning the East Asia miracle, the fact of their transformation of their societies remains. Even as they enter the twenty-first century their GDP is fast recovering, and is already a multiple of what it was a half-century ago, and far higher than that of countries that have pursued alternative development strategies. Equally important, poverty rates are a fraction of what they were a half-century ago, although somewhat higher than at the beginning of the 1990s. Literacy remains near-universal, and health standards remain high. A careful reading of the East Asian experience over the last several decades—of what strategies led to those remarkable achievements—reveals that many of the views advocated in this chapter were, in fact, incorporated in the development strategies of the fastest developers (World Bank 1993, Stiglitz 1996).

The East Asia Crisis

This is not the place for an extended exegesis either of the crisis' cause or its depth, and we have spoken or written extensively about these matters elsewhere.[5] Nevertheless, there are important lessons to be learned from the crisis concerning the design of development strategies. These lessons have not been completely lost on both developing and developed countries, and by international agencies, over the past five years or so, even if they have at times become, in our view, somewhat muddled.

To show how views about development have begun to change because of the crisis, it is worth thinking back to 1997—the year before the crisis exploded. How much the world has changed since then! In 1997, in Hong Kong, there was a debate about extending the IMF charter to include a mandate for capital market liberalization. Critics of hedge funds were seen as financial Luddites who wished to reverse the course of history and the inevitable domination of free markets.

Today, in 2002, there is widespread recognition that even countries that pursue good economic policies can suffer from the volatility of short-term capital flows. While the risks and market failures (including externalities associated with contagion and systemic failures[6]) associated with short-term capital flows have now become apparent, the benefits, especially for countries like those in East Asia with high savings rates, remain unproven.[7] But the East Asia crisis has raised questions about the Washington Consensus itself, as the source of the problems were items that were simply not emphasized in the earlier policy prescriptions. Ironically, in identifying these new sources of potential problems, much of the popular discussion in the later 1990s shifted attention away from another set of problems—those associated with the financial and capital market liberalization, which were a central part of the Washington Consensus.

Thus, while the countries of East Asia that encountered economic problems were widely chastised for having inadequate or weak financial institutions, the Washington Consensus had failed to stress that such institutions could be as important a source of macro-instability and excessive government deficits. And many of the recent discussions have failed to note the role that financial market liberalization—often under pressure from outsiders—played in contributing to the weaknesses in financial institutions.[8] What is now quite clear is that it is far easier to strip away regulations than to create the requisite institutional infrastructure for financial markets to function efficiently. For a recent reminder of the difficulties of regulating financial institutions (including banks)—even in the most developed economies—we need only consider the bail-out (in 1999) of Long-Term Capital Management, the huge US-based hedge fund that reportedly had an exposure of more than a trillion dollars before its crash.

Indeed, it may be argued that excessively risky lending and inadequate supervision of the financial sector in the developed countries contributed to the crisis. We now realize that for every borrower there is a lender, and the lender is as much to blame as the borrower. Thus, if the borrowers in East Asia are to be held to account, so too should the lenders from developed countries. And to the extent that the foreign banks were marginal lenders, they deserve even more of the blame. Foreign lenders to Korea's highly leveraged firms (or to banks that had, themselves, made extensive loans to highly leveraged firms) knew that these enterprises' debt–equity ratios were far higher than any financial analyst would have called prudent. Yet supposedly well-managed banks, supervised by supposedly sophisticated regulatory authorities, made these loans. Moreover, these loans were not driven by government pressure. Is there a suggestion that in some countries bad loans result only from unacceptable crony capitalism, while in others, they result from the acceptable natural working of market processes?[9]

The East Asia crisis has not only put a sharper spotlight on financial institutions, but on broader aspects of political and economic life. A lack of transparency has been widely identified as contributing to the crisis, for instance. There is little econometric evidence in support of that conclusion[10]—and our scepticism is reinforced when we remember that the previous three major crises occurred in Scandinavian countries, which are amongst the most transparent in the world. But the emphasis on transparency and accountability is welcome, in that it raises the importance of broader societal issues. Both institutional elements are necessary for effective participation in decision making, and participation, we shall argue, is an essential part of successful development as a transformation of society. At the same time, the East Asian economic crisis has exposed several deficiencies in the moral ecology underpinning the capitalist system of both East Asian and Western economies, as identified, for example, by such commentators as George Soros (1998) and other contributors to this volume. These too need to be addressed if the kind of development, we are setting forth in this chapter, can be successfully achieved.

4.4 THE PRINCIPLES OF THE NEW DEVELOPMENT STRATEGY

The new development strategy takes as its core objective development, the transformation of society. It recognizes that an integral part of successful development is the increase in GDP per capita. But this is only part of the story, and even this will not be achieved unless the country adopts a broader and more socially oriented development focus. If successful, the new development strategy will not only raise GDP per capita, but also living standards, as evidenced by standards of health and literacy and a reduction of such bads as crime and drugs. It will reduce poverty—our goal should be its elimination, a goal that the more successful economies have actually attained (at least by the *absolute* poverty standard). It will be sustainable, strengthening the environment. And the real societal transformations will enhance the likelihood that the underlying policies will be durable, withstanding the vicissitudes sometimes accompanying democratic processes.

The following discussion of principles is divided into three sections: what development strategies are, and how they differ from plans; how we can catalyse society-wide change; and why participation and ownership are crucial.

4.4.1 The Concept of Development Strategies

Corporations have increasingly found corporate strategies of use in guiding their thinking and longer-term investments. Development strategies need to be thought of in a similar light, rather than as the detailed programming models and development plans of the past, which originally grew out of an attempt to make central planning work. Development strategies, which in some ways are less detailed than these planning documents, are, in many ways, more ambitious, for they set out a strategy not just for the accumulation of capital and the deployment of indigenous resources and capabilities, but for the transformation of society.

A development strategy, first, needs to set forth the vision of the transformation, i.e. what the society will be like ten to twenty years from now. This vision may embrace certain quantitative goals, such as a reduction in poverty by half, or universal primary education, or an increase in life expectancy by ten years, or a fall in crime by 30 per cent, but these are elements in or targets for the transformation process, not the vision of the transformation itself.

This vision needs to include a view of the transformation of institutions, the creation of new social capital and new regulatory or incentive mechanisms. In some cases, this will require new institutions to replace traditional institutions that will inevitably be weakened in the process of development. In other cases, the new institutions will contain within them elements of the old, and there will be a need for a process of evolution and adaptation. Some of these transitions may be difficult, either to articulate or to implement. For example, how will societies that have traditionally discriminated against women achieve a higher degree of equality at the same time that they maintain traditional values?

A development strategy has sometimes been likened to a blueprint, a map of where the society is going. But this metaphor is misleading, and understanding why helps us to see the difference between plans of the past and development strategies of the future. The contemporary development process is too complex and difficult to allow us to prepare a blueprint or a map of where the economy will be going over the next ten years, let alone the next quarter of a century. Doing so requires too much information and knowledge that is not currently available. In the past, planning documents have failed to take into account virtually any of the major uncertainties facing the development process. While, in principle, a development plan could map out how the economy would respond to the myriad of different contingencies that might occur in the coming years, in practice this is seldom done.

By contrast, a development strategy is a living document. It needs to set forth how it is to be created, revised, and adopted; the process of participation; the means by which ownership and consensus is to be obtained; how the details will be fleshed out. Such a development strategy would fulfil several functions as it sets forth its vision for the future.

Development Strategies and Priorities

All societies—and particularly poor countries—are resource-constrained. Beyond general resource constraints are the constraints on the capacity of government, including the limitations on the number of issues which it can pursue. While there are many pressing needs, it is imperative that any development strategy should set priorities. A key aspect of prioritization is an awareness of sequencing: *viz.* what tasks have to be done before other tasks. It may, for instance, be essential to establish formal priority systems[11] and a competition and regulatory framework before the privatization of production. It may be no less vital to establish a financial regulatory framework *before* capital market or financial sector liberalization. A prerequisite for a successful industrial relations system is the freedom to engage in collective bargaining, but also it requires a constructive, honest, and trustworthy relationship between employers and employees.

Development Strategies and Co-ordination

In traditional economic theory, prices perform all the co-ordination that is required in an economy. But this requires a full set of markets and the absence of uncertainties and information asymmetry—conditions that patently are not satisfied in less developed countries. Having a sense of where the economy is going is essential: if, for instance, an economy is to move to the 'next' stage of development, the appropriate infrastructure, human capital, and institutions all have to be in place. If any of the essential ingredients is missing, the chances of success will be greatly reduced. Not only must there be co-ordination of different agencies within and among levels of government: there must be co-ordination between the private sector and the public, and among various parts of the private sector.

The kind of co-ordination provided by this kind of development strategy is markedly different, both in spirit and detail, from that envisioned (but never actually achieved) in indicative planning. While indicative planning saw itself as a substitute for missing markets, in its attempts to provide detailed co-ordination of input and output decisions of various industries, development strategies focus more on the broader vision, including entry into new technologies or new industries.

Development Strategies as Consensus Builders

The process of constructing a development strategy may itself serve a useful function in helping build a consensus not only about a broad vision of the country's future, and key short- and medium-term objectives, but about some of the essential ingredients for achieving those goals. Consensus building is not only an important part of achieving political and social stability (and avoiding the economic disruption that comes when claims on a society's resources exceed the amount available[12]), but it also leads to an 'ownership' of policies and institutions, which in turn enhances the likelihood of their success.

4.4.2   Catalysing Society-Wide Change:
Beyond Enclaves and Projects

If the transformation of society is at the heart of development, the question now arises of how to bring these changes about. One of the major roles of a holistic development strategy is to serve as a catalyst, for example by identifying the areas of a country's (dynamic) comparative advantage both in goods and services. Identifying these areas and publicizing such information is a *public good*, and, as such, is a responsibility of government.

Transforming Whole Societies

To be effective, any role of governments to serve as catalyst to development will need to embrace the ambitious goal of encouraging *society-wide* transformation. Earlier, we noted that, all too often, development efforts succeeded in transferring technology without transforming societies. In the process they created dual societies with pockets of more advanced technology but little more. In a sense, duality—in which only isolated enclaves are developed—represents a failure rather than a success of the development process. What went wrong, and why did these enclaves not serve as 'growth poles', catalysts of development beyond their narrow confines?

The same could be said about many development projects. A project may be 'good' in the sense that it yields high project returns, but it may disseminate few of its benefits to the majority of consumers or workers. Of course, high returns are better than low, but if its benefits do not spread throughout society, then the project cannot be judged a true success.

Part of a government's role as a catalyst is to undertake projects that can lead to social learning—that is, projects from which the country can draw widely applicable lessons, for instance about the viability of an industry. The benefit of the investment is not just the direct returns from the project, but also what can be learned for other projects from its success or failure. Because these learning benefits cannot be appropriated fully by private agents, there will be too little of this kind of experimentation within the private sector. A critical aspect, then, of the government's decision to undertake a particular project should be whether it can be scaled up. A project that succeeds only because of massive investment of resources that could otherwise have been mobilized more generally, or only due to an input that is not generally available, is not a good candidate for scaling up.

To make this point more concrete, let us cite a couple of examples. A project that provides more textbooks to a school may, for instance, be able to increase the effectiveness of that school, but if there are no resources available to provide similar textbooks to all schools, the project will have very limited development impact. By contrast, a project that develops a new curriculum, one that is better suited to the conditions of the country, and motivates children and their parents more effectively, can have nationwide impact. A project that demonstrates that local participation in education and local control of rural schools increases school accountability (as in El Salvador[13]) or student performance (as in Nicaragua[14]) could be replicated nationwide (or indeed, even worldwide), with limited additional resources. Indeed, such local involvement can itself be a catalyst for civic-related development efforts that go well beyond education. There are strong externalities associated with such projects. Not only do others learn directly from how the project itself performs, but in the process of learning to interact to address educational problems, the community learns how to deal with other issues as well, how to engage each other in a process of consensus formation. We would argue that this concern with scaling up must be at the core of government's involvement with projects, if that involvement is really to have the desired transformative effect.

4.4.3 Participation, Ownership, and the Role of Outsiders

Seeing development as a transformation of society also has clear implications for where the locus of development efforts must be, and how the process of assistance must be organized, as we will explain in the following section.

Why Imposing Change from the Outside Cannot Work

This much is surely clear: effective change cannot be imposed from outside. Indeed, the attempt to impose change from the outside is as likely to engender resistance and give rise to barriers to change, as it is to facilitate change. At the heart of development is a change in ways of thinking of the individuals of the countries concerned, and individuals cannot be forced to change how they think. They can be forced to take certain actions. They can be even forced to utter certain words. But they cannot be forced to change their hearts or minds; or, indeed, their basic attitudes and values.

This point was brought home forcefully in 1998, at a meeting of finance ministers and central bank governors from the countries of the former Soviet Union. All could articulate perfectly the requirements of sound macroeconomic policy, as each announced that he (or she) subscribed to those policies 100 percent—including those whose practices deviated markedly from the professed beliefs. Each, however, was noticeably deficient in his or her understanding of the institutional requirements necessary to bring about the kind of change they needed.

Indeed, interactions between donors and recipients may sometimes actually impede the transformation. Rather than encouraging recipients to develop their analytic capacities, the process of imposing conditionalities may undermine both the incentives to acquire those capacities, and the recipients' confidence in their ability to use them. Rather than involving large segments of society in a process of discussing change—thereby changing their ways of thinking—excessive conditionality is likely to reinforce traditional hierarchical relationships. Rather than empowering those who could serve as catalysts for change within these societies, it demonstrates their impotence. Rather than promoting the kind of open dialogue that is central to democracy, it argues, at best, that such dialogue is unnecessary, at worst that it is counterproductive.

Ownership and Participation

Thus, key ingredients in a successful development strategy are ownership and participation. We have seen again and again that ownership is essential for successful transformation. Policies that are imposed from outside may be grudgingly accepted, but will rarely be implemented as intended. But to achieve the desired ownership and transformation, the process that leads to that strategy must be participatory. Development cannot be just a matter of negotiations between a donor and the recipient government. Development must reach deeper. It must involve and support groups in civil society. These groups are part of a social fabric that needs to be strengthened, *inter alia* by giving voice to the often-excluded members of society, facilitating their participation and increasing ownership of the development process.

By involving these groups, the process of strategy formulation may be able to elicit the commitment and democratic involvement that is necessary for development to be socially acceptable and sustainable. Ownership and participation are also necessary if the development strategy is to be adapted to the particular circumstances of the country. Recent research has clearly shown that projects with higher levels of participation are more successful, probably in part because those projects make fewer erroneous assumptions about the needs and capabilities of beneficiaries (World Bank 1995, 1998*b*; Isham, Narayan, and Pritchett 1995).

Outside agents, including donors, can encourage ownership through persuasion—i.e. through presenting evidence, both theoretical and empirical, that particular strategies and policies are more likely to bring success than other approaches. But the degree of ownership is likely to be even greater when the strategies and policies are initiated by institutions within the country itself, i.e. when the country itself is in the driver's seat.

Some scholars, in their enthusiasm for ownership and participation, have implied that these participatory processes by themselves would suffice. But while individuals within a community may actively participate in discourse about what to do and how to do it, there must be more to this process than simple discourse. First, for participation to be fully meaningful, it should be based on knowledge; hence the crucial role of education and of capacity building. Second, merely calling for participation does not resolve the issue of incentives. Individuals (and groups of individuals or organizations) need to be motivated to be involved. In particular, it will be difficult to sustain participation if participants sense that they are not being listened to, and that their views are not taken into account in decision making. There also has to be a sense that the process of decision making is a fair one, and this, in turn, requires participation in the process that constructs institutional arrangements for decision making. Even if there has been full representative participation, each individual has to be offered appropriate incentives to take the desired actions. Indeed, one of the reasons for participation is so that policymakers can have a better understanding of what incentives are necessary. Institutions, incentives, participation, and ownership can be viewed as complementary development tools; none on its own is sufficient.

The Need for Inclusion and Consensus Building

One of the obstacles to successful development in the past has been the limited ability of some countries to resolve conflicts. The willingness and ability to resolve disputes is an important task of social and organizational capital. Reforms often bring advantage to some groups while disadvantaging others. There is likely to be greater acceptance of reforms—and a greater participation in the transformation process—if there is a perception of equity, of fairness, about the development process; if there is a spirit of trust, commitment and reciprocity abound; and there is a sense of ownership derived from participation if there has been an effort at consensus formation. For example, there have been numerous cases (such as Ghana) which have shown the importance and the promotion of solidarity and of consensus formation in achieving macroeconomic stability. By contrast, a decision to, say, eliminate food subsidies that is imposed from the outside, through an agreement between the ruling elite and an international agency, is not likely to be helpful in achieving a consensus, and therefore, in promoting a successful transformation.

4.5 THE COMPONENTS OF A NEW DEVELOPMENT STRATEGY

While, as we have said, the details of a development strategy will strongly differ from country to country, one constant is that, since a development strategy outlines an approach to the transformation of society, it must address all components of society.

4.5.1 Loci of Development

In particular, a strategy must include components aimed at developing the private sector, *viz.* international agencies, the state (the public sector), the constituents, the family, and the individual. The different components of the development strategy are intricately interrelated. For instance, at the centre of the strategy for the development of the individual is education and training; but enhancing skills is also critical for the private sector strategy, and the increase in wages for women that results from improved female education has a strong bearing on the family.

Private Sector Development

In the past, too often the responsibility for development strategies has been placed upon the shoulders of government. To a certain extent this was understandable, given that in the main, the 'plan' was a plan for public action, a blueprint for the government. But given the broader role that we envision for development strategies, it is natural to begin our discussion with the private sector, which, after all, typically is at centre stage in our globalizing economy.

A key objective then must be the creation and sustenance of a strong, competitive, stable, and efficient private sector. Among the elements of strategies which advance that objective are:

- a *legal infrastructure*, providing (and enforcing) competition laws, bankruptcy laws, and more broadly commercial law
- a *property system* which allows for the production of tangible and intangible assets, and for the creation of wealth from these assets
- a *regulatory framework* which encourages the private provision of infrastructure where possible, which maximizes the extent of feasible competition, and which ensures that, where competition is not possible, or desirable, there is not abuse of market power
- a *public provision of infrastructure*, where the private provision of infrastructure is not economically feasible
- a *stable macroeconomic framework*
- a *stable and effective financial system*, which requires a regulatory framework that not only ensures safety and soundness, but also enhances competition, protects depositors, creates confidence that there is a 'level playing field' in securities markets by protecting investors from abuses, and identifies underserved groups within society
- an *adjustment strategy* for the elimination of those distortions in the economy that interfere with the efficient deployment of resources.

The failure to establish some of the key institutional underpinnings to a market economy is perhaps one of the main factors contributing to the slow and painful transition to a market economy of many of the countries of the former Soviet Union. The inability (or unwillingness) to establish a sound legal and regulatory environment for banks, securities markets, and the financial sector more broadly is now recognized to have played a large role in the East Asia crisis.

If the private sector is to flourish, the environment must be conducive to private sector development. A key part of that environment is the quality of the labour force—an educated, healthy, well-motivated, and participating workforce is essential for an efficient upgrading of indigenous resources and capabilities.

Public Sector Development

The development strategy needs to pay particular attention to the public sector. After all, if the government cannot manage its own affairs, how can it be expected to manage (or even affect in an appropriate way) the affairs of others? The key question behind the strategy for the public sector is to identify the role of the government—both *what* the government should do and *how* it should do it. Moreover, the question should not be whether a particular activity should be carried on in the public or private sector, but how the two can best complement each other, acting as partners in the development effort. Related issues include what tasks should be undertaken at what level of government, and how governments can most effectively interact with civil society, and create or encourage the conditions that are most conducive to the transformation of the whole society.

Central ingredients to the public sector strategy are: (*a*) a focus of the public sector on the unique functions that it must perform, such as: creating the enabling environment for the private sector, ensuring that health and education are widely available, and spearheading the drive to eliminate poverty; (*b*) a strengthening of the capabilities of the public sector, including the development of an effective civil service, and a restructuring of the public sector to make more effective use of incentives and of market and market-like mechanisms; and (*c*) a matching both of responsibilities and modes of operation to the capabilities of the state (World Bank, 1997*b*).

Community Development: The Role of Civil Society

While certain activities are most effectively undertaken at the national (or international level), much of life centres around local communities and particular interest groups. Such institutions are often the most effective vehicle for both initiating and implementing the transformation of society. National governments are simply too cumbersome and remote, and the opportunities for meaningful participation are too limited. Well-designed development projects (such as those that have been financed through social funds) can be an important catalyst for community development. Participation at the local level (be it a region, district, city, or village) allows the project choice to reflect the needs and preferences within the community. It also allows the project design to reflect the local information, ensuring that local conditions, and the preferences and circumstances of local producers and consumers are taken into account. Equally importantly, local participation engenders commitment, which is necessary for project sustainability over the long run. And participation in the project itself becomes part of the transformation process. There is growing evidence among both sociologists and economists of the positive relationship between participation and development effectiveness.

Family Development

A major determinant of success in raising income per capita is population growth, which stems from decisions made within the family. Another important determinant is the extent and quality of female education—also a decision made within the family. The impact of female education is reflective of the key role that women play in educating the next generation. During the formative years of a child, the family is responsible not only for education, but for nutrition and health and the inculcation of moral values and behavioural patterns. More broadly, we have become increasingly aware of the importance of family development—of what goes on within the household. And just as we have become aware of the power of the family as an instrument for development, we have also become aware that in both developed and developing countries there are frequent instances of dysfunctional behaviours, including intra-family violence, drug abuse, divorce, and alcoholism.

Individual Development

In the end, the transformation of society entails a transformation of the way individual persons think and behave. Development entails the empowerment of individuals, so that they have more control over the forces that affect their lives, so that they can have a richer, healthier life. Education and health—including moral health—are at the centre of efforts at individual development. Jack Behrman takes up these and related issues in Chapter 5 of this volume.

4.5.2   Resources, Knowledge, and Institutions

We have provided a framework for thinking about development strategies that focuses on five levels—the private sector, the government, the community, the household, and the individual. A second cut at identifying the requirements of a holistic development strategy approach emphasizes not the levels on which it operates, but on what it must provide.

Resources and Capabilities

As we have already observed, development entails more than the possession of indigenous resources and capabilities. Returns to capital, even defined broadly to include human capital, depend heavily on the availability of complementary inputs such as a well-managed economic environment and honest, transparent, and well-functioning institutions. Nevertheless, it is clear that such resources and capabilities are an important ingredient of the development process. A development strategy must outline plans for developing indigenous physical capital, innovating systems and human capital, as well as preserving natural resources; plans for encouraging saving and investment, and for filling the gap between the two; plans for schools and for financing them; and plans for an ecologically friendly use and renewal of natural resources.

Entrepreneurship and Economic Management

One of the defining characteristics of less developed countries is their paucity of indigenous resources, including entrepreneurship. This is why it is all the more important that the resources that are available are both well utilized and upgraded. Comprehensive development strategies must set out to identify the most important distortions in the economy—particularly as far as the use of capital is concerned (DeSoto 2000)—and how they are to be addressed, taking full account of the social costs and distributional impacts of policies. Accordingly, the ingredients in economic management need to be both more comprehensive and more institutionally oriented than the traditional lists, which focused largely on liberalization, privatization, and macro-stability.

Knowledge Management

Development requires closing the gap not only in 'objects', in human and physical capital, but also in knowledge. Knowledge and capital in fact complement any assets. Improved knowledge enhances the return to capital, while additional capital provides the opportunity to make use of recently acquired knowledge. Incorporating knowledge into any development strategy requires creating capacities to absorb and adapt knowledge (through investments in human capital and in innovating capacity), investing in technologies to facilitate the dissemination of knowledge, and creating knowledge locally. Thus, a development strategy needs to outline a strategy of knowledge management. The World Bank is increasingly thinking along these lines, conceiving of itself as a knowledge bank, with one of its central tasks being to help countries to reduce the knowledge gap between rich and poor countries (Wolfensohn 1998; World Bank 1998*a*). It can provide the cross-country experience that, when melded with local knowledge, makes possible effective choices of development policies, programmes, and projects.

Sector and Sub-National Strategies

In many cases, it is useful to narrow one's focus from the whole economy to a sector or some industry (the health care sector, or agriculture), to some interest group, or to some region, to city or rural area. The cities represent an arena in which a cluster of concerns jostle together forcefully—infrastructure, the environment, health, finances. In some ways, cities are microcosms of the economy as a whole, and integrated solutions to a city's problems may provide insights into integrated solutions for the national economy. Moreover, many cities have been more successful in achieving modernization than rural areas, and it is thus nat-ural to focus development policies particularly on the former in trying to achieve societal transformation. The role of clusters of related industries in economic development is now receiving increasing attention by scholars.[15]

Social and Organizational Capital

Another form of capital, beyond physical capital, human capital, and knowledge, is also essential for a successful transformation. This embraces various forms of social and organizational capital, which includes the institutions and relations that set values or encourage value formation, mediate transactions and resolve disputes. In recognition of the theme of the volume and because it is too often given short shrift in policy discussions, we will elaborate on this point a little fur-ther. Traditional societies often have a high level of organizational and social cap-ital, though this capital may not be of a form that facilitates change. But in the process of development, this organizational and social capital is often weakened or destroyed—as indeed it was in early nineteenth-century Britain. The transforma-tion may weaken traditional authority relationships, and new patterns of migra-tion may sever community ties. The problem is that this process of destruction may occur before new organizational and social capital is created, leaving society bereft of the necessary institutional structures and the moral ecology with which to function well.[16]

Social and organizational capital and its underpinning ethical framework can-not be handed over to a country from the outside. It must be developed from within, even if knowledge and moral suasion from outside bodies can help facil-itate the creation of this social/organizational capital. The pace of change and the pattern of reforms must be adapted to each country's willingness and ability to create social/organizational capital; and, in particular, to its cultural heritage. This factor may, in fact, be the most important constraint on the speed of transformation. In the earlier development literature, in the days when it was thought that the main factor separating developed from less developed countries was physical capital, there was considerable discussion of countries' absorptive capacities (Rostow 1960: 143–4). From our particular perspective, the issue is not the pace of absorbing capital, but that of societal transformation and the recon-figuration of values and norms which change—and particularly technological change—demands.

China has demonstrated that a country can absorb enormous amounts of physical capital quickly. In the early stages of development, the need for roads, schools, energy, telecommunications, and other elements of the infrastructure is huge, and it is hard to believe that more resources could not be productively used. But simply providing these ingredients does not constitute development.

There has been much talk of late about capacity building. The (relatively) easy part of capacity building is upgrading the quality of human capacity, the educa-tion, the skills, the knowledge required for development. The hard part of capacity building is the development of the organizational and social capital, and the identification and promulgation of new codes of conduct that will enable a society to function well. There are many dimensions to this; they include:

- the *enabling* environment for the private sector, which includes markets and the legal infrastructure that is necessary for markets to function well
- the *knowledge* environment, which enables new knowledge to be absorbed, adapted to the circumstances of the country, and put to use in an efficient and socially acceptable way
- the *policy* environment, which includes the capacity to make key decisions concerning development strategies

4.5.3 Consistency, Coherence, and Completeness

We have described the various pieces that constitute an effective development strategy, from two points of view: *viz.* the levels on which it must operate, and the building blocks that it must provide. But the whole is more than the sum of the parts, and the parts must not only be consistent with each other, but must also fit together, and together set forth a road map—a vision of the future combined with a framework for realizing that vision.

The kind of development strategy we advocate is not a one-year plan, or even a five-year plan. The fruits of enhancing nutrition or education to a pre-school child and of institutional development will not be fully felt until a decade or more later. The reconfiguration of the moral ecology to meet the needs of the twenty-first century may take a generation to achieve. The vision must be long-term, while, at the same time, it must point to the actions to be taken today. To be meaningful, the vision and actions must be set within a coherent framework, which requires setting priorities, encouraging partnership, and taking into account the global economic and political environment.

Priorities

We know that so much is needed for successful development, including the actions listed above and more. Earlier, we emphasized that, given the limitations on resources and capabilities—particularly those of the poorer countries—there is a need to set priorities. We argued earlier that one of the purposes of an integrated and holistic development strategy was to establish these priorities. We can now flesh out in greater detail both the principles for setting priorities and what are the priorities, which most less developed countries will share. In particular, the global community needs to focus on identifying areas where the actions of markets, governments, civil society, and the international agencies can have large-scale effects, and where the absence of the requisite action part can have disastrous effects. Although the particular priorities will differ from country to country, there are some common elements:

- Among the most important is *education*, because without education a country cannot develop, cannot attract and build modern industries, cannot adopt new growing technologies as rapidly in the rural sector. But most fundamentally, if development represents the transformation of society, education is what enables people to learn, to acquire values and standards of behaviour, and also to accept and help engender this transformation. Education is at the core of development.

- *Infrastructure*—and in particular property protection, communications, and transportation—is vital for the conduct of business in the modern world. It is also necessary to reduce the sense of isolation of those in developing countries, which is one of the most crippling aspects of underdevelopment. But today, we realize that much of the infrastructure can be provided privately, provided that the government establishes the appropriate regulatory/legal environment. Doing so must be given a high priority.

- *Health.* Because an unhealthy population cannot be a productive labour force, and because a basic quality of health should be viewed as a fundamental human right, upgrading health standards must be an integral part of any holistic development strategy. Today, however, we recognize that actions exist that are at least as important as the provision of medical services in maintaining overall health—including warning against dangerous behaviours (such as undue stress, smoking, and drug taking) and encouraging good behaviour (such as responsible citizenship and suitable eating and drinking habits).

- *Knowledge*—because, like education, it enriches the human spirit, and because, like education and health, it leads to a more productive society. The power of knowledge is enormous: with increased knowledge, the output that can be produced with the limited amounts of resources can be multiplied by orders of magnitude.

- *Capacity building*—because, in the end, successful development and a successful transformation must come from within the country itself, and to accomplish this, it must have institutions, entrepreneurship, and leadership to catalyse, absorb, and manage the process of change, and the changed society.

Partnership and Country Assistance Strategies

A country's own development strategy provides, then, the overall framework for thinking about a country's plan for change. Within that framework, various donors, including the World Bank, can act as partners in the development effort by identifying where they can be most effective. These roles will include not only creating, transferring, and disseminating capital, but also providing knowledge that is essential for development and capacity building.

But partnership goes beyond the country and the aid donors. Recall that development entails transformation of the whole society; hence the whole society must be engaged. Any comprehensive development strategy must then need to identify how this engagement will occur. It should set forth, for instance, a view about the role of government, and within the public sector, a framework for decentralization (i.e. subsidiarity). It needs to describe areas where the private sector and civil society should take the lead, and more broadly the 'terms of the partnership' among government, private sector, and civil society.

Consistency with the Global and Regional Environments

We have emphasized that all five components of the development strategy are interrelated. Strategies for the private sector must be integrated with and complemented by strategies for the public sector; strategies at the national level must be complemented by strategies at the community level. At each level, the strategy must be consistent with the capabilities and needs of institutions of the environment within which it is embedded. At the same time, it must be embedded within an ever-changing global environment. This global environment is constantly opening up new opportunities—both in respect of markets for goods and services, and access to new sources of knowledge and capital, organizational skills and entrepreneurship.

But these opportunities have also been accompanied by new challenges. For example, a heavy dependence on exports of goods or imports of capital exposes a country to the vicissitudes of foreign markets, such as a foreign economic downturn that may close off opportunities for exports or a sudden change in investor sentiment that may reduce sharply capital inflows from abroad. The magnitude of these risks may depend little or much on how well the country manages its own economy. The exposure to the cultures, standards, and norms of foreign countries may be seen as a threat to indigenous religions, teachings, or ideologies. It takes strong government actions, and powerful economic institutions, and a plentiful supply of social capital to weather these challenges—and even then there may be large costs to the economy and its traditional values. For many less developed countries, the impact may be—and experience has shown it frequently is—disastrous. An essential part of the new development strategy must be to take advantage of the new global environment while, at the same time, to reduce any country's vulnerability to the inevitable downsides and uncertainties that are associated with global engagement.

All countries, developed and less developed, share our planet, and thus must husband together our globe's scarce resources, including the atmosphere. The preservation of our atmosphere—e.g. avoiding the build-up of greenhouse gases—is an example of an international public good, the benefits of which accrue to all people (Stiglitz 1995). A development strategy needs to set forth a vision of how these international collective needs are to be addressed.

There is another aspect of global development, which becomes particularly important when one views development through the lens of a societal transformation. We have seen that some countries have had remarkable success in making that transformation, and that there is much those who are in the early stages of a transition can learn from those experiences. As more successes (and failures) occur, these successes (and failures) have impacts on others, as each extracts the lessons that can be learned from these various experiences. The spreading of the learning curve no doubt played a role in the successive development of the countries within East Asia.

At the same time, many countries' economic and social strategies must be set within the context of development within their region. This is especially true of small countries, and even more so of land-locked countries, for whom access to outside markets is critical. But it is not only transportation issues that have to be dealt with on a regional level. There are, for instance, a myriad of environmental and natural resource issues (most notably those dealing with water) that can only be addressed at a regional level. Issues of social justice and the inclusivity of countries and regions presently ill affected (or perceived to be ill affected) by the globalization of economic activity, must also be built into any development programme. These, in turn may be affected by the influence of such countries and regions at the international negotiating table. To this latter consideration, we now turn.

4.6 LEARNING FROM OPENNESS: TRADE, FOREIGN CAPITAL, AND THE NEW DEVELOPMENT STRATEGY

Where does openness to the outside world fit into this vision of a new development strategy? Our new understanding of development as a transformation of societies—rather than just the accumulation of physical or even human capital—gives us a lens with which to examine this question. It reveals that trade, FDI, and cross-border co-operative alliances can play a crucial role, although not always through the mechanisms that economists have traditionally stressed.

4.6.1 Trade and the Development Transformation

In the standard textbook model of international trade, openness to foreign goods is supposed to bring benefits primarily through its effects on the market price of imported goods. If Indonesia produces midsize automobiles domestically at a cost of $40,000 each but can import them at $20,000 apiece, then an opening up to auto imports yields a net gain in welfare. In so far as the increase in consumer surplus more than offsets the fall in profits enjoyed by indigenous manufacturers, Indonesia can then move the resources formerly employed in producing cars—the idle labour, human and physical capital, and land—into an economic activity in which the country has a comparative advantage (textiles, in the classic story). Barring terms-of-trade effects, the resulting increase in efficiency will allow Indonesia to be better off as a result of trade liberalization, even without the assumption that foreign countries respond with market-opening of their own. The magic of comparative advantage is that a poor country benefits from trade even if, in absolute terms, its productivity is lower than its trading partners' across the whole range of goods.

This standard model tells an important tale, but one that is far from the complete. There is much more going on, in ways that contribute directly to the transformation of society. Consider the gaps between the standard Hecksher–Ohlin trade model and what we observe in practice. First, both rigorous empirical research and country experience suggest that the growth effects of engagement in the global market place are far larger than would be predicted by the standard model (Romer 1994). Many specifications of empirical growth regressions find that some indicator of external openness—whether trade ratios or indices of price distortions or average tariff level—is strongly associated with per-capita income growth (Sachs and Warner 1995). And countries (especially small, poor ones) that have tried autarky have typically found themselves lagging far behind in their development, for reasons that apparently stem in part at least from their closed borders. Yet the standard Hecksher–Ohlin model predicts gains from trade are relatively small, consisting only of the well-known Harberger triangles in the supply–demand diagrams. Clearly, something is missing from the standard story.[17]

A second problem is that industry-level evidence is also inconsistent with the standard model. In this model, trade causes economies to shift inter-sectorally, moving along their production frontier. But in reality, the main gains from trade seem to come from an *outward shift* of that production frontier, with little inter-sectoral movement. In essence, trade makes it possible for the economy not just to consume a given basket of goods at lower cost, but also to produce a given pre-opening set of goods at lower cost.

What then is going on here? The evidence suggests strongly that opening up to the outside world leads to an improvement in the technology of production. When we say 'technology', we have in mind something far broader and more important than the technical blueprints that lie behind the production of any given good. *'Technology' here means anything that affects the way in which inputs are transformed into outputs—not just blueprints, but also market and non-market institutions and modes of organizing production.* A major difference between developed and less developed countries is the difference in the efficiency with which inputs are transformed into outputs. Trade is one of the most important vehicles that reduces discrepancy.

If, then, what we are concerned with is the transformation of society, it follows that both governments and international agencies must adopt policies that ensure that openness leads to that broad transformation. It is crucial that trade, FDI, and the cross-border activities of firms not be confined to small enclaves, even if those enclaves give a temporary boost to our statistical measures of national output. For example, a wealth of gold resources in an area far from a country's population base might well be successful at attracting FDI and increasing mineral exports, but may do little to spur the kind of development we are advocating over the long term. In designing policies to spur openness and capture its potential benefits, we need to focus on realizing the transformative power of interaction with the outside world. To put it succinctly, the goal of development should be not a dual economy, but a developed economy.

All forms of international commerce have important roles to play here. Our understanding of how these roles work remains incomplete, but it is growing. We have already alluded to the benefits of trade. FDI is of even greater importance, because when capital enters a country through direct investment, it typically comes in a package with management expertise, technical human capital, product and process technologies, and overseas marketing channels—all of which are in scarce supply in the typical developing country. Evidence suggests that if the society puts in place the appropriate complementary policies and structures, FDI can give a boost to the technological level and growth of the host country. The fears about FDI in the 1960s and 1970s were based largely on the notion of FDI as an enclave phenomenon. In its more modern incarnation, which is typically better integrated into the surrounding society, FDI is something to welcome, not to fear. International competition among MNEs has become more robust, so that the foreign corporation receives fewer monopoly rents and the host country gets a larger share of the benefits from investment. At the same time, recipient countries need to be aware of the values and standards introduced by foreign firms, even if the exposure to these is likely to be much less than through other means e.g. TV and the Internet, tourism and trade.

4.6.2   Implications for the International Architecture and Financial Flows

In the last half-decade, the rethinking and soul-searching that has followed the global financial crisis has led to much discussion of how to redesign the international financial architecture. The new development strategy outlined in this chapter has important implications for that design process. How, for example, should we think about short-term capital? First, we should note that short-term capital is especially volatile, as the experience of the past year has reminded us repeatedly. Even as FDI flows have continued largely unabated until the global recession and the events of 11 September,[18] short-term capital flows have completely reversed in many of the crisis countries. Second, short-term capital offers few of the added benefits brought by FDI—benefits that seem ancillary in the old view of development as accumulation of capital, but that are recognized as central when we view them through the lens of the new development strategy. With today's volatility of short-term capital, one cannot make good long-term investments based on this short-term capital. But equally important, short-term capital does not, in or of itself, bring development transformation. Indeed, in societies with high domestic saving rates and hence relatively low quality of marginal investments, short-term capital may retard that transformation. The high development costs exacted by abrupt capital-flow reversals—the lost years of education, the rise in infant mortality, the job losses—can easily swamp any marginal benefit derived from such flows, as happened in East Asia.

4.6.3   Implications for the Developed Countries: What are their Responsibilities?

It is clearly in the interest of developing countries to engage fully with the rest of the world through trade and through attracting FDI. But the trade policy agenda for the developing world—or at least the agenda advocated for developing countries by the West—has in recent years suffered from its single-minded focus on liberalization through reduction of trade barriers in those countries. To complement this argument, important as it is, we need to ask also, what responsibilities does the developed world have in the area of trade policy? It is not for us to lay out all those responsibilities. Gordon Brown touches on some of these in Chapter 14, but let us content ourselves with identifying some recent developments that have clearly helped delay the progress towards transformative development through openness.

First, the Uruguay Round trade agreement—for all the benefits it brought to the world's consumers, producers, and taxpayers—did too little to ensure the opening of markets to exports from developing countries. Consider the empirical estimates of net benefits by region, calculated just after the agreement was signed: according to these estimates, sub-Saharan Africa was a net *loser* as a result of the Uruguay Round (Harrison, Rutherford, and Tarr 1996). To be sure, Africa failed to gain largely because it did too little to liberalize its own barriers to trade, thus depriving itself of the opportunity to lower costs and spur efficiency and innovation domestically. But the Round also offered relatively little in the way of new market access for the products that Africa is most able to export. As suggested by the experiences of East Asia's economies, much of the learning opportunity offered by trade takes place in export markets, as developing-country firms build relations with sophisticated customers and compete head-to-head with the best producers in the world. Moreover, success in export markets requires learning, and the export champions can then bring these lessons home to apply in the domestic markets. We are not claiming that lack of market access is the only, or even most important, barrier to African exports. African countries can still do much to make life easier for exporters, whether by improving communications infrastructure, revamping transportation facilities, or reducing unnecessary bureaucratic obstacles to exports. But market access is one area where the developed world is uniquely positioned to give a boost to the development transformation that this chapter has urged.

A second, and related point, is that we must continue working to stem the tide of the new protectionism in the West. The last two decades have seen a rise in the use of creative new measures to block imports. Examples include nuisance anti-dumping claims, lodged under laws that often make little economic sense; countervailing duties that similarly lack objective justification (Finger 1993; Stiglitz 1997a); and barriers to genetically altered products, which are likely to become steadily more important as developing-country exports make greater use of those products. Developed countries often have the luxury of large and well-paid legal and lobbying industries in their capitals, and firms that can be quite innovative in devising new means of restricting competition. From an equity standpoint, it is essential that we stamp out these innovations as energetically as we work to lower developing-country barriers to trade.

Third, we believe that international protection of intellectual property rights (IPRs) should strike a balance between the interests of producers and users. The users include not only many firms and consumers within the developing world—who are more often technological adapters and users than innovators—but also the academic community throughout the world. We accept that it is important to give incentives to innovators by ensuring them a fair return on their investment in R&D. But we must also remember that knowledge is a crucial input into production processes, whether in agriculture or high-tech industry, and that, unlike physical inputs into production, knowledge can be shared *ad infinitum* without any additional cost. Thomas Jefferson likened the creation of knowledge to the lighting of a candle in the darkness: many other candles can draw their light from that first candle without diminishing its power or brilliance. Excessive protection of IPRs may end this virtuous cycle of knowledge transmission and regeneration in the developing world. There is no easy answer to this particular problem, but that should not stop us from asking questions. It is for this reason that a section in *World Development Report* 1998/9 was devoted to the issue of IPRs.

In all these cases, governments and international agencies should seek to construct not just good policies, but also a sense that the process by which policies are devised is itself fair and open. Without such a sense of fairness, the developing world will retreat from its reforms of recent decades. Worse still, the perception of hypocrisy reinforces the sense of unfairness. Even as the more developed countries preach the doctrines of openness, they engage in restrictive practices. Even as they preach that countries must undertake the painful measures of liberalization— which may entail losses of jobs and industries—all too frequently developed countries use anti-dumping and safeguard measures to protect their own industries that are adversely affected. Moreover, they do so even when their economies are at full employment, so that the risks of extended unemployment are minimal. This is in marked contrast to the situation in many less developed countries, where unemployment is high and safety nets are inadequate. And even as the developed countries dismiss the political problems facing less developed countries, they justify their own resort to these protectionist measures as necessary to overcome even worse protectionist sentiments within their own countries. Here it's clear that a new moral ecology is called for by developed countries if they are to help their less prosperous neighbours engage in the kind of economic and social transformations that, at the end of the day, will be to the benefit of all.

As we have observed elsewhere (Stiglitz 1998d) the pendulum of opinion has swung before, and it now risks swinging too far back in opposition to openness. We believe that the current need is to lessen the momentum of this pendulum swing, by increasing the equity of the international architecture for trade and finance. Retreat from openness in the developing world would unacceptably delay the development transformation that it so sorely needs.

4.7 CONCLUDING COMMENTS

We have learned in the last half century that global development is possible, but also that such development is not inevitable. We have also learned that global development is not just a matter of technical adjustments, but a transformation of society. It requires an holistic and co-ordinated approach to the reconfiguration of social and economic goals, and of the methods and modes by which these goals are advanced.

In our opening paragraphs, we referred to the disillusionment with the Washington Consensus, which provided a set of prescriptions that failed to foster this development transformation. We argued that that consensus was too narrow both in its objectives and its instruments. We have tried to set out the foundations of an alternative paradigm to the Washington Consensus. In a way, our views and prescriptions are far from revolutionary. Within the World Bank and the development community more broadly, there has been increasing attention in recent decades to issues of health, education, and environmental and changing social values, and we have moved beyond measures of GDP to look at life spans and literacy rates. We have recognized the importance of economic security, and stressed the creation of safety nets. There has been a growing consensus behind the objectives of democratic, equitable, and sustainable development. The issue of moral responsibility of both the developed and developing world is being increasingly aired. Here, we have tried to argue that the whole is greater than the sum of the parts, and that successful development must focus on the whole—the transformation of society. We believe the global community is well prepared for this task, precisely because its various institutions are increasingly addressing themselves to these and similar issues.

But we have also argued that a successful development transformation affects not only what we do, but how we do it. This broader perspective not only affects the strategies and policies, but it also affects the processes of development. It argues for openness, partnership, participation, and moral responsibility—words that too often sound like appeals to the politically correct nostrums of the day. We have suggested that there lies behind these words a theory of development, as well as evidence that these processes can lead to more successful development efforts.

Our final word specifically relates to the theme of this volume. In calling for a transformation of societies, we have alluded to a central question: What sort of transformation do we want, and for what ends? We have observed that many commentators are concerned lest that development will destroy traditional values and norms. In some cases, there will be a clash between science, certain features of global capitalism, and traditional beliefs. But development today often focuses on the preservation of cultural values, partly because these values serve as a cohesive force at a time when many other such forces are weakening. Maintaining social organization and enhancing social capital are essential to successful development transformations. Moreover, it is important to remind ourselves that much of the progress that is associated with successful development—the mothers who do not have to see their children die in infancy, the opening of minds to new knowledge, and the increased opportunities—also reflects almost universally held desires and values.

But there is a further reason that the present writer believes in openness, especially openness in processes and the exchange of values. It is that these processes, when properly conducted and assimilated, contribute to a more open, tolerant, democratic society. For these, we believe, are critical values in their own right.

NOTES

1. Throughout this chapter, we have in mind a somewhat different conception of the Washington Consensus than the one originally outlined by my colleague John Williamson (1990), who coined the term. As Williamson (1997) himself notes, the term has evolved over time to signify a set of 'neoliberal' policy *prescriptions*, rather than the more descriptive usage that he originally intended in discussing reforms undertaken by Latin American economies in the 1980s. The policies that now fall under the 'Washington Consensus' rubric are often—and we believe incorrectly—taken to be both necessary and sufficient for substantial development. (See also Stiglitz 1998*a*.)

2. While the fraction of the world's population in absolute poverty (living on under $1 a day) has declined from an estimated 30.1 per cent in 1987 to 29.4 per cent in 1993, the total number of poor has increased, from 1.23 billion to 1.31 billion (World Bank 1996). The soaring population in some of the poorest countries makes the battle against poverty an uphill fight.

3. For instance, Deininger and Squire (1996) find that 77 out of 88 decade-long periods of growth were accompanied by reductions in poverty. While from today's vantage point this may not seem surprising, it seems at odds with the conventional wisdom of the Kuznets curve. Kuznets argued that in the early stages of development, growth would be associated with increases in inequality; in fact, Deininger and Squire find that inequality fell as often as it rose during periods of growth. Kuznets, however, lacked the extensive cross-country datasets we have today, and his conclusion was based on data from only a handful of countries.

4. The inadequacy of the traditional perspectives is nowhere more apparent than in the experience over the past decade of the former Soviet Union (discussed below), particularly in contrast to the successful experiences in China, which managed to find strategies well adapted to its particular situation. One measure of China's success in devising such a strategy is that, if the separate provinces of China were treated as separate 'data' points, the twenty fastest-growing economies in the world between 1978 and 1995 would all have been Chinese (World Bank 1997*a*).

5. See e.g. Furman and Stiglitz (1998) and Stiglitz (1998*b* and 1998*c*).

6. The arguments for bail-outs, as well as the presence of bail-outs themselves, provide overwhelming support for the view that there may be marked discrepancies between private and social net return to short-term capital movements. These discrepancies at the very least call for a review of feasible government actions to redress this market failure, which has imposed such huge costs on millions and millions of people (though to be sure, some of these costs might have been reduced if the crisis-response polices had been better designed).

7. See Furman and Stiglitz (1998) for a discussion of both the evidence and the theory explaining why the result that liberalization does not yield higher growth (see e.g. Rodrik 1998) should not come as that much of a surprise.

8. Research by Demirgüç-Kunt and Detragiache (1998) in fact shows the systematic relationship between financial market liberalization and economic crises.

9. For instance, there is no evidence that government pressures caused the excessive real-estate lending in Thailand.

10. See, in particular, Furman and Stiglitz (1998). They show that transparency in East Asia on average (at least as gauged by standard measures) was no less than in other countries that did not experience a crisis; the crisis countries of East Asia had had

three decades of remarkable growth, yet if anything transparency had increased rather than decreased prior to the crisis.

11. See e.g. De Soto's analysis of the need of a formal property system if the entrepreneurship and 'dead' assets of many individuals in the developing world can be unleashed and translated into productive capital (De Soto 2000).

12. For an analysis of the effects of hyperinflation, often caused by such an imbalance between resources and objectives, see Bruno and Easterly (1998).

13. See Jimenez and Sawada (1998).

14. See King and Ozler (1998).

15. See e.g. various essays in Dunning (2000) for a review of the literature.

16. As occurred, for example, in the early years of the Industrial Revolution (see Ch. 1 of this volume). The Russian Federation's experience offers an excellent, if sobering, more recent example. Almost a decade after the process of transition to a market economy began—after the inefficient system of central planning was replaced by a more decentralized, market-oriented system, after the distortive pricing patterns were, by and large, eliminated, and after private property was supposed to restore incentives that seemed so lacking under the previous regime—output remains a third below what it was before the transition started. The underlying resources may have deteriorated slightly, but the human capital and knowledge base remains. The explanation: the destruction of organizational and social capital, a process which had in fact begun under the previous regime, continued. Policymakers made inadequate efforts to develop new bases, and to provide the the legal infrastructure necessary for markets, including bankruptcy, competition, and contract laws and their effective enforcement.

17. The most important gains from trade may come from the increased variety of goods—particularly goods that are inputs into production processes—to which an open trading system offers access (Rodriguez-Clare 1996 and Stiglitz 1997*b*). That is, rather than just reducing the price of goods that are already available domestically, trade also offers access to many goods (such as semiconductors or numerically controlled machine tools) that simply were not available *at any price* under autarky. The new inputs bring down costs and spur innovation in the importing economy.

18. Since then they have started to recover and are predicted to reach their 1999 levels by 2006 (Kekis 2002).

REFERENCES

Bruno, M., and Easterly, W. (1998), 'Inflation Crises and Long-Run Growth', *Journal of Monetary Economics* 41(1) Feb.: 3–26.

Deininger, K., and Squire, L. (1996), 'A New Data Set Measuring Income Inequality', *World Bank Economic Review* 10(3): 565–91.

Demirgüç-Kunt, A., and Detragiache, E. (1998), 'Financial Liberalization and Financial Fragility', Paper presented to the Annual World Bank Conference on Development Economics, Washington, DC, 20–1 Apr.

De Soto, H. (2000), *The Mystery of Capital* (London and New York: The Bantam Press).

Dunning, J. H. (ed.) (2000), *Regions Globalization and the Knowledge Based Economy* (Oxford: Oxford University Press).

Finger, J. M. (ed.) (1993), *Anti-Dumping: How It Works and Who Gets Hurt* (Ann Arbor: University of Michigan Press).

Furman, J., and Stiglitz, J. E. (1998), 'Economic Crises: Evidence and Insights from East Asia', *Brookings Papers on Economic Activity*, vol. 2.

Harrison, G. W., Rutherford, T. F., and Tarr, D. G. (1996), 'Quantifying the Uruguay Round.' In W. Martin and L. A. Winters (eds.), *The Uruguay Round and the Developing Economies* (Cambridge: Cambridge University Press), 215–84.

Isham, J., Narayan, D., and Pritchett, L. (1995), 'Does Participation Improve Performance? Establishing Causality with Subjective Data', *World Bank Economic Review* 9(2): 175–200.

Jimenez, E., and Sawada, Y. (1998), 'Do Community Managed Schools Work? An Evaluation of El Salvador's EDUCO Program', Impact Evaluation of Education Reforms Working Paper Series, Development Economics Research Group, World Bank, Feb.

Kekis, L. (2000), 'Global Foreign Direct Investment: Recent Trends and Forecasts.' In *Economist Intelligence Unit, World Investment Prospects 2002* (London: EIU), 15–20.

King, E., and Ozler, B. (1998), 'What's Decentralization got to do with Learning? The Case of Nicaragua's Education Reform', Impact Evaluation of Education Reforms Working Paper Series, Development Economics Research Group, World Bank, Apr.

Rodriguez-Clare, A. (1996), 'Multinationals, Linkages, and Economic Development', *American Economic Review* 86(4): 852–73.

Rodrik, D. (1998), 'Who Needs Capital-Account Convertibility?' *Essays in International Finance* 207, International Finance Section, Department of Economics, Princeton University (May): 55–65.

Romer, P. (1994), 'New Goods, Old Theory, and the Welfare Costs of Trade Restrictions', *Journal of Development Economics* 43(2): 5–38.

Rostow, W. W. (1960), *The Stages of Economic Growth. A Non-Communist Manifesto* (New York: Cambridge University Press).

Sachs, J. D., and Warner, A. M. (1995), 'Economic Reform and the Process of Global Integration', *Brookings Papers on Economic Activity*, vol. 1.

Soros, G. (1998). *The Crisis of Global Capitalism* (London: Little, Brown and Company).

Stiglitz, J. E. (1995), 'The Theory of International Public Goods and the Architecture of International Organisations', United Nations Background Paper 7, Department for Economic and Social Information and Policy Analysis, July.

—— (1996), 'Some Lessons from the East Asian Miracle', *The World Bank Research Observer* 11(2): 151–77.

—— (1997*a*), 'Dumping on Free Trade: The U. S. Import Trade Laws', *Southern Economic Journal* 64: 2(Oct.): 402–24.

—— (1997*b*), 'Trade and Technology: Links and Problems', Paper presented to the Annual World Bank Conference on Development in Latin America and the Caribbean. Montevideo, Uruguay: 29 June–1 July.

—— (1998*a*), 'More Instruments and Broader Goals: Moving Toward the Post-Washington Consensus', Presented as the WIDER Annual Lecture, at the World Institute for Development Economics Research in Helsinki (January).

—— (1998*b*), 'Responding to Economic Crises: Policy Alternatives for Equitable Recovery and Development', Presented at the North-South Institute Seminar. Ottawa, Canada: 29 Sept.

—— (1998*c*), 'Must Financial Crises Be This Frequent and This Painful?' Presented as the McKay Lecture, University of Pittsburgh, Pennsylvania: 23 Sept.

—— (1998*d*), 'Towards a New Paradigm of Development: Strategies, Policies and Processes', Geneva: The 9th Raúl Prebisch Lecture, UNCTAD.

Wolfensohn, J. D. (1998), 'The Other Crisis', World Bank/IMF Annual Meetings Address (6 Oct.).

Williamson, J. (1990), *Latin American Adjustment: How Much Has Happened?* (Washington, DC: Institute for International Economics).

——(1997), 'The Washington Consensus Revisited', In L. Emmerij (ed.), *Economic and Social Development into the XXI Century* (Washington, DC: Inter-American Development Bank), 48–61.

World Bank (1993), *The East Asian Miracle: Economic Growth and Public Policy*, World Bank Policy Research Report (New York: Oxford University Press).

——(1995), *Structural and Sectoral Adjustment: World Bank Experience, 1980–92*, World Bank Operations Evaluation Study (Washington, DC: World Bank).

——(1996), *Poverty Reduction and the World Bank: Progress and Challenges in the 1990s* (Washington, DC: World Bank).

——(1997a), *China 2020: Development Challenges in the New Century* (Washington, DC: World Bank).

——(1997b), *World Development Report 1997: The State in a Changing World* (New York: Oxford University Press).

——(1998a), *World Development Report 1998/99: Knowledge for Development* (New York: Oxford University Press).

——(1998b), *Assessing Aid: What Works, What Doesn't, and Why*, World Bank Policy Research Report (Washington, DC: Oxford University Press).

5

Transformation of Society: Implications for Globalization

JACK N. BEHRMAN

5.1 INTRODUCTION

Further movement towards globalization will require rethinking the nature and role of capitalism in meeting the goals of mankind, including its melding with both social and political objectives and institutions. A more open world economy will not be acceptable unless there is broad agreement on objectives, processes, and fundamental values buttressing civil societies. In the last half century, capitalism has changed as it has moved from a focus on national wealth and power to growth and integration of regional associations of nations; and it will have to be adapted further as diverse countries are brought into an open and integrated global system—one founded on roughly similar values expressed in freedom and social justice. These changes must address the recurring problems of poverty and an inequitable distribution of benefits and burdens (including unemployment and increasing uncertainty) within and among nations.

Up to now, capitalism has only been partially effective in meeting these problems and others that have come in its wake—such as environmental degradation and visible corruption. To make appropriate changes will require new mind-sets, attitudes, and relationships among people as well as a reconfiguration of institutions and policies to address these socio-political problems. Both individual and societal changes are needed. New societal forms discussed in other chapters in this volume must be supported by orientations, behaviour, and attitudes of individuals that foster a creativity that offers progress, and is seen as co-creation with The Creator, furthering the evolutionary development of mankind. Individual behaviour can also thwart broad economic and social reforms, so a renewed and intensified morality to support societal ethics is needed (Behrman 1988). Co-operation among individuals and societies will be required for this. And for those not able to participate in or fully benefit from the new economy and society, compassion and understanding will need to be extended at both individual and societal levels.

What the 'New Global Capitalism' will look like is not the subject of this chapter. Rather, it addresses the societal and individual transformations that will be required to make a global system acceptable. Such transformations go to the root of the moral and ethical foundations of society and the socio-economic-political institutions they support. In turn, these transformations will modify a globalizing capitalism and ease any movement toward it. The potential benefits appear to be well worth the effort, for those who are discontented with the prospects or are concerned about their roles will be satisfied only if the ills of capitalism as they know it today are addressed, and especially the 'social problem', in ways that offer opportunities to all able and willing to take them.

A New Economy Needs a New Morality... there's a moral vacuum at the heart of the New Economy that needs to be filled. (Michael J. Mandel)[1]

5.2 CRITERIA OF ACCEPTABILITY OF GLOBALIZATION

Globalization involves creating a 'new international economic order', extending beyond the traditional modes of capitalism and requiring realignment or establishment of the institutions of 'civil society'. If progress toward a more open world economy is to be made, it will require a complementary overhaul of the entire socio-economic-political arenas of participating countries, and in ways that authoritarian governments will find difficult, as it would essentially leave them outside the new world economy. Though the process of globalization appears inevitable from some viewpoints—e.g. the advance of modern communication technologies—it is not imperative and is unlikely to be all-inclusive in the early stages (Behrman and Rondinelli 2000). All nations involved will seek to gain conditions and positions acceptable to their interests, reducing co-operation and making the road to globalization long and difficult. Traversing it satisfactorily can be accelerated only by a transformation to socio-economic-political systems based on broadly accepted value systems. From an assessment of national policies and preferences in international and intergovernmental negotiations in and outside of official organizations, it appears that at least seven criteria will be sought by countries willing to accommodate to deeper and wider integration within an open world economy. These relate respectively to demands for *efficiency, equity, participation, creativity, risk adjustments, human rights,* and *environmental protection*—discussed below.

These criteria are not restricted to economics, which has too long been separated analytically from social and political disciplines. But this isolation must also change so that economic systems are seen holistically, as part of the total global society, founded on value-based cultures. Only then can the world move to a more equitable and socially acceptable global order with the freedom and opportunities offered by democratic capitalism.

The failures of capitalism as presently practised are pushing the West to seek solutions through repeated modifications that will assist in the solution of the 'social problem' and in the establishment of 'civil society' in countries willing to adopt it. This will involve the widening of a global community opening opportunities for all and emphasizing the three Cs urged by John Dunning (Chapter 1), *viz. creativity, co-operation,* and *compassion.* Creativity is pervasive and, at its root, is in co-operation with The Creator; co-operation must modify competition under capitalism so that the latter does not destroy but becomes a means of improvement; and compassion is needed to ameliorate the harsh judgements of the market in the creation of community. These must be done by and among individuals and by and among institutions of society and government. If these cannot be practiced sufficiently, the world will continue to face three opposing Cs of *corruption, conflict,* and *conflagration,* arising out of greed and the aggressive drive for 'success'. The observation by William James is apropos, especially in the light of the corporate scandals in the US that surfaced in mid-2002: 'The exclusive worship of the bitch-goddess success! That—with the squalid cash interpretation put on the word success—is our national disease.' Men and women are given free will to choose a new way, which involves a reasonable detachment from the temptations of materialism. The seven criteria of acceptability encompass aspects of civil society that require urgent attention in the early years of this century.

5.2.1   Efficiency

The major benefit claimed for capitalism was, and is, its greater efficiency in directing the use of resources to the demands of consumers—individuals, organizations, or governments—as signalled by market forces. Such efficiency is desired (but not always sought) as a means of accelerating economic growth, conserving resources, and mitigating the social ills of poverty, squalor, disease, and ignorance. Any acceptable global system based on the use of resources should pursue high levels of efficiency, including the optimum use of human resources through equality of opportunity for individuals to apply their talents and acquired capabilities. Efficiency creates less costly facilities for the rapid communication of ideas and information—both within and among countries—and hastens the spread of technologies. It results from a greater mobility of peoples and resources, moving employment to appropriate endeavours globally, as cross-border integration progresses. Efficiency, then results from a reliance on and application of the comparative advantages of each country, as resources move, expanding trade and investment both domestically and internationally and opening new opportunities for employment.

However, as Dunning points out in Chapter 1, efficiency in production and distribution of goods and services (GNP) is not in itself an adequate goal, for mere economic growth is not a good measure of improved economic and social welfare. Too much is included in GNP that is mere 'repair' of 'dis-benefits', and much desirable social improvement is left out.

Progress has many dimensions, one of the most important is that indicated by higher living standards for the poorest ranks. Rising average incomes (per capita GNP) can mask a wide dispersion of incomes, saying nothing about economic welfare or greater happiness. Happiness is not necessarily produced by greater GNP; it depends on *how* it is produced (treatment of workers and sound work environment) and *what* it is used for. If the view of George Bernard Shaw that 'Happiness is being used in a cause greater than oneself' is correct, increases in

GNP do not necessarily lead to happiness. On the contrary, they may increase the angst of those excluded from the system or not accorded equal opportunities—as seems to be demonstrated today by the increasing gap between rich and poor. The greater current attention given to 'quality of life' by mobile managers and workers over 'quantity of consumption' is a reflection of the diminishing attention to mere additions to GNP. Yet, efficiency is desirable for upgrading both the quality and quantity of goods and services and is a key component in achieving real progress.

5.2.2 Equity

Greater efficiency in production and distribution of goods and services tells us nothing about the distribution of benefits in income and wealth and in the burdens of adjustment. These are major concerns among governments, societies, organizations, and individuals. Past experience has shown that equality of material welfare cannot be a measure of equity without having an adverse effect on efficiency and growth. As shown by the demise of socialist systems, motivations of most individuals and 'for-profit' organizations will remain strongly materialistic rather than service oriented. But, equity—appropriately reflecting differences in the contributions of individuals and motivation to societal good (both in and outside the market)—must be a characteristic of the worldwide system to be acceptable. At the same time greater equity in this sense will lead to greater efficiency and progress because of the satisfaction with positions and results, and a greater willingness to attack social ills in general. It also would generate facilities and learning opportunities for a continuity of diverse cultural orientations by not yielding to the pressure for unification arising out of the drive for efficiency.

As John Stuart Mill noted in his *Principles of Political Economy*, though there are 'laws of production' showing how to gain efficiency in the use of resources, there are no 'laws of distribution of income'. Since the mid-nineteenth century, how and how much the factors of production were to be paid has been seen to be a matter of the market, negotiating ability, organizational strength, and government intervention. Mill, and later economists of the same mind, approved of a degree of 'socialism' as a compassionate transfer of income and wealth through government in order to achieve greater equity.

Such transfers are a mark of contemporary capitalism throughout the West, at least. They can be accomplished only through a system of 'political economy' based on a community of interest. Without a 'world community' or a supranational government through which to make appropriate transfer payments, there can be no established process for achieving global equity. However, it is clear that 'equality of opportunity' is a primary element of equity both within and among nations. Although equity will inevitably be perceived differently among countries and individuals, based on their value systems, efforts must be made to approach acceptable levels of equity for progress to be made toward a worldwide community needed to underpin globalization. But pursuit of equity is itself based on moral and ethical values—an intent to seek justice and do what is 'right'.

This pursuit is hampered by the lack of ethical behaviour in many countries, as seen in widespread public and private corruption by individuals and groups (e.g. the recent example of ENRON in the US[2]), seeking to acquire wealth and power far beyond their contributions to society in production or service.[3] The observation by Luigi Barzini is telling: 'Civilization and the graces of life flourish best where there are dedicated and intelligent people... who prefer dignity, fame, authority, prestige or ease of conscience more than money.' Such anti-social behaviour is seen in corporate and personal greed, bribery, extortion, fraud, theft, lying, deception, and a simple breaking of the rules—whether legislated or conventional—and also as 'cowboy capitalism' in mafia-run markets in countries transforming from socialism. Despite laws and social conventions in every country against bribery of and extortion by public officials, pervasive corruption is reported in over half the countries of the world, making it impossible to develop the behavioural requisites for a global community—such as honesty, promise, truthfulness—that combine to produce the virtue of *trust* that is a foundation stone of a free, civil society (Sztompka 1999; Tomkins and Passey 2000).

At present, even national communities are not always held together by common behaviour or objectives, and the criterion of equity is ill-met. Several are under the ultimate bonding mechanism of force by the ruling authority. But there is no such ruling power at the global level—nor, as yet, even within regional associations. So, the needed community of interest must come through volition, extended to agreed (ethical) patterns of behaviour. Such conduct would turn individuals and nations to a 'high purpose' that unifies a community through pervasive loyalty and collaboration, rather than the 'lower purpose' of mere material advancement, which has been recognized as a divisive objective.[4] This suggests that to achieve societal goals, less attention needs to be given to value in the market and more to values underlying socially acceptable capitalism and whatever system emerges from it.[5]

5.2.3 Participation

Not only must the citizens and organizations of each country share to an acceptable degree in the process of production (opportunity to gain income and wealth) and in the distribution of benefits and burdens (equity), but also each will naturally demand an appropriate role in decision making in the globalization process. Not all countries will be accorded the same voice globally, but means must be found to make the role of each acceptable, or they will seek to exercise sovereignty to reshape the benefits and burdens of globalization. It is only through an acceptable decision making process—co-operation and collaboration—that the compromises necessary to come to agreement will themselves be acceptable.

A major benefit is that a closer sense of community is developed out of which differences of views on efficiency and equity can be reconciled in a continuous opportunity to rectify any perceived imbalance from prior decisions. These, in turn, gain greater openness and security in one's affairs, and assure wider sharing of progress through a concern for equity. Active participation will encourage educational programmes preparing for continued participation by individuals and organizations, and will potentially reduce openings for authoritarian or populist governments.

Without the opportunity for appropriate participation being offered to all, the process of 'balancing' will be in danger of being decided by an unrepresentative minority or authority. Consequently, neither the results nor that process will be acceptable to the majority of players in globalization. Their angst can thwart what could be desirable global progress.

5.2.4 Creativity

Modern Western cultures have encouraged the view that 'being human means to be creative'—not simply living in response to Nature. But the opportunities to be imaginative and creative in the economic arena (essentially through science and technology but also in a myriad of other ways, including the various arts and academic research) are not spread evenly around the world. The geographic location of facilities, academic preparation, cultural stimulus, and sponsorship by foundations and governments is mainly concentrated in advanced countries. If nothing else, globalization will demand a greater effort by the international community to open creative opportunities and provide encouragement. The potential yield from such efforts in enhancing the contributions that each individual and nation can make to the progress of mankind is very great indeed.

In economics and business, creativity for a nation means to be involved in scientific discovery and technological innovation and preceding educational programmes. The present concentration in a few countries challenges the acceptability of globalization. Under global capitalism, the several phases of the knowledge-based economy will be developed in different countries, according to comparative advantages in specific sectors. But a number of countries, potentially capable of efficiently conducting industrial R&D, will find it unsatisfactory for a few countries to continue to be the inventors and innovators while they merely commercialize the technologies. Thus, means will need to be found of spreading the stages of industrial progress more widely (Behrman 1980; Behrman and Fischer 1980). Again, this involves a process of sharing (requiring moral decisions) modifying the market solution. The role of MNEs and cross-border inter-firm coalitions could be constructive in making creative opportunities more equitable. The benefits of creativity include not only the satisfaction of discovery but also greater rein to curiosity in science by both individuals and institutes, with the result that the quality of life may be enhanced.

5.2.5 Risk Adjustments

Tying the economies of the world more closely together means that there will be even greater uncertainty and volatility in national economies than previously. This situation imposes a new responsibility on the richer nations to bear a larger burden of the risks, for they are not only the source of the risks but are the beneficiaries when the risks pay off.[6] Not only will employment opportunities change more readily over the working life of individuals but also periods of unemployment are likely to be more frequent. The result is a 'risk society' with characteristics different from the 'full employment' economies sought after World War II. Not only will positions change but also some jobs may have to be shared in order to provide a living income to all able and willing to work and provide greater equity. And, to fill the slack periods of employment, individuals may need to be encouraged to volunteer their services, expanding the 'non-profit' (NGO) sector. These civic services could well play an important role in filling a gap in the supply of social work, and provide rewarding experiences for those volunteering and those served (Rifkin 1995). Such career shifts will require a change in our value system from greater income and wealth in marketed goods and services to greater wealth in non-market services, reduction of social ills, and greater equality of opportunity for both economic and socio-political employment (Beck 2000).

Those making career shifts should be respected for work done, be it for-profit or not and regardless of type or duration—so long as it is ethical and legal. The moral dimension is to see all work as equally rewarding and useful, so long as it is demanded legitimately by society or is seen as a service to it.

5.2.6   Respect, Dignity, and Human Rights

Historically, national governments have sought to gain respect, dignity, presence, and negotiating strength through autonomy and the exercise of sovereignty. As globalization proceeds, the sovereign role of government will be mitigated, at least in setting the rules for international affairs. No country will accept being 'lost' in the process—each must be respected if they are to be encouraged to play positive roles within the world community.

At the individual level, there must be means of extending respect and treating others with dignity and deference in all phases of life and in death. *Inter alia* this means non-discrimination by all nations, by race, gender, creed, or age. Persons of all walks of life are to be respected and, at the end, offered a non-violent 'death with dignity'. Tolerance of differences in human relations is imperative if bland uniformity is to be avoided and diversity in cultures is to be celebrated and enjoyed. Tolerance should be virtually absolute, with the exception that it cannot tolerate 'intolerance' that harms others. The first admonition to the medical profession—'Do no harm'—should be extended to all human relationships. If pervasive, it would eliminate or mitigate greatly the present levels of conflict, crime, and corruption, and it would reduce the need for governmental and social controls through regulatory agencies, police, and the judiciary.

Although through its various Charters, the United Nations has endorsed the universal protection of individual human rights, the coverage and interpretation of human rights and the priority given to their extension varies among countries. Implementation within nation states is considered a domestic (not intergovernmental) matter, and, in fact, the principles continue to be violated in roughly half the UN countries. At present, there is a move by some countries to consider the death penalty a violation of the right to life. However, it is not yet written into the Human Rights agreement, and the US remains opposed. Frequently, the rights extended to foreigners are often less than those granted to nationals. For globalization to be complete, however, greater harmonization of human rights will be necessary, so as to provide similar protections as people move around the world. Human rights are fundamentally based on moral values, which are still not sufficiently similar to provide equal protection among all countries. This is likely to become an obstacle to realizing the benefits of globalization.

5.2.7   Environment

Protection of the environment has also been given a raised profile by the United Nations, with most nations recognizing a threat through several areas of pollution and direct damage, such as air–water–noise pollution, deforestation, desertification, global warming, wastage of water, and the erosion of land. The benefits are the conservation of resources, improvement in the quality of life, and care for future generations. Again, however, special interests and varying value systems have led to quite different treatment of the environment by national authorities. The US is less concerned than others over the threat of global warming; Brazil is determined to cut the Amazon forest regardless of the impact on rainfall; attitudes to the conservation of fishing stocks varies among EU countries, and so forth. But, it is difficult to open trade and permit the free movement of capital and technology when cross-border attitudes towards, and the costs of, environmental protection are significantly dissimilar. A move to harmonization is again required if globalization is to yield its full benefits; this can often be accelerated through multinational enterprises (Behrman and Carter 1975). Any agreement will be based on emergence of an agreed value system.

Each of these seven criteria of acceptability has been partially met at national levels, at least in civil societies, where a 'community of interest' has been formed, and it, in turn, provides the basis for a peaceful life. They are less fully attained at regional levels—e.g. Europe or South-East Asia—and hardly at all on a global scale. Some elements, at least, partly exist within the UN, but most of its decisions are implemented (or not) by national governments, at their volition. To fulfil these criteria will require a transformation of both individuals and societies in terms of objectives and means of achievement. But they are necessary in the pursuit of *peace*, which is itself a requisite for successful establishment of global capitalism; a free-enterprise system serving buyers and sellers through market signals cannot withstand the pervasive intervention of government in wartime.

Once there is agreement on the collective pursuit of the seven criteria, the *how* of implementation becomes the most important step. At the system level, this involves the formation of appropriate institutions to buttress an effective and acceptable global capitalism. Given the major issues involved, merely marginal adjustments by governments will not sufficiently advance the world to meet the demands of globalization as seen in these seven criteria.

If the world is to move strongly against the pervasive ills of war, crime, corruption, violence, deceit, greed, licentiousness, and the desire for power, it must now attack the root causes more successfully than it has done in the past. Reformers in the eighteenth and nineteenth centuries sought to free individuals to pursue their own development (even to enlightenment) and to change governmental and social institutions, but they feared that the self-restraint and self-discipline required for a system of individual freedom to function peacefully would be lacking. In this fear they were prophetic.[7] Neither systemic reform (from the *top down*) or reformed individual behaviour (from the *bottom up*) has achieved its objectives; and neither has gone deeply enough or functioned in an integrated manner. What is needed is nothing less than a process of transformation of both individuals and society— preferably in tandem and holistically. Hopefully, the peace promised from such fundamental change is a *cause* sufficient to catalyse both leaders and followers to pursue the requisite transformations.

This chapter attempts to show that blueprints for transformation exist, both in and outside of religious sources, as in the 'Ancient Wisdom' (Cheng 1981; Fung 1989; Grof 1984; Huxley 1970; Ni 1979; Wilhelm 1962), in the counsel of Masters and Sages (as referenced below) and in current analysis of the plight of and prospects for mankind (Csikszentmihalyi 1993; Etzioni 1998; Fukuyama 1999; Nicoll 1984*a*, 1984*b*,1985; Sen 1999*a*; Steiner 1984; Zukav 1989). At the foundations, all this advice and counsel and the underlying values are the same. The lack of appropriate response and the differing interpretations continue to engender conflicts—most of which could be avoided by a wider adherence to common values and assumption of responsibility by both individuals and social institutions.

5.3 VALUES AND RESPONSIBILITY

Global implementation of the above criteria would itself involve a transformation of governance within and among nations based on a wider acceptance of fundamental values and norms of behaviour. Any move toward greater integration globally will be more readily accommodated if basic values are understood and agreed upon.[8]

However much scholars may dispute the existence of absolute versus relative virtues or disagree about the need for virtue, leading to proper and acceptable (ethical) behaviour in society, it has long-since been urged by all religions. Virtue is seen in all countries to emanate from the Law of Creation, the Will of God, or the Law of Love—which requires the recognition of the existence of a basic Unity of All with multiple manifestations in diversity (Smart and Flecht 1982). And religio-philosophies that do not include a covenant God rely on an Original Source of laws and virtues, or the ability of man to 'think-out' the appropriate modes of behaviour.

5.3.1 Values

Values are the fundamental principles or patterns of behaviour by which people guide their lives. They may be good or evil in intent, but no community can sustain itself on evil values (except toward those outside that community). *Virtues* are guides to 'the good life' and stem from fundamental morality, however derived. In this chapter, *morals* are distinguished as values adopted by individuals *voluntarily* to guide their own behaviour. When a society selects from them to form acceptable patterns of behaviour, they become *ethical* values. Morals reflect personal *intent to do good*; ethics are societal in origin and evidenced in actions. Morals, then, are seen here as absolute, applying to personal intent anywhere; action may or may not follow. Ethics are relative and situational depending on the cultural setting and expectations of a society or community.

In his study of *The Perennial Philosophy*, Aldous Huxley (1970) shows that a set of virtues have been considered absolute over millennia, overarching all of mankind's diverse interpretations. The *Book of Proverbs* (one of the three 'wisdom books' of the Bible) contains forty-four value-laden prescriptions for proper individual behaviour, dependent on individual will, making ethical behaviour 'obedience to the unenforceable'. Thus, to sustain a community, individuals should be taught to act responsibly and appropriately (i.e., ethically) within the social norms.

Among them are at least four that form the basis for trust that is required for global capitalism (indeed all forms of capitalism) to function effectively and equitably: *viz.* honesty, sincerity, truthfulness, and integrity. These virtues may be applied to such tasks as the acquisition and dissemination of information (in which transparency is critical); to purchases and sales of products and services in the market (in which quality is important); and to agreements (which require promises to be fulfilled). And, if followed, they reward the person practising them. In support of honesty, Benjamin Franklin reportedly asserted that 'If rascals knew the profitability of honesty, they would be honest out of rascality.' Ethical behaviour is, then, a cure for corruption and crime—far better to have self-regulation under ethics than to expend resources in penalties and punishments.

Ethical behaviour clearly predominates around the world, but it appears grossly lacking among key players who flout it in each society or community. What is missing is an understanding of the pervasive unity underlying all 'higher values', as reflected in the fundamental unity of all major religions (Schoun 1984; Smart and Hecht 1982). Reflecting this, many teach their *beliefs* and interpretations of the Masters as dogma, brooking no disagreement—as with some Imam or Ayatollah in the Islamic religion, the Pope in the hierarchy of Catholicism, and leaders of some of the fundamentalist sects or cults in diverse societies—each claiming unique validity for their beliefs.

The conflict over *what* values should be taught or encouraged, and the unwillingness to 'inculcate' any set pattern in 'secular' education, has caused several Western, and particularly the US educational system, to abandon their responsibility to teach values. But, as one sage put it, 'Teaching a student without values is to create a menace to society.' In his *Laws*, Plato wrote: 'Education in virtue is the only education which deserves the name.' Such teaching today is often seen as restricting the student's freedom to pursue an inquiry into values on his/her own; it also often reflects teachers' recognition of their own lack of understanding. But, as Hoetler (1993) has pointed out, the freedom to inquire about values does not imply the freedom to act irresponsibly or to be intolerant of others, for that removes *their* freedom.

Freedom is, itself, a guarantee provided by and to members of a civil society—it does *not* exist in nature, for 'the happy savage' is still 'savage' and fully subject to the highly constraining 'law of the jungle', which will treat his life lightly. Societies are formed, in fact, to protect its members, hopefully in freedom. But, as Lincoln said 'The price of freedom is eternal vigilance'—against all incursions, even from the government. Freedom is prized because it permits each individual to pursue his/her development and happiness as he/she sees fit—so long as he/she accepts the obligation to extend the same freedom to all others in the society (Sen 1999*a*). Obligations, therefore, come *before* rights; the latter are contingent on the former—in the 'loyalty-culture' of Japan, the language had no words for 'rights', 'ego', or 'individual'. And, in no society are there individual rights *against* society except those that society offers for the protection of the individual.

A concern for ethics and its role in peaceful accommodation to globalization arises from frequently reported instances that unethical behaviour has entered into all walks of life—including science communities, university research, the medical profession, the classroom, financial institutions, government, churches,[9] business, and family life. This is true over much of the world, where political, business, and church scandals are reported among leaders in these fields (*The Economist* 2002). In each instance, corruption is a reflection of the pursuit of personal wealth, power, or pleasure, over service to the community, and a threat to democratic capitalism. Yet, an ethic that puts material satisfaction of individuals and society first is not one on which a global community can be built. It is impossible to form a strong community without an ethic of mutual service, as Mikhail Gorbachev found in trying to move the USSR towards 'glasnost' and 'perestroika'. Indeed, his failure to change Soviet culture was due in part to his inability to root out corruption and crime— a culture of 'beating the system for personal survival and gain'.

Since time immemorial, it has been recognized that ethics *must* be taught— rather, learned!—and nurtured into continuing practice. President Putin of Russia recently announced a determined effort to eliminate corruption in that country in order to establish behaviour that would permit it to grow internally and to join more fully in world trade and finance (*Business Week* 2002: 46–8). Ethics *can* be learned, but it is group learning—not just individual—since they are a societal construct, guiding relations among citizens and with foreigners.[10]

But learning and employing ethical rules of the past is not enough: the evolution of mankind requires improvement in ethical standards towards the highest levels of virtue. As G. B. Shaw reportedly said, 'Virtue does not lie in not doing vice, but in not wanting to do it.' The move towards globalization means that the 'society' becomes worldwide—or, at least encompassing those countries that intend to abide by the 'unenforceable rules'. This is the major challenge in the application of the criteria of acceptability—to extend the arena of their application.

5.3.2 Responsibility

Responsible behaviour by both individuals and organizations must be added to the criteria that are requisite to acceptance of global capitalism, even though it has not been demanded at national or intergovernmental levels. The reason for this is that it is the corollary to freedom and is, therefore an essential part of a functioning civil society. And, it must be understood in its value sense, rather than a mere legal construction. It has long been recognized as a requisite within communities, having an ethical basis wider than the law and as an integral part of mankind's development. The sages of Egypt 4,000 years ago taught that the acquisition of knowledge of the ultimate causes and understanding of the unity of all men and things requires individual commitment to awakening one's 'latent consciousness. This they claimed was best achieved by the cultivation of the power of observation [to discern cause and effect, science and Nature], the recognition of values [to advance spiritually and buttress community], and a strong sense of *responsibility* [to guide behaviour and action].'[11]

However, responsibility is not always woven into mankind's behaviour on a daily basis. It is seen more widely in times of emergency or disaster. It has a pervasive value foundation in the widely shared maxim to 'Do unto others as you would have them do unto you' (Christian expression) or 'Do not do to others what you would not want them to do to you' (Confucian expression). This 'golden rule' of responsibility is found in virtually every religion in one form or another, making it one of the absolute virtues. (Das 1947; Schuon 1984; Dalai Lama 1999) and one that must be woven into the process of globalization, as is argued by other authors in this volume.

Obviously, the specific expression of 'responsibility' will vary among societies and cultures as they put 'morals into action' through their own ethical systems. But, from Christ's parable of 'the good Samaritan' (Luke 10: 30–7), it can be considered that one's responsibility is *for* oneself and family for sustenance and personal development and *to* all others to maintain their freedom and opportunity, to assist those in need to learn how to care for themselves, and to extend aid in times of emergency or distress. Among those able, each and all are to learn, in freedom, to develop their own capabilities, interests, compassion and contributions that result in benefits to both themselves and others.

Governments, representing society as a whole, should be responsible for providing elements not attainable by individuals or groups within it as necessary for freedom and opportunity. Any greater responsibility assumed by government and private organizations is a matter of choice among its citizens, exercised in a democratic fashion. But, it is important that, as far as practicable, each responsibility assumed by governments should be assessed in terms of its effect on the freedom of individuals and their social responsibility.

Virtue, then, encompasses our responsibility *for* ourselves—to maintain 'moral intent'—and *to* others in 'ethical conduct'. As explained in more detail by David Loy in Chapter 10, Buddha offered an 'Eightfold Path' of righteousness, which one should follow to gain enlightenment—right views, right mindfulness, right intentions, right concern, right speech, right action, right effort, and right livelihood—and to 'do the right, because it is right' for no recompense. Righteousness, then, is its own reward. Or, to put it in Christian terms: it requires us to first love ourselves [Know Thyself—little self—as part of the larger Self of Mankind] and then to love others and treat them as members of the same Self.

Virtually all peoples of the world are represented in North American society, with each having their own religious institutions—including Christian (Catholic and Protestant), Jewish (and Hasidic), Muslim (and Sufi), Hindu (and Sikh), Buddhist (and Zen), Mormon, Mennonite, American Indian, Eskimo, Hawaiian, and others from Africa, China, India, Japan, and Korea. Each is founded on the understanding that the world is God's (by whatever name or concept), that man is His steward, and that life's purpose is to develop into 'wholeness' individually and collectively (Bohm 1980). All religions or religio-philosophies emphasize the need for man to better understand the purpose of life and proper rules of its conduct.[12]

Each of these views points to the conclusion that mankind is individually and collectively *responsible* for its evolution to higher forms and powers (Tulku 1990). Each individual must pursue his or her own personal enlightenment; but the entire educational system should focus on this movement out of darkness into light—the development of the soul—as the lifelong goal of learning (Zukav 1989).

Responsibility for oneself extends to all phases of life, beginning with one's health (as discussed below) if individuals are to progress as far as they can in each turn of the wheel of life. Otherwise, to be dependent on others is to be limited by their view of the purpose of life and its pursuit. This concept of responsibility should be thoroughly imbued throughout all educational levels, and made most apparent in the universities (or any terminal level of education) within societies and nations seeking to mould a global society.

Responsibility must also be exercised collectively—in public and private organizations, governments, and societies. Social responsibility is not merely the collective of individual responsibilities, for these may not always form a coherent basis for action. Rather, organizations and governments have wider and different responsibilities than those of individuals, as they reflect the goals and objectives of society, expressed through participatory decision making under democracy. However while the responsibility of a national government is essentially to its citizens, it also encompasses its relations with foreign governments and their citizens—including, at the extreme, abiding by 'the rules of war'.

In a civil society, the moral responsibility of corporations or organizations includes playing by the rules of market behaviour and competition, as promulgated by the government. These include abiding by agreements (promise), truthfulness in advertising, packaging, and lending, transparency of information, good governance, and honest dealings. Broad exercise of these responsibilities would greatly mitigate corruption and crime.

With greater individual and collective responsibility, the 'criteria of acceptability' of global capitalism would be more readily achieved, and peace would be more readily obtained. But exercise of both individual and social responsibility seems unlikely without some fundamental transformations in attitudes and orientations.

5.4 NECESSITY OF TRANSFORMATION

Transform: to change the form or outward appearance; to change the nature, condition, or function; to change the personality or character.

(*Webster's New World Dictionary, 1984*)

Transformations—both personal and institutional—have occurred throughout history, and are repeatedly occurring—more or less extensively and intensively. Some are voluntary or guided, and others, like evolution, are involuntary. Voluntary or guided transformations take the form of 'paradigm shifts' in which events or knowledge accumulate until key relationships are seen quite differently—as, for example, happened during the Copernican revolution. More often the process of change is more gradual—albeit significant—as in the case of the agricultural and commercial revolutions. The responses to transformations may be reactive (letting events influence society) or proactive (taking the opportunity to influence the direction and pace of change).

A number of observers have noted that the world is currently in a transition that reflects a 'sea-change' in which events are redirected at right angles (Harman 1988). Such a change will involve several transformations on the world scene. Globalization, as presented in Dunning's introductory chapter, is one such movement. However, if it is to be socially acceptable and sustainable, it must be accompanied by complementary moves in social and political orientations and institutions—all of which will require reconfiguration of existing value systems.

Already a small group of people (leaders from many quarters and disciplines) have asserted that change *must* be directed towards a more beneficent and compassionate world if mankind is not to destroy itself in a violent confrontation. If and when a critical mass of such observers and leaders arises, changes will accelerate. This is the way radical social change so frequently occurs—out of extreme situations and under the leadership of a few visionaries. But, despite major socio-economic-political transformations in the evolution of mankind, we do not believe they have proceeded far enough to buttress and sustain globalization. To accomplish this will require more widespread agreement on fundamental values than is presently in evidence. For this, nothing new needs to be created—merely an acceptance of received wisdom. Over the millennia, despite major changes in many arenas, the moral issues have remained the same, as have the prescriptions for transformation of both individuals and societies (Huxley 1970).

5.4.1 Individual Transformation

Of all the creatures on earth, only human beings can change their patterns. Man alone is the architect of his destiny...human beings, by changing the inner attitudes of their minds, can change the outer aspects of their lives.

(William James)

The transformation of society that must precede, or at least accompany, successful globalization is dependent on the transformation of individuals. Personal transformation has been urged by major religions as the means of resolving fundamental conflicts in both the inner and outer life (Cohen and Phipps 1993). And, the sages warn that 'no one is fully enlightened until all are'; since we are interdependent. Starting on the path to enlightened responsibility is a matter of individual will and choice and is open to everyone[13] (Murphy 1992). Some start earlier in life; others later; some not in one lifetime.

This transformation is not easy since it requires dedicated self-discipline. But it involves little sacrifice because the benefits are greater than what one gives up, such as:

- the agony of trying to protect one's Ego (self-pride or vanity)
- the unhappiness of anger and negative thoughts (envy and covetousness)
- temptations of over-indulgence (gluttony and licentiousness)
- worry and stress (frustration and depression)
- the aching desire for worldly success (greed and prestige)
- the corruption of living off others (sloth and theft)
- the fear of death[14] (Foos-Graber 1989)

One gains a joy in life itself—whatever the task, including service to others—and a 'peace that passes understanding', so that nothing ruffles one's calm.[15] *Balance* in life becomes the overriding means of responding to all events equably and appropriately, which leads to holistic health—as taught by Chi Kung, the martial arts, and other Eastern approaches.[16] Energy increases, since 'blockages' are removed, and 'peak performance' is frequently achieved. One becomes 'open' to others, extending and receiving *love, respect*, and *compassion*. Life, simply, is transformed, and the price is merely that which has been agonizing us through the past—a continuously frustrated desire for more and more—for there is never 'enough' to quell desire! As Buddha concluded, it is *desire* that causes suffering. To give up suffering is *no sacrifice*.

For a journey 'through the narrow gate' and onto the path of transformation, guidance can be found in the 'wisdom books' within and stimulated by the major religions (Molinos 1647), religio-philosophies (Huxley 1970), and the more recent 'consciousness' literature. (cf. publications by Lindisfarne Press, Quest Books, Random House, Samuel Weiser, Shambala, Sounds True Catalog, St. Martin's, and Tarcher). It is not necessary to begin an entirely new investigation of how to meld basic value systems around the world. It requires only an understanding of the essential unity of the major religions as seen within these books and the sacred texts (Smart and Hecht 1982)—to learn and to act!

Guided transformations have mostly been directed at external affairs and not at pursuing individual absolute moral virtues. But many sages have concluded that inner and outer transformations are complementary in the pursuit of true knowledge. ('Ali al-Jamal of Fez 1977) Transformation of the individual self—from a self-centred to an other-centred personality—requires change along physical, emotional, intellectual, and spiritual dimensions. Without such development, sustainable progress is not likely in the socio-economic-political arenas, though some halting measures are certainly feasible for a time. In the present context, transformation of the individual also demands cross-cultural sensitivity and leads to a new set of cross-border relationships which help create the sense of community necessary to accommodate appropriate adjustments to technological and socio-cultural change.

Support for the transformation of the individual exists in the views of human nature and the ability to change one's personality (Nicoll 1985; Fukuyama 1999). Different societies have been built over the centuries on diverse assumptions as to the nature of man and the 'nature of human nature'—i.e. is it fixed, malleable, or changeable by oneself? There are two opposite views on this question. One which is predominantly Western and *neo*-Christian avows that 'man is sinful' and will always be so and can be 'saved' into the next world only by the grace of God, by which his (inevitable and endemic) sins are forgiven. The second is the Eastern (and Confucian) view which asserts that 'man is good' and that his virtue should be encouraged by education so that he will form the 'perfect society'. These two assumptions lead to quite different concepts of society: the Western, which requires statutory laws and punishment to keep order, because left unconstrained man will act against the interests of the society (*vide*, American corporate scandals, Russian mafia, Colombian drug lords, Chinese corruption, and so on); the Eastern, which relies on innate virtue and the resulting shame when a person acts improperly. (Judaism and Islam are less concerned with this question than that man should obey the ordinances of God.) The different results from the two extremes was noted millennia ago by Confucius in his *Analects*:

Govern the people by laws, and regulate them by penalties, and they will try to do no wrong but they will lose the sense of shame. Govern them by virtue and restrain them by rules of propriety and the people will have a sense of shame and be reformed by themselves.

Of course, neither view has been sufficiently put into practice to achieve 'the good society'; for this, both require a large measure of individual responsibility. Yet, both Christians and Confucians have strayed from the teachings of their Masters on the need for *transformation* through self-discipline, as a prerequisite for the transformation of society. What has been lacking is the *will* to change our *acquired* nature—to give up the *persona* we have accumulated during our lifetime in order to find the *essence* which is ours from birth. This change is individually accomplished (Molinos 1647). But, over the centuries formal dogmas, ceremonies, and loyalties to a particular institution have been developed by its leaders to control the 'believers' and extend that institution's power—in Confucianism through the hierarchy under the emperor, and in Christianity through the hierarchies of the Catholic and Protestant churches.[17]

But Christ did not teach such organization or institution-building based on dogma and rigid ceremony. He taught *surrender* to God (as Islam means surrender to Allah and obedience to His ordinances, following the Judaic Torah which set forth God's teachings for Israel). Human nature is usually identified with personality and is seen as difficult, if not impossible, to change. But, development of the soul raises a person's understanding of their essential tie to the goodness of God, making a transformative change in personality. The 'nature of Human Nature' in Christ's view is *not* fixed; mankind is in evolution and is himself able to participate in the development of higher forms of conduct and consciousness. This view is echoed in more recent books on the development of higher levels of behaviour and consciousness (Aurobindo 1971 and 1977; Csikszentmihalyi 1993; Murphy 1992; Nicoll 1984*a* and 1984*b*; Sheldrake 1981; Steiner 1994). One aspect of a current change in human nature is seen in a new concordance between economics and biology, characterized by one observer as 'evo-economics' in which evolutionary 'biology meets the dismal science' to form a new and encouraging view of human nature (*The Economist*, 1994).

Encouragement to change our 'Nature' was given clearly by Christ (and by others):[18]

> 'Ye must be born again' (John 3: 7).
> 'Be ye perfect (whole)' (Mathew 5: 48).
> '. . . be ye transformed' (Romans 12: 2).
> 'Awake—out of spiritual sleep' (Romans 13: 11; Ephesians 5: 14).

Thus, rather than seeing human nature as inevitably and innately sinful, the expectation from these visions is that men and women should seek 'the Kingdom Within' and pursue the transformation from individual egoism, and the seven deadly sins of avarice, covetousness, envy, gluttony, pride, sloth, and vanity[19] to be the servant of all through following God's will.

5.4.2   Societal Transformations

Some societal transformations occurred in the late twentieth century. Most notably among these was the rapid shift from socialism and central planning to market-type economies in the former Soviet Union and China. Others that have moved more slowly include the reduction in racial discrimination in the US (which began with the freeing of slaves in the nineteenth century), the transition from British Empire to Commonwealth, the end of colonial empires, and the ridding of apartheid in South Africa. Each of these events involved paradigm shifts—from one way of operating in the world to another diametrically opposed way. But, the shifts in personal mind-sets which had to accompany each of these changes took place (or are taking place) still more slowly (Fisher 1988). The more fundamental shifts discussed here as a necessary base for responsible global capitalism are not yet regarded as high priorities—though the present popularity of the 'consciousness literature' signals a potential focus on such changes.

Most socio-economic-political adjustments and changes are hard for most people to accept. But, those imposed by technological advances are easier for they seem impersonal and inevitable, despite their social consequences—as happened at the time of the Industrial Revolution. The adjustments to the shifts from monarchy to democracy under the American and French Revolutions were broadly welcomed, despite the abrupt changes in governmental and social structures. Many countries and peoples have yet to go through some of these stages—*viz.* South American, Eastern European, and Central and South-East Asian countries—notably in respect of the redistribution of land ownership and institution of private property.

Still more major shifts are now both being called for and are likely to occur. The anticipated transformations have also been the subject of ancient wisdom. They are related to the widest concepts embodied in our views of our world and the universe, the relations among nations, the purpose and evolution of mankind, and our perception of our individual and collective identities and destinies (Csikszentmihalyi 1993).

Societal transformation starts from high dissatisfaction with the extreme insecurity and violence that threatens mankind. A paradigm shift—a new way of looking at things, a different mind-set, a new formulation, a new design for life and living, a new *purpose*—will be required to reject conflict and to embrace unity and wholeness as major characteristics of a more desirable existence.[20] This assessment is increasingly being promulgated by thinkers in fields as diverse as astrology, astrophysics, biophysics, bioelectromagnetics, sociology, ecopsychology,[21] engineering, economics, medicine, management, and mythology[22] (Harman and Clark 1994). The perceived changes touch all aspects of life—from cosmology and the earth's survival,[23] to the evolution of mankind, international relations, sustainable economic growth, social reform, security, and individual behaviour, down to the role and use of living cells.[24]

These observations about the likely direction of future events are not unrealistic. The imperatives and underlying forces may be fairly readily identified. What is more difficult to envision is their precise timing and the effects. In fact, if one thinks on a somewhat grand scale, it is impossible to know the full consequences of anything we do. For example, the collapse of the Soviet Union was foreseeable—but not when, nor its precise repercussions—as soon as Gorbachev renounced the use of force and opened up the country to wide communication with the West. Gorbachev failed to change Russian culture (as Mao failed in China) because culture cannot be changed from a *top-down* approach. It requires *bottom-up* support, if not initiative. But unanimous support is not required for fundamental change. Some historians have calculated that only 5 per cent of Northerners opposed slavery in the US; yet they were sufficient to lead to its abolition. This phenomenon of a vocal and vibrant minority causing a paradigm shift has been repeated often in Western countries. Examples include women's suffrage, women in business, racial discrimination, environmental concerns, drunk driving, and more recently street crime. In each case, once a critical mass of opinion was formed, others joined and society followed, if only slowly.

At the level of societies, a few transformations are now proceeding that require recognition and energy to complete them before irreparable damages from their unwanted repercussions occur. *Inter alia*, these involve turning from (*a*) 'excessive individualism' and libertarianism to a more communitarian society—that is, from a desire for a risk-free society to an acceptance of mutual solidarity between and obligations of, citizens in an uncertain world; (*b*) irresponsible treatment of our physical, emotional, and mental qualities to an understanding of self-health (or health for the whole person), including our spiritual self; (*c*) education for egalitarian mediocrity (*or* the preparation of tunnel-vision specialists) to preparation for life, and (*d*) crime and corruption to honesty, trust, and transparency.

The major social transformations—in world-views, in socio-economic-political relations, and in spiritual development—are interdependent upon each other. The resolution of one contributes to, and requires, the resolution of the others. Moreover they have a widespread impact on social issues. For example, a solution to crime or periodic health crises depends on resolving the welfare problem, which is linked to unemployment and job-training policies; better jobs are dependent on education, and that, in turn, on a sense of community and its purpose. The resolution of these relations will depend on the form and robustness of collaboration within each local community and on the role business is permitted or urged to play in fostering such co-operation (Harman 1990). Both work and political action influence our view of ourselves (our identities), and our willingness to assume responsibility. To deal with the critical and pressing problems and issues of the early twenty-first century, we are being forced to change social behaviour fundamentally in order to remove or counter the unwanted consequences of what we have been doing in the search for hedonistic pleasures.

5.4.3   Shifts in World-Views

Support for societal transformation is arising in a shift in world-views. History has recorded several changes of world-views about the earth itself and its place in space—from perception of a flat to a round earth, from an earth-centred universe to a solar-centred system and latterly to a complex, curved-flat, and expanding universe. Changes in the radius of human relationships have moved from family-centred groups, to tribal societies composed of multiple families, to villages and cities, to city-states, to nations (composed of tribes and tribal alliances or cities and alliances), to nation states, and more recently to regional associations of nations. Each and all of these changes have required shifts in mind-sets—in our concept of who we are, our 'identity' as individuals and societies[25]—that have usually been opposed strongly by 'conservative' elements, as in Russia where the former Communist Left is now seen as the 'Conservative Right'.

Despite appearances to the contrary, some contemporary observers now see the world on the verge of yet another series of transformations, involving the rejection of violence and intolerance of other cultures and peoples into a more peaceful world and a more symbiotic relationship with Nature (Lovelock 1979; Thompson 1987 and 1991; Zoeteman 1991). The increasing recognition—reinforced by views from space-shots—that the world, itself, is a single, integrated entity, that there are no natural geographic borders, and that distinctions among groups are man-made is the fundamental shift in mind-sets that will buttress a global mind change. This, in turn, is a requisite for useful progress towards socially acceptable and sustainable globalization, which is likely to move faster in the economic realm than in the social, political, or moral. But this requires a shift in our 'identity' (Sen 1999*b*). We must begin to see ourselves as belonging to a more encompassing society—as the nations participating in the European Community are now trying to do without giving up 'too much' of their national identity.

This shift is matched at the level of cosmology where the universe is seen not only as a single whole but also as a potentially living, thinking entity, which is itself 'one big thought'. (Foster 1975; Hoyle 1983; Briggs and Peat 1984) In this view, all of its parts are a result of 'mentation' by The Creator and are simply complex bundles of energy, which have been projected out of The Creator—'and God said…'—subject to His will and to the 'One law' and, ultimately, pursuing His purpose. The unity of science and spirituality is occurring as knowledge of the universe increases—thus, Einstein: 'You will hardly find one among the profounder sort of scientific minds without a religious feeling of his own'; and Harides Chaudhari: 'We know too much about matter today to be materialistic any longer' (*Discover*, March 2002, 38–42; Harman and Clark 1994).

Unity, place, composition, interdependence, fit and meshed behaviour of all parts (or participants) are characteristics of this 'Oneness'. But the achievement of this unity is also subject to the will of humans, who have been given the ability to make choices between good and evil or unity and separation; and each choice tends to be cumulative. A choice of social good yields more in return, for unity enhances that unity; anger receives anger in return and conflict more conflict. The Buddhist Law of Karma (of cause and effect) states that consequences are eventually returned in the same mode as what was extended, and the Christian caution is 'whatsoever a man soweth, that also shall he reap' (Galatians 6: 7). But, we do not know *when* the returns will arrive or how much they may be magnified. Still, it behoves mankind to practise virtue to improve the chances of gaining a virtuous (civil) society and a more peaceful world.

5.4.4   Transformation to Health

Will Durant, the philosopher, concluded after his work on the history of civilizations, that 'The health of nations is more important than the wealth of nations.' One cannot buy health with wealth, for health requires individual time and effort, though wealth can 'buy' such time. Wealth is not required, however, for health is also available to the poor—though access to a cure for illness may not be so available. With enhanced health, the individual and nation can prosper. It is a concept, according to Laura Tyson (former Chairman of the Council of Economic Advisers to the President of the US) whose time has come (*Business Week* 2002: 20), in that it gives particular emphasis to the kinds of private and public goods and services people are seeking. These include (1) education for life and lifelong learning, (2) promotion of self-health and disease prevention compared to illness cure, and (3) assistance in local communities for development of mental health in all its facets.

A fundamental problem facing the modern society, however, is to understand what 'health' really is; and this itself will require a transformation in the way minds and bodies are viewed (Locke and Colligan 1986; Wilson 1987). The usual medical (allopathic) concept of health is merely the absence of illness. But this is far from the meaning employed in the major theologies or social philosophies of the world, beginning with Plato's view of health as holistic in his advice to doctors[26]—i.e. that they address the whole person at each stage in one's development *and* in relation to others. Health, then, is a matter not only of physical condition but also of sound emotional, intellectual, and spiritual development.[27]

These four dimensions of health encompass all human characteristics, which *must be balanced* in order for evolution to occur toward higher forms of understanding, and the power to improve (Kuhlewind 1988). This is understood by the Masters of the martial arts of the East, for their goal is to help the practitioners achieve such a *balance* in physical, emotional, mental, and spiritual development that they are able to meet all challenges and to protect themselves against *any and all* threats from within and without.[28]

Balance in these four aspects offers a degree of protection (immunity) against all threats to health. Balanced persons are not easily brought to 'dis-ease' by illness, stress, or invective, for they are always 'at ease' in all dimensions. Imagine the increased productivity at work, performance in games, and joy in living that would arise from a community that was healthy in this manner! These results can be envisioned as ingredients of transformation.

This concept of health is not one that can be left to the medical profession alone. To properly understand its characteristics requires continuing education and the development of higher levels of understanding by individuals and those in the society encouraging health of the whole person. Can such a community be contemplated and pursued by appropriate means? (Etzioni 1998)—that is, can a *vision* of health be described so that it is both understandable and desirable, and the *means* be seen by which it can be accomplished? The effort is imperative if the benefits of global society are to be gained.

Attaining health (wholeness) requires a shift in our view of ourselves and our relation to each other and to Nature, for we have long viewed our bodies as *separate* and distinct carriers of the five senses and that we must *learn how to think*. What is increasingly evident from the research of scientists, from astrophysics to biophysics, is that 'thinking' exists first (Thompson 1987 and 1991; Zoetemann 1991). Awareness is already there—then body *and all matter* arise from thought energy—i.e. out of 'an intelligent universe'.[29] Thus, 'a thought is nothing but a quantum event in the same unified field from where nature creates everything' (Chopra 1993: 18). Many doctors consider that we can *think* our way into illness (Shorter 1993)—for energy follows thought; it is asserted by some that we can also think our way *into* health (Wilson 1987). This is because 'the immune system is a circulating nervous system. It thinks, it has emotions, it has memory, it has the ability to make choices and to anticipate events' (Chopra 1993: 18). Dis-ease is a result of how we think and live our lives, which are our individual responsibility. In Rosenfield's words 'the diagnosis and treatment of diseases are your doctor's main concerns. Prevention, learning what to do to stay healthy, is your responsibility. You must think prevention, act prevention and know all about prevention. No one can or will do that for you' (1986: 19). This responsibility is individual, though general education is necessary (Behrman 1994).

Health, then, has to do not only with breathing, eating, drinking, and the resulting digestion and metabolism, but also with our impressions—the movement of our consciousness. For this reason, meditation, as prescribed by most religions and in recent guides on stress-management, is a necessary starting point. It has long since been taught by the Vedantists, Buddha, Christ, and Yoga masters; and it is now gaining support in the medical profession. Yet, people seem to turn to holistic approaches to health only when life is too stressful and 'becomes sufficiently painful... [causing them] to choose and maintain lifestyles that are life-enhancing rather than self-destructive... one that's based on altruism, compassion, and love' (Ornish 1993: 9).

Health of the individual and of society are threatened by personal illness and epidemic diseases. And it may be objected that illness and disease will always be with us, but this is not inevitable. It is inevitable *only* if we continue not to learn about its causes and remedies and fail to exercise our *will.*

Illness plays a positive role in learning about health—it shows that something is wrong and that learning and action are required. Pain has the purpose of identifying where a particular health problem is manifesting itself. However, the cause and the remedy may be elsewhere in the body, and they must be sought. It is not enough to stop the pain, though this may be the immediate need; the cause must be addressed, and this is *the learning process.* Illness, therefore, is necessary to help us learn about health, telling us what health is *not* and, in its avoidance, guiding us to a more healthy condition (Dossey 1984). *Life is Learning.* (Krishnamurti 1994) We can pursue it pro-actively or re-actively; the latter is the general tendency, for it appears to require less effort, but this is not so over the long run, for lessons not learned must be repeated. The former requires self-discipline and collective education; both seem to be in short supply in our modern society. A disciplined life requires taking responsibility for oneself (Foster 1987). How we develop along these dimensions indicates our readiness for a global community.

5.4.5   Role of Violence in Transformation

The renowned monk and palaeontologist, Teilhard de Chardin, was once asked from his audience what he thought of the Holocaust. His reply shocked them— 'It was as God intended for us to learn.' Yet, if we understand that all life is learning and that it is only by learning that we can start to remove the ills of society, his view is sound. And the continued violence and 'inhumanity of man to man' is ample evidence that we have not learned.[30]

Violence, of itself, is not evil. It exists throughout the Universe, and on Earth it is evident in the 'great food chain' within which each life form consumes and is consumed by another. Thus, the caution to 'Do no harm' is restricted to mankind and the other life forms it chooses to protect. And, even within human society, violence is acceptable when used to stop those seeking to harm others. But, intentional violence in any form—including intolerance, corruption, and crime—damages the sense of community that is necessary for the progress of mankind, and is evil. Accidental violence is not evil despite the undesirable results. It is *intent* that determines the morality of violence.

The purpose of intentional violence, as seen by those perpetrating it, is to force others to do what the perpetrators want them to do, to remove an undesired element in society (below or above), to achieve their view of 'justice', or even to carry out the 'Will of Allah'. Such violence is the final act of intolerance, vengeance, or desire for power and wealth. It indicates that *moral reason has broken down* and that a *sense of community* is absent. The only justifiable intentional violence is to protect oneself (or society) against unwarranted incursions by others. To wilfully kill members of our own species and to destroy the marvels of Nature and man, 'fouling our nest', is neither rational nor communal. And there is no nation today about which one would say: 'That is a sensible society; people in that country are living as we all should—rational, loving, tolerant and at peace with each other.'

The *role* of violence in the greater scheme is to show that *this is not the way to a fuller life*—one of creativity, co-operation, and compassion, which are 'unifying factors' in a community.[31] (Krishnamurti 1980). Violence among humans has never *solved any* problem without creating new ones; enduring solutions arise from continuous voluntary co-operation. But, as a reaction to the massacres in Africa and Yugoslavia, the continued civil strife in Northern Ireland, Sri Lanka, the Kashmir, Israel/Palestine, and the terrorist attacks in the US (11 Sept. 2001), attitudes are emerging that point to a widening disgust with and rejection of violence in society.[32]

Violence and war are *not* inherent in mankind; they are learned activities, just as is anger, jealousy, and all the other anti-virtues. A distinguished British military historian (Keegan 1993) concluded that man in not warlike by nature, that 'Unless we unlearn the habits we have taught ourselves, we shall not survive', and that the means of war have made it a 'scourge' and a 'menace' to mankind's very existence, and that a reversal of the violent trends requires nothing less than a 'cultural transformation'. Another military historian, added in his review, 'this voice from the heart of the military establishment seems to be exhorting us to make love, not war... All that is missing is a blueprint for the cultural transformation that is necessary to save us from extinction' (*The Washington Post National Weekly* 1993).

If members of mankind can take their identity from being a part of *humanity* and 'created in the image of God, then a new identity will be formed' (Aurobindo 1977). And, the realization that all will play by the same basic rules reduces intolerance. If we could all see ourselves and others as responsible members of a global society, our identities would reform and conflicts diminish. And violence would cease when we have realized that *each individual and group has the responsibility to grow*, and must be given the opportunity to do so, with the full support of the society. This realization is more likely to arise when we learn that *there is only one law* and we all live under it.[33]

5.5 REQUISITES FOR GUIDED CHANGE

The thinking that got us into this situation is inadequate to get us out of it.

(Albert Einstein (and others))

Whether the transformations are societal or individual, and if they are to be guided by participation in the process of co-creation, there are four sequential prerequisites for success:

1. strong *dissatisfaction* with the present situation—followed by
2. a *vision* of a more desirable condition, society, or world—followed by
3. recognition of a *means* for achieving it—catalysed by
4. the *will* to act.

Several sources in modern society provide ample evidence of a widespread *dissatisfaction* with conditions of work and life and with the lack of personal or political *will* to respond effectively. But there is much less agreement on a *vision* or appropriate *means* to achieve societal transformation. Yet these latter two prerequisites are as necessary as the other two. Any transformation of society must be accompanied by a transformation of individuals so that they voluntarily seek the same vision, abide by the rules, and practise virtue.

Thus, dissatisfaction that tolerates an undesirable condition means that correctives will not be sought or applied, for they are always difficult and seemingly costly to implement. 'The worst of all evils is surely tolerable evil', for it will be permitted to continue. But, in fact, the cost of continuation is probably much more than the perceived costs of transformation. One reason for the perceived high short-run sacrifice is that societal costs and benefits do not track with individual costs and benefits. Part of the transformation of both society and individuals, therefore, must involve a greater identity of each with others—i.e. a greater sense of community.

Note, for example, the 'unacceptable' conflicts, assassinations, and massacres in the former Yugoslavia, Somalia, Congo, Chechnya, Afghanistan, and so on; plus the 'unacceptable' aspects of the political systems in the US, Japan, Italy, France, Brazil (and others), which law-makers have promised to reform but do not—not to mention the corruption in many countries, both developed and developing (*Business Week* 1993: 133; *The Economist* 2002: 37, 44). To effect change, dissatisfaction must come to the point of a critical mass of people saying 'We will not take it any more!'—as in the case of the violent revolt in Romania against its leader, the 'Velvet Revolution' in Czechoslovakia, the peaceful breakaways from the USSR, the student demonstrations in Tiananmen Square in Beijing, and the smaller but more effective repeated protests in Chinese villages, and the shocked response to paedophiles among Catholic priests. The evidence of impending transformation is seen in increasing dissatisfaction and disillusion, which may fester before boiling over.

A *vision* is necessary. As the *Book of Proverbs* asserts: 'Where there is no vision, the people perish' (29: 18). Unfortunately, a lack of a vision often characterizes contemporary governments. For example, later comments by two members of

President Bush's Administration (1988–92) were that 'he was in fact a president without a vision who predictably employed a staff without vision, and that was the undoing of his presidency' (*The Christian Science Monitor* 1994, reviewing Kolb 1993 and Podhoretz 1994).

The required vision is not difficult to describe, since visions of a more perfect world have been offered since millennia before Christ and after, in several utopias, and are embodied in all major religions and philosophies urging a virtuous and righteous life, based on love, compassion, and service to others.[34] These are the source of the call for 'transformation'—from worldly to spiritual values, from worldly to spiritual guidance in the economic and social needs of mankind—that is being heard more insistently in many quarters in recent years (Krishnamurti 1980; Collin 1984*b*; Etzioni 1988; Nicoll 1985; Steiner 1994; Sen 1997). But it is warped when carried to rigid extremes by 'fundamentalists' in any religion or philosophy. Such intolerance has no place in an acceptable global society. For the 'not so fundamental' vision is less rigid and can accommodate differences in behaviour—so long as they do no harm.

The *means* are the most difficult to come by, for they give rise to strong disagreements among elements of society. They require a shift in relationships, power positions, perquisites and privileges, and the distribution of benefits and burdens. The very structure of society will need to be re-configured, in ways which not all members will like. To be successful, such a fundamental change requires also a transformation by individuals themselves. Millennia ago, Confucius presented the sequence in achieving a more perfect society:

> To spread illustrious virtue around the world, the ancients first governed their own estates well;
> to govern their own estates, they first regulated their families;
> to regulate their families, they first cultivated their own person;
> to cultivate their own person, they first rectified their hearts;
> to rectify their hearts, they first sought sincerely in their thoughts;
> wishing for sincerity in their thoughts, they first extended their knowledge.
>
> (*The Analects*)

Similarly, in the words of Socrates: 'To fix the world, first fix yourself.'

The exercise of individual *will*, therefore, is to forswear the temptations of mammon and to use God's blessings of progress to further the improvement (education and health) and (spiritual) evolution of all (individuals and communities). The recognition of the same processes and goals by Confucius and Buddha, 500 years before Jesus, and the many heroic stories and myths around the world recounting the pursuit of spiritual development, indicate that there is fundamental and generally accepted truth in these concepts.[35] But their universal *practice* will not occur without the exercise of the *will* of key individuals who set an example for the entire society. As Robert Davies will demonstrate more fully in Chapter 13, business can play a key role, but to do so, it will have to get into the vanguard of the process—as is now being urged by several management gurus (Hoffman and Frederick 1995; Pruzan 2001).

5.6 CONCLUSIONS

All civilizations have encompassed, and do encompass, with more or less emphasis, the three central aspects of any culture—*contemplation, work,* and *action* (Arendt 1958; Gellner 1988). Any move to globalization of society must show, first, that it offers renewed and reformed education with opportunities for creativity in science, art, and literature (contemplation and creativity); second, that it provides for co-operative competition in a free-enterprise system under market capitalism (work and opportunity); and third, it allows for participation in decision making under democracy at all levels of community (action and justice). And it should meet the demands for the seven criteria of acceptability of a new global order, as earlier identified in this chapter. If these are offered and implemented, the need for government regulation to enforce proper behaviour in the several institutions of capitalism would be reduced, since this would be replaced by greater self-regulation.

In countries where civil society (especially the rule of law) does not yet exist and the institutions of capitalism are absent or embryonic, their gradual establishment would be easier and more readily accepted within a wider world which was acting responsibly with similar values. Assistance should be given the 'late bloomers' in their adoption of a private enterprise system and the formation of a level of small and medium enterprises (SMEs) that form the core of dynamic growth in both developing and advanced countries. This assistance should be on a person-to-person basis and *inter alia* should embrace the promotion of SMEs and trade associations, regulatory and statutory constraints on market activities, taxation, accounting and information systems, financial institutions, and corporate governance.

Many different elements of society have roles to play both in the process of globalization and, especially, in the help needed to reduce the gap between the rich and the poor. NGOs, churches, foundations, non-profit organizations, educational and medical groups, supranational and regional agencies, and regional economic associations—all can offer substantial contributions to the new global society to make it equitable and sustainable. In this way, bridges can be built between national economies, government policies, and value systems, and as a result cross-border integration and mutual understanding could be enhanced.

With global capitalism founded within national civil societies and buttressed by the transformations discussed in this chapter, the results would be visible not only in economic growth but also in progress along a continuum of desirable dimensions—such as reduction of poverty and disease and stress, improved quality of life, protection of the environment, extension of human rights, an increase in trust, and a reduction of conflict. These results would produce *not* a perfect global society but a world in which peace (a requisite to democratic capitalism) could be sustained and evolutionary progress made through individual freedom, encouraging creativity, co-operation, and compassion.

With recognition and practice of common virtues, societies would progress toward peace, and nations and the global economy would make more effective use of resources, saving billions from reductions in military establishments, police, medical costs, and unemployment. These gains would be available to all nations as they improve their cultures in an integrated fashion to provide the foundation for both individual and national health that would permit sustainable progress toward a global community. The recognition of shared *values* would arise from the processes of the transformation of individuals and societies. These would undergird a sense of community strong enough to overcome adversities, mitigate conflicts, encourage enjoyment of diversity, and provide 'great causes' with which citizens could become identified and find the happiness that results from the individual and collective pursuit of a High Purpose.

NOTES

1. Mandel concludes: 'no matter what laws are eventually passed, moral foundations are critical to reassure jittery investors and workers, and to put the New Economy on a firm footing' (Chief economist, *Business Week* 2002: 115).
2. Management attitudes and policies were the major cause of its bankruptcy, deceiving, hiding information, and putting an emphasis on immediate success. *Business Week* (2002: 118–20, 150) concluded that: 'Enron's unrelenting stress on growth and its absence of controls helped push execs into unethical behavior.'
3. The debilitating focus on material progress was stressed by Derek Bok, former President of Harvard, who deplored the prevailing materialistic ideology in America as being inadequate to lead to an elevation of life; he quoted a Rabbi—'It behooves us to be careful of what we are worshiping, because what we are worshiping we are also becoming' (*The Christian Science Monitor* 1992: 18).

    Millennia earlier, the Sages of Egypt cautioned against the degradation of materialism: 'For when luxury becomes a necessity preponderance is given to wealth. Society is no longer governed by quality but by favoritism and greed.' ... 'When the governing class is not chosen for quality it is chosen for material wealth: this always means decadence, the lowest stage a society can reach.' (de Lubicz 1956: 46).

    The quantitative emphasis is seen as separating rather than integrating society: 'Two tendencies govern human choice and effort: the search after quantity and the search after quality ... Quantitative mentality ... consists in the analytical consideration of the parts without vital connection' (de Lubicz 1956: 46).
4. T. S. Eliot, in his *Choruses from 'The Rock'* queried: 'When the Stranger says: "What is the I meaning of this city? I Do you huddle close together because I you love each other?" I What will you answer? "We all I dwell together I To make money from each other" or I "This is a community"'.
5. In an assessment of 'The Failures of Capitalism' a former Deputy Undersecretary of Commerce for International Trade under President Carter recently asserted that, left uncorrected, the failures would stimulate attempts to form alternative economic systems that would likely be populist (*Washington Post National Weekly Edition* 2002). An attempt to formulate a worker-oriented capitalism can be found in Melman (2002).
6. Michael Mandel concludes that a 'new morality' that fits the 'new economy' carries a 'moral imperative for the riskiest projects and activities to be taken on by those best able to bear the uncertainty, while poorer people should have more income and job security. Wealthy corporations have a responsibility to fund risky innovations even if it doesn't immediately help the bottom line. Rich countries such as the US are morally bound to make investments in the developing world even if the risks are high' (*Business Week* 2002: 115).

7. A. O. Hirschman (1977) records that the philosophers proposing individual freedom in church, state, and economic life feared that those relishing their freedom would succumb to three lusts—power, greed, and licentiousness (debauchery and excessive sex). They wanted to rely on democracy to curb power, on capitalism to harness greed for the good of society, and on the church to constrain the sinfulness of man, but they were not sanguine. In fact, no society has yet contained these lusts, which can be restrained effectively only from within—that is, by individual transformation.

8. Joan Robinson, in her acceptance of the Presidency of the American Economic Association, pointed out that policy agreements were easy at the factual level, and only slightly more difficult at the level of logical analysis. Both, she argued, could be resolved by observant and thinking officials, but value differences were almost impossible to resolve in policy formation. Thus, accommodations in value foundations become a prerequisite for agreements on policies.

9. At an extreme, clergymen in Rwanda were involved in genocide (*The Economist* 2002: 44).

10. One of the major problems today is the approach used in presenting ethics to students. More often than not it takes the form of a study of 'ethical analysis', meaning that one is to learn how to analyse a situation to determine what if any ethics are to be applied—leaving it to the student to make the determination. This approach leads to a conclusion that a wide variety of answers are permissible and virtually any would be acceptable to society. This makes a mockery of standards of ethical behaviour.

11. These are the preliminary steps as reported in a commentary on the legacy of the ancient wisdom of Egypt by de Lubicz 1978: xiv (italics in original). She continued her commentary, contrasting modern thought with 'the conditions which are indispensable for understanding the ancient Wisdom.' These are: 'The uncovering of the "inner ear" '; 'Simplicity of heart and mind (the factor opposed to the complexity of modern thought), and finally the spirit of synthesis, opposed to our analytical mentality'; 'the understanding of this [ancient Wisdom] calls for a mental outlook so different from our modern way of thinking that it requires a considerable effort of adaptation. . . . we have to free ourselves from the distortion wrought by prejudice, ready-made theories, and other restrictions on our mental processes' (de Lubicz 1978: xv).

12. A young Russian observed that the Soviet leadership and most of the populace have no understanding of the fact that Western democratic capitalism is grounded on Christian principles, requiring certain responsibilities while providing freedom. But, then, many in the West seem to have forgotten this tie.

13. According to Buddhist teaching, says Segyal Rinpoche: 'Enlightenment is real. It is something not exotic, not fantastic, not for an elite, but for all of humanity.' He continues with the observation that death is certain, but Westerners consider that life should go on forever and tell each other to 'Take care of yourself'. But, 'Which self: is it the one that is going to die or the one that will survive?' Living in order to die well is an important part of transformation and the resulting enlightenment (*The Tibetan Book of Living and Dying and Tibetan Wisdom for Living and Dying* (a series of six cassettes) *The Sounds True Catalog*, Boulder, Colo., 1994.)

14. Robert. N. Butler (1975: 421–2), later the first director of the National Institute of Aging, encouraged a fuller life as a means of removing the fear of death: 'What can be done about humankind's uneasy knowledge that life is brief and death inevitable? There is no way to avoid our ultimate destiny. But we can struggle to give each human the chance to be born safely, to be loved and cared for in childhood, to taste everything the life cycle has to offer, including adolescence, middle age, perhaps parenthood and

certainly a secure old age; to learn to balance love and sex and aggression in a way that is satisfying to the person and those around him; to push outward without a sense of limits; to explore the possibilities of human existence through the senses, intelligence and creativity; and most of all to be healthy enough to enjoy the love of others and a love for oneself. After one has lived a life of meaning, death may lose much of its terror. For what we fear most is not really death but a meaningless and absurd life.'

15. Advice from a Zen Master on living—adopt the following 'Calm, Peace, Balance, Think, Act, and Gain'.

16. One may listen to a Chi Kung Master, Ken Cohen, discuss this Chinese system for healing the mind, body, and spirit, and why it is growing in popularity in the West on several tapes offered by *The Sounds True Catalog* (Boulder, Colo.), as 'The Way of Chi Kung'. A variety of Eastern systems for holistic health are provided by practitioners.

17. The extent to which the Catholic Church went to squelch independent religious practice is seen in the Inquisition and in its persecution of Michael Molinos (a monk in the seventeenth century) who wrote a widely read guide encouraging individual pursuit of spirituality through direct surrender to God, not through the church hierarchy or its ceremonies (Molinos 1647). And, of course, the Protestant churches in America had their 'witch hunts'.

18. For example, Epictetus (AD 60): 'Dare to look up to God and say, "make use of me for the future as Thou wilt; I am of the same mind; I am one with Thee. I refuse nothing which seems good to Thee. Lead me whither Thou wilt. Clothe me in whatever dress Thou wilt. Is it Thy will that I should be in a public or a private condition; dwell here, or be banished; be poor, or rich? Under all these circumstances I will testify unto Thee before men...". Expel grief, fear, desire, envy, intemperance. But these can be no otherwise expelled than by looking up to God alone, as your pattern; by attaching yourself to him alone, and being consecrated to his commands. If you wish for anything else, you will, with sighs and groans, follow what is stronger than you; always seeking prosperity without, and never able to find it. For you seek it where it is not; and neglect to seek it where it is.'

19. 'Enron's failure was due to the vanity and villainy of its bosses' (*The Economist* 2002: 13).

20. Anna Lemkow (1993) shows that the principle of wholeness underlies both science— in modern physics and biology—and all religions and argues that it can transform society and bring beneficial global change.

21. 'Ecopsychology' is the study of the needs of the planet and of the person as an integral whole, a continuum. It is a combination of cosmological influences on humans and the environment, combining the Anthropic Principle and the Gaia hypothesis into a new 'wild science' susceptible to 'bizarre formulations' and therefore entering on an uncertain voyage (Roszak 1992).

22. The many changes in economics and business are noted by Singer and Wildavsky (1993) as 'a gradual change in the technical basis of power, the continuing triumph of quality over quantity, of brain power over muscle power, of mind and imagination over physical resources, of the uncontrolled order of freedom over the rigid order of central control and planning,' which will lead to political democracy and diminished use of force among nations (*Financial Times* 1994).

23. *Newsweek* (1988: 98–9) warned more than a decade ago that 'The Earth is One Big System' and that it can live without man but man cannot live without a balanced environment from the earth, but we still have not responded adequately.

24. Two popular news magazines discussed new medical discoveries ten years ago: 'Miracle Cures may be in your Cells' (*Business Week* 1993: 76) and 'New discoveries linking the brain to the immune system suggest that state of mind can affect us right down to our cells' (*Newsweek* 1988: 88–97).

25. The issue of identities is bound up with the concept of culture and its underlying values. Both Europe and Asia are repelled by some American values that permit freedom to portray violent acts by firearms and to carry guns, which are prohibited in their countries. The traditional communitarian values of Asia are challenged by the individualistic orientation of the US, so that strong reactions are arising, which do not embrace the same concepts of democracy held in the West (*Christian Science Monitor* 1993).

26. Plato's *Seventh Epistle* states that a doctor 'who advises a sick man, living in a way to insure his health, must first effect a reform in his way of living. . . . And if the patient consent to such a reform, then he may admonish him on other points.' And in Plato's *Republic*, Socrates rebukes those who become ill as a result of their unwholesome regimen: 'And isn't this a charming trait in them [the licentious ones] that they hate most in all the world him who tells them the truth, that until a man stops drinking and gorging and wenching and idling, neither drugs nor cautery nor the knife, no, nor spells nor periapts nor anything of that kind will be of any avail.'

    Plato also wrote that physical wholeness must be supported and balanced with spiritual wholeness as well—a proper proportion between body and soul. In *Charmides*, Plato wrote: 'you ought not attempt to cure the eyes without the head, or the head without the body, so neither ought you to attempt to cure the body without the soul. And this is the reason why the cure of many diseases is unknown to the physicians of Hellas, because they disregard the whole, which ought to be studied also, for the part can never be well unless the whole is well.'

    Plato went further to suggest that the ultimate source of physical illness might well be a spiritual disorder. (Bryan and Naso 1989: 8—quoted from William B. Naso and Thomas H. Woollen, Jr., 'Holistic medicine in ancient Greece'.)

27. The very concept of salvation has been warped from its first meaning of 'salving' or 'healing into wholeness' in this life (the word 'heal' comes from the Indo-European word 'to make whole'). And the word 'perfect' in Christ's admonition—'Be ye perfect, even as your Father in heaven is perfect'—is better translated as 'Be ye whole.' (Compare Briggs and Peat 1984.) Christianity was meant as a prescription for complete health—in all dimensions. Instead, the concept was shifted into one relating to an after-life—'saving from hell-fire'. The 'salving' process was intended to be from the 'dis-ease' that attacks those who have not attained a balance of the physical, emotional, mental, and spiritual aspects of their lives, which leads to the 'blessed' conditions of the Beatitudes, or learning to live now in the promised peace, for 'The Kingdom of God is within you' (Luke 17: 21).

    As defined in the late 1940s by the World Health Organization, health is 'a state of complete physical, mental, and social well-being' (LeShan 1982). Later, the WHO added the spiritual dimension. This is well beyond the normal (allopathic) concept of the 'absence of illness', but a number of doctors have moved into the spiritual realm as well. (Dossey 1984)

28. 'Always more vital to karate than techniques or strength is the spiritual element that lets you move and act with complete freedom. In striving to enter the proper frame of mind, Zen meditation is of great importance. Though we say that this meditation involves a state of impassivity and complete lack of thought, we mean that through

meditation we can overcome emotion and thinking and give freer reign to our innate abilities than ever before. The Zen state of selflessness is the same condition of disregard for selfish thoughts and concern for personal welfare that the artist experiences in the heart of creation. The man who wants to walk the way of karate cannot afford to neglect Zen and spiritual training' (Oyama 1967).

29. Giridal Jain, former editor of the *Times of India*, wrote: 'as I have pursued the philosophical implications of modern science, especially quantum physics, it has become reasonably clear to me that the basis on which the Western perception of reality rests has disappeared and that instead of the world of matter (inanimate, in the Western view), we live in a world of energy—or spirit, as we Hindus would say' (*World Press Review* 1990: 80).

30. In commenting on the angst and violence of 'The New Angries', who are willing to protest almost anything in society, Melvin Maddocks quoted Ortega y Gassett, who foresaw the present situation some seventy years ago, calling it the 'blight of the century' and a result of the prevailing philosophy of materialism: 'Life is reduced to mere matter, physiology to mechanics' and such a 'reality' has 'a violent temper' for there is never 'enough' (*World Monitor* 1990: 12–14).

31. In the Japanese tradition, one of the greatest lessons of accommodation was taught through the action of two leaders of warring factions; as they moved to a negotiated peace, each sought to give the other the responsibility for writing the terms. Each considered that the other, knowing that peace would come only from a real accommodation of interests, would write terms acceptable to both sides.

32. M. J. Rozenburg, Director of Policy for the Israeli Policy Forum writes in his weekly newsletter of a conversation with another Israeli: I asked him if most Israelis are so anxious for peace that they would, despite a year of almost incessant violence, make major concessions. 'Of course, we would. That is what the polls all show. Ask me if I want to give up the West Bank and I will tell you that I don't. But ask me again after we go a few months or—I am dreaming now—years of peace and quiet, and I will tell you that I'd sacrifice my Zionist dreams just so I can feel that my daughters are safe at the mall. Once you taste a few days without fear, it is unimaginable to go back. It is like a remission from a terrible illness. You know the disease may come back but you keep yourself going by telling yourself it cannot and that you are disease free. The disease here is the violence.' This Israeli who would prefer not to compromise but would, for the sake of his daughters' safety, is typical of those people on both sides who would give up cherished political and ideological aspirations for the reality of security (email from Israel, 19 Jan. 2002).

33. Scientists have concluded that there is one Unified Force comprising the four evident ones—therefore, only *one* law of creation exists, covering all manifestations (Miller 1993). We and Nature *are* one; our identity *is* with each other and the universe, which is seen by one theoretical physicist as a thinking, evolving entity, able to experiment with different routes: 'The universe is evolving, and matter and energy are free to enjoy some degree of spontaneity. In other words, the universe is free to explore different pathways of evolution' (Davis 1992: 35).

According to a professor of theoretical physics (University of Adelaide), the act of creation in the universe is taking place all the time, and in more and more complex ways. The result is that not even the universe knows where it is going nor could predict the future of even a small part of itself—but it is moving to higher forms of itself, and man is a necessary participant because *consciousness* is a necessary component of that creation; and consciousness implies *purpose*, which is itself manifested in quite different ways from eon to eon (Davies 1992). Thus, physics is opening a perception of an active God, whose existence it cannot prove or disprove, but constant creation requires a thinker, who has promulgated 'a law'. Its promulgation means that there is *purpose for the universe and man*, for the design of a law requires fore-knowledge of how it is intended to operate.

However, despite the existence of purpose (Wiener 1964), the route to the goal is not mapped—'there are many routes up the mountain but only one summit'. Mankind, and maybe Nature, has been given the ability to exercise *will* (Prigogine and Stengers 1984). But, to be effective in evolution, it must be exercised to a High Purpose that protects and sustains mankind (Murphy 1992).

34. See e.g. the instructions of Ptahhotep (a high officer of the court of King Assa in the fifth dynasty of Egypt, approximately 2750 BC) to his son on how to live a proper and useful life. They are similar to those in Confucius' *Analects* and in the Book of Proverbs of the Old Testament (Breasted 1933: 115–31, on 'Conduct, Responsibility, and the Emergence of a Moral Order').

35. Joseph Campbell in his many studies of mythology noted that the major defining myths around the world were of the 'hero' or 'heroic god' being tempted by all manner of earthly attractions, but finally making his way to righteousness as demanded by God—the transformation by struggle that is man's basic test and which he is destined (eventually, if he exercises his own will) to pass (1949; 1972). (Campbell can be heard on several cassettes released by the *Sounds True Catalog*, Denver, Colo.).

REFERENCES

'Ali al-Jamal of Fez, S. (1977), *Meaning of Man: the Foundations of the Science of Knowledge* (Norfolk, UK: Diwan Press).

Arendt, H. (1958), *The Human Condition* (Chicago: University of Chicago Press).

Aurobindo, S. (1971), *The Mind of Light* (New York: E. P. Dutton).

——(1977), *The Human Cycle, The Ideal of Human Unity, War and Self-Determination* (Pondicherry: Sri Aurobindo Ashram).

Beck, U. (2000), 'A Global Prospect: Beyond the Work Society,' *Global Focus* 12(1): 79–88.

Behrman (1980*a*), *Industry Ties to Science and Technology Policies in Developing Countries* (Cambridge, Mass.: Oelgeschlager, Gunn, & Hain).

——(1988), *Essays on Ethics for Business and the Professions* (Englewood Cliffs, NJ: Prentice-Hall).

——(1994), 'Responsibility: the Key to Resolving the Crisis in Health Care', *Business & the Contemporary World* 6(1): 84–101.

——and Carter, G. (1975), *Problems of International Business Cooperation in Environmental Protection*, for the U.S. Environmental Protection Agency (New York: Fund for Multinational Management Education).

——and Fischer, W. (1980*b*), *Science and Technology for Development: Corporate and Government Policies and Practices* (Cambridge, Mass.: Oelgeschlager, Gunn, & Hain).

——and Rondinelli, D. A. (eds.) (2000), 'Economic Globalization: Who Gains and Who Loses?' *Global Focus-An International Journal of Business, Economics, and Social Policy*, Millennium Issue.

Bohm, D. (1980), *The Implicate Order and Wholeness* (Boston: Ark Paperbacks, 1980).

Breasted, J. H. (1933), *The Dawn of Conscience* (New York: Charles Scribners & Sons).

Briggs, J. P., and Peat, F. D. (1984), *Looking Glass Universe: The Emerging Science of Wholeness* (New York: Simon & Schuster).

Bryan, J. A. II, and Naso, W. B. (1989), *What About Being a Physician?* (Chapel Hill, NC: University of North Carolina, School of Medicine).

Business Week (1993), 6 Dec.: 76 and 133.

—— (2002), 14 Jan.: 20 and 46–8; 25 Feb.: 114–15.

Butler, R. N. (1975), *Why Survive? Being Old in America* (New York: Harper & Row).

Campbell, J. (1949), *The Hero with a Thousand Faces* (New York: Pantheon).

—— (1972), *Myths to Live By* (New York: Viking Press).

Cheng, M. (1981), *Lectures on the Tao Te Ching* (Richmond, Va.: North Atlantic Press).

Chopra, D. (1993), 'Timeless Mind, Ageless Body,' *Noetic Sciences Review* 28 (Winter): 49.

Cohen, J. M., and Phipps, J. E. (1993), *The Common Experience* (Wheaton, Ill.: Quest Books).

Collin, R. (1984), *The Theory of Conscious Harmony* (Boulder, Colo.: Shambala).

Csikszentmihalyi, M. (1993), *The Evolving Self* (New York: Harper).

Dalai Lama (1999), *Ethics for a New Millennium* (London: Riverhead).

Das, B. (1947), *The Essential Unity of All Religions* (Benares, India: Ananda Publishing House).

Davies, P. C. W. (1992), *The Mind of God* (New York: Simon & Schuster).

Davis, P. (1992), 'The Open Universe,' *Noetic Sciences Review* 22 (Summer): 35–6.

De Lubicz, E. S. (1956), *HER-BAK: Egyptian Initiate* (New York: Inner Traditions International; Eng. trans., 1978).

—— (1978), *HER-BAK: The Living Face of Ancient Egypt* (New York: Inner Traditions International).

Dossey, L. (1984), *Beyond Illness: Discovering the Experience of Health* (Boston: New Science Library).

Etzioni, A. (1988), *The Moral Dimension: Toward a New Economics* (New York: Free Press).

—— (1996), *The New Golden Rule: Community and Morality in a Democratic Society* (New York: Basic Books).

—— (1998), *The Essential Communitarian Reader* (Lanham, Md.: Rowman and Littlefield).

Financial Times (London) (1994), 1–2 Jan., sect. ii: PAGES?

Fisher, G. (1988), *Mind Sets* (Yarmouth, Me.: Intercultural Press).

Foos-Graber, A. (1989), *DEATHING: An Intelligent Alternative for the Final Moments of Life* (York Beach, Me.: Samuel Weiser).

Foster, D. (1975), *The Intelligent Universe: A Cybernetic Philosophy* (New York: G. P. Putnam's Sons).

Foster, R. I. (1987), *Celebration of Discipline: The Path to Spiritual Growth* (New York: Harper & Row).

Fukuyama, F. (1999), *The Great Disruption: Human Nature and the Reconstitution of Social Order* (New York: The Free Press, Simon & Schuster).

Fung, Y.-L. (1989), *CHUANG-TZU* (Beijing: Foreign Languages Press).

Gellner, E. (1988), *Plough, Sword, and Book: The Structure of Human History* (London: Collins-Harvill).

Gleick, J. (1987), *Chaos: Making a New Science* (New York: Viking).

Grof, S. (1984), *Ancient Wisdom and Modern Science* (Albany, NY: SUNY Press).

Harman, W. W. (1988), *Global Mind Change: The Promise of the 21st Century* (Sausalito, Calif.: Institute of Noetic Sciences).

—— (1990), *Creative Work: The Constructive Role of Business in a Transforming Society* (Indianapolis: Knowledge Systems).

—— and Clark, J. (eds.) (1994), *New Metaphysical Foundations of Modern Science* (Sausalito, Calif.: Noetic Sciences Institute).

Hirschman, A. O. (1977), *The Passions and the Interests: Political Arguments for Capitalism before its Triumph* (Princeton: Princeton University Press).

Hoetler, S. (1993), *Freedom: Alchemy for a Voluntary Society* (Wheaton, Ill: Quest Books).

Hoffman, W. M., and Frederick, R. E. (eds.) (1995), *Business Ethics: Readings and Cases in Corporate Morality* (New York: McGraw-Hill).

Hoyle, F. (1983), *The Intelligent Universe* (New York: Holt, Rinehart, and Winston).

Huxley, A. (1970), *The Perennial Philosophy* (New York: Harper-Colophon Books).

Keegan, J. (1993), *A History of Warfare* (New York: Knopf).

Kolb, C. (1993), *White House Daze* (New York: Free Press).

Krishnamurti, J. (1969), *Freedom from the Known* (New York: Harper & Row).

—— (1980), *From Darkness to Light* (New York: Harper & Row).

—— (1994), *On Learning and Knowledge* (San Francisco: Harper).

Kuhlewind, G. (1988), *From Normal to Healthy* (Hudson (NY: Lindisfarne Press).

Lemkow, A. (1993), *The Wholeness Principle* (Wheaton, Ill.: Quest Books).

LeShan, L. (1982), *The Mechanic and the Gardner* (New York: Holt, Rinehart & Winston).

Locke, S., and Colligan, D. (1986), *The Healer Within: The New Medicine of Mind and Body* (Sausalito, Calif.: Institute of Noetic Sciences).

Lovelock, I. E. (1979), *GAIA: A New Look at Life on Earth* (Oxford: Oxford University Press).

Melman, S. (2002), *After Capitalism: from Managerialism to Workplace Democracy* (New York: A. A. Knopf).

Miller, R. C. (19931. *As Above, So Below: Paths to Spiritual Renewal in Daily Life* (San Francisco: Tarcher).

Molinos, M. (1647), *The Spiritual Guide* (repub. by Seed Sowers, Sargent, Ga., n.d.).

Murphy, M. (1992), *The Future of the Body: Exploration into the Further Evolution of Human Nature* (Los Angeles: Tarcher).

Ni, H.-C. (1979), *The Complete Works of LAO TZU* (Malibu, Calif.: Shrine of the Eternal Breath of Tao).

Nicoll, M. (1984*a*), *Psychological Commentaries on the Teaching of Gurdjieff and Ouspensky*, vols. i–iv (Boston: Shambala).

—— (1984*b*), *Living Time and the Integration of the Life* (London: Shambala).

—— (1985), *The Mark* (Boston: Shambala).

Newsweek (1988), 'The Earth is One Big System', 7 Nov.: 88–97 and 98–9.

Ornish, D. (1993), 'Opening Your Heart: Physically, Emotionally, and Spiritually', *Noetic Sciences Review* 28 (Winter).

Oyama, M. (1967), *Prelude to Vital Karate* (Tokyo: Japan Publications Trading Co.).

Podhoretz. I. (1994), *Hell of a Ride* (New York: Simon & Schuster).

Prigogine, I., and Stengers, I. (1984), *Order out of Chaos: Man's New Dialogue with Nature* (New York: Bantam Books).

Pruzan, P. (2001), 'The Question of Organizational Consciousness: Can Organizations have Values, Virtues and Visions?' *Journal of Business Ethics* 29(3): 271–84.

Rifkin, J. (1995) *The End of Work* (New York: G. P. Putnam's Sons).

Rosenfeld, I. (1986), *Modern Prevention: The New Medicine* (New York: Linden Press/Simon & Shuster).

Roszak, T. (1992), *Voice of the Earth* (New York: Simon & Schuster).

Schuon, F. (1984), *The Transcendental Unity of Religions* (Wheaton, Ill.: Theosophical Publishing House).

Sen, A. K. (1997), *Human Rights and Asian Values* (New York: Carnegie Council on Ethics and International Affairs).

—— (1999*a*), *Development as Freedom* (New York: Knopf).

—— (1999*b*), *Reason before Identity* (Oxford: Oxford University Press).

Sheldrake, R. (1981), *A New Science of Life: The Hypothesis of Formative Causation* (Los Angeles: Tarcher).

Shorter, E. (1993), *From the Mind into the Body: The Cultural Origins of Psychosomatic Symptoms* (New York: The Free Press).

Singer, M., and Wildavsky, A. (1993), *The Real World Order* (Chatham, NJ: Chatham House).

Smart, N., and Hecht, R. D. (eds.)(1982), *Sacred Texts of the World: A Universal Anthology* (New York: Crossroads).

Steiner, R. (1994), *How to Know Higher Worlds: A Modern Path of Initiation* (Hudson, NY: Anthroposophic Press).

Sztompka, P. (1999), *Trust: A Sociological Theory* (Cambridge: Cambridge Press).

The Christian Science Monitor (1992), 22 May: 18.

—— (1993), 15 Dec.: 11–12.

—— (1994), 24 Jan.: 13.

The Economist (1994), 25 Dec.–7 Jan.: 39–42 and 93–5.

—— (2002) 16–22 Feb.: 13, 37, 44.

Thompson, W. I. (1987), *GAIA: A Way of Knowing: Political Implications of the New Biology* (Hudson, NY: Lindisfarne).

—— (1991), *GAIA-2: Emergence—The New Science of Becoming* (Hudson, NY: Lindisfarne).

Tomkins, F., and Passey, A. (2000), *Trust and Civil Society* (New York: St. Martin's Press).

Tulku, T. (1990), *Knowledge of Time and Space* (Berkeley, Calif.: Dharma Publishing).

Washington Post National Weekly (1993), 29 Nov.–5 Dec.: 35.

—— (2002), 28 Jan.–3 Feb.: 21.

Wiener, N. (1964), *God & Golem, Inc.* (Boston: MIT Press).

Wilhelm, R. (1962), *The Secret of the Golden Flower* (New York: Harcourt, Brace & Jovanovich).

Wilson, O. H. (ed.) (1987), *The Mind as Healer: The New Heresy* (Fremont, Calif.: Insights and Sources Corp.).

World Monitor (1990), June: 12–14.

World Press Review (1990), March: 80.

Zoeteman, K. (1989), *Gaiasofie* (Stuttgart: Deventer; trans. *Gaiasophy: The Wisdom of the Living Earth* (Hudson, NY: Lindisfarne, 1991).

Zukav, G. (1989), *The Seat of the Soul* (New York: Simon & Schuster).

PART II

6

An Ethical Framework for the Global Market Economy

HANS KÜNG

6.1 SUCCESS OR FAILURE OF GLOBAL MARKET ECONOMY? THE MORAL DIMENSION

After the breakdown of the Soviet empire in 1989, the market-based economy became generally accepted as the global economic model. While on the European continent, most people today only reluctantly acknowledge the benefits of socialism, it is widely agreed that a free market economy has to be both socially inclusive and ecologically responsible if it is to be both inclusive and sustainable over time.

The very latest experiences have proved that the sustainability of the market economic system is by no means guaranteed. The Asian financial crisis of the 1990s clearly demonstrated that a free market economy is not without its costs, and the continuing crisis in Russia's economy is an excellent, albeit an unfortunate, example of how a transformation to a market-based system is not without its problems. Indeed, one cannot escape the fact that the emergence of global capitalism brings with it an entirely new set of risks. We wisely have to expect an 'endangering of the system as a whole in the case of intensified crises, e.g. so-called system risks in the financial markets' (Tietmeyer 2001).

Trying to find a single reason for, or solution to, the challenges of the global market economy in a particular country or in a particular region is unlikely to be successful. In fact, what we often observe is that, in such a situation, mutual recriminations occur: economists accuse politicians and politicians accuse economists; while the average citizen frequently sees the moral defects of both protagonists. In any case, it is already evident that if one of the three elements, whether it be economics, politics, or morality, does not work, it can cause serious difficulties for the capitalist system.

In seeking to present my own views on this issue, I am heartened to find that my analyses are largely confirmed by the views and explanations of John Dunning in his recent book *Global Capitalism at Bay* (Dunning 2001). In particular, Dunning distinguishes between three types of failures of the capitalist system.

1. A failure of markets: moral hazard, inappropriate macroeconomic politics, excessive speculation (property and stock market), an inappropriately valued currency, manipulated exchange rates, cross-border and intra-firm transfer prices, bad timing of short-term debts, presence of a strong black market, and the abuse of monopoly power.

2. A failure of institutions: inefficient functioning of the regulatory and supervisory systems, an inadequate legal and financial infrastructure, shortcomings in the protection of ownership rights, lack of accountability and/or transparency, and inadequate standards in financial reporting.
3. A deficiency of moral virtues, which lies at the core of the failure of the markets and institutions. Such failures include crony- and Mafia-capitalism, bribery and corruption, lack of truthfulness, trust and social responsibility, and excessive greed of the investors or institutions.

Dunning investigated these different factors as they affected the recent economic crises in seven countries, *viz.* Japan, Korea, Indonesia, Thailand, Hong Kong, Malaysia, and Russia. He found out that each of them demonstrated failures on all three levels. While each had its own particular imperfections, all demonstrated serious systemic defects in their particular brand of capitalism. In his original diagram presented here as Figure 6.1, Dunning tried to connect the failures in the economic and institutional fields with the failure of morality.

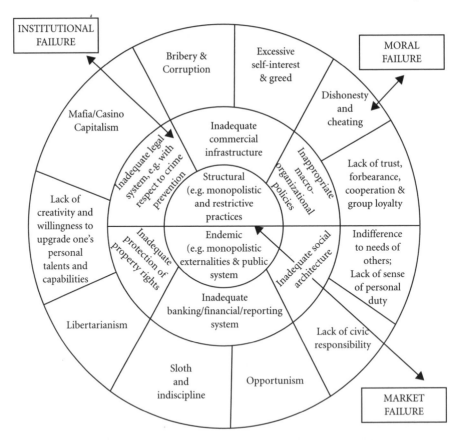

Figure 6.1. *Illustrations of three ways in which global capitalism might fail.*
Source: Dunning 2000, 2001.

In this context, he was able to identify the following relationships.

- The inadequate infrastructure for international commercial transactions is often associated with bribery and corruption and with excessive self-interest and greed.
- Bad functioning at the macro-organizational level is often correlated with dishonesty and fraud, a lack of trust, or the ability to compromise, and inadequate group loyalty.
- Inadequacies in the legal system, e.g. regarding crime prevention, are frequently related to Mafia- and casino-capitalism.
- An insufficient banking, finance, and accountability system can sometimes be a nesting ground for opportunism, slackness, and lack of discipline.
- An ineffective social architecture with indifference towards the needs of others can encourage a lack of personal sense of duty and social responsibility.
- The shortcomings in the protection of the rights of ownership are often associated with a carelessly irresponsible attitude.

All this leads Dunning to conclude that moral virtues are not marginal or artificially put on features in shaping global capitalism, but that it is justified to talk of a moral ecology which is both interactive and interdependent with the economic function of the main institutions of capitalism, *viz.* markets, governments, civil society, and supranational organizations.

6.2 NECESSITY FOR AN ETHICAL FRAMEWORK

One conclusion we draw from the Dunning model is that ethics do not only denote moral appeals, but moral action. Nevertheless a strain is often present in the economy, as within the contemporary stock market, in order to create the pressure to reform which can turn into a political agenda. Meanwhile, the recent protests against globalization have raised the question of the social acceptability of the new globalized economic system. This acceptance would still not be guaranteed even if the global companies and markets, the national governments, national institutions, and intermediate organizations worked efficiently. For today, it is the ethical framework on which they are based which is being increasingly questioned, even though this framework must not be equated with an overadministration of ethics in every detail.

We strongly believe that in the long run, global capitalism will only be sustainable if it is socially acceptable. After all, in a democratic society the majority of the electorate has to be repeatedly convinced on at least three issues:

1. that the economic system is rewarding for themselves and for those for whom they feel responsible in any way;
2. that economic participation ('inclusiveness') and social justice are integral parts of the objectives of this economic system; and
3. that a strong ethical framework supports both the operation and effects of the global markets and the extra market institutions and that this framework

influences the behaviour and the decisions of those who are directly involved in the process of production and distribution.

Not least does a look at history show that successful economies have always been supported by a strong moral basis (Lal, Chapter 2 of this volume). The economic systems, valid up to a certain point, started to collapse at the very moment their ethical basis was undermined, or a new social system appeared as a feasible alternative. In the words of Dunning again,

It is necessary for individual and social moral virtues to be strengthened and reconfigured in a way that is consistent with a knowledge-intensive, alliance-based, multicultural society, and will best enable market and extra-market institutions to work together to promote efficient growth and social justice. Only then will the global market place be an acceptable servant of individuals and society and not an unacceptable master. (Dunning 2001: 40)

6.3 CROSS-CULTURAL ETHICAL VALUES AND STANDARDS. IS A GLOBAL CONSENSUS POSSIBLE?

Every word can be understood and every term interpreted in different ways. One should not then be surprised that morally loaded terms like 'integrity' may have various meanings depending on the cultural context in which they are used. It is generally known that the word 'integrity' stems from the Latin 'tangere' = 'to touch'. The Latin 'integer' means 'untouched', 'unscathed', 'respectable', 'unharmed', 'whole'. Integrity can therefore be interpreted as being free from moral or ethical misdemeanours and being respectable and incorruptible. (This, incidentally, is not to be confused with being completely free of faults or errors or even being infallible.) However, most Americans tend to construe the term integrity as keeping to given laws rather than interpreting them in the wider Latin or German sense.

How can this difficulty be resolved? We may offer two suggestions.

1. It is not necessary to use such terms formally, but rather to fill them with meaning. If, in German, the meaning of the word 'integrity' extends to being incorruptible, honest, and truthful, and there is a general agreement of the words and actions spoken or written, then this is a clear example for the necessity to start interpreting 'global ethic' with a more concrete and comprehensive meaning.
2. It will be possible to interpret even a single expression unambiguously if it is not used in an absolute manner, but with respect to a specific situation. If, in a particular context, people are reminded of 'integrity' in the face of a particular event of corruption, then it will be obvious in Germany as well as in America what this means. Or, to widen the question and quote an example given by the American sociologist Michael Walzer:

When the citizens of Prague took to the streets in the revolutionary year of 1989 and their banners simply demanded 'justice' or 'truth', the special situation made their intentions completely clear: 'Justice' referred to the abolishment of particular party privileges, an unbiased legislation and the termination of random imprisonment, and 'truth' demanded an end to the official lies and persistently misleading information through the media. Across all national, cultural and religious boundaries, these words were understood so well in all the world that an international solidarity with the people in Czechoslovakia evolved. (Michael Walzer 1994: 1)

In this way, such terms can, and do express something like a bundle of elemental ethical values and standards, or core ethics. Nevertheless, abstract terms cannot suffice in the formulation of a global ethic that is capable of implementation; rather the moral values and standards have to be filled with meaning.

6.4 CONTENTS OF A CROSS-CULTURAL ETHICAL FRAMEWORK

The UN Global Compact, which was initiated by the general secretary Kofi Annan in 1999 offers a valuable starting point.[1] The claims it makes on the global economic system are threefold: (i) respect of, and support for, human rights, (ii) the elimination of all forms of forced or child labour, and (iii) a response to ecological challenges. These claims are based on the conviction that everywhere on earth—i.e. in all societies, cultures, and religions—people need to recognize and accept comparable ethical pillars which allow them to live together peacefully without conflict or compromise to their interests and concerns.

In this respect, the contents of the UN Global Compact are very much in accord with the ideas of the Chicago *Declaration Toward a Global Ethic* of the Parliament of the World's Religions in 1993. Both documents focus on the absolute respect of human dignity. But whereas the UN Global Compact takes human rights, the outline of general working conditions, and environmental protection as its starting point, and presupposes the broad acceptance of the underlying ethical principles, the Declaration of the Parliament of the World's Religions starts from a number of ethical principles, and then seeks to tackle social and ecological demands from this perspective. In consequence, the Global Compact does not directly embrace such concepts as truthfulness or fairness which are the prerequisites for trust, which, in its turn, is an indispensable attribute not only of true democracy and a state founded on the rule of law, but also of a sustainable market based economy. Trust or mistrust are then the outcome of truthful or untruthful, fair or unfair behaviour.

At this point, the OECD guidelines for multinational enterprises (MNEs) (OECD 2000) can be quoted. These contain very specific ethical guidelines, notably

- how any claim for disclosure requires the will to truthfulness, honesty, transparency;
- how any claim for environmental protection as well as public health and safety requires reverence for life, all life including that of animals and plants;
- how any claim to refrain from slush corruption and bribery requires both a basic attitude towards justice and fairness and the will to encompass a just economic system;

- how any claim to avoid any kind of sex, colour, or age discrimination at the workplace, implies the ethical conviction of the partnership of man and woman and the necessity for equal rights.

Lest anyone assumes that we are making only abstract and general statements they should read the already mentioned *Declaration Toward a Global Ethic.* There, principles stemming from ancient ethical and religious traditions are applied to contemporary situations (see for example the chapter about 'solidarity and just economic systems'). Alternatively one should read the suggestion for a *Universal Declaration of Human Responsibilities* as it was presented in 1997 by the Inter-Action Council of former heads of state or government, then chaired by the former German Bundeskanzler Helmut Schmidt. The nineteen articles of this document express the same principles in more legal terms. They deserve to be thoroughly discussed at a future UN general assembly. Even an exchange of views on the content and form of such principles would help to raise the awareness in the world community about shared values, standards, and attitudes. However, the declaration also deserves to be taken as a broad basis for the ethical charter of every large company.

All this leads us to conclude that the question of upgrading cross-cultural global values and behavioural standards, which is crucial for the success of global capitalism, can indeed be satisfactorily addressed.

6.5   WHICH ARE THE COMMON HUMAN BASIC VALUES AND STANDARDS?

The elementary human values and standards of the major ethical-religious traditions, as they are expressed in the declarations mentioned above, were formed by individuals who, themselves, are part of a highly complex socio-dynamic process in the course of evolution. This means that where needs of life and human urgencies revealed themselves, regulations for human behaviour became unavoidable; and with these, priorities, conventions, laws, precepts, regulations, ethical values, and social norms took root. And thus, a lot of what is proclaimed as God's commandment in the Hebrew Bible, in the New Testament, and in the Koran can also be found in the religions and philosophies of Indian and Chinese origins.

But this also means that people have to continuously experiment with ethical norms and solutions within developing concepts and models; and practise and test them over generations. After periods of such testing and practice, new norms are eventually recognized, but sometimes—e.g. when times change completely— they are undermined and abolished again. In other words, morality, like economic systems and technological advances, goes through frequent periods of creative destruction. The question is whether or not we are currently living in such a time.

Throughout the planet, there is great concern about events as they are unfolding; and, more than anything else, 11 September 2001 brought these vividly to the fore. It is commonly felt that despite, and partly because of, globalization, the world in which we live is religiously and politically torn apart, full of military conflicts and lacking in moral inspiration or orientation. We also live in an age in which many traditional mores have lost their credibility; when many institutions have been drawn into deep identity crises; and when ethical standards and norms are frequently either marginalized or unstable, with the result that many, particularly young people, hardly know what is good and bad in different areas of life.

All this points to the need for a new moral consensus within global society, and a return to an acceptance and practice of minimum human values and standards. For this, the whole armoury of spiritual and intellectual resources available to humanity from all religious and philosophical traditions should be used, as it has been in the respective declarations of a global ethic. No single religion or philosophy can force its particular values and standards upon the others. But from the richness of their spiritual and intellectual resources, each religion or philosophy can contribute to a new and sustainable moral ecology underpinning global society.

Therefore, the reception of the idea of a global ethic at the highest levels of the Christian churches, and the agreement between them which is beginning to emerge, gives cause for hope.

In his report at the eighth general assembly in Harare 1998, the Moderator of the World Council of Churches, Catholicos Aram I, explained:

We are committed to the development of a basic common ethic that may lead societies from mere existence to meaningful co-existence, from confrontation to reconciliation, from degeneration of moral values to the restoration of the quality of life that restores the presence of transcendence in human life. Global culture must be sustained by a global ethic that will guide the relations of nations with each other and with the creation, and will help them to work together for genuine world community. Such a global ethic, the idea of which was launched by the Parliament of the World's Religions in 1993 should not reflect the Western Christian ethos; it must be based on a diversity of experiences and convictions. The church, together with other living faiths, should seek a global ethic based on shared ethical values that transcend religious beliefs and narrow definitions of national interests. Human rights must be undergirded by ethical principles. Therefore dialogue among different religions and cultures is crucial as the basis for greater solidarity for justice and peace, human rights and dignity. Religions must work together to identify areas and modes of cooperation in human rights advocacy.[2]

Again, in his speech to the Papal Academy of Social Sciences on 27th April 2001, Pope John Paul II declared in the context of globalization:

As humanity embarks upon the process of globalisation, it can no longer do without a common code of ethics. This does not mean a single dominant socio-economic system or culture which would impose its values and its criteria on ethical reasoning. It is within man as such, within universal humanity sprung from the Creator's hand, that the norms of social life are to be sought. Such a search is indispensable if globalisation is not to be just another name for the absolute relativization of values and the homogenization of life-styles and cultures. In all the variety of cultural forms, universal human values exist and they must be brought out and emphasised as the guiding force of all development and progress.[3]

So what are the human values and standards which, in our contemporary and globalizing world, can be regarded as universally valid and acceptable? On the basis of our previous observations on the concept of a global ethic, we have shown that the basic values which underlie all other values are: humanity and reciprocity. Derived from them are a number of *core* values which are identified and explained in Table 6.1. We present these without comment.[4]

Table 6.1. *Table of values, with arguments from the 'Declaration Toward a Global Ethic' by the Parliament of the World's Religions, Chicago 1993*[5]

Basic Values

• **Humanity**
In the face of all inhumanity it should be a shared basic ethical principle that *every human being must be treated humanely!* This means that every human being without distinction of age, sex, race, skin color, physical or mental ability, language, religion, political view, or national or social origin possesses an inalienable and *untouchable dignity*, and everyone, the individual as well as the state, is therefore obliged to honor this dignity and protect it. Political and economic power must be utilized for *service to humanity* instead of misusing it in ruthless battles for domination.

• **Reciprocity**
There is a principle which is found and has persisted in many religious and ethical traditions of humankind for thousands of years: *What you do not wish done to yourself, do not do to others.* Or in positive terms: *What you wish done to yourself, do to others!* This should be the irrevocable, unconditional norm for all areas of life, for families and communities, for races, nations, and religions.

Core Values

• **Respect for life**
A human person is infinitely precious and must be unconditionally protected. But likewise the *lives of animals and plants* which inhabit this planet with us deserve protection, preservation, and care. As human beings we have a special responsibility—especially with a view to future generations—for earth and the cosmos, for the air, water, and soil. We are *all intertwined together* in this cosmos and we are all dependent on each other. Each one of us depends on the welfare of all. All people have a right to life, safety, and the free development of personality insofar as they do not injure the rights of others. No one has the right physically or psychically to torture, injure, much less kill, any other human being.

• **Non-violence**
Wherever there are humans there will be conflicts. Such conflicts, however, should be resolved without violence within a framework of justice. This is true for states as well as for individuals. Persons who hold political power must work within the framework of a just order and commit themselves to the most non-violent, peaceful solutions possible. And they should work for this within an international order of peace which itself has need for protection and defense against perpetrators of violence.

• **Solidarity**
No one has the right to use her or his possessions without concern for the needs of society and earth. Property, limited though it may be, carries with it an obligation, and its use should at the same time serve the common good. Humankind must develop a spirit of compassion with those who suffer, with special care for the children, the aged, the poor, the disabled, the refugees, and the lonely.

Table 6.1. *(continued)*

- **Justice**

  The world economy must be structured more justly. Individual good deeds, and assistance projects, indispensable though they be, are insufficient. The participation of all states and the authority of international organizations are needed to build just economic institutions. A distinction must be made between necessary and limitless consumption, between socially beneficial and non-beneficial uses of property, between justified and unjustified use of natural resources, and between a profit-only and a socially beneficial and ecologically oriented market economy.

- **Tolerance**

  No people, no state, no race, no religion has the right to hate, to discriminate against, to 'cleanse', to exile, much less to liquidate a 'foreign' minority which is different in behavior or holds different beliefs. Every people, every race, every religion must show tolerance and respect—indeed high appreciation—for every other. Minorities need protection and support, whether they be racial, ethnic, or religious.

- **Truthfulness**

  Everybody should think, speak, and act *truthfully*. All people have a right to information to be able to make the decisions that will form their lives. Without an ethical formation they will hardly be able to distinguish the important from the unimportant. Freedom should not be confused with arbitrariness or pluralism with indifference to truth. *Truthfulness* should *be cultivated* in our relationships instead of dishonesty, dissembling, and opportunism. Truth should be *constantly sought* and incorruptible sincerity instead of spreading ideological or partisan half-truths.

- **Equality**

  The relationship between women and men should be characterized not by patronizing behaviour or exploitation, but by love, partnership, and trustworthiness. All over the world there are condemnable forms of patriarchy, domination of one sex over the other, exploitation of women, sexual misuse of children, and forced prostitution. No one has the right to degrade others to mere sex objects, to force them into or hold them in sexual dependency.

- **Partnership**

  Partnership is expressed through mutual respect and understanding, mutual concern, tolerance, readiness for reconciliation, and *love*. Only what has already been experienced in personal and family relationships can be practiced on the level of nations and religions.

6.6   ETHICALLY FOUNDED MANAGEMENT

All this is not to suggest we are proposing a moralism which is specific to the needs of global capitalism. Indeed, it is not an ethic which is imposed on the economy deductively, but rather one which suggests itself from the economic processes. The market economy and the ethic which underpins it are not mutually exclusive. No ethic can demand that an employer acts against his own interests, permanently and systematically. On the contrary (as Chapter 13 will demonstrate in more detail), ethically responsible managerial strategies have a chance of success today since the public's attention has been drawn to the issue of the morality of the market place, and often shows disapproving reactions to morally questionable conduct.

It is not an easy question, how under rational criteria of costs and benefits, the conduct of companies can be reconciled with the ethical standards we are recommending. Dr Wolfram Freudenberg, a member of the board of trustees of the Global Ethic Foundation, has briefly reflected upon this question (oral intervention at the Symposium *Globale Unternehmen und Globales Ethos*, Baden-Baden, Germany, 23 March 2001). Let me summarize his views, dealing first with some doubts expressed about the desirability or practicality of a global ethic for corporations, and then turning to the perceived advantages.

Objections: The doubts most often expressed refer to the competitive pressures and the primacy of striving for efficiency and profit. Generally the reasoning goes as follows.

- It is indeed legitimate to show tolerance towards different customs, and to adapt to them—especially if these amount to 'proper selfishness' (Dunning, Chapter 1 of this volume).
- If the insistence on high ethical standards is too strong, competitors with less scruples will win.
- The management will tend to avoid risks (and not endanger their own careers) rather than search for unconventional and new solutions.

Advantages: Here the central contentions are as follows.

- Striving for profit is subject to spontaneous behaviour and not just in response to ethical externally imposed regulations. Thus, long-term goals tend to gain more importance compared to short-term ones. A negative public opinion is avoided and the chance of social acceptance of the business in question increases.
- The prerequisites of co-ordinated and calculable behaviour within the cultural and social diversity of a global economic environment, are improved. The stability and consistency of complex units, which—depending on size and diversity—are increasingly organized and managed at a subsidiary level are enhanced.
- Putting ethical standards into practice emphasizes long-term goals. Thus, the management concentrates more intensely on the fundamental and strategic interests of the company and its stakeholders. This entails a move away from hectic day-to-day routine.
- Qualified personnel, not only with professional but also with social competences, are attracted to the business.
- There is a positive influence on prices, goals, composition, and character of shareholders. Since the introduction of the Dow Jones Sustainability Group Index, in the US in 1999, a trend towards ethical–ecological investments has spread; thus, more transparency and public interest in ethical–ecological questions has been created.
- There is likely to be more stability and reliability of business relations with suppliers and buyers who operate according to similar principles.
- If the company has a good image and its long-term commitment to ethical standards is credible, an improvement in dealing with ecologically and politically delicate projects can be expected.

All this leads us to conclude that there is likely to be a positive relationship between a corporation's ethical standards and (i) its performance in the long run, (ii) its socio-political acceptance and image, (iii) the quality (including the environmentally friendly quality) of its products, and (iv) its ability to recruit and retain productive and co-operative employees. Moreover, such a strategy is entirely in conformity with the principles of social market economy, since it allows a balance between the freedom and responsibility of management, a long-term view of corporate goals, and a better appreciation of the objectives and opinions of the most important 'stakeholders', in the value-added process.

6.7 ETHICAL COMPETENCE

Only somebody who possesses a strong ethic himself can give clear and instructive orientation to others, as is required by strong leadership. This is achieved through pre-set goals and values, the strict observance of standards and regulations, and a positive and sympathetic approach towards both employee participation and customer satisfaction. As one successful manager, Professor Reinhold Würth has recently put it,

Whether a company is run more in the style of a big family or a strictly rational organization or a monarchical hierarchy, the decisive prerequisite for its survival and its long-term success is, after all, 'integrity', which very concretely means: that one can rely on the company in every respect, that one is never fooled, lied to or outmanoeuvred, but that despite all business efficiency one feels always treated in a decent and honest manner. (Oral intervention at Baden-Baden 2001)

All this means that the management of a company should promote a clearly defined stance on the question of ethics. And this should be done in the awareness that in today's global environment the spirit of a company will increasingly depend strongly on the entrepreneurial and co-operative spirit of the labour force, in addition to that of senior managers and the board of directors. A descriptive picture of the ethical competence of a company based on the extent and composition of its human resources and capabilities is presented in Figure 6.2.

In taking our argument further, let us give an analogy. Anyone who has had to navigate a large ship through a stormy sea at night, knows the risks of navigational errors which may lead to the destruction of the vessel, a loss of human lives, and environmental damages. Today, however, there are many navigational instruments for all kinds of measurements and calculations, which help direct and control the ship's movements to an optimal extent, so that it can reach port as fast, economically, and safely as possible. Indeed, the modern 'integrated' navigation systems frequently employ more informational measuring devices than necessary, in order to ensure this objective is met.

At the same time, even with the most sophisticated equipment, a navigator, steersman or pilot still depends on a navigational chart. This chart, which is veined with unchangeable co-ordinates, is determined by a certain scale and marked by the north–south direction as given unalterably by the compass. Only

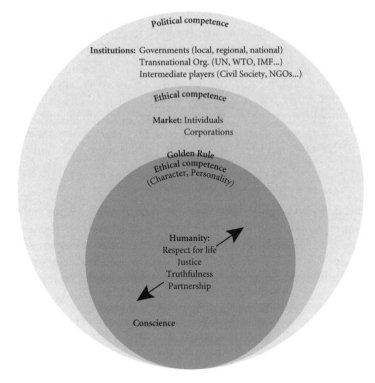

Figure 6.2. *Leadership based on competence: an ethical framework for the individual person.*

on this basis can the position at a given moment and the course which is to be steered be determined, and the necessary decisions be correctly made.

This image may be easily applied to the economic dimension. A chief executive who has to navigate a global enterprise through the storms of globalization, and is not only responsible for a single department but for the course of the company in general, has at his disposal a variety of technical, financial and organizational information, and technical aids, so that he can regularly assess its condition and position. Indeed, a visual image of the project is often projected on a screen for him with the different options—supported by statistics, diagrams, and prognoses—and they help to make the decisions. For those decisions, analytical skills, judgemental competence, and the ability to assert oneself are undoubtedly essential if complex connections are to be recognized and dealt with in the shortest possible time, and for both human and physical resources and capabilities to be utilized efficiently.

But also in managing a company, certain qualities beyond technical and organizational instruments and a solid psychological constitution are required. Referring to the navigational image again, these include:

1. A clear identification and awareness of the goals of the company. Such an identification and awareness is not only necessary for the well-being of the

company and its shareholders, but that of its other stakeholders, e.g. the clients, employees, and suppliers. Indeed, the function of business aims should be viewed in a wider context, which comprises the welfare of the citizens of the societies in which they operate (for example in the form of creating work-places, paying taxes, supporting the cultural scene).

2. A sense of orientation, which is more than mere knowledge of information, and which in an integrated perspective keeps the overview, thus making a realistic evaluation and promotion of the appropriate business strategy a workable proposition.

3. A system of co-ordinates which embrace globally valid, unchangeable ethical standards; and which are independent of time or space, and encompass as their standards the principle of humanity together with the Golden Rule.

4. A set of ethical guidelines which includes an uncompromising conscience, which works irrespective of upheavals and changes in global, economic and political events (fusions, takeovers, trimming, decentralization, mismanage-ment), and which may exert a critical influence on important decisions in the tough reality of everyday business.

An awareness of the aims, a sense of orientation, high moral standards, and an inner compass—all of these are structural elements of the ethics of business behaviour and of the individuals managing and working within corporations.

6.8   HOW CAN A GLOBAL ETHIC BECOME GENERALLY ACCEPTED?

This is a question repeatedly asked, and not only by sceptics. The answer is in no way other than by an acceptance and practice of the UN Global Compact, which is now claimed to have gained UN status. But it is worth remembering, it was a long process before this international consensus with respect to human rights, humane working conditions, and demands for the protection of the environment, was reached. For all these questions—similar to those about peace and disarmament and gender equality and the absence of racial discrimination—to be tackled ser-iously at a global forum took a long time. Yet such changes as these are the prereq-uisites for a change in the awareness of humankind towards a general human ethic.

Many people can help in this matter; not only the intellectual, spiritual, and political leaders of the world, but the mass of ordinary people of goodwill who already do what they can to promote and practise an understanding of a new global ethic. For the sake of a peaceful social existence on a local (in innumerable 'multi-cultural' and 'multi-religious' towns and villages), as well as at a national and global level, the need for a shared common ethic is now more important than ever.

Thus what happens in their narrower or wider areas of life largely depends on the individual person and his or her motivation. When some time ago I asked the magnanimous founder of our Global Ethic Foundation—Count von der Groeben—about the impulse for his initiative, he reached for his wallet and showed me a small old piece of paper. It carried words by Mahatma Gandhi about the 'Seven social sins in today's world', which reads as follows:

> Wealth without work,
> Consumption without conscience,
> Knowledge without character,
> Business without morals,
> Science without humanity,
> Religion without sacrifice and
> Politics without principles.

NOTES

1. As described for example by Kell and Ruggie (1999).
2. Website: www.wcc-coe.org/wcc/assembly/modrep-e.html
3. Website: www.vatican.va/cgi-bin/w3-msql/news_services/bulletin/news/8998.html
4. For further details the reader is invited to consult Küng 1991, 1998, and 2002.
5. Published in German in Küng 2001: 154–6.

REFERENCES

Dunning, J. H. (2000), 'Whither Global Capitalism', *Global Focus* 12(1): 117–36.

——(2001), *Global Capitalism at Bay* (London: Routledge).

Enderle, Georges (ed.) (1998), *International Business Ethics: Challenges and Approaches* (Indiana: Notre Dame University Press).

Kell, G. and Ruggie G. (1999), 'Global Markets and Social Legitimacy: The Case of the Global Compact', *Transnational Corporations* 8(3): 101 ff.

Küng, Hans (1991), *Global Responsibility: In Search of a New World Ethic* (Munich: Piper).

——(1998), *A Global Ethic for Global Politics and Economics* (Oxford: Oxford University Press).

——(ed.) (2001), *Globale Unternehmen—Globales Ethos* (Frankfurt: FAZ-Verlag).

——(2002), *Tracing the Way: Spiritual Dimensions of the World Religions* (London and New York: Continuum).

——and Schmidt, Helmut (eds.) (1998), *A Global Ethic and Global Responsibilities: Two Declarations* (London: SCM Press; New York 1999).

Tietmeyer, H. (2001), 'Gestaltung von Rahmenbedingungen für globale Märkte.' In Küng, H. (ed.), *Globale Unternehmen und Globales Ethos* (Frankfurt: Rahmenordnung).

Walzer, M. (1994), *Thick and Thin: Moral Argument at Home and Abroad* (Indiana: Notre Dame University Press).

Further information including a bibliography can be found on the website: www.weltethos.org.

7

The Challenge of Global Capitalism:
A Christian Perspective

BRIAN GRIFFITHS

7.1 INTRODUCTION

Ten years after the fall of the Berlin Wall, the 'battle of Seattle' in December 1999 marked the beginning of a series of large protests against global capitalism. In the following two years, in Washington, Nice, Quebec, Gothenberg, and Genoa, students, intellectuals, single-issue interest groups, trade unionists, committed activists, religious groups, and anarchists left no one in any doubt of their views of the IMF and World Bank, the neo-liberalism of the EU, the Free Trade Area of the Americas, the G7 and G8 conferences or the WTO. They were protesting at what they perceived to be the inequities and injustices of the current global economic system, and that was capitalism.

Much of their rhetoric has been couched in neo-Marxist language. Capitalism is after all a word invented by Marx and the protest movement is above all anti-capitalism. The major drivers of change are perceived as technology, through the revolution in computing, information, and communications, and the introduction of policies of de-regulation, privatization, and liberalization. The result is a world of inequality and conflict. Global companies are cast in the role of the exploiting class, using their superior know-how and 'monopoly' power to capture international institutions such as the IMF, World Bank, and WTO, and influence Western governments, especially the US, who in turn bend the rules of trade and investment in their favour. The exploited are the world's proletariat, the dispossessed, the excluded, and the poor and, as with Marx, there is an inevitable conflict between the capitalists and the proletariat. For a minority the cry is for revolution, for the majority engagement, activism, and protest; in the words of Anita Roddick 'spread the word, campaign, change your life style, make ethical consumer choices, be a proactive employee, invest ethically, above all connect to other people'.

The anti-capitalist movement however does not depend on a neo-Marxist framework. After the rhetoric has been stripped of its ideology, the protest movement is making a number of quite specific charges against the current global economic system: that it results in an increasing inequality of income and wealth, both within countries and between countries; that the trade policies of the WTO are unjust and penalize developing countries; that, compared to democratically elected governments, international institutions take decisions behind closed doors and lack accountability; that global companies pay insufficient attention to the environment, exploit cheap labour, infringe human rights, and spur governments on to a 'race to the bottom' in standards; and that globalization is resulting in the development of a homogeneous, *laissez-faire*, and materialistic culture, which is threatening the very existence of minority cultures and the survival of their languages.

Even among those who would not take to the streets and would welcome aspects of globalization, there remains an unease about the way capitalism is developing in the West. People are suspicious about the growing power and influence of large corporations, and the way in which the language and methods of business have penetrated the provision of public services. Many find it impossible to justify the salaries and compensation of the winners in the new economy and, over recent years, the feeling has grown that society has become increasingly impersonal and less human, and that this is a product of the way capitalism has developed since the 1980s.

At one level, the challenge of global capitalism is about economic issues, encouraging increased trade and investment flows to developing countries, increasing the transparency of their fiscal and monetary management, enabling the transition to competitive market economies and strengthening the poverty reduction programmes of individual governments. But these subjects raise questions of morality which cannot be answered within the context of economics. They require an explicit framework of ethics or religion. Hans Küng argues that the emerging global economy needs a new global ethic (see Chapter 6). Because they are easily perverted and breed hypocrisy, George Soros is sceptical about invocations of moral principles. Yet he is adamant that because no society can exist without morality, we need to define the new responsibilities which must accompany the growth of global markets and global society (Soros 2002: 164). The report to the Catholic bishops of the European community, chaired by Michel Camdessus, the former managing director of the IMF, stated that,

In the future world of globalisation, mankind will need to accept new values in order to alleviate the plight of the poor. (COMECE 2001: 6)

The Christian faith is a source of just such values. They have relevance to the issues raised by global capitalism and the purpose of this essay is to explore them.

7.2 FOUNDATIONS FOR A CHRISTIAN PERSPECTIVE

Any attempt to develop a Christian approach to these issues faces a major problem, namely the contradictions which exist at a theological level between different Christian approaches. These range from creation ethics, which grounds an ethical response in the nature of the created world and the moral principles contained in the Decalogue; to the ethics of the Kingdom, which focuses on the radical change brought about by the life and teaching of Jesus; and to situation ethics, which rejects any attempt to apply universally valid and prescriptive rules, and emphasizes in their place the uniqueness of each situation and the need for a response based on love and not rules (Bultmann 1935; Fletcher 1966; Robinson 1964).

Situation ethics is surely right to emphasize the importance that should be paid to the particular characteristics of each situation in which an ethical decision is made, as well as the overriding significance of love in Jesus' teaching. Nevertheless, it is difficult to read the text of scripture without recognizing that certain absolute standards are set out clearly, and held to be universally valid. The uniqueness of the Incarnation must be at the centre of any Christian approach, but the limitation of Kingdom ethics is that, while they are relevant to those who belong to the Kingdom, they lack universal validity. Creation ethics have universal validity, but they are criticized for being remote and abstract, and taking too little account of the changing secular world in which we now live.

On the basis of the texts of the Old and New Testaments, a Christian perspective must take into account three elements: the nature of the world God has created, the covenants and the moral law of the Old Testament, and the Incarnation itself. We need to expand on each of these.

7.2.1 Creation and Fall

The opening words of the Old Testament, 'In the beginning God created the heavens and the earth' (Genesis 1: 1) are bold and unambiguous. The act of creation is the work of an infinite, all wise, all loving, and personal creator so that the universe is not the result of some chance process with an impersonal beginning. The Judaeo-Christian claim is that men and women have been created in the image of God, and it is this that accounts for our capacity for thinking, moral awareness, creativity, responsibility, the authority over creation, and the ability to know God. It is because each human being has been created in the image of God that he or she possesses dignity, worth, and the freedom to choose. Creation is not a once for all act, but an ongoing process, which in the poetry of the Psalms, is described as God working to uphold the universe. It comes as no surprise then that human work is a natural part of the created order. It is both a God-given responsibility and a source of satisfaction.

The tragedy of the created order however is that it has been marred by our rebellion against God. The world in which we live is a fallen world and at the heart of human life is a self-centredness which puts ourselves in the place of God. The Christian understanding is that while sin has affected every aspect of our world, the image of God is still evident.

This understanding of creation and the fall has profound implications for economic life. One is that wealth creation is a process which is necessary, legitimate, and beneficial. The creation mandate is clear and unambiguous. It is that we are to be fruitful, to increase in number, to subdue the earth, and to rule over the creation. The original Hebrew words which describe this mandate, subdue (*rabach*) and rule (*radah*), are strong words, meaning to stamp out, to bring into subjection, to tread on. In the Garden of Eden the task of wealth creation was straightforward. It was to till the land and to maintain it in good order. In different economies—agricultural, manufacturing, knowledge, global—the techniques of wealth creation will differ. In each case however, the force of the original Hebrew words suggests that the transformation of the material world involves the physical and intellectual challenge of hard and productive work, while at the same time it confirms human authority in directing the process. As part of wealth creation each human being has the potential for creativity, so that even in a fallen world, work will provide an element of personal fulfilment. Implicit also in the creation mandate is personal responsibility. God has made us trustees of his creation. We are given the task of using our physical and creative powers to transform the resources of the physical world for our benefit, but this is not a license to permanently damage and destroy the physical universe in the process.

7.2.2   Covenant and Law

Another element of a Christian perspective derives from the political economy of Israel, which is described in detail in the Pentateuch. When the Jewish people crossed the river Jordan into the promised land, the Pentateuch describes an 'experiment' in which a social, economic, political, and religious order was constructed which reflected the will of God. At the heart of this 'experiment' was the moral law, the ten commandments, which summarized the basic religious and moral principles which were to guide the Jewish people. In the Torah these are then applied in great detail to every aspect of their life. The economic prescriptions were tailored to the specific needs of a nomadic Middle Eastern people who were in the process of becoming settlers, but the structures of economic life which were laid down for Israel embodied principles of lasting significance. For example, the Jubilee 2000 campaign for debt relief to the poorest of third world countries was inspired by the Jewish year of Jubilee, in which debts were cancelled and property returned to its original owners. The concept of the Sabbath as a legislated day of rest has been at the heart of the movement to impose restrictions on Sunday trading. The obligation to provide assistance to the less fortunate, 'the widow, the orphan, and the stranger' of the Old Testament, has been an inspiration for many welfare programmes to relieve poverty.

The basis of the early Jewish economy was land, and when the promised land was settled, each family was allocated a plot of land. The laws took great care to protect property rights, but these rights were never absolute. The ultimate ownership of the land belonged to God and property rights carried obligations. Freed slaves were not to be released empty handed but given resources to look after themselves. Those with wealth were to give generously to those in need. Those who borrowed were not to be treated as debtors. When fields were harvested the edges of the field were to be left unharvested for the poor and the stranger.

The right to property gave each family the freedom to buy and sell, to save and invest, to take risks and innovate. But it was not a *laissez-faire* system. Restrictions were imposed on the labour, capital, and property markets to ensure that each individual and family was treated on the basis of justice. The sabbatical year was an occasion when the land was to lie fallow, slaves were to be freed, and debts were to be cancelled, and the year of Jubilee one in which land was returned to its original owners. One of the consequences of this redistribution was that each family retained a permanent stake in the economic life of the community. It was a way of preventing the development of a permanent underclass. Restrictions were also imposed on the capital markets to prevent the exploitation of people in need. In the labour market, wages were to be paid daily, so that labourers could afford to pay for their lodgings that night.

Of course this was an idealized system, and there is no evidence to suggest that certain laws, such as the law of the year of Jubilee, were ever implemented. But it was God's standard for economic life, and because of that, it contained principles which have relevance for us even today. It respected the dignity of the individual, their right to own private property and their freedom to do business. It was organized by way of a simple market economy set in the context of an agricultural background. Yet it was not a libertarian, free market economy: it was hedged about with regulations to ensure justice.

7.2.3 The Incarnation

The third and crucial element in developing a Christian perspective is the Incarnation itself. The claim of Jesus to be the Messiah, the Son of God, and the inauguration of his Kingdom, which extended the covenant to include Gentiles as well as Jews, marked a radical break with the Jewish tradition. Yet it was not a total break. There is an important continuity between the Old and New Testaments, and in terms of an ethic for economic life, two strands are important.

First, Jesus is recognized as God, the creator of the world. The Gospel of John starts with the declaration

In the beginning was the Word, and the Word was with God, and the Word was God. He was in the beginning with God; all things were made through him and without him was not anything made that was made. (John 1: 1–4)

St Paul stated clearly that Jesus is the image of the invisible God, the creator of all things visible and invisible and the source of meaning for the whole of life (Col. 1: 15–20). The Incarnation confirms the goodness of creation and the mandate given to men and women to exercise authority over the physical world. Implicit in the Incarnation is the necessity, legitimacy, and value of wealth creation. The Christian faith has no truck with dualism.

Second, Jesus confirmed the significance and the continuing importance of the moral law of the Old Testament. Sometimes the impression has been given in Christian writings that while the Old Testament ethic is based on law and commandments, summed up in the expression 'thou shalt not', the Christian ethic introduces a new freedom based on love, grace, and the Holy Spirit.[1] I believe this is to misunderstand the ethical teachings of Jesus.

Jesus taught that the whole of the Jewish law and the prophets, including the 'thou shalt nots' of the moral law could be summed up in two precepts:

'Love the Lord your God with all your heart, with all your soul and with all your mind.' This is the first and greatest commandment. And the second is like it, 'Love your neighbour as yourself.' All the Law and the Prophets hang on these two commandments. (Matt. 22: 37–40)

This statement of Jesus' shows that, at its heart, the Mosaic law was the injunction to love God and our neighbour. Jesus went out of his way to emphasize that he never rejected the moral law of the Old Testament. For him it had permanent validity as the word of God. At the beginning of the Sermon on the Mount, he made it very clear that he had come to confirm and fulfil the law,

Do not think that I have come to abolish the Law or the Prophets: I have not come to abolish them but to fulfil them. (Matt. 5: 17)

It was because of this that he never set out a moral code dealing with such things as the family, theft, adultery, and murder because that had already been done in the Old Testament. His teaching in the Sermon on the Mount was not in opposition to the moral law, but to a narrow and legalistic interpretation of it, which depended on hair-splitting and fastidious obedience to an ever increasing number of rules. He said that the law had become a yoke and a burden, and in his teaching he challenged the motives underlying a person's actions, contrasting obedience to the law based on love towards God, with conformity to a set of rules which were little more than an empty regard for tradition. The confirmation by Jesus of the moral law of the Old Testament is, in terms of economic life, an endorsement of its teaching regarding wealth creation, the freedom of exchange, the ownership of private property, the obligations which ownership brings, and the importance of economic justice.

Against this background, a number of his parables and teaching emphasized the way in which wealth creation could so easily become the worship of money. He posed the stark choice, 'You cannot serve God and Mammon', and in using the Aramaic word for money, he both personified and deified it. He never questioned that the material world was anything other than the blessing of God, but stressed that our material life needed to be set in the context of the spiritual life, and touched lightly. His mission was to preach the good news to the poor, the hungry, and the excluded, something the rich would find difficult to comprehend, because of their self-assurance and self-satisfaction.

The harshest of all the parables he taught was that of a rich man and Lazarus, in which the rich man is ultimately judged, not because of his wealth, but because of his indifference to Lazarus, a beggar suffering from malnutrition and hunger, who pleaded unsuccessfully for help and camped daily outside his property. In the story of the final judgement, Jesus pictures the judge separating people and nations from one another as a shepherd might separate sheep from goats. The basis of judgement is that it is in feeding the hungry, giving drink to the thirsty, welcoming the stranger, clothing the vagrant, caring for the sick, and visiting those in prison that true faith is shown. Faith is important, but it must be judged by deeds and not just by words.

In view of the continuity between Jesus' teaching and that of the Old Testament, it may be argued that in terms of ethical teaching, there is little difference between

Judaism and Christianity. There is clearly a great deal in common. Yet while Jesus confirms the permanent validity of the moral law, his life nevertheless expresses the moral ideal, in a way in which a set of rules never could. It is because of this that, throughout the New Testament, Christians are urged to follow him and to make His life their example. This is particularly true of the way he practised virtues such as love and humility, seen most clearly when, as their lord and master, he washed the disciples feet, and in his constant self-giving and service to others, which found its ultimate expression on the cross. The church, which is made up of those who follow him, and which is described as the 'body of Christ', is to stand out as a community in which extremes of wealth and poverty have no place, and in which those with material resources are to give generously to those in need.

7.3 A CHRISTIAN FRAMEWORK FOR GLOBAL CAPITALISM

I have always had difficulty in using the word capitalism to describe the economic system of the Western world. This is largely because capitalism carries with it such baggage from the nineteenth century that it is not something I would wish to defend, especially from a Christian perspective. It is used as the title to this section, however, following Professor Dunning's use of the word, so that it includes not just the market economy but those social and legal institutions, as well as certain values, on which the market economy itself depends.

A Christian framework has a number of distinctive features. First, it gives the whole of life, including economic life, meaning. Its starting point is the existence of a personal, yet infinite God, who is creator, sustainer, and redeemer and who became incarnate in Jesus Christ. The life and teaching of Christ provides the individual with the supreme example of the balance to be struck between the material and the spiritual and the way in which all of life must be in the service of others. At the heart of economic life, it affirms the importance of the person and relationships, not the thing and transactions. It is because of this that, if God is excluded, and the purpose of work is no more than making money or increasing shareholder value, personal fulfilment will prove elusive.

Second, the Christian faith emphasizes personal responsibility. Each person created in the image of God is accountable for their actions, whether in government, business, NGOs, international institutions, or in private life. Globalization has brought into sharper relief our global responsibilities. Today, it is unthinkable that any Christian could be indifferent to the needs of the extremely poor, to world hunger, or to ecological disaster.

Third, within this structure, the global market economy has legitimacy. Wealth creation is a direct implication of the creation mandate. The existence of markets in which people can buy and sell goods and services freely, and in which property rights are protected by the rule of law, strengthens personal freedom. This is something valuable in itself in that it allows individuals and families to develop and prosper, and creates a buffer against the control of economic life by the state.

In this context A. K. Sen captures the nature of markets well,

> To be generically against markets would be almost as odd as being generically against conversations between people. The freedom to exchange words, or goods, or gifts does not need defensive justification in terms of favourable but distant effects: they are part of the way human beings in society live and interact with each other (unless stopped by regulation or fiat). (Sen 1999: 6)

In the context of globalization, increased trade and investment extend the benefits of markets to developing countries, and in the process help reduce poverty.

Fourth, the kind of global capitalism that a Christian will wish to see develop is one which encourages responsibility, fairness, and widespread ownership. This implies legally enforceable contracts, the adoption of generally accepted accounting practices, an effective competition policy, transparent systems of corporate governance, and an education system, at least one objective of which will be to prepare people to thrive in a market economy. The ability of each individual and family to own or lease property, to invest in the wealth creation process, and to pass on their assets to their children is a basis for freedom and a safeguard against economic adversity. In place of the Darwinian economic jungle, a social market economy will ensure that a series of safety nets are in place to help those who find themselves casualties, or are excluded, from the economic system.

Fifth, a Christian perspective will place a strong emphasis on economic justice. The world is God's creation, but through human self-centredness it is in rebellion against God. In a fallen world there will be exploitation, corruption, and injustice. Those with power will seek to bend the rules in their favour. The Christian must be prepared to stand up and confront injustice, and work to change the rules, structures, and ethos in order to create a more just society. The Christian understanding of justice will embrace wealth creation as much as wealth redistribution.

Sixth, individuals live and develop not in isolation but in communities, and so a Christian will emphasize the importance of communities such as the family, the village, the church, the school, and the corporation. Global capitalism cannot exist without vibrant communities. Strong and robust communities help people live fulfilled lives, but if these communities are to be effective, they need the ability to operate independently of government control. Effective communities depend on trust. In static cultures, trust rarely extends beyond the family and because of this, the lack of trust is a barrier to removing poverty. In a culture which seeks to affirm Christian values, trust will extend beyond the family to other mediating structures, some of which are crucial for successful development.

7.4 AUTONOMY AND GREED

One implication of a Christian perspective is that the whole of economic life, including globalization, can never be considered autonomous. For the Christian, it is God, not economics which is the starting point. The fact that God's world is a moral order means that the whole of economic life is included within this order, and therefore all of the issues raised in the globalization debate—the plight of the world's poor, the fairness of trading structures, the meaning of economic justice, the process of environmental degradation, the exhaustion of renewable resources, the accountability of the IMF, World Bank, and WTO and the power of global companies—must be judged by a set of moral reference points which are part of the world God has created.

By contrast, in liberal economics the market is autonomous. It is conceived of comprising rational, maximizing individuals, who, as buyers or sellers, are free to choose independently of any moral constraint. The unambiguous conclusion of market economics is that extending choice will improve the efficiency of markets and lead to a gain in economic welfare. In fact, the triumph of modern liberal economics, and indeed the reason for its success, is precisely because it has escaped the confines of medieval thought and become part of a thoroughly modern post-Enlightenment world view.

Perhaps the clearest contemporary exposition and defence of this position is the work of F. A. Hayek. Although the origins of economic life are 'cloaked in the mists of time' (Hayek 1988: 38), Hayek views the growth of capitalism, by which he means not just economic life but also the moral systems and institutions which underpin it, as a spontaneous order, namely something which evolved without there being any overall plan or design to it, and without having to be propped up by any external system of morals. This spontaneous order in the economic sphere is comparable to the growth of language, money, and law in the social sphere and to the growth of crystals, organic compounds, and the evolution of biological species in the physical world. A spontaneous order has no purpose. It has no end to which it is working. In its development it will simply express the wishes of a myriad individuals in the pursuit of their particular objectives. As a consequence, the outcomes of a spontaneous order, namely what is produced and what is consumed and the consequent distribution of income and wealth, will have no relationship to any concept of morality or social justice.

Within this framework, globalization is a natural and spontaneous process and is independent of any reference to morality. It is best left to itself and not subject to regulation by government, or interference by international institutions. It has no need for governance. The state and the church should keep out of economic life and allow the 'invisible hand' the freedom to allocate resources to maximum global benefit. The fact that in certain poorer countries, legal, environmental, health, and safety standards are low or poorly enforced should be the concern of their governments not global corporations. Providing they operate within the law, global companies will have discharged their responsibilities. Attempts to interfere with the natural process of globalization by imposing environmental standards, enforcing minimum standards for employment, or demanding social audits by companies, are seen as a tax on the activities of companies, a disincentive to foreign investment and job creation and therefore ultimately detrimental to the interests of third world countries.

Hayek is right to point out the complexity which economic development involves, as well as the unintended consequences of well-meaning politicians in their attempt to improve the lot of humanity. His basic thesis, however, regarding the autonomy of the market economy, presents great difficulty to Christians, and is something which ultimately they must reject. Hayek is very clear in recognizing that his approach to economic development is based on assumptions which are a rejection of a Christian world-view. He rejects any external moral standard by which economic activity should be judged. Ethics are not 'immutable and eternal', determined outside of the system, but the result of a process of adaptation to changing circumstances, namely cultural selection. It is precisely because there is no external moral standard that globalization is considered an autonomous and amoral process, without the need for any system of governance.

If global capitalism were allowed to develop within a free market Hayekian framework it would suffer from three weaknesses: there would be no external standards of what was right and wrong, just and unjust, moral and immoral, by which its results could be judged; there would be no guarantee that even in the absence of outside intervention, globalization would be a benign process; and there would be no assurance that in a free society left to itself, we could count on an evolution of moral beliefs to generate values which would continue to under-pin the market order. For the Christian, global capitalism requires an ethos within which globalization can develop, and it is precisely this which the Christian faith can provide.

A second implication of a Christian perspective is that it is difficult to accept the views of writers such as Ellul, Tawney, Tillich, and Newbigin who make such sweeping judgements on capitalism,[2] views which incidentally are echoed in the globalization debate, though not from a theological perspective, by campaigners such as Roddick, Hertz, and Benoit. For example, Bishop Newbigin is scathing about the market:

The driving power of capitalism is the desire of the individual to better his material con-dition. It is the unleashing of this power from the restraints imposed by traditional morality that has transformed static societies into the dynamic and growing society of which we are a part. No one can deny either the reality of the motive force or the mag-nitude of what it has achieved. The name the New Testament gives to the force in question is covetousness. The capitalist system is powered by the unremitting stimulation of covetousness. (Newbigin 1986: 113)

This is a sentiment which could have come straight from the streets of Genoa or Seattle. It is inadequate for three reasons. First, it makes no attempt to distinguish different varieties of capitalism. The worlds of *laissez-faire*, monopoly capitalism, the social market economy, the casino economy, and the robber barons are all tar-nished by the same label and written off as immoral. This is much too simple, and makes no attempt to recognize the ways in which the regulation of markets has evolved in different countries to ensure transparency and justice. Second, it fails to imagine any motive which drives the marketplace other than avarice and greed. Within markets, people's behaviour may be guided by the highest as well as the lowest of ideals, by standards of honesty as well as dishonesty and by the desire to serve, as well as the need to control. The one thing which market behaviour is not is uni-dimensional. Third, in terms of New Testament teaching, it fails to strike any balance between Jesus' teaching on the false god of materialism with his teaching on the responsible management of those talents with which we have been entrusted by God. More than that, it makes little attempt to recognize any continuity between the Old and New Testaments. It is as if the Old Testament were wholly redundant to Christian ethics, a view which, based on the teaching of Christ himself, is simply not tenable.

7.5 GROWTH BENEFITS THE POOR

So far the argument has been that a global market economy which operates within the rule of law and with a safety net to help those who are disadvantaged, has a moral legitimacy and should, from a Christian perspective, be defended on the basis of human dignity, personal freedom, and social justice.

The proponents of globalization go further, and argue that liberalizing markets in developing countries and opening up these economies to trade and investment, will increase economic growth and reduce poverty. Lower trade barriers will increase competition, reduce prices to domestic consumers, and allow resources to be used more effectively. Increased foreign direct investment will bring access to new technology, superior management, and new markets. Countries which open themselves to the world economy are more likely to de-regulate their labour and capital markets, reform their systems of corporate governance and regulatory frameworks, and improve their standards of company law and accounting.

The research evidence on these subjects is extensive, and points to three important conclusions. The first is that economic growth unambiguously benefits the poor. A comprehensive study by two World Bank economists, David Dollar and Aart Kraay, using evidence from eighty countries and with income data covering a period of over forty years, showed that internal economic growth in developing countries benefited the poor as much as the rich (Dollar and Kraay 2002). More rapid growth meant more rapid growth in the income of the poorest 20 per cent of the population, and rising per capita income overall meant rising per capita income for the poorest 20 per cent of the population. Their results are corroborated by other research findings. The World Bank estimates that, between 1993 and 1998, the extremely poor in the new globalizing developing countries declined by roughly 120 million. In China for example, due to its rapid growth, the best estimate is that those suffering from extreme poverty fell from 32 per cent to 17 per cent of the population (Dollar and Kraay 2002). Research evidence suggests that there is no example of a country reducing poverty without long-term internal growth. As a way of permanently reducing poverty, an increase in government to government development aid will never be a substitute for more rapid internal economic growth in developing countries. The evidence of the past twenty years also suggests that those countries which have grown more rapidly have also experienced a greater reduction in infant mortality, illiteracy, and hunger, as well as a growth in life expectancy.

A second conclusion of this research is that more rapid economic growth in developing countries is associated with trade liberalization and increased foreign investment. Economists are careful to argue that this is not a direct causal connection, even though there are good reasons why it should hold. Consider the following two pieces of evidence. One is that between 1900 and 1950, the living standards of the world measured by GDP per capita grew by roughly 1 per cent per year, while population grew by about 1 billion. Between 1950 and 2000 GDP per capita grew by more than 2 per cent per year, despite population growth of 3.5 billion. One major reason is that between 1950 and 2000 world trade grew by 1700 per cent (Browne 2002).

Another is a piece of research based on a World Bank study of two groups of developing countries over the past two decades. One group is the 'globalizing' countries which includes China, Mexico, Vietnam, Uganda, and India. They doubled the ratio of their exports to GDP over the 1980s and 1990s. In the 1990s the per capita GDP in these countries rose to 5 per cent a year. The other group, the 'non-globalizing' countries which includes Myanmar, Nigeria, Ukraine, and Pakistan experienced a fall in the ratio of exports to GDP over the 1980s and 1990s, with the result that per capita GDP fell by an average of 1 per cent per year in the 1990s. More open economies benefit from trade and foreign investment (Dollar and Kraay 2002).

A third conclusion is that, contrary to much of the rhetoric in this debate, globalization has not, on average, resulted in greater inequality in the distribution of income within developing countries. On average, the incomes of the poorest 20 per cent of the population have grown at the same rate as GDP growth. In some countries the income of the poor has grown less (China), in others slightly more (Philippines and Malaysia). But even in a country such as China, although inequality between urban and rural areas has grown, the number of rural poor has declined from 250 million in 1978 to 34 million in 1999. The change in inequality is less related to integration in the world economy than it is to domestic policies on education, taxes, and welfare.

7.6 GOD AND THE POOR

Global capitalism will increase wealth and reduce poverty in developing countries, if they are prepared to liberalize and are appropriately equipped to benefit from it. But within a Christian perspective three serious problems still remain, namely the plight of the extremely poor who are barely touched by globalization, the repeated charges regarding the injustice of world trading rules, and the potential impact of global corporations on sustainable development. This section will deal with the first of these problems, and the next two sections with the other two.

President Clinton in his 2001 BBC Richard Dimbleby Lecture, quoted the statistics regarding the extreme poor in an arresting manner:

Half the people on earth live on less than two dollars a day, a billion people, less than a dollar a day. A billion people go to bed hungry every night—and a billion and a half people—one quarter of the people on earth never get a clean glass of water. One woman dies every minute in childbirth. (Clinton 2001)

While globalization has raised living standards in those countries which have been drawn into its orbit, the really poor live in countries which are marginal to the world economy, where incomes have been falling and poverty rising over recent years. In sub-Saharan Africa over the 1990s, the undernourished grew from 89 million to 180 million. James Wolfensohn, the President of the World Bank, claims that unless we address the problem of exclusion, by 2030 there will be 5 billion people living on less than $2 per day. Although inequality *per se* is not a measure of poverty, the fact that of the 6.1 billion people in the world, the richest one per cent receive as much income as the poorest 57 per cent is an unacceptable state of affairs.

One of the unmistakable facts of the Christian faith is that the God of the bible is the God of the poor. Poverty undermines the dignity and worth of individuals created in the image of God. The Exodus was the liberation of poor and oppressed slaves. Many of the laws and regulations of the Jewish economy in the Pentateuch were specifically intended to help the poor, the dispossessed, the impoverished, and the deprived. One of the recurring themes of the prophetic texts of Isaiah, Jeremiah, Amos, Micah, and Hosea is the judgement of God on societies in which the poor are oppressed by the rich. Jesus' mission was to preach good news to the poor, and one evidence of faith is our response to the poor.

It is because of this that Roman Catholic thought has emphasized 'the preferential option for the poor', stressing that the poor, the vulnerable, and the excluded have a special place in Christian teaching. David Sheppard, the former Bishop of Liverpool has had a major impact in the Anglican Church through his work in the inner cities and especially through his book *Bias to the Poor* (Sheppard: 1983). Reflecting on a life spent in ministry in the inner city, he writes of God identifying in a special way with the poor and of there being a divine bias to the poor. Professor Ronald Sider has taken up the same themes in his book, *Rich Christians in an Age of Hunger*, in which he presents the scandal of world hunger and the challenges individual Christians face in making a response to it (Sider 1997).

What should be the Christian response to poverty? First, to support global capitalism by encouraging the governments of developing countries to privatize state-owned industries, open up their economies to trade and investment and allow competitive markets to grow. Global poverty cannot be tackled without the market economy and the involvement of the private sector. The private sector has a key role to play in creating jobs and transferring management skills to developing countries. The process of growth will inevitably involve change, and change is nearly always painful for some. If poverty is to be tackled however, then change is inevitable and cannot be avoided. What is important is that governments face up to their responsibilities, namely to devise policies which tackle structural adjustment in these situations.

Next, allowing the market the freedom to be effective will not by itself be sufficient to deal with the challenge of eliminating poverty. The removal of global poverty requires a redistribution of resources to help the developing world adjust to the enormous changes which the process of opening up their economies to globalization demands. The path from poverty to prosperity involves pain, but through a range of policies from debt relief, to more focused development assistance, to special help in constructing basic infrastructure such as roads, electricity, and telecommunication, the journey for developing countries can be made easier. In certain countries, the poor are seriously handicapped in participating in a market economy, because of the lack of property rights, poor access to credit, and little or no savings to cushion adversity. These can be put right. In this context, the proposals made by Gordon Brown, in Chapter 14 of this volume, as well as the World Bank Report (2002) on building institutions to support the market economy deserve serious consideration.

Apart from supporting trade and government assistance, the church has always sought through charities and personal initiatives to build hospitals and schools, to relieve poverty and hunger, to provide emergency relief and to initiate a variety of humanitarian programmes in developing countries. From a Christian perspective, the challenge today is to find a fresh vision which inspires a new generation to serve the world's poor in meaningful ways.

Finally, there is the good news which Jesus himself announced, and which he made very clear was spiritual as well as material. Pope John Paul II, in a visit to the Lixào de Sào Pedro shanty town in October 1991, reflected on the first beatitude of the gospel of Saint Matthew, 'Blessed are the poor in spirit, for theirs is the kingdom of heaven' (Matt. 5: 3). He explained the link between poverty and trust in God and between happiness and total surrender to the Creator, and then he continued,

> But there also exists another poverty, which is quite different from the poverty that Christ declared to be blessed, and which affects a multitude of our brethren, hampering their integral development as persons. Faced with this kind of poverty, which is the lack and deprivation of the material things they need, the Church speaks out... This is why the Church knows that all social changes must necessarily come about through the conversion of hearts, and she prays for this. That is the first and main mission of the Church. (Pontifical Council 1996: 71)

Indeed, many of the miseries of society result from the self-centredness which lurks in the heart of every person, and which is seen in the structures of sin. For these to be changed and poverty itself dealt with, a reformation of the individual is required, a turning to God and a commitment to love and serve others. The Pontifical Council document goes on to argue that

> the Church knows that this deep-seated and intimate change in people will encourage, in daily life, a look beyond immediate interests, to gradually change the way of thinking,

working and living, in order to learn to love in daily life, fully exercising faculties in the world as it is. (ibid. 73)

7.7 JUSTICE AND TRADE

The next issue which global capitalism must address is the justice of the rules affecting world trade. International institutions such as the IMF, the World Bank, and the WTO are an important part of global capitalism. They were established (the WTO was initially established as GATT) at the end of the Second World War, in order to create a new international order, which would avoid the pitfalls of the nineteen twenties and thirties. In the past decade, however, they have come under increasing attack, because of the lack of transparency in the way they operate and the ways in which they are perceived to be controlled by rich countries.

For example, the WTO stands charged with propping up an unjust trading system, which is biased against poor countries and in favour of rich countries. Two examples are frequently given. One is agriculture, where existing rules are biased in favour of the EU and the US and against developing countries. Developing countries have had to reduce protection against cheap food imports, while the advanced countries currently spend some $360 billion a year subsidising their agriculture. By contrast they spend only $53.7 billion a year on foreign aid.

Another area of concern relates to intellectual property rights. The Agreement on Trade-related Intellectual Property Rights (TRIPS) covers patents, copyrights, trademarks, industrial designs, and so on, and makes it obligatory in all countries to confer rights on existing patent holders for a period of twenty years. This is seen as bio-piracy. Pharmaceutical companies from rich countries have been able to patent the natural resources (such as indigenous plants and trees in third world countries discovered for medicinal purposes) of poor countries without paying any royalties and making it less likely for developing countries to gain access to new science and technology. The matter came to a head over the issue of drugs needed for the treatment of HIV/Aids in Africa. The fear was that the prices of branded drugs would remain high, that there would be less transfer to third world pharmaceutical production and that pharmaceutical companies would invest less resources in finding cures for diseases which affect very poor countries. Médecins sans Frontières estimate that between 1975 and 1997, out of 1,223 new medicines brought to market, only thirteen were for the treatment of tropical diseases commonly found in poor countries.

Some critics argue that, within the present world trading system, free trade will never result in fair trade. Free trade will result in a more unequal distribution of income. Large foreign companies will drive small companies out of business, so that free trade will create a barrier to third world countries building up comparative advantage in technological fields. Because WTO agreements do not deal with trade-related labour rights (except prison labour), trade-related environmental protection and trade-related health measures free trade will not produce a fair trading system. Not only that, but because current trading rules do not cover human rights, trade policy is given priority over health and education policies.

In judging the present WTO system, the first point to make is that if we wish to see trade grow, then it is better to have a World Trade Organization than no trade organization. The experience of the inter-war years of the last century showed all too clearly the problems created by protectionism, trade wars, and competitive devolutions between countries. It was a disaster and contributed to the severity of the great depression. The reason the GATT, precursor to the WTO, was established in the late 1940s was to ensure that the world economy never again returned to the chaos of the 1930s. It now has a rules-based system for liberalizing trade, which is a vast improvement on the past.

A second point is that when it comes to complaints by one country against another country, the WTO has proved to be a very effective judicial institution which has built up an impressive body of international law. It has a strong enforcement mechanism as well, such that the injured party can retaliate or receive compensation unless the practice is discontinued.

Some attacks on the WTO are misdirected. The WTO is an organization which enforces rules for trade. It is not an organization which is able to lay down the law on other trade related issues such as employment practices, child labour, labour rights, environmental protection, health and safety regulations, anti-corruption measures, or human rights themselves. It is surely asking too much of any one organization to tackle all these issues simply because they have some relationship to trade. The WTO exists to oversee trade, which is an important objective in its own right. It should not be burdened by other objectives. These should be dealt with by other means. The danger is that if we add other responsibilities to the WTO, countries will withdraw or use blocking measures and prevent the reduction of trade barriers. That raises legitimate questions, such as whether we should have a world environmental body, some institution to oversee competition, and whether the ILO itself, which is meant to deal with labour issues, should be strengthened and have new life breathed into it.

Perhaps the single most important decision that the rich countries could take to improve justice in trade would be to dismantle their hopelessly inefficient system of agricultural subsidies. This is especially true for the EU Common Agricultural Policy (CAP), which is the most inefficient way of supporting farm income and rural communities imaginable. For most of its life, CAP farm prices have been supported at roughly twice world market levels and consumers have faced the double penalty of higher prices and higher taxes. The CAP has accounted for the major part of the EU budget, has created friction with our trading partners and most ironical of all is very inefficient at transferring incomes to farmers. In this respect Gordon Brown's comments in his Marshall Plan for the developing world deserve wholehearted support.

With three-quarters of the worlds poor living in rural areas, opening up agricultural markets offers the best and quickest route for reducing poverty. Subsidies to agriculture which run at one billion dollars a day—six times the amount spent on development assistance—are in urgent need of reform. So we welcome the agreement at Doha to open up trade in agriculture and, in particular, to negotiate reductions in export subsidies with a view to phasing them out. (HM Treasury 2002: 25)

The EU has taken, at least in principle, the unprecedented step of unilaterally and completely opening its agricultural markets to imports from the poorest countries. All that remains is that the decisions are implemented effectively.

7.8 GLOBAL CORPORATIONS AND SUSTAINABLE DEVELOPMENT

The third issue which global capitalism must address is the environment. The challenges posed for the environment raise questions of technical complexity which we cannot begin to discuss. But at the heart of this concern is a moral issue. It is simply not possible for science, ecology, or economics to find a reason for subscribing to a concept such as sustainable development. One is forced to turn to ethics or religion. In the Christian understanding of creation, God has created the world but entrusted human beings to be co-creators with Himself. We are given freedom, but we are also accountable for our exercise of dominion. We have a responsibility to current generations but also to future generations. As people created in the image of God, future generations need to be provided with a world in which things are hopefully better and certainly not significantly worse than they are for us.

As has been clear from the debate started by the 'Bruntland Report' of 1987 (United Nations World Commission on Environment and Development), it is impossible to define the word 'sustainable' precisely. In general terms it is development compatible with the current standards of living being an option for future generations.

The goal of sustainable development has been taken up by the business community in a major way. The World Business Council for Sustainable Development was set up in 1995, and consists of leading multi-national corporations such as ABB, AT&T, BP Amoco, Deloitte Touche Tomatsu, Ford, General Motors, Glaxo Wellcome, Monsanto, Nestlé, Procter and Gamble, Rio Tinto, and Volkswagen. In a major report in 2000 they defined corporate social responsibility as

the commitment of business to sustainable development, working with employees, their families, the local community and society at large to improve their quality of life. (World Business Council 2000: 10)

They then broke down the concept of sustainable development into three areas, economic, environmental, and social, with the recommendation that

Companies...need to demonstrate, more quickly and with increasing levels of detail, that their operation enhances economic development, ensures environmental protection and promotes social equity. (World Business Council 2000: 16)

From this, companies have been encouraged to accept responsibility by accounting for their activites to stakeholders in terms of a 'triple bottom line', and developing a metric of specific targets and obligations for the business. After noting the continuing deterioration of the environment and the exhaustion of resources, such as fresh water, forests, plants, and animal species, the UK government, in its report on eliminating world poverty, committed itself to reducing harmful climate change, pollution, and resource depletion, as well as moving to more sustainable consumption and production patterns through a strategy for sustainable development (HMSO 2000).

In 1999 the OECD made the pursuit of sustainable development a key objective for its member countries, recognizing that this required the integration of economic, environmental, and social concerns in policy making, the diffusion of environmentally sound technologies. In its *Guidelines for Multinational Enterprises* the OECD also specified that enterprises should aim to achieve sustainable development. In 1999, the UN Secretary General launched the idea of a Global Compact, covering human rights, labour, and the environment, through which companies were invited to embrace and enact a set of nine principles in their operations, which would support appropriate public policies.[3]

Most recently, the European Commission recommended that to support sustainable development, all publicly quoted companies, with 500 staff or more, should publish a 'triple bottom line' in their annual reports to shareholders. They then issued a consultative document, a 'Green Paper' promoting a European framework for corporate social responsibility, which recommended greater disclosure on employment, training, and working conditions. Because values should be translated into action, they argued that

this involves practices such as adding a socially (*sic*) or environmental dimension in plans and budgets and evaluation corporate performance in these areas, creating 'community advisory committees', carrying out social or environmental outfits and setting up continuing education programmes. (European Commission 2001: 15, 16)

The business community has embraced the concept of sustainable development in an important way, but it has also come in for heavy and repeated criticism (Friedman 1962; Brittain 1995; Barry 1995; Henderson 2001). Much of the criticism is based on Hayek's approach which we examined earlier.

Few trends could so thoroughly undermine the very foundations of our free society as the acceptance by corporate officials of a social responsibility other than to make as much money for their stockholders as possible. This is a fundamentally subversive doctrine. If businessmen do have a social responsibility, other than making maximum profits for stockholders, how are they to know what it is? Can self-selected private individuals decide what the social interest is? (Friedman 1962: 133)

and:

How is it possible for a firm to 'demonstrate' or even to be sure itself, that its policies and operations promote the goals of 'economic development, environmental protection and social equity'? (Henderson 2001: 45) and again:

Is it really the case that what the overwhelming body of public opinion now wants and expects from companies is that they should (1) embrace the objective of sustainable development, (2) recognize that this explicitly has three dimensions, economic, environmental and social, and (3) run their affairs in close conjunction with an array of different 'stakeholders', primarily with a view to meeting specific targets and obligations under each of these heads, even if this results in higher costs and prices for the products and services they are selling? (Henderson 2001: 74)

The critics argue that the task of business leaders is to maximize shareholder value, not to set standards regarding employment and the environment. That is the task of parliaments, who have been elected through the democratic process.

The questions raised by the critics are important, and should not be dismissed lightly. The danger is that the movement to encourage corporate social responsibility will involve inappropriate and costly regulation, such as the introduction of new accounting and reporting systems and the excessive use of management time in consultation and negotiation with outside groups, with no obvious corresponding benefits. This danger is seen clearly in the EU Green Paper which recommends an enormous number of new procedures, systems, monitoring and committees, with no attempt to identify costs or benefits.

One weakness in the argument of those who dismiss corporate social responsibility, however, is that, too often, they give the impression that business is an amoral activity and a modern corporation little more than a nexus of contracts dominated by incentives and rewards, so that the concept of social responsibility becomes simply another constraint on maximizing shareholder value. However, research evidence on companies demonstrates conclusively that a corporation is more than just a set of contracts. It is a community held together by shared values, to which those working in the business will subscribe and of which they can be proud. Because a commitment to shared values will typically have a positive impact on a business, it could be argued that this emphasis is no different from maximizing long-term shareholder value. But there will be times when, because a company adheres to its values, decisions have to be taken which will result in reduced long-term shareholder value.

Another weakness of the opposition to social responsibility is the sharp distinction it draws between the activities of corporations and parliaments. In principle this distinction seems clear-cut but in practice it is far from easy. In return for the privilege of incorporation, corporations will wish to abide not just by the letter of the law but also by its spirit. This may well involve corporations taking initiatives which are not required by law. For example the CEO of BP, John Browne, has agreed with the President of Angola that in his company's development of the country's oil reserves, BP will make public all payments it makes to the Angolan government. If this were followed by other companies it could make a significant contribution to reducing corruption in developing countries.

Within a Christian framework, the emphasis on shared values by business, including the concept of sustainable development, is to be welcomed. While it is for parliaments to set down the law, there is a great deal corporations can do in looking for new ways to reduce the environmental impact of their operations and in managing natural resources more efficiently. Encouraging companies to publish their business principles and core values, and then be held to account for the way in which they have implemented them, is an important development which should be encouraged. At the same time the bureaucracy and box ticking approach of the EU, which is simply a dead hand on enterprise needs to be resisted. This will be done most effectively only if business is prepared to take the lead in making its contribution to sustainable development.

7.9 CONCLUSIONS

I have sought to argue in this essay that from a Christian perspective, globalization should not be viewed as an autonomous economic process which is best left to itself. Without it being placed in some form of moral framework, the risk will remain that extreme poverty, injustice, and the threat to the environment will continue. Governments, international institutions, corporations, NGOs, and individuals must relate their activities to a moral framework, and it is this which is provided by the Christian faith.

A number of specific points need to be made in conclusion.

The first is that global capitalism has moral legitimacy. The Christian faith affirms the right to private ownership, the freedom to do business in the market place, and the rule of law. These are the basic institutions of global capitalism and the foundation of economic freedom, something which is valuable in itself. They provide the basis for innovation and creativity and, along with trade and cross-border investment, they are the source for the growth of prosperity and the reduction of poverty in developing countries. It is inconceivable that global poverty could be eliminated without the private sector playing a major role. The appeal by Christians to economic justice must embrace wealth creation as well as wealth redistribution.

Second, to support the key institutions of global capitalism is not to advocate *laissez-faire* economics or to subscribe to a libertarian philosophy. Within a Christian perspective, free markets must be set within a framework of laws and regulations which aim to ensure fairness and justice, and be anchored in the values of integrity and trust which respects the dignity of each individual.

Third, global corporations are at the heart of global capitalism and the process of globalization. In the way they do business, global corporations express certain values. They should be encouraged to develop core values, to set out these values explicitly and then to be held accountable for them. By taking the initiative to act responsibly, the business community will prevent unnecessary and cumbersome legislation by governments or supra-governmental bodies, which would simply impose higher costs on companies and disincentives for their investment in developing countries.

Fourth, global capitalism needs global governance, but not global government. Global capitalism is a process which must be managed and global governance improved in the interests of fairness. International institutions such as the IMF, the World Bank, and WTO have important roles to play in facilitating globalization. Each has a specific objective: to help countries manage financial crises, to support economic development, to ensure fairness in world trade. They were intentionally, and for good reason, not established as democratic institutions. But they were established as accountable bodies. They have undertaken major reforms in the 1990s. There is still room for improvement. The ILO should be strengthened to deal with labour trade related issues, environmental issues would be better handled through a new World Environmental Organization and the WTO needs to be expanded to deal with competition and anti-trust issues.

Fifth, the global market economy has its limitations. Following the example of Christ, the Christian will identify in a special way with the poor, the hungry, and the excluded. Unless specific initiatives are taken by NGOs, governments, and international institutions, the extremely poor of the world will remain barely touched by global capitalism. The Christian church worldwide, which historically has been a major source of voluntary and charitable initiatives, is still committed to the task of serving the needy. More than ever global capitalism is challenging the church to face the full implications of its calling.

NOTES

1. In the Sermon on the Mount he contrasted the received interpretation of the law 'you have heard that it was said', with his own teaching, 'but I say unto you', and in the epistles, St Paul stated that 'we are not under law but under grace' (Rom. 6: 15) and that 'a man is not justified by works of the law but through faith in Jesus Christ' (Gal. 2: 16).
2. For a review of the evolution of Christian thought towards capitalism from the seventeenth century onwards see Novak (1982) and Dunning (2001).
3. See also Chapter 6 of this volume.

REFERENCES

Barry, N. L. (1995), 'What Moral Constraints for Business?' in S. Brittan, and A. Hamlin (eds.), *Market Capitalism and Moral Values* (Aldershot: Edward Elgar), 57–78.

Browne, J. (2002), 'The Role of Multinational Corporations in Economic and Social Development of Poor Countries', Lecture at Harvard University, Boston, Mass.

Bultmann, R. (1935), *Jesus and the Word* (London: Nicholson & Watson).

Clinton, W. (2001), 'The Struggle for the Soul of the 21st Century' (London: BBC Richard Dimbleby Lecture 2001).

COMECE (Commission of the Bishops' Conference of the European Community) (2001).

Dollar, D. and Kraay, A. (2002), *Globalisation, Growth and Poverty* (Washington, DC: World Bank and New York: OUP).

Dunning, J. H. (2001), *Global Capitalism at Bay* (London and New York: Routledge), esp. ch. 2, 'The Christian Response to Global Capitalism', 48–80.

European Commission (2001), *Promoting a European Framework for Corporate Social Responsibility* (Brussels).

Fletcher, J. (1966), *Situation Ethics* (London: SCM Press).

Friedman, M. (1962), *Capitalism and Freedom* (Chicago: University of Chicago Press).

Hayek, F. A. (1979), *Law, Legislation & Liberty*, vol. 3 (London: Routledge & Kegan Paul).

—— (1988), *The Fatal Conceit* (London: Routledge).

Henderson, D. (2001), *Misguided Virtues* (London: IEA).

HMSO (2000), *Eliminating World Poverty: Making Globalization Work for the Poor* (London: HMSO Cmd. 5006).

HM Treasury (2002), *Tackling Poverty: A Global New Deal* (London: HM Treasury).

Newbigin, L. (1986), *Foolishness to the Greeks* (London: SPCK).

Novak, M. (1982), *The Spirit of Democratic Capitalism* (Lanham, Md., and New York).

Pontifical Council, (1996), *Cor Unum—World Hunger* (Vatican City: Libreria Editrice Vaticana).

Robinson, J. A. T. (1964), *Christian Morals Today* (London: SCM Press).

Sen, A. K. (1999), *Development as Freedom* (Oxford: Oxford University Press).

Sheppard, D. (1983), *Bias to the Poor* (London: Hodder and Stoughton).

Sider, R. (1997), *Rich Christians in an Age of Hunger* (London: Hodder & Stoughton).

Soros, G. (2002), *George Soros on Globalisation* (Oxford: Public Affairs Ltd.).

World Bank (2002), *World Bank Report: Perspectives and Development* (Washington, DC: World Bank).

World Business Council (2000), *World Business Council Report.*

8

The Challenge of Global Capitalism:
An Islamic Perspective

KHURSHID AHMAD

8.1 INTRODUCTION

Global capitalism, like globalization in general, is not that new, despite its new attire and idiom. This is not to deny what is really new, particularly with respect to the *speed* as well as the *extent* and depth of capitalism's global reach in the post-Cold War world. Nor is the impact of the newly enhanced role of human capital and the micro-chip in any way being minimized. These and the geographic dimensions are important, but the substantive issues are more crucial. While the present writer shares the deep concerns of the other contributors to this volume, and the need to focus on the moral, humanitarian and egalitarian dimensions of our globalizing economy, we shall suggest in this chapter that the issues involved are even more fundamental and complex. Put in question form, 'Is globalization inevitably leading mankind towards one dominant economic system—global capitalism, notwithstanding its many variants in different geographical and cultural contexts? Or would humanity be better off with a genuinely pluralistic world with the prospect of many flourishing economic systems?'

Capitalism has been a great historic force for the last six centuries, passing through many stages of evolution and innovation; from merchant capitalism, to industrial capitalism, financial capitalism, welfare capitalism, state capitalism, and now global capitalism. The premise that mankind has now reached a stage that may be described as the 'end of history' with one global economic model for the entire human race as the only alternative, deserves to be critically examined. In this chapter an effort is being made to offer a somewhat unorthodox interpretation of the ethos of capitalism. To this end, a critique of global capitalism from an Islamic perspective is provided, together with a vision of a global economy and society where many economic and social systems can coexist, each with its set of shared values, priorities, common goals, and areas of co-operation, yet each with its unique characteristics and its ability to pursue different paths and explore new avenues to face ever-emerging challenges. This may sound like a voice of dissent, but therein, we submit, may lie the usefulness of this contribution.

8.2   CAPITALISM: AN OUTSIDER'S CONCEPTUALIZATION

Capitalism may be described as an economic system based on private property and private enterprise in which at least the greater proportion of economic life is undertaken by private individuals and institutions, primarily through a process of economic competition, via a myriad of market transactions. The principles on which capitalism is founded are those natural values and premises which, taken individually, pre-date capitalism, yet which were adumbrated, consolidated, and given a new identity and direction under the influence of powerful intellectual, political, cultural, technological, and economic forces in the era of post-Renaissance Enlightenment in Europe. Eight of these might be specifically identified. These are (1) self-interest, (2) private property and enterprise, (3) the profit motive, (4) the market mechanism, (5) civil society ensuring institutional support for free enterprise, (6) the availability of a juridico-legal framework for business rights and enforcement of contracts, (7) the intermediation of money, and (8) good governance and political stability providing domestic and external security. Each of these, taken individually, in some form or another, has been present ever since the emergence of the post-barter economy. They were there, although their specific form and direction were very much conditioned by the religio-moral and politico-economic context of different societies and times. The decline of feudalism and the flowering of the Renaissance, Reformation, and Enlightenment in Europe, and the emerging technologies and expanding political frontiers of major European powers, provided the background in which modern capitalism emerged. The specific role of certain cultural trends and ethical attitudes, as suggested by scholars like Sombart, Max Weber, and Richard Tawney, and the influence of new thought currents, promulgated by such thinkers as Kant, Voltaire, Hume, Rousseau, Hobbes, Bentham, and Adam Smith, played a critical role in creating a new civilizational ethos that helped pave the way for a new economic system which was christened 'capitalism'—not by its advocates, but by its adversaries.[1] The new paradigm was characterized by an overpowering acquisitive urge for profit making, wealth creation, and the pursuit of affluence and power.

The defining character of this new system was not only this dominant ethos but also the fact that the real builders of the system were a class of entrepreneurs. They were able to amass wealth through trade and imperialistic exploits, and were instrumental in innovating and harnessing new technologies and new organizational modes, which were leading to the precursors of the Industrial Revolution, urbanization and global trade. The balance of power shifted in favour of this new class and all other relations, particularly economic and political, were redefined in the light of the critical role of capital and capitalists. Competition became the mode of economic behaviour, and the market mechanism emerged as the effective process for decision making. Society became increasingly polarized between the bourgeoisie and the working classes.

The intellectual premises on which the new system rested were such that (1) the individual became the cornerstone of the economy and (2) that individual's self-interest as expressed in terms of the maximization of satisfaction for pecuniary rewards acted as the real élan of the system. *Inter alia* it was claimed that this would lead to the most efficient allocation of resources at all levels in the economy, and to optimum rewards for participants in the wealth creation process. Naturally self-interest also became the *dominant* if not the *sole* moving force for all economic effort. Increasing the output of goods and services became the greatest virtue and the highest prize in life. The spirit of acquisitiveness and achievement motivation became the cardinal values of society. The role of governments was limited to creating an appropriate instrumental infrastructure and a congenial climate for the operation of the system. *Laissez-faire* was accepted as the major guiding principle both within the nation state and at global level. As the new system unfolded, a powerful coalition between the class of entrepreneurs and the ruling powers struck root. This enabled the system to operate at high speed and achieve an unprecedented rate of growth and global outreach. Capitalism and imperialism became twins, each providing support and strength to the other.

With a host of cultural, intellectual, and social factors to the fore, the secularization of society took place, and the hold of religion and of traditional moral values was weakened. New-found affluence provided new lifestyles resulting in consumerism, the flaunting of wealth and hedonism. Furthermore, the pursuit of unbridled individualism as the chief pillar of the social system created a society strewn with conflicts, disparities, and injustices. This new-found freedom and opportunity also released powerful streams of creativity, innovation, enterprise, and management, which resulted in unprecedented economic development and material affluence. But as John Dunning points out in Chapter 1 it also led to many downsides. Indeed Victorian society became ripped apart as inequalities of income, wealth, and influence created a scenario described by sociologists as 'Social Darwinism'. A new maxim of 'the ends justify the means' further aggravated this process, and all this resulted in the creation of a society wherein the fruits of development could not be shared equitably by all its members. Globally, the system was characterized by imperialistic exploitation.[2]

At the advent of this twenty-first century, humanity is faced with a scenario where capitalism occupies the position of the dominant economic system in the world; yet the greater part of humanity remains in the grasp of poverty, hunger, disease, and deprivation, particularly in Sub-Saharan Africa, and parts of Latin America and South Asia. The roller-coaster movements of the financial markets of East Asia and financial convulsions that have devastated many parts of the world have exposed the clay feet of the system's security and stability. Frustrating experiences in Russia and some East European countries with privatization and liberalization have highlighted the dangers of thrusting capitalism upon countries ill-prepared for it. In our view, the challenge of global capitalism is two dimensional: (1) it poses a challenge to countries in the non-Western world, and (2) it poses a challenge to its own very existence as to how to deal with its inherent problems. The only silver lining is that every challenge also provides an opportunity.

8.3 GLOBAL CAPITALISM: ACHIEVEMENTS AND FAILINGS

Three centuries of capitalistic experiment present a mixed picture of unprecedented achievements in the fields of economic development, productivity, creativity, and innovation, as well as unpardonable disasters and inequities in social and human realms. Advocates and adversaries of capitalism (including Karl Marx), agree on its tremendous wealth creating contributions. It has been claimed, for example, that the volume and variety of economic achievements under its aegis, have surpassed those of humanity in the entire pre-capitalist era. The alternatives to capitalism that have been tried and tested during the last one and half centuries, despite some positive contributions, have lagged far behind in their wealth creating potential, and have disintegrated under the weight of their own follies.

Capitalism on the other hand, seems to have survived all the vicissitudes of time. By and large, the system has maintained a high standard of efficiency, if efficiency is defined in physical and materialistic terms. The pivotal role of the individual and the infrastructure of freedom, effort, opportunity, and meritocracy have established the credentials of the system and demonstrated its relative superiority over the alternatives that challenged it. The market mechanism, despite its weaknesses and failures has turned out to be a more efficient arrangement for economic decision making. Moreover, capitalism has also shown remarkable inner resilience and a capacity to change, adapt, adjust, and create new forms, instruments, and structures to face new challenges both from within and without. The system has also shown a capacity to transcend geographic boundaries. While it is difficult to establish a causal relationship between capitalism and democracy, *inter alia* because of the different interpretations of the two concepts on the appropriate distribution of power,[3] by and large it can be inferred that the prospect of compatibility between capitalism, democratic processes, and freedom are relatively great (Sen 1999). The above features represent the positive side of capitalism.

There is however another side which is rather ugly and distressing. The affirmation of individualism is a great human achievement, but individualism alone cannot ensure a healthy and harmonious social system. Society and state are important dimensions of human life. Individuals do not live in a vacuum. They live in the context of other humans and a network of institutions. A healthy, just, and sane society comes into being only if there is a balanced relationship between the individual and society. Individualism run amok, can be as disastrous as totalitarianism, collectivism, and unbridled statism.[4] Individual gain and social welfare must go hand in hand. In any society there are bound to be conflicts of interest between individuals, but every system worth its name needs to develop mechanisms to resolve those conflicts in a manner that the well-being of the individual and the welfare of society are simultaneously achieved. Personal good and public good make up the matrix of a balanced contented society. Neglect of either is bound to be deleterious socially and economically. If socialism erred on the side of collective extremism, capitalism's failures can be traced to its emphasis on an unbridled individualism.

While over the last century, from time to time, serious efforts have been made by national governments and supra-national entities for harmony between personal and societal objectives, dichotomy and clashes between them remain unresolved at almost all levels. The pillars of capitalism, namely competition and the market economy, are based on the assumption of the availability of information and symmetry in the capacity and bargaining power of all the participants, producers and consumers, employers and employees, profit takers and wage earners. The vision of economic individualism expounded by Adam Smith and Ricardo and incarnated in the assumptions of the market economy are found only in economic textbooks and mathematical models of capitalism. In the real world, where gross inequalities prevail and many players are in a position to manage and manipulate market forces, they are all too conspicuous by their absence. Big fishes not only control the pond; they even eat the small fish! Monopolistic and oligopolistic forces call the shots. Market imperfections and distortions plague both the domestic and global economy. This has led to accentuation of class conflicts, regional rivalries, national clashes, and global confrontations. Asymmetry of power and influence are at the root of a system that all too frequently thrives on distortions, imperfections, exploitations, and inequities (Thurow 1996; Greider 1997; Shutt 1998; Sklair 1994; Hayter 1991; Bell and Kristol 1971; Hertz 2001).

This brings me to the central issue of the exclusion or marginalization of justice and equity as a critical concern of all levels of the economy and society. Within the national economy and at global level, a kind of centre periphery relationship has emerged. The distribution of wealth, income, and resources between different strata of society and between different nations and regions is grossly unequal. The theory that all boats rise when the water level rises has not held true for most of the poorer countries in the world. The theory of the trickle-down effect of benefits has also proved ineffective. Poverty amidst plenty, hunger amongst affluence, deprivation along with conspicuous consumption are just some of the festering sores of the capitalist system (Amin 1974, 1976; Frank 1979; Emmanuel 1972; Kenton 2000).

Major capitalist countries today and most of the third world countries were roughly at similar levels of economic development and well-being around the mid-eighteenth century. A review of literature on the historical comparisons of per capita income suggests that around 1760 disparities were almost non-existent (Kennedy 1988; Fogel 2000; Alam 2000).[5] Three centuries of capitalist development have changed the situation to such an extent that, at the advent of the twenty-first century, the richest countries of the world with only 20 per cent of the world's population, own 87 per cent of the world's GDP; the corresponding share of the remaining 80 per cent of the world's population is only 13 per cent. Disparities both at global level between rich and poor countries within developed and developing countries and between rich and poor sections of every capitalist society were increasing.[6] This seems to be the unavoidable result of the logic of the market place, and underpins the need for *extra*-market arrangements to redress the situation, as for example documented by Thurow 1996; Shutt 1998; Marris 1997; Ellwood 2001; Küng and Schmidt 1998; Gray 1998, and several contributors to this volume.

Economic development has been a positive achievement, yet there are strong reservations as to how far this has led to the welfare and well-being of *all* sections of society. Human needs have an objective dimension, but needs as such are not of direct relevance to the calculus of capitalism. What is relevant are wants, that is needs backed by purchasing power. This, then introduces a major new dimension into the equation. Purchasing power is determined by the distribution of income and wealth in society. But when an economy suffers from gross inequalities, its priorities of production and consumption are not in keeping with the needs of the majority of people in that society. This is the dilemma of capitalism. The market responds to subjective wants, not objective needs. While some inequalities of income and wealth are acceptable, even inevitable, in order to maintain effective incentives and achievement-oriented rewards, extreme inequalities distort the entire spectrum of a society's productive and consumptive priorities, rendering the system unbalanced and exploitative (Lutz and Lux 1979; Roepke 1977; Gray 1998; World Bank 1997; Sachs 2000).

Capitalism claims to be a universal system based on a set of natural principles. Its global reach is undeniable. But its inclusiveness and social desirability is open to question. How far its politico-cultural context remains an unalienable part of its economic ethos remains debatable. What is universal and adoptable by others, and what is specific to its Euro-American historical background and cultural ethos? Is it possible, then, to detach its principles and precepts from the moral values and traditions that acted as the womb for the gestation of the embryo of self-interest into its economic imperative? Self-interest, as such, has been a great creative force. But once it is promoted as the *only* motivating force, the normative considerations that could safeguard social interests are marginalized. Consequently, the focus shifted from society to economy and economy was reduced to the market.

When the market mechanism becomes the sole arbiter of the desirable and the undesirable—a virtual source of values—the result is that ethical norms are gradually eroded and the dimensions of justice grossly violated. In short, capitalism's claim to be the natural order is not shared by those who have strong apprehensions about its deleterious performance on social and moral grounds. The realities about different countries' varied levels of development and socio-cultural aspirations do not admit the relevance of one economic model for all societies or provide a mosaic for contemporary mankind. The global economy, like global society, cannot be encased in one model. Instead, an open and just world would have to be genuinely pluralistic, with link-ups and interrelations that enable all people, societies, and states to reap benefits through co-operation as much as through healthy competition.

This view of the vast majority of intellectuals of the third and Muslim worlds is shared by several enlightened thinkers in the West. According to Lester Thurow of the Massachusetts Institute of Technology,

the danger is not that capitalism will implode as communism did. Without a viable competitor to which people can rush if they are disappointed with how capitalism is threatening them, capitalism cannot self-destruct. Pharoanic, Roman, Medieval and Mandarin economies also had no competitors and they simply stagnated four centuries before they finally disappeared. Stagnation, not collapse, is the danger... The intrinsic problems of capitalism visible at its best (instability, rising inequality, a lumpen proletariat) are still out there, waiting to be solved, but so are a new set of problems that flow from capitalism's growing dependence upon human capital and man-made brainpower industries. In an era of man-made brainpower those who win will learn to play a new game and this will require new strategies. Tomorrow's winners will have very different characteristics than today's winners. (Thurow 1996: 325–6)

The issue is not merely one of brainpower. More importantly it relates to the whole moral, social, cultural, spiritual, and political context of mankind. The shift of emphasis from machine to mind represents a qualitative shift in the global human situation. This brings the moral question to the centre of the debate and consequently concerns for justice become the real focal point, as against exclusive obsession with material affluence, development, and efficiency.

Robert Fogel, winner of the 1993 Nobel Prize for Economics, also addresses this issue in his work *The Fourth Great Awakening and the Future of Egalitarianism*. His formulation of the real problem is succinct and perceptive. In his words:

At the dawn of the new millennium the critical issues are no longer whether we can manage business cycles or whether the economy is likely to grow at a satisfactory rate. It is not even whether we can grow without sacrificing the egalitarian advances of the past century. Although the consolidation of past gains cannot be ignored, the future of egalitarianism in America rests on the nation's ability to combine continued economic growth with an entirely new set of egalitarian reforms that adhere to the urgent spiritual needs of our age, secular as well as sacred. Spiritual (or immaterial) inequity is now as great a problem as material inequity, perhaps even greater. (Fogel 2000: 1)

Fogel emphasizes that 'in a world in which immaterial assets are becoming the dominant form of wealth, equity, (justice) in the cultural sphere becomes an issue, both domestically and internationally' (Fogel 2000: 230). He concludes his book with a significant warning:

Although the world that our grandchildren will inherit will be materially richer and contain fewer environmental ills it will be more complex and more intense than that of my generation. Ethical issues will be at the centre of intellectual life and engagement with those issues will form a larger part of the fabric of daily life than is the case today. The democratisation of intellectual life will broaden debates and insinuate spiritual issues more deeply into political life. Clashes between old and new religions may become more acute, but the average age of the population will rise significantly and with that ageing will come, one hopes, a maturity and intellectual vitality that will help our grandchildren find better solutions than we found. (Fogel 2000: 242)

John Gray, a British commentator, focuses on the political dimensions of capitalism. He writes:

A reform of the world economy is needed that accepts a diversity of cultures, regimes and market economies as a permanent reality. A global free market belongs to a world in which Western hegemony seemed assured. Like all other varients of the Enlightenment

Utopia of a universal civilization it presupposes Western supremacy. It does not agree with a pluralist world...It does not meet the needs of a time in which Western institutions and values are no longer universally authoritative. It does not allow the world's manifold cultures to achieve modernizations that are adapted to their histories, circumstances and distinctive needs. (Gray 1998: 20)

8.4 PLURALISM OR ONE GLOBAL CAPITALISM?

This being the cultural and political context of the debate on globalization and the future of capitalism, it is a very healthy and promising development that a group of intellectuals belonging to all parts of the world and all faiths and cultures is looking upon the issue from a moral perspective. Whatever the merits and failings of capitalism, when one looks into its historical performance one cannot fail to notice the capacity of the system to innovate change and respond to internal and external stimuli. The many forms and shapes that capitalism has assumed during its chequered history is a testimony to the system's capacity for resilience and adaptation.

For much of the last 150 years, socialism has presented a major challenge both to the concept and content of capitalism. However, the initial socialist challenge did not build its case on purely economic grounds. Robert Owen, St Simon, and others challenged the system on its moral and egalitarian failures. Marx and Engels gave the critique a different twist. Their so-called scientific socialism transformed the language and substance of the challenge into exclusively materialistic and historical terms. In the name of science, a new form of economic and historical determinism was unfolded. The national socialisms of Germany, Italy, and Spain represented another challenge. Liberal governments responded to these challenges and to those generated internally by a free market system, by introducing more socially acceptable or welfare based, economic policies; by accepting the concept of the mixed economy; or recognizing the possibilities of a convergence scenario between different varieties of capitalism.

The current phase of global capitalism may also be scanned and examined from many perspectives. Critiques from moral and humanitarian perspectives are enriching the debate. A trend that was initiated by the emergence of revolutionary theology in the 1950s and 1960s in Latin America, the upsurge of Christian democratic movements in post-Second World War Europe and a number of humanistic, communitarian, and green groups in America and other parts of the world is now assuming global proportions. These concerns are genuine and widespread, notwithstanding untoward expressions and unacceptable violent aberrations from the extreme left. What began as outbursts of dissent at Seattle, Washington, Budapest, Ottawa, and Genoa is now influencing the tone and temper of current intellectual and inter-government discourse. The search for some kind of new consensus can be discerned from discussions at a recent UN Conference at Durban (2001) and the WTO Summit at Doha (2002). The fact that the World Economic Forum, moved from Davos to New York in 2002 in search of some common ground is meaningful. Concurrently with this meeting, another platform, the World Social Forum, stole the show in Posto Aleger, Brazil, addressing some of the burning issues. The Monterrey Consensus (March 2002) also had a flavour markedly different from that of Washington Consensus (see also Chapter 5 of this volume). All this points to the capacity of global capitalism to be flexible in the face of internal and external challenges.

Global capitalism is now being challenged on two fronts (1) by its own internal weaknesses, contradictions, and inequities, and (2) by the response of Muslim and third world countries, which have culturally different world-views, social and moral aspirations, and traditions of civilization, and make up four-fifths of the world's population. With capitalism riding the current wave of globalization, the real challenge lies not in 'Unity in Diversity' but in establishing an open society with a genuine plurality of systems and options, and which offers a diversity with unlimited scope for co-operation in the pursuit of shared values and common interests.

In this connection I draw upon some thinking about hegemony. A matrix for global society is the need for the hour. John Rawls has recently come up with some new thoughts in his latest work on the *Law of Peoples* (Rawls 1999). Here he extends his earlier idea of 'justice as fairness' (Rawls 1972) to peoples and societies which may not be strictly within the conceptual framework of (what Western thinkers regard as) political liberalism. Rawls admits the plurality of civilized societies, which he classifies according to their modes of organization. Along with the category of 'liberals' and 'reasonably liberal peoples', Rawls introduces the notion of 'decent people' which allows, in his words

that there may be other decent people whose basic structure does not fit my description of a consultative hierarchy, but who are worthy of membership of a society of people. (Rawls 1999: 4)

He also wants to make it clear that there is

no single possible Law of People, but rather a family of reasonable such laws meeting all the conditions and criteria. I will discuss and satisfy the representatives of people who will be determining the specifics of law. (Rawls 1999: 4)

Rawls' exposition of this dimension of liberalism is an important step towards a vision of a world in which genuine pluralism might prevail, and a global political, economic, and cultural matrix established that could provide humanity with opportunities for coexistence, co-operation, and competition. The future vision of such a global society would hinge on the concept of 'reasonable pluralism'. To quote Rawls once more:

the parallel to reasonable pluralism is the diversity among reasonable people with their different cultures and traditions of thought, both religious and non-religious. (Rawls 1999: 11)

The conclusion I would like to draw for this discussion is that global capitalism is capable of coexisting with other systems; and because of this there is no need to assume that all societies and cultures must try to become a variant of capitalism. This does not preclude the possibility of vast areas of shared values, interests, and aspirations, and also scope for co-operation, interaction, and competition. Even interdependence, prompted by variations in resource-endowments, specializations, and comparative advantage is not ruled out. Instead, what is being questioned is the hegemony of one system, and a relation of dependence that impinges upon political freedom, cultural integrity, economic self-reliance, and—perhaps most important of all—moral and spiritual identity.

8.5 MUSLIMS AND THE ISLAMIC APPROACH TO LIFE

Muslims constitute one-fifth of the human race. At the end of 2001, there were 1.3 billion Muslims in the world today—some 900 million in fifty-seven independent Muslim states and 400 million in over 100 communities in the rest of the world. While there is a concentration of Muslim populations in countries in Central and South East Asia and in large parts of Africa, Muslims are a part of the demographic landscape of the entire world. With over 30 million Muslims in Europe, and more than 7 million in North America, Islam is the second largest religion in Europe and America. Fifty-seven Muslim states straddle over 23 per cent of the land surface of the world. Strategic land, air, and sea routes pass through the Muslim world and there is strong interdependence between the Muslim countries and the rest.

In the main, Muslim countries are resource rich, but they presently lag behind in economic and industrial capabilities. They have huge financial resources, but are weak in the fields of technology, management, and advanced modes of production. Around 13 per cent of Muslim countries' trade takes place amongst themselves, and 87 per cent with the rest of the world. This shows their strong linkages with the global economy. It may also be noted that while most of the Muslim countries today belong to the group of developing countries, five are in the high human development group, twenty-five in the middle human development group and the rest in the low human development group (UNDP 2000: 156–60).

The Muslim world was a global economic power for several centuries,[7] and it was not until the time of the Western Enlightenment that economic stagnation or decline began to occur: and this lasted for more than 300 years. The re-emergence of the Muslim world as a powerful political and economic force is a recent phenomenon, and a lot of critical thinking is taking place examining what originally went wrong and how the Muslim world can set its house back in order. The rediscovery of its moral and ideological roots is a critical part of this exercise.[8]

Islam is a universal religion and the Muslim *ummah* is a global community. Faith is the foundation that defines the global nature of Islam for the Muslim *ummah*. *Tawhid* (the Oneness of God) establishes the unity of the universe, the oneness of humanity, the unity of life and the universality of law. Islam is not the religion of any particular nation, people, ethnic group, linguistic or territorial entity. Islam does not claim to be a new religion: rather it stands for Divine Guidance, provided by the Creator of mankind through all His prophets from the moment life began on earth. In that sense, Islam has been the religion of all Godly prophets and their followers. Indeed, Muslims believe in all the prophets from Adam through Noah, Abraham, Moses, and Jesus to Muahmmad (peace be upon them all).

Islam, literally means 'peace' and 'submission'. It stands for faith in God, as the only object of worship and obedience. It stands for faith in His Prophet as a model and source of guidance. It demands a firm commitment among its followers to live in obedience to the Divine Will and Guidance. *Shari'ah* (literally the Path) is a set of norms, values, and laws that go to make up the Islamic way of life.

Islam believes in freedom of choice and does not permit any coercion in matters of faith and religion.[9] It spells out a genuinely pluralistic religious and cultural landscape for mankind. It is by free will and dialogue that ideological borders can be crossed. Acceptance of each other, despite differences, is a cardinal principle of Islam. Islam concerns all aspects of human life—faith and worship, personality and character, individual and society, economy and community, national and international concerns. However, overarching these aspects is its moral approach to life and the universe. The physical and the secular have been brought together under the umbrella of the spiritual and the sacred. It does not exclude the worldly dimension; it does not pit the secular as against the sacred. Rather, it integrates all dimensions of life under one moral and spiritual approach. The Islamic approach, therefore, is primarily a moral and ideological approach directed towards all human beings, irrespective of faith, colour, creed, language, or territory. It regards plurality of culture and religion as genuine and respectable. There is also diversity within the Muslim *ummah*. Islam does not stand for any artificial unity, forced conformity, or syncretism. It provides an authentic base for coexistence and co-operation.

Another important aspect of the Islamic faith and civilization relates to its emphasis on values which are absolute and universal, and the identification of certain key institutions which act as permanent pillars for the system and a vast area of flexibility which could cater for the demands of changing times. While its value framework is based on human nature and universal realities, it also acknowledges the need to work out details and develop modalities for the application of this value framework in the context of changing political, economic, and cultural scenarios. While Islam provides an overall regulatory mechanism, it avoids rigid instructions in respect of detailed human formulations. It regards the individual as the cornerstone of society, nay of all creation. Each individual is personally accountable to God. As such, individuals are not merely cogs in the social machine. Society, state, nation, and humanity are all important and have a specific role to play; yet final accountability is at the individual level. This ensures the centrality of the individual in the Islamic system. *Yet it also relates the individual to the society and its institutions and seeks a balanced network of relations between them.*

Islamic morality is based on the concept of life fulfilment, and not of life denial. It is through moral discipline that all dimensions of human activity become a part of virtuous conduct. Personal piety and public morality contribute towards the enrichment of life and the pursuit of personal and social well-being and welfare for all. Wealth is not a dirty word; in fact wealth creation is a desirable goal, subject only to moral values and imperatives. A good life (*hayat al-tayyebah*) is one of the major objectives of human pursuit. Welfare in this world and welfare in the life-to-come are co-dependent, representing two sides of the same coin. It is this spiritualization of the whole secular realm, and an encasement of the entire gamut of worldly life and activities within a moral framework, that enables human beings to simultaneously seek to fulfil their own needs and to create a society wherein the needs of all are also fulfilled. Individual freedom, the right to property and enterprise, the market mechanism, and distributive justice are inalienable parts of the economic framework of Islam. However, there are moral filters at different levels—individual motivation, personal behaviour, social mores and manners, employer–employee conduct, and individual–state relationships. The state has a positive role to play, particularly in the nature of supervision, guidance, and essential regulation; yet also to ensure freedom, economic oppor-tunity, and property rights.

Islam emphasizes a more need-oriented approach, and is committed to estab-lishing a society in which the basic necessities of life are ensured for all members of the human race primarily through personal effort, and reward orientated activity, but to do so in an environment in which those who are disadvantaged are helped to live an honourable life and become active participants in society. While Islam emphasizes wealth creation activities, its real focus is on the creation of a just and egalitarian society where genuine equality of opportunity exists for all. This is only possible if society provides effective support mechanisms for the weaker members of the community. This is done both through the institution of the family and through other organs of society and state. The distinctive con-tribution of Islam to the economic approach lies in integrating freedom with responsibility and efficiency with justice. Justice is one of the key values and has been described as one of the objectives for which God raised His prophets (The Quran, 57: 25). Guidance does not merely relate to man's spiritual relationship with God: it is no less concerned with man's just relationships with all other humans and the universe.

8.6   THE ISLAMIC APPROACH TO ECONOMICS

The major characteristics of an Islamic approach to economics can be summed up as follows.

1. Life is an integrated whole. A people's culture, like an individual's person-ality, is indivisible. The entire social order is an organic unity. Economic life and the system of resource allocation cannot be taken in isolation. Specialization and division of work are important, but all elements have to be interrelated, making

a wider matrix. The economic approach is rooted in the faith, the worldview and the moral and cultural framework of a people. It is only through a holistic, integrated approach that all aspects of human life can be taken care of.

2. The Islamic world-view is based on *tawhid* (the Oneness of God), *risalah* (God's prophets as the source of Divine Guidance), *akhirah* (life-after-death, that is the continuity of life beyond death and a system of accountability based on Divine Law). The position of man and woman on the earth is that of God's *khalifah* (representative/vicegerent). He (or she) has been given discretion, will, knowledge and limited authority. His (or her) role, position and mission is described as *istikhlaf*, that is fulfilling God's Will on earth, promoting what is good, forbidding what is wrong, establishing justice (*'adl*) and promoting beneficence (*ihsan*), resulting in attaining high levels of good life (*hayyat al-tayyebah*), both individual and collective. The objectives of the Shari'ah (the Islamic way and code of conduct) in the words of al-Ghazali (d.AD 505), one of the greatest scholars of Islam, are: 'The obligation of the Shari'ah is to provide the well-being of all mankind, which lies in safeguarding their faith, their human self (*nafs*), their intellect (*'aql*), their progeny (*nasl*) and their wealth (*mal*).'[10]

3. The core value in the Islamic system, after loyalty to God (*taqwa* or God-consciousness and abidance of His commands), is *'adl* (justice) tempered with beneficience (*ihsan*). '*Adl*, in Islamic terminology, means giving everyone their due. Jurists and other thinkers throughout Muslim history have held justice as the defining characteristic of Islamic life and society, and as an indispensable part of the legal, social, and economic process. In the economic context, Abu Yusuf (d.AD 798) advising Caliph Harun Al-Rashid (d.AD 809) proclaimed that rendering justice to those wronged and eradicating injustice accelerates development. Al-Mawardi (d.AD 1058) argued that comprehensive and multi-dimensional justice promotes solidarity, law and order, development of the country, expansion of wealth, growth of the population, and the security of the country, and that 'there is nothing that destroys the world and the consciousness of people faster than injustice'. Ibn Taymiyyah (d.AD 1328) considered justice to be an essential outcome of *tawhid* (belief in One God). According to him 'justice towards everything and everyone is imperative for everyone and injustice is prohibited to everything and everyone. Injustice is absolutely not permissible irrespective of whether it is to a Muslim or a non-Muslim, or even to an unjust person'. Ibn Khaldun (d.AD 1406) states unequivocally that it is not permissible to engage in economic development without justice and that 'oppression brings an end to development' and that 'decline in property is the inevitable result of injustice and transgression' (Chapra 2001).[11] Justice, then is the very soul and breath of the Islamic economic system.

4. The Islamic scheme for social change and regeneration of human societies is unique as it is based on a methodology that is different from the one pursued by all major economic and political ideologies of post-Enlightenment Europe and America. The methodology and strategy of this change, as developed and practised in contemporary secular societies, has assumed that a radical transformation of humans can be brought about by changing the environment and society's

institutions. That is why emphasis has always been placed on external restructuring. The failure of this method lies in ignoring individual persons as its real
focus—their beliefs, motives, values, and commitments. It ignores the need to
bring about change within men and women themselves, and concentrates more
on change in the outside world. What, however, is needed is a total change—
within people themselves as well as in their socio-economic environment. The
problem is not merely structural, although structural arrangements may also
have to be remodelled. The starting point must be the hearts and souls of men
and women, their perception of reality, and their own place and mission in life.

5. The key elements of the Islamic approach to social change are:

- Social change is not a result of totally predetermined historical forces.
  Although the existence of a number of obstacles and constraints is a fact of life
  and history, there is no historical determinism. Change has to be motivated,
  planned, and achieved through individual and collective effort. And this
  change should be purposeful, that is, a movement towards the ideal.
- People are active agents of change. All other forces have been subordinated to them
  in their capacity as God's vicegerent and deputy (*khalifah*) on earth. Within the
  framework of the divine arrangement of this universe and its laws, it is human
  beings themselves who are responsible for making or marring their destiny.
- There needs to be change not only in the environment, but also within the
  hearts and souls of men and women—their attitudes, motivation, and commitment, and their resolve to mobilize all that is within them and around them
  for the fulfilment of their objectives.
- Life is a network of relationships. Change means some disruption in some
  relationships somewhere. So there is danger of change becoming an instrument
  of dis-equilibrium in society. Islamically oriented social change would cause
  the least friction and disequilibria, as it is a planned and co-ordinated movement from one state of equilibrium to a higher one, or from different states of
  disequilibria towards equilibrium. Hence, change has to be balanced, gradual
  and evolutionary. Innovation is to be coupled with integration.

It is this unique Islamic approach which leads to revolutionary changes along an
evolutionary trajectory.

6. Self-interest is a natural motivating force in all human life. But self-interest
has to be linked to the overall concept of good and justice. Reward for effort and
suffering for failure in effort provide the best framework for human society and
the economy.[12] Islam acknowledges it and accepts it as a first principle for
economic and social effort. But Islam also lays down a moral framework for
effort, spelling out values and disvalues, what is desirable and what is reprehen-
sible from a moral, spiritual, and social perspective. *Halal* (permissable) and
haram (forbidden) provide a moral filter for all human actions. Moderation and
concern for the needs of others, along with ones own, become an integral part
of the scheme. The concept of reward is also broadened by incorporating within
it reward in this world and reward in the life-to-come. This provides a strong

and self-propelling motivation for good and just behaviour, without denying the natural instincts for personal gain. Private property and private enterprise are affirmed as inalienable rights and a natural mode for economic activity. But the very concept and function of property is transformed by the provision of moral and legal filters, and instilling in people's minds and hearts the notion that in all its forms—physical and human, machine power and brain power—property is a *trust* (*amanah*), and as such, property rights are subject to moral limits and used as a means of fulfilling ethical objectives—the *Maqaasid al-Shari'ah* (objectives of the Islamic way).

7. Economic effort takes place through the processes of co-operation and competition. The market mechanism is the natural corollary of private property, freedom of enterprise and motivation for profit and reward. Scriptural guidance and historical evidence establish that trade, the promotion of production and the exchange of goods and services, the pursuit of genuine profit, protection of the market mechanism, and a legal framework for the fulfilment of contracts, are pillars of the Islamic economic scheme. Effort, innovation, creativity, division of labour, technology, and skills development have been emphasized by all major Muslim thinkers along with co-operation, compassion, justice, charity, and solidarity. Shams al-Din al-Sarakhsi (d.AD 1090), almost 700 years before Adam Smith, stated

the farmer needs the work of the weaver to get clothing for himself, and the weaver needs the work of the farmer to get his food and the cotton from which the cloth is made ... And thus everyone of them helps the other by his work.[13]

A century after Al-Sarakhsi, another scholar, Jafar al-Dimashqi (d.AD 1175), further developed the idea by saying that,

no individual can, because of the shortness of his lifespan, burden himself with all industries. If he tries to do so, he may not be able to master the skills of all of them from the first to the last. Industries are all inter-dependent. Construction needs the carpenter and the carpenter needs the iron smith and the iron smith needs the miner and all industries need premises. People are therefore necessitated by force of circumstance to be clustered in cities to help each other in fulfilling their mutual needs.[14]

Ibn Khaldun (d.AD 1406) three centuries before Adam Smith emphasized the crucial role of the division of labour and specialization in economic development and human progress:

It is well-known and well-established that individual human beings are not themselves capable of satisfying all their economic needs. They must all co-operate for this purpose. The needs that can be satisfied by a group of them through mutual co-operation are many times greater than what individuals are capable of satisfying themselves.[15]

He also gave a scientific explanation of why trade would promote development when he argued that development does not depend on the stars (i.e. luck) or the existence of gold and silver mines. Rather, it depends on economic activity and the division of labour, which is then dependent on the largeness of the market and tools. Tools, however, require savings which he defined as the

surplus left after satisfying the needs of the people. Increase in the size of the market boosts the demand for goods and services which promotes industrialisation (*sana'i*), raises income, furthers science and education, and accelerates development. (Chapra 2000: 7)

8. The market mechanism is a fundamental pillar of the Islamic economic scheme. But Islam demands actions by *extra*-market institutions to ensure that the market does not degenerate into 'market fundamentalism' (Soros 1998), and that 'self-interest' and the 'profit-motive' do not create a situation that is socially disruptive and in violation of the norms of justice and fair play. These needs and actions include:

- A moral filter at the level of personal motivation, define limits of permissible (*halal*) and impermissible (*haram*) behaviour by the individual, while institutional arrangements in the form of *hisbah* (ombudsman), social sanctions and specific legal rules and regulations.
- To encourage the family as a social and economic unit to provide an initial system of social security and solidarity.
- Governments to provide: (i) a set of moral, social, and legal provisions for the equitable distribution of wealth in society and laying guidelines for a just incomes policy; (ii) a comprehensive system of social security, both through private philanthropic activities (*sadaqat*—voluntary charity) and a state managed system of public support for the needy and underprivileged (*zakat*—obligatory poor-due); and (iii) in cases where there is market failure in respect of essential utilities and supplies, by way of monitoring, supervisory and regulatory functions, and public support programmes, so that every member of society, irrespective of religion, race, gender, or age is enabled to be in a position to participate in the dynamics of economic life.
- A network of voluntary organizations for the provision of *waqf* (public endowments). Non-commercial provisioning (i.e. by civil society), in an integral part of the Islamic economic scheme, along with provisioning through the market.
- Islam is deeply concerned about the problem of waste, over-utilization, and the excessive exploitation of non-renewable natural resources and the ecological and environmental aspects of economic activity. Its concept of a good life is based on moderation, balance and harmony. It is equally cognizant of the inter-temporal and interpersonal dimensions of economic life. The Islamic economic system is not selective; it is rather comprehensive. On the one hand, it aims to guarantee individual liberty, freedom of choice, private property and enterprise, the profit motive and possibilities of unlimited effort and reward: on the other it seeks to provide effective moral filters at different levels of life and activity and established institutions in the voluntary sector, as well as through state-apparatus to ensure economic development and social justice in society. Even the concept of charity is transformed by making part of it a legal obligation (*haq*—a right in the words of the Quran: 70: 24). As such, distributive justice and social security have become *structured* elements of the Islamic economic system and not merely *voluntary* supplements, as in other systems of life.

Voluntary and obligatory transfer payments are safety nets against poverty and exploitation in society.[16]

- The prohibition of certain sources of income is a particularly distinctive plank of the Islamic economic system. The most important prohibition is that of *riba* (usury/interest). Others relate to gambling, speculation, fraud, exploitation, and extortion. Islam lays down an elaborate code of business ethics to ensure honesty, transparency, and equity in business and financial dealings. It should be emphasized that prohibition of interest does not mean that Islam does not allow any reward on capital. Islam is well cognizant that capital, when used productively, is entitled to an appropriate reward. It does, however, oppose a guaranteed, fixed and pre-determined reward for capital. Islam believes that capital and entrepreneurs are both entitled to a share from the profit on the basis of the successful deployment of the investment. Instead of a fixed reward, there will be a variable reward based on actual return. It follows, then, that Islam would prefer to promote an equity-based, risk-sharing, and stake-taking economic system to a debt-based system. Were this to occur, it would have far-reaching implications for the economic and financial organization and management of the economy. An economy based on Islamic principles would be more oriented towards real asset creating economic activities, as against a focus on virtual money rewards. Such an economy is more likely to be more stable, real growth oriented, egalitarian, and participatory.

- Islam has no quarrel with the concept of globalization. *Tawhid* (the Oneness of God) implies the oneness of mankind. The Muslim *ummah* is a universal community both conceptually and historically. The global reach of the human race began at the time of the Prophet Noah in the Bible and the Qur'an. Contemporary changes transforming the entire world into one global city provide unprecedented opportunities, provided the process and its outcome is fair and just. Islam's concern is about the nature, direction, and socio-moral consequences of the manner and consequences of globalization. Globalization as such is not worrying; it could, indeed, be a great blessing for mankind. What must be ensured, however, is that the process is equitable, and does not become a camouflage for hegemony and exploitation of the weak by the powerful.

I would like to conclude this part of the chapter by giving a summary of the interdisciplinary dynamic model for socio-economic organization that Ibn Khaldun suggested to the ruler in the fourteenth century (eighth century Hijri). I believe this is of great relevance for our day and age:

The strength of the sovereign (*al-mulk*) does not become consummated except by implementation of the Shari'ah...;
The Shari'ah cannot be implemented except by a sovereign (*al-mulk*);
The sovereign cannot gain strength except through the people (*al-rijal*);
The people cannot be sustained except by wealth (*al-mal*);
Wealth cannot be acquired except through development (*al-imarah*);
Development cannot be attained except through justice (*al-adl*);
Justice is the criterion (*al-mizan*) by which God will evaluate mankind; and
The sovereign is charged with the responsibility of actualizing justice.

(Chapra 2000: 147–8)

8.7 TOWARDS A JUST MODEL FOR A GLOBAL ECONOMY AND SOCIETY

Global capitalism is a reality only in the sense of the global reach of Euro-American capitalism. Nor is it in dispute that several different kinds of capitalism exist within the many countries and regions that are pursuing its particular credo. Yet it is too chivalrous and unrealistic to expect that all the countries of the world should want to come under its umbrella. For example, I feel sure that despite changing political and economic precepts, several European countries and intellectual and political forces would be unhappy about a monogamous commitment to American style capitalism. Japan remains a unique case. The West counts it in its camp. Japanese thinking over the last two decades is not very clear. The prolonged stagnation that has taken hold in Japan since the late 1980s has cast a shadow of doubt and uncertainty over the future of this post-Second World War experiment. Russia, after the collapse of communism, went the whole hog for the capitalist option, but finds itself in a mess. China is pursuing a distinctly Chinese path. East Asian cultures are smarting under the 1997–8 crisis and are having second thoughts about the benefits of market fundamentalism. Third world countries have their own reservations.

The overall picture is, then, hazy and confusing. It is the submission of the present writer that the global economy and society are too fractured and lacking in homogeneity to admit any one model of wealth creation and distribution. The realities as well as the moral, social, cultural, and political aspirations of people belonging to the non-Western world make it imperative that we should all try to cultivate the vision of a genuinely pluralist world, an open society with the free exchange of ideas, technologies, goods, services, finance, and of the movement of human beings. The process, if it is to be successful and respectable, should be transparent and reciprocal. It should not be based primarily on the interests of particular groups or institutions; and certainly not the powerful and the dominant. It must ensure justice, fair play, and consensual arrangements. Hegemonic systems last only as long as the power equation remains undisturbed. And, as history clearly demonstrates, power equations can and do change.[17] Otherwise, once dominant, a power would always have remained dominant. The fact is that history is a graveyard of dozens of superpowers, and, in our own lifetime, we have witnessed quite a few such changes. The message therefore, is that instead of envisaging one dominant system, even with some built-in variations, concerned thinkers and policy makers of the world would better direct their attention to constructing the elements of a genuinely pluralistic world, wherein co-operation as well as competition could play their respective roles.

I have strong reservations as to whether the Muslim world would ever willingly accept the hegemony of global capitalism as it is now evolving, despite their openness to mutually beneficial co-operation and cross-fertilization of ideas and experiments. Capitalism does contain *some* elements that are universal and as such common with other economic systems. But it also contains a great deal that is specific to its historical and cultural context. Its identification with the once imperial powers of the West, and its present association with the only world superpower, make its incursions into the non-Western world suspicious and destabilizing. The divergence of interests, aspirations, and value frameworks possess not only formidable obstacles to a single over-arching global system, but also raises a range of questions about its desirability.

Western-style capitalism has not been an unmixed blessing in all parts of the world. In particular, many people in the third world have been excluded from its benefits. Neither has its performance in Europe and America been entirely satisfactory. The spectre of poverty is haunting half of the human race. Unemployment is rife in mature capitalist countries. Debt mountains are breaking the bones not only of people in poorer regions of the world, but also of those in many industrialized countries. The genie of financial instability cannot be put back in its bottle. Excessive inequalities remain festering sores on humanity's body. Capitalism has to do a lot to set its own house in order, before it can catch the imagination of the rest of humanity. That is why, in John Dunning's words, the present study seeks to develop a vision, not of classical or contemporary capitalisms, but of Responsible Global Capitalism. Capitalism has yet to prove that it can become responsible in every sense of the word. The moral dimensions that are missing in the present set-up could improve the prospects of capitalism: but we also need the vision of a more responsible world system, where equal opportunities for belonging to other economic alternatives, based on different faith systems and cultures, would exist.

As far as the Muslim *ummah* is concerned, it shares the perception of interdependence between the West and the Muslim world. Dialogue, joint economic ventures, increased trade, and the movement of ideas, goods, and humans can be the building blocks for future co-operation. But as Ibn Khaldun has emphasized, without the pursuit of justice and without establishing political and management infrastructures which could operationalize and actualize justice in relations between states, economies, and peoples of the world, a peaceful, prosperous, and co-operative global human society may remain a dream.

In this chapter, I have made a humble effort to present an Islamic perspective on the challenge of global capitalism, and have tried to identify some of the challenges that capitalism will have to squarely face if it is to be both sustainable and socially inclusive. If capitalism could become *responsible*, the chances of the healthy coexistence of many social and economic systems would increase. The test would very much lie in the extent to which capitalism could transform itself into a responsible global system, not necessarily the system. Otherwise, capitalism will remain very much an umbrella for Euro-American hegemony, unable to win over the hearts of people of the other world. Furthermore, the possibilities for dissent and challenges from within the Western world cannot be ruled out.

The Muslim world may be politically and economically weak, but there are a significant number of Muslim people who believe that the Islamic economic system is based on a set of universal values and lays down its own foundational principles and institutions. It contains some of the major elements of a natural economy, i.e. individual freedom, the right of property, a market mechanism, the profit motive, and legal and institutional arrangements for wealth creation, wealth distribution, and individual and social well-being. Though it shares many features with that of other religion-dominated economic systems, taken as a whole, it is unique. It is not autonomous; it is part of the Islamic system and civilization. It envisages an open society within Muslim lands and an open global society of which it would like to be an integral part. This would make the global society a matrix where different cultures and systems can coexist.

While some similarities do exist between certain core values of capitalism and the Islamic system, significant differences do remain, primarily, because of the unique ethos of the Islamic faith and culture. The Islamic economic system operates in the context of the Islamic culture and civilization. This is why Muslim economists do not visualize any variant of capitalism being the dominant economic system in their part of the world. Peripheral concessions or variations based on religion and culture cannot change basic realities. There is vast scope for co-operation among different ideologies and beliefs in the global arena. Certain values are common to all faiths and civilizations; they can act as anchors for a framework for contact, co-operation, and confluence. The idea of one capitalistic system becoming the dominant system over the globe would be a violation of the vision of a genuinely pluralistic world, free from hegemony and clash between warring civilizations. What inspires persons like myself is the vision of a world where all participants have the confidence that they can live according to their own values and yet be partners in a global enterprise.

The tragedy of contemporary global capitalism is that it has become global without winning the confidence of the peoples who inhabit the globe; without developing understanding about shared values and limits of agreement and disagreement; without opting for a path which reduces asymmetries, paving the way for greater harmonization of interests and concerns; and without caring for an international order which has institutions and architecture which could ensure freedom, participation, and the well-being of all. Even some of the icons of global capitalism, like George Soros, acknowledge that, while the market mechanism, individual freedom, and democratic values are essential for human well-being and for the establishment of a peaceful, prosperous, and just world community, 'market fundamentalism' and gross disparities in levels of economic development, financial resources, technological skills, and political power are bound to be obstacles and not aids to healthy globalization (Soros 1998). Free trade is welcome but it has also to be fair trade. Development is a desirable goal but it should be development for all. Wealth is a source of well-being, but it should ensure well-being for all human beings and all regions. This is possible only if the primacy of the moral dimension is established and the pursuit of justice along with efficiency become the cornerstones of the global system.

8.8 CONCLUSIONS

For much of the past two hundred years the capitalist system has been fuelled by the self-interested profit-motive of its participants, with the market being the predominant (if not the sole) economy. Communism shifted the focus to modes of production under centralized planning or control. The market was superseded by a command economy. Both, despite containing some elements of reality about the most desirable organizational mode of wealth creation and distribution, erred because of their one-sidedness, sometimes brilliant, yet spiritually and morally deficient.

The Islamic approach to economic activity focuses on both men and modes of production, but harnesses them into a balanced and harmonious whole. Mankind remains the focal point, and his well-being is its primary objective. Self-interest, private property, enterprise, and the profit motive are fully safeguarded. The market remains a critical institution for economic decision making. Yet Islam is concerned beyond the market, looking to moral principles, values, and commands influencing human motivation, institutions, and processes at all levels. It is equally concerned with moderating 'self-interest', so as to harmonize the personal with the public good. The ethical orientation of the individual and society supported by social and legal institutions provide the socio-economic matrix for the fulfilment of human objectives. Individual freedom, human rights, and unlimited opportunities for economic action take place within the context of moral norms, ethical imperatives, and a juridico-legal framework. National governments and supra-national entities play a positive role without becoming authoritarian or totalitarian. All economic activity takes place in the context of culture and society permeated by the pursuit of higher goals in life.

I suggest that, in this framework, John Dunning's three Cs[18] should be supplemented by four more Cs and their connotations are also given a wider orientation. The seven Cs propelling the Islamic system then are:

- *Commitment*, based on faith (*iman*) and a world view rooted in *tawhid* (the Oneness of God), and the unity and equality of mankind. Sharing this commitment is the cementing force for community and society.
- *Character*, aiming at the development of a balanced personality in every man and woman, building blocks of a society, on the basis of the Islamic concept of *taqwa*, i.e. God-consciousness, moral discipline, and a firm sense of accountability before God and people.
- *Creativity*, based on knowledge, self-interest, technological innovation, and management with an ambition to serve not only one's self and one's family but also other human beings, good causes, and the noble pursuits of life.
- *Competition*, signifying the centrality of freedom, opportunity, effort, and continuous striving to harness physical and human resources for the achievement of personal and social, worldly and moral, objectives. The Quran emphasizes the principle of healthy competition in the pursuit of good and virtue (The Quran: 2: 148; 5: 48).
- *Co-operation*, to complement the forces of competition, and safeguard it from degenerating into cut-throat economic fratricide. Welded together, competition and co-operation bring solidarity and social cohesion to society and

humanity, along with admitting unlimited opportunities for innovation and progress. The primary institution which acts as the cradle for this unique combination of competition and co-operation is the family. Further, through a network of institutions in society from local to national, regional, and global levels, it enables human beings to have a more sharing and caring model for their interrelationships and for economic and social excellence. The Prophet Muhammad described the entirety of humanity as the 'family of God'.

- *Compassion*, which in an Islamic framework represents a combination of '*adl* and *ihsan*. '*Adl* stands for justice in all matters and implies rendering to everyone what is their due, respecting and fulfilling each others' rights. The protection of faith, life, property, and honour is integral to the dispensation of justice. *Ihsan* goes beyond justice. It stands for beneficence, excellence, mercy, affection, and sacrifice. It even goes beyond wishing for others only what one wishes for one's self. It also goes beyond reciprocity which means expecting from others what they should expect from us. *Ihsan* means wishing and doing for others more than what one expects from them. This involves *sacrificing* ones rights for the well-being of others. Pareto's optimality gives way to a higher level of human *choice*. Tempering justice with beneficence gives the true concept of compassion in Islam.

- *Coexistence*, which underpins the idea of freedom, tolerance, mutual respect, and a commitment to live together. This is a genuine plurality which accepts diversity as authentic without compromising on ones own vision and fundamental principles. This means plurality with integrity—a plurality which provides ample scope for interaction without any form of syncretism, hegemony or arbitrary interference. This model holds for all levels: individuals, communities, interest groups, nations, regions, cultures, and ideologies. Dialogue, and not compulsion or obtrusive intervention, is the natural corollary. Coexistence also assumes the presence of effective processes in society for the articulation and resolution of differences and conflicts, and, a commitment to live together despite all differences. This could be a model for peace with justice and freedom.

As for the strategies '*top-down*' and '*bottom-up*', identified by Dunning, these are not mutually exclusive. In an Islamic framework both strategies are expected to be pursued simultaneously, blending one with the other. Moral values, monetary incentives, rewards and punishments, altruism, sacrifice, compassion, custom, traditions and public opinion, social institutions, the law and the state all play definite but limited roles. The hierarchy of rights and obligations with self-enforcing processes is the sheet anchor of Muslim society. It is only through a comprehensive and more integrated approach that a just and harmonious society can be established; and with it, a sustainable set of wealth creating and distributing institutions.

The Western liberal paradigm has freedom as its centrepiece. Everything else hovers around it and emanates from it. The Islamic paradigm has freedom, justice, and solidarity rolled into one as its defining character. Justice also means balance and harmony. All three are inalienable complements to each other, and it is in their harmonious integration that the real flowering of the human genius takes place at individual and collective levels. This is what makes the Islamic paradigm distinct.

Islam, like all revealed religions, adds one more very crucial and decisive dimension to the galaxy of strategies—that the final reward is destined for the life-to-come. Material affluence, social well-being, spiritual bliss, and eternal salvation become different aspects of one model of success (*falah*). Spiritual and material dimensions become two sides of the same coin. Life becomes one organic whole. Death no longer remains the end of life; it only represents the beginning of a new phase of existence. Life and life-after-death become two phases of the same stream. Man's position in the world and every man and woman's relationship with each other and the universe assume a very different significance in this purpose-oriented, holistic vision of human destiny. The secular and the sacred are fused, and transcendence comes within human reach. This makes the system unique. It is not possible to place Islam with any other 'ism' in juxtaposition with each other, seeking some integrated religious doctrine. It is however, possible for various 'isms' and Islam to coexist, compete, co-operate and contribute towards the betterment of the human race.

NOTES

1. G. D. H. Cole in his entry on 'Capitalism' observes: 'the word Capitalism was largely popularised by socialists as a name for the economic system they were attacking' (Cole 1964: 70); Robert Hessen goes a step further and says: 'Capitalism, a term of disparagement coined by socialists in the nineteenth century is a misnomer for "economic individualism" which Adam Smith earlier called "the obvious and simple system of natural liberty" ' (Hessen 1993: 110).
2. 'Indeed, Herbert Spencer and others equated the competitive market forces of supply and demand with Darwin's biological forces of natural selection: market competition, too was survival of the fittest. This connection—"Social Darwinism"—is not accidental' (Dalton 1974: 45). In another context Keynes writes: 'The Economists were teaching that wealth, commerce, and machinery were the children of free competition—that free competition built London. But the Darwinians could go one better than that—free competition had built man ... The principle of Survival of the Fittest could be regarded as a vast generalisation of the "Ricardian Economics" ' (Keynes 1926: 13–14).
3. 'Democracy and capitalism have very different beliefs about the proper distribution of power, one believes in a completely equal distribution of political power, "One man, one vote", while the other believes that it is the duty of the economically fit to drive the unfit out of business and in to economic extinction.... Survival of the fittest and inequality in purchasing power are what capitalist efficiency is all about' (Thurow 1996: 242; see also pp. 245–8).
4. George Soros underpins this point extensively in his book *The Crisis of Global Capitalism*. The central contention of this book, he claims 'is that market fundamentalism is today a greater threat to open society than any totalitarian ideology' (Soros 1998: xxii).
5. Kennedy (1988: 190); Bairoch (1982: 269–333); Alam (2000).
6. Branca Milanovic, of the World Bank, gives the following summary of his findings on income distribution based on household surveys: world income inequality is very

high: the Gini coefficient is 66 if one uses incomes adjusted for differences in countries' purchasing power, and almost 80 if one uses current dollar incomes. World inequality has increased (using the same sample of countries) from a Gini of 62.8 in 1988 to 66.0 in 1993. This represents an increase of 0.6 Gini points per year. This is a very fast increase, faster than the increase experienced by the United States and the United Kingdom in the 1980s. (The Gini coefficient is scale-invariant: thus larger and smaller units can legitimately be compared.) The increase of inequality between 1988 and 1993 occurred both between-country and within-country. However since their relative proportions remained the same, it was the between-country inequality which, being much larger, drove overall inequality up. The bottom 5% of the world grew poorer, as their real incomes decreased between 1988 and 1993 by one-quarter, while the richest one-fifth grew richer. It gained 12% in real terms, that is its income grew more than twice as much as mean world income (5.7%), A number of other statistics can be generated from world income distribution. These are some examples: The richest 1% of people in the world receive as much as the bottom 57%, or in other words, less than 50 million of the income-richest people receive as much as 2.7 billion poor people. An American having the average income of the bottom US 10% is better off than two-thirds of the world's population. The top 10% of the US population has an aggregate income equal to the income of the poorest 43% of people in the world, or put differently, the total income of the richest 25 million Americans is equal to the total income of almost 2 billion poor people. The ratio between the average income of the world's top 5% and the world's bottom 5% increased from 78 to 1 in 1988 to 114 to 1 in 1993. 75% of the world's population receive 25% of world $PPP income; and the reverse. 84% of the world's population receive 16% of world (unadjusted) dollar income; and the reverse.(Milanovic 2002: 51–92).

7. Muslim countries were engaged in international trade throughout the Middle Ages and the economic relationships spread from Morocco and Spain in the West, to India and China in the East, Central Asia in the North, and Africa in the South. Available historical documentation is supported by the discovery of Muslim coins of the seventh to eleventh centuries found through excavation in countries like Russia, Finland, Sweden, Norway, the British Isles, and countries that were outside the immediate realm of the Muslim political entity which itself spread over three continents (Kramer 1952 and Udovitch 1981).

8. As dealt with in detail by Ahmad (1994); Chapra (1992); Chapra (2000); and Siddiqui (1983).

9. The Quran explicitly lays down the principles that 'there is no compulsion in religion' (The Quran 2: 256). Freedom of choice is the defining element of the human situation. God has given His guidance, but now it is the choice of the humans to accept and follow, or reject it and suffer the consequences of rejection. The message and the warning via the first prophet and guide, Adam, spells out the rules of the game: 'Thus shall come to you from Me the Guidance, then whosoever will follow My Guidance need have no fear, nor shall they grieve. But those who refuse to accept this (Guidance) and reject the signs as false, are destined for the Fire, where they shall abide forever' (The Quran 2: 38–9). 'O Mankind! We created you from a single (pair) of a male and a female, and made you nations and tribes, so that you may know each other, verily the most honoured of you in the sight of God is the one who is most righteous' (The Quran 49: 13), 'If God had so willed, He would surely have made you one community. Instead (He gave each of you a law and a way of life) in order to test you by what He gave you. Vie then, one with another in good works. Unto God is the return of all of you', (The Quran 5: 48).

10. Al-Ghazali, Abu Hamid, *Al-Mustasfa*, quoted by Chapra (2000: 118).
11. References to the original source of this article can be seen in Chapra (2001).
12. Lester Thurow writes: 'All societies need a mixture of self control and social control but even social control is socially instilled… Yet Capitalism has no basis for demanding even self-constraint unless individual actions directly harm someone else. Even Adam Smith two hundred years ago saw that something more was needed. Men could safely be trusted to pursue their own self-interest without undue harm to a community not only because of Utilitarian laws. But also because they were subject to built in restraint derived from morals, religion, customs and education' (Thurow 1996: 30).
13. References to the original source of this article can be seen in Chapra (2001).
14. Ibid.
15. Ibid.
16. There is ample historical documentation for the fact that poverty was totally eliminated from Muslim lands during the periods when the Islamic economic system was in practice. Even now, when obligatory poor-due is not in force, zakat and *sadaqat* are the most effective and widespread sources for helping the poor. A recent study by the Agha Khan Foundation about Pakistan revealed that the budget of the Federal Government in Pakistan is around Rs 6 billion ($100 million) and support to the needy through religious charitable endowments and the like (zakat, *sadaqat* and voluntary payments) are responsible for providing Rs 70.5 billion ($1.2 billion), an amount equating to 11% of the Federal budget. Source: Agha Khan Foundation (2000: 46).
17. Paul Kennedy concludes his study on the *Rise and Fall of Great Powers* as follows: 'In the largest sense of all, therefore, the only answer to the question increasingly debated by the public is of whether the United States can preserve its existing position is 'no'—for it simply has not been given to any one society to remain *permanently* ahead of all others, because that would imply a freezing of the differentiated pattern of growth rates, technological advance and military development which has existed since time immemorial.' (Kennedy 1988: 689).
18. John Dunning, Chapter 1, this volume. The reader might also like to compare these 'C's' to those offered by Jonathan Sacks in Chapter 9.

GLOSSARY OF TERMS

'*Adl*: Justice, straightness, balance, impartiality, fairness, equilibrium, probity, uprightness, equitable composition, fulfilment of each others' rights.
Akhirah: Belief in life-after-death; the Hereafter
Amanah: Trust, reliability, honesty, good faith.
Halal: Permitted, that which is allowed in the Shari'ah, i.e. lawful.
Falah: Well-being, welfare, salvation, moral and material, in this world and after death.
Haram: Forbidden, prohibited, i.e. unlawful in the Shari'ah.
Hisbah: The process and institution of social accountability, ombudsman. In theology this equates with examination of one's conscience, self-evaluation, and accountability.
Hayat al-Tayyebah: Good life, balanced satisfaction of the material and spiritual needs of human beings, individual and collective.
Ihsan: Beneficence, charity, performance of good deeds, being magnificent towards others.
Istikhlaf: The concept that man is God's deputy, representative and vicegerent, assigned to fulfil God's will through his own voluntary actions and to establish individual and social life based on divinely revealed values and principles.

Islam: Submission, resignation and reconciliation to the will of God, peace.

Khalifah: Vicegerent.

Quran: The divine guidance revealed to the Prophet Muhammad and preserved in the form of the Book. The chief source of Islamic guidance and law.

Risalah: Message, the process of guidance God has laid down for mankind through His representatives known as prophets/messengers. Divine guidance is revealed to the prophets to be conveyed to human beings.

Sadaqat (sing: *sadaqah*): Charitable gifts, alms, voluntary contributions for good causes.

Shari'ah: The way, the Islamic way, the divine guidance given in the Quran and the *Sunnah*, providing a comprehensive code of conduct for different aspects of living, including beliefs and practices, individual and social.

Sunnah: The sayings, actions, and things that were approved by the Prophet Muhammad; the life example of the Prophet, the second major source of Islamic guidance and law.

Taqwa: Godliness, devotedness, God fearing, piety, perfection, discipline, and control over one's self to do what is good and restrain from what is undesirable.

Tawhid: The Oneness and Unity of God, the only Being worthy of worship and obedience.

Ummah: Nation, in the terminology of Islamic law, the whole global Muslim community irrespective of colour, race, language, nationality, or territory.

Waqf: Endowment, Endowment fund, Religious Endowment, Unalienable property committed to certain specific good causes.

Zakat: Legally prescribed alms, obligatory poor-due, which the rich pay for the welfare of the poor and the needy: categories of payers and causes for which the amount can be used are laid down by the Shari'ah. Ideally collected and dispersed through state channels or social institutions.

REFERENCES

Agha Khan Foundation (2000), *Philanthropy in Pakistan* (Islamabad: Agha Khan Foundation).

Ahmad, Khurshid (ed.) (1980), *Studies in Islamic Economics* (Leicester: The Islamic Foundation).

—— (1994), *Islamic Approach to Development: Some Policy Implications* (Islamabad: Institute of Policy Studies).

—— (2000), 'Islamic Finance and Banking: The Challenge and Prospects', *Review of Islamic Economics* (Leicester) No. 9, 2000/1421H.

—— (2002), *The Contemporary Economic Challenges and Islam* (Islamabad: Institute of Policy Studies).

Ahmad, Ziauddin, et al. (eds.) (1983), *Money and Banking in Islam* (Jeddah: International Centre for Research in Islamic Economics, King Abdul Aziz University).

Alam, M. Shahid (2000), *Poverty from the Wealth of Nations: Integration and Polarisation in the Global Economy since 1760* (London: Macmillan Press).

Amin, Samir (1974), *Accumulation on a World Scale: A Critique of the Theory of Underdevelopment* (2 Volumes) (New York: Monthly Review Press).

—— (1976), *Unequal Development* (New York: Monthly Review Press).

Ariff, Mohammad (ed.) (1982), *Monetary and Fiscal Economics of Islam* (Jeddah: International Centre for Research in Islamic Economics, King Abdul Aziz University).

Arighi, Giovanni (1994), *The Long Twentieth Century* (New York: Verso).

Arnold, Thomas, and Guillaume, Alfred (eds.) (1952), *The Legacy of Islam* (London: Oxford University Press).

Bairoch, P. (1982), 'International Industrialization Levels from 1750 to 1980', *Journal of European Economic History* 11: 269–333.

Barberton, Peter (1999), *Debt and Delusion* (London: Allen Lane/The Penguin Press).

Bell, Daniel, and Kristol, Irving (eds.) (1971), *Capitalism Today* (New York: Mentor Book/New American Library).

Brittan, Samuel, and Hamlin, Alan (eds.) (1995), *Market Capitalism and Moral Values* (Aldershot: Edward Elgar Publishing Company).

Burkett, Lary (1991), *The Coming Economic Earthquake* (Chicago: Moody Press).

Chapra, M. Umer (1985), *Towards a Just Monetary System* (Leicester: The Islamic Foundation).

——(1992), *Islam and the Economic Challenge* (Leicester: The Islamic Foundation).

——(2000), *The Future of Economics: An Islamic Perspective* (Leicester: The Islamic Foundation).

——(2001), 'Islamic Economic Thought and the New Global Economy', *Islamic Economic Studies* (Jeddah: Islamic Development Bank), vol. 9, no. 1, Rajab 1422H (September 2001).

Cole, G. D. H. (1964), 'Capitalism.' In J. Gould, and W. L. Kolb (eds.), *A Dictionary of the Social Sciences* (London: Tavistock), 70–2.

Dalton, George (1974), *Economic Systems and Society: Capitalism, Communism and the Third World* (Harmondsworth: Penguin Education).

Donaldson, Thomas (1995), 'Moral Minimums for Multinationals.' In Joel H. Rosenthal (ed.), *Ethics & International Affairs: A Reader*, 2nd edn 1999. (Washington, DC: Georgetown University Press), 455–80.

Dunning, John, H. (2001), *Global Capitalism at Bay?* (London and New York: Routledge).

Ellwood, Wayne (2001), *Globalization* (London: Verso/New Internationalist).

Emmanuel, Arrighi (1972), *Unequal Exchange: A Study of the Imperialism of Trade* (New York: Monthly Review Press).

Etzioni, A. (1998), *The Moral Dimension: Towards a New Economics* (New York: Free Press).

Fogel, Robert, W. (2000), *The Fourth Great Awakening and the Future of Egalitarianism* (Chicago and London: The University of Chicago Press).

Frank, Andre Gunder (1979), *Dependent Accumulation and Underdevelopment* (New York: Monthly Review Press).

Giddens, Anthony (1990), *The Consequences of Modernity* (London: Polity Press).

Gorringe, Timothy (1999), *Fair Shares: Ethics and the Global Economy* (London: Thames & Hudson).

Gray, John (1998), *False Dawn: The Delusions of Global Capitalism* (London: Granta Books).

Greider, William (1997), *One World, Ready or Not: The Manic Logic of Global Capitalism* (New York: Simon & Schuster).

Grindle, Merilee S. (2000), 'Ready or Not: The Developing World and Globalization.' In Joseph S. Nye, and John D. Donahue (eds.), *Governance in a Globalizing World* (Washington: Brookings Institution Press).

Hayter, Teresa (1981), *The Creation of World Poverty* (London: Pluto Press).

Hessen, R. (1993), 'Capitalism.' In D. R. Henderson (ed.) *The Fortune Encyclopedia of Economics* (New York: Warner Books), 110–14.

Hertz, Noreena (2001), *The Silent Takeover: Global Capitalism and the Death of Democracy* (London: William Heinemann).

Kung, Hans and Schmidt, Helmut (1998), *A Global Ethic and Global Responsibilities: Two Declarations* (London: SCM Press).

Kennedy, Paul (1988), *The Rise and Fall of the Great Powers*: (London: Fontana Press).

Kenton, Jeffrey (2000), *Capitalism and Coercion: The Economic and Military Processes that have Shaped the World Economy 1800–1990* (New York and London: Garland Publishing).

Keynes, J. M. (1926), *The End of Laissez Faire* (London: Hogarth Press; quoted by Dalton 1974: 59).

Kramer, J. H. (1952), 'Geography and Commerce.' In Arnold and Guillaume, op. cit. (1952): 79–107.

Lutz, Mark, and Lux, Kanneth (1979), *The Challenge of Humanistic Economics* (Menlo Park: Benjamin/Cummings).

Maddison, Angus (1995), *Monitoring the World Economy 1820–1992* (Paris: OECD).

Marris, Robin (1997), *Ending Poverty* (London: Thomas and Hudson).

McCracken, Grant (1990), *Culture and Consumption* (Bloomington: Indiana University Press).

Milanovic, Branca (2002), 'True World Income Distribution, 1988 and 1993', *The Economic Journal* 112 (January 2002): 51–92.

New International (2001), *The World Guide 2001–2002* (Oxford: New Internationalist Publication).

Nye, Joseph S., and Donahue, John D. (eds.) (2000), *Governance in a Globalizing World* (Washington, DC: Brookings Institution Press).

Paterson, Matthew (1999), 'Globalization, Ecology and Resistance', *New Political Economy* 4(1): 129–45.

Rawls, John (1972), *A Theory of Justice* (Oxford: Clarendon Press).

—— (1999), *The Law of Peoples* (Cambridge, Mass.: Harvard University Press).

Roepke, Willhelm (1977), 'Ordered Anarchy.' In Lawrence S. Steplevich (ed.) *Capitalist Reader* (New Rochelle, NY: Arlington).

Rosenthal, Franz (1967), *Ibn Khaldun: The Muqaddimah, An Introduction to History*, 3 vols. (London: Routledge & Kegan Paul),

Rowbotham, Michael (1998), *The Grip of Death: A Study of Modern Money, Debt Slavery and Destructive Economics* (Oxford: John Carpenter Publishing).

Sachs, Ignacy (2000), *Understanding Development* (New Delhi: Oxford University Press).

Sen, Amartaya (1999), *Development as Freedom* (Oxford: Oxford University Press).

Shutt, Harry (1998), *The Trouble with Capitalism: An Enquiry into the Causes of Global Economic Failure* (London and New York: Zed Books).

Siddiqi, M. Nejatullah (1983), *Muslim Economic Thinking: A Survey of Contemporary Literature* (Leicester: The Islamic Foundation).

Sklair, Leslie (ed.) (1994), *Capitalism and Development* (London and New York: Routledge).

Soros, George (1998), *The Crisis of Global Capitalism: Open Society Endangered* (London: Little, Brown & Company).

Tawney, R. (1926), *Religion and the Rise of Capitalism* (London: John Murray).

Thurow, Lester (1996), *The Future of Capitalism* (London: Nicholas Brealey).

Udovitch, A. L. (ed.) (1981), *The Islamic Middle East, 700–1900: Studies in Economic and Social History* (Princeton: Darwin Press).

UNDP (2000), *Human Development Report 2000* (Oxford: Oxford University Press).

UNCTAD (1997), *World Investment Report 1997: Transnational Corporations, Market Structure and Competitive Policy* (New York: United Nations).

US Arms Control and Disarmament Agency (1995), *World Military Expenditure and Arms Transfer 1993–1994* (Washington, DC: Government Printing Office).

Wallerstein, Immanual (1974), *The Modern World System I*; (1980) *The Modern World System II*; (1989) *The Modern World System III* (New York: Academic Press).

Weber, Max (1930), *The Protestant Ethic and the Spirit of Capitalism* (London: George Allen & Unwin).

World Bank (1999), *Attacking Poverty: World Development Report 2000–2001* (Oxford and New York: Oxford University Press).

—— (2000), *Entering the Twenty First Century: World Development Report 1999–2000* (Oxford and New York: Oxford University Press).

9

Global Covenant: A Jewish Perspective on Globalization

JONATHAN SACKS

9.1 INTRODUCTION

The events of 11 September 2001—a defining moment in the history of the twenty-first century—were freighted with symbolism. Two icons of global capitalism, the jumbo jet and the twin towers of the World Trade Center, were turned into instruments of destruction. Office workers going about their daily routines found themselves suddenly implicated in a conflict whose epicentre was thousands of miles away, and of whose very existence they may have been unaware. The terror itself was plotted by means of the Internet, encrypted emails, and satellite phones. It was planned, almost certainly, with global television coverage in mind. The terrorists may have been driven by religious ideas centuries old, but their methods were quintessentially of our time. Nothing could have demonstrated more vividly the vulnerability of our hyper-connected world and the tensions, conflicts, and resentments it contains.

The concept of globalization is not new. Almost four hundred years ago, John Donne gave it one of its most memorable expressions:

All mankinde is of one Author, and is one volume . . . No man is an Iland, intire of it selfe; every man is a peece of the Continent, a part of the maine; if a Clod bee washed away by the Sea, Europe is the less, as well as if a Promontorie were, as well as if a Mannor of thy friends or of thine owne were; any mans death diminishes me; because I am involved in Mankinde; And therefore never send to know for whom the bell tolls; It tolls for thee. (Donne 1930: 537–8)

International commerce, practised extensively by the Phoenicians, goes back almost to the dawn of civilization.[1] The great maritime adventures, beginning in the fifteenth century, of Zheng He, Vasco de Gama, Magellan, and Columbus created new trade routes and a growth of long-distance exchange. Further momentum was added by the development of accurate navigation instruments, the growth of banks and the funding of risk, and the birth of giant international businesses such as the Dutch East India Company. Industrialization, the spread of railways, and the invention of the telegraph added impetus in the course of the nineteenth century. The integration of distant regions into a single international economy has been a continuous process, extending back for many centuries.

A restless spirit has led mankind to travel ever further in search of the new, the remote and the undiscovered. In one sense, then, the world we inhabit is a logical outcome of the world of our ancestors.[2] It is the latest stage in a journey begun millennia ago.

But there are changes in degree which become changes in kind. The sheer speed and extent of advances in modern communications technology have altered conditions of existence for many, perhaps most, of the world's six billion inhabitants. The power of instantaneous global communication, the sheer volume of international monetary movements, the internationalization of processes and products, and the ease with which jobs can be switched from country to country have meant that our interconnectedness has become more immediate, vivid, and consequential than ever before.

Global capitalism, as described by John Dunning in Chapter 1, is a system of immense power, from which it has become increasingly difficult for nations to dissociate themselves. It heralds potential blessings, most significantly economic growth. Countries that have embraced the new economy—among them Singapore, South Korea, and Thailand—have seen spectacular rises in living standards (Hertz 2001: 36–7). Improvements in agriculture have meant that while, prior to industrialization, it took the majority of a country's workforce to produce the food it needed, today in advanced economies the figure is around 2 per cent (Barber 2001: 27). Throughout the developed world, advances in medicine and healthcare have reduced infant mortality and raised life expectancy. The average supermarket in the West sets before consumers a range of choices that, a century ago, would have been beyond the reach of kings.

But globalization also carries effects that are perceived as deeply threatening, especially to traditional cultures. Jobs become vulnerable. Whole economies are destabilized. Inequalities within and between nations grow larger, not smaller. One-fifth of the world's population subsists on less than a dollar a day. Throughout Africa and parts of Asia, poverty, disease, and hunger are rife. Developing countries find themselves vulnerable as never before to sudden economic downturns, currency fluctuations, and shifts in production, leaving behind them vast swathes of unemployment. Local cultures are often overwhelmed by predominantly American forms of music, food, and dress conveyed by cable and satellite television, the Internet, and multinational corporations. The power of corporations has grown while that of nation states ('too big for the small problems, too small for the big problems') has declined. Questions multiply as to the accountability of mega-businesses and whether control mechanisms exist for balancing the pursuit of profit with the common good.

One of the most significant changes is the acceleration of the rate of change itself. Scientific knowledge doubles in every generation. Computing power grows faster still, doubling every two years. I have on my shelves a book of futurology, published in 1990, entitled *Megatrends 2000*. One word is conspicuous by its absence—the word 'Internet'. In a post-presidential address, Bill Clinton noted that when he took up office in 1993, there were fifty registered websites. By the time he left office in 2000 there were upwards of 350 million. Already in the early twentieth century Alfred North Whitehead observed that 'in the past the time-span of important change was considerably longer than that of a single human life'. The result was that most people inhabited a world whose character was recognizably the same when they were old as it had been when they were young. 'Today,' he noted, 'the time-span is considerably shorter than that of a human life' (Whitehead 1942). Change has become part of texture of life itself, and there are few things more disorienting than constant flux and uncertainty.

9.2 CONTROL: THE HUMAN PROTEST AGAINST FATE

Globalization raises vast, even protean issues: too complex, perhaps, for any single mind or group to conceptualize, let alone confront in practice. What, then, can a religious perspective contribute? It cannot lie at the level of detail. The world's great faiths arose at the so-called 'axial age' of civilization, long before the rise of modernity. Yet there is much that a religious voice—more precisely, a range of religious voices—can add to the collective conversation on where we are, or should be, going. Faced with fateful choices, humanity needs wisdom, and religious traditions, alongside the great philosophies, are our richest resource of wisdom. They are sustained reflections on humanity's place in nature and what constitute the proper goals of society and an individual life. They build communities, shape lives, and tell the stories that explain ourselves to ourselves. They frame the rituals that express our aspirations and identities. In uncharted territory one needs a compass, and the great faiths have been the compasses of mankind. In an age of uncertainty, they remind us that we are not alone, nor are we bereft of guidance from the past. The sheer tenacity of the great faiths—so much longer-lived than political systems and ideologies—suggests that they speak to something enduring in human character. Above all, as Francis Fukuyama (1999: 231–45) points out, it was religion that first taught human beings to look beyond the city-state, the tribe, and the nation to humanity as a whole. The world faiths are global phenomena whose reach is broader and in some respects deeper than that of the nation state.

Judaism is one of those voices. The prophets of ancient Israel were the first to think globally, to conceive of a God transcending place and national boundaries and of humanity as a single moral community linked by a covenant of mutual responsibility (the covenant with Noah after the Flood). Equally, they were the first to conceive of society as a place where 'justice rolls down like water and righteousness like a never ending stream' and of a future in which war had been abolished and peoples lived together in peace. Those insights remain valid today.

No less significantly, Judaism was the first religion to wrestle with the reality of global dispersion. During the destruction of the First Temple in the sixth century BCE, Jews were transported to Babylon in the East or had escaped to Egypt in the West. By the time of the destruction of the Second Temple, in 70 CE, they had spread throughout much of Europe and Asia. For almost two thousand years, scattered throughout the world, they continued to see themselves and be seen by others as a single people—the world's first global people. That experience forced Jews to reflect on many problems that are now the shared experience of mankind: how to maintain identity as a minority, how to cope with insecurity, and how to sustain human dignity in a world that seems often to deny it.[3] Judaism eventually gave rise to two other monotheisms, Christianity and Islam, that represent the faith of more than half of the 6 billion people alive today. There is much in common in the ethics of these three faiths, though each speaks in its own distinctive accent. What can we learn from Judaic teaching and the Jewish experience about the complex issues raised by a global age?

Perhaps the most important is the simple idea of *responsibility*. There has been a perennial temptation in human history to see the forces that surround us as inexorable and fundamentally indifferent to mankind. In ancient times they were the forces of nature: the sun, the wind, the rain, the flood, and the sea. Today we would probably speak of global ecology, evolution, the march of science, the ebb and flow of the economy, and the shifting balance of international power. Every era has produced its own myths, philosophies, or quasi-scientific systems to show that what is could not have been otherwise; that the march of history is inevitable; that it is hubris to believe we can fight against fate. All we can do is to align ourselves to its flow, exploit it when we can, and render ourselves stoically indifferent to our fate when we cannot. Mankind is alone in a world fundamentally blind to our presence, deaf to our prayers and hopes.

The great leap of the biblical imagination was to argue otherwise. Nature is not all there is. There is a personal dimension to existence. Our hopes are not mere dreams, nor are our ideals illusions. Something at the core of being responds to us as persons, inviting us to exercise our freedom by shaping families, communities and societies in such a way as to honour the image of God that is mankind, investing each human life with ultimate dignity. This view, shared by Judaism, Christianity, and Islam, sees choice, agency, and moral responsibility at the heart of the human project. We are not powerless in the face of fate. Every technological advance can be used for good or evil. There is nothing inevitably benign or malign in our increasing powers. It depends on the use we make of them. What we can create, we can control. What we initiate, we can direct. With every new power come choice, responsibility, and exercise of the moral imagination. This view has always been opposed by determinisms of different kinds, among them the Hegelian, Marxist, and neo-Darwinian versions. The assumption of this chapter will be that the biblical insight remains true. Global capitalism is not a juggernaut that no one can steer. It can be turned this way or that by collective consent. Our aim must be to maximize human dignity and hand on to future generations a more gracious, less capricious world.

In what follows, we begin by telling the story of an ancient revolution in information technology to show how simple changes can have immense social, moral, and political implications. History is helpful here because, though great inventions change our world, it is only after they have done so that we can see how. One obvious example is the development of printing in mid-fifteenth-century

Europe (China had invented it several centuries earlier, but the technique had not spread). This led, in the course of time, to the Reformation, the spread of literacy, the rise of science, the secular nation state, and the Industrial Revolution (Landes 1998). None of these could have been foreseen in advance, nor did they happen because of printing alone, but they would not have been possible without it. We are living through a comparable revolution, and the past is our only available guide to the future. We then turn to biblical tradition to see how some of its values might guide us as we navigate through an age of uncertainty. To John Dunning's helpful idea of three Cs (creativity, co-operation, compassion) set out in Chapter 1, we have already added one (control) and will suggest three others: conservation, coexistence, and covenant. First, though: how does technology change society?

9.3 INFORMATION TECHNOLOGY AND SOCIAL STRUCTURE

The great leaps in civilization occur when there is a fundamental change in the way we record and transmit information. There have been four such changes. Printing was the third. Our current era of instantaneous global communication via computer, email, and Internet is the fourth. The first was the invention of writing in Mesopotamia some 6,000 years ago (Diringer 1962). Its origin is lost in the mists of time, but it came as a result of new building materials, specifically the making of bricks from clay tablets dried in the sun. Marks made by a wedge-shaped stick while the clay was still wet would become indelible once the tablet had become hard and could thus serve as permanent records. The first signs to be inscribed were schematic representations of objects. Art, specifically the making of pictures, preceded writing by tens of thousands of years. As time went by, however, the pictures became simpler to the point where they had become symbols whose meaning was determined by convention. The wedge-shaped sticks used to make impressions in the clay gave this first of written languages its name: cuneiform.

The settlement of populations, the development of agriculture, and the birth of complex economies with their division of labour and growth of exchange, gave writing its earliest and most immediately practical use, namely to record transactions. But the power of the system was soon apparent. It could do more than keep a note of who owed what to whom. It could capture for posterity the great narratives—myths, cosmologies, and epic histories—that explained the present in terms of the past, and whose telling in oral form had been a central feature of ancient religious rituals. While cuneiform was being developed, a parallel process was taking place in ancient Egypt, giving rise to the family of scripts known as hieroglyphics. In all, writing was invented independently seven times—in India, China, and Greece (Minoan or Mycenean 'Linear B') and later by the Mayans and Aztecs as well in the ancient Mesopotamian city-states and the Egypt of the Pharaohs (Ong 1988: 85).

The birth of writing was the genesis of civilization. For the first time knowledge could be accumulated and handed on to future generations in a way that exceeded, in quantity and quality, the scope of unaided memory. Few things have been more significant for the development of *homo sapiens*, the being whose period of dependency is longer, and whose genetically encoded instincts are fewer, than any other. Humanity's great evolutionary advantage is that we are, *par excellence*, the learning animal. Writing was the breakthrough by which the present could hand on the lessons of the past to the generations of the future. It led to a quantum leap in the growth of knowledge and skills and to a huge acceleration in the pace of change in human affairs.

The early forms of writing, however, suffered from one significant disadvantage. Because each character represented a word or at least a syllable, their symbol-sets were huge. The time it took to master them—to learn to read and write—was such that literacy was bound to remain the preserve of a cognitive elite, a knowledge class. Bacon's famous observation that knowledge is power applies with especial force to the ancient world. A civilization in which literacy is available only to the few—an administrative class, usually the priesthood—inevitably gives rise to a stratified society in which the many are denied access to education and information.

The second revolution—the invention of the alphabet—was therefore more than a mere technical advance. It heralded far-reaching social and political possibilities. For the first time the entire universe of communicable knowledge was reduced to a symbol-set of between twenty and thirty letters, small enough to be mastered, at least in principle, by everyone. Again origins are shrouded in mystery, but we know that the first alphabets were semitic and that they emerged in the territory known today as Israel or to the south of it, in the Sinai desert. The most likely scenario is that they were developed as a simplification of the hieroglyphic script or its abbreviated cursive form, known as hieratic. The inventors may have been Canaanites or Phoenicians or the wandering folk known as Apiru, from which the word 'Hebrew' may be derived.

The alphabet appeared early in the second pre-Christian millennium, in the age of the biblical patriarchs.[4] There is evidence from the turquoise mines of Serabit in the Sinai desert that it was there, among the slave workers or their supervisors, that the breakthrough came. William Flinders Petrie, the British archaeologist of the early twentieth century, speculated that the first alphabetical scripts were used by the Israelites while they were slaves in Egypt and later on their way to the promised land. This much we know: that the alphabet was one of those inventions whose origin can be traced to a single source. All alphabetical systems derive directly or indirectly from these first 'proto-Sinaitic' scripts. To be sure, it was not until they were transferred, probably by trading Phoenicians, to Greece, that for the first time symbols were added to represent vowels (Hebrew to this day is a consonantal script). But the semitic origin of the alphabet is still evident in the word itself: a combination of the first two Hebrew letters, *aleph* and *bet* (*alpha-beta* in Greek).

The pre-alphabetical world was, and could not be other than, hierarchical. At its top was a ruler, king or pharaoh, seen as a god, or a child of the gods, or as prime intermediary between the people and the gods. Below him and holding much of the day-to-day power was the cognitive elite, the priesthood. Below them was the mass of the people, conceived as a vast work- or military force. The cultures of the ancient world were mythological, or what Eric Voegelin called 'cosmological'.[5] Central to this way of thinking is the idea that the divisions in society mirror the hierarchy of the gods or planets or elemental forces. They are written into the structure of the universe itself. Nor was this an abstract idea. It was manifest in the monumental architecture of the age—the ziggurats of Babylon, the pyramids and temples of pharaonic Egypt, each a statement in stone of the power structure of the ancient world. William Shakespeare has left us a memorable statement of this world-view:

> The heavens themselves, the planets, and this centre,
> Observe degree, priority, and place,
> Insisture, course, proportion, season, form,
> Office, and custom, in all line of order...
> Take but degree away, untune that string,
> And, hark, what discord follows![6]

This is, needless to say, a deeply conservative vision, an 'organic' view of society in which the individual's status is a given of birth and cannot be changed without disturbing the fundamental order on which the world depends.

By contrast, the invention of the alphabet heralded an entirely new possibility, namely of a society in which each individual has access to knowledge, and thus power, and hence ultimate dignity in the presence of God. A world of potential universal literacy is one in which everyone has equal citizenship under the sovereignty of God. That is the significance of the most revolutionary of all religious utterances, the declaration in the first chapter of Genesis that not only kings and pharaohs but every human being is God's 'image and likeness'. Though it would take thousands of years for it to work its way into the culture of the West, it is here that the idea is first given expression that would become, in the American Declaration of Independence, the famous statement: 'We hold these truths to be self-evident, that all men are created equal, that they are endowed by their Creator with certain unalienable rights, that among these are Life, Liberty and the pursuit of Happiness...' The irony is that these truths are anything but self-evident. They are the negation of a view, held universally by the ancient world, given philosophical expression by Plato and Aristotle, and maintained throughout the Middle Ages, that people are *not* born equal. Some are born to be rulers, others to be ruled.

The politics of ancient Israel begins with an act inconceivable to the cosmological mind, namely that God, creator of the universe, intervenes in history to liberate slaves. It reaches its climax in the nineteenth chapter of the Book of Exodus with an event unique in the religious history of mankind, in which God reveals Himself to an entire people at Mount Sinai and enters into a covenant with them. One detail in the narrative deserves reinterpretation in the light of the story we have told. In proposing the covenant, God invites the Israelites to become *mamlechet cohanim vegoi kadosh*, 'a kingdom of priests and a holy nation' (Exodus 19: 5). In fact Israel did not become, literally, a kingdom of priests. That role was reserved, initially for the first-born, later to the descendants of Aaron. Once we remember, however, that the functional uniqueness of the priesthood in pre-modern times was its ability to read and write—an association still present in the English word 'clerical'—it becomes possible to translate *mamlechet cohanim* not as 'a kingdom of priests' but as 'a society of universal literacy.'

Ancient Israel was the not always successful, but nonetheless historically unprecedented, attempt to envisage and create a society as a covenant of equal citizens freely bound to one another and to God. As Norman Gottwald puts it, the God of Israel was:

the historically concretized, primordial power to establish and sustain social equality in the face of counter-oppression from without and against provincial and nonegalitarian tendencies from within the society...Israel thought it was different because it was different: it constituted an egalitarian social system in the midst of stratified societies. (Gottwald 1980: 692–3)

This, we have argued, would have been impossible without the existence of the alphabet, which, for the first time, made universal literacy a conceivable idea. Whether or not the first alphabetical script, proto-Sinaitic, was invented by the Israelites, they were certainly the first to meditate on and explore the new social and political possibilities it heralded. The alphabet gave rise to the book and thus to the people of the book.

We have told this story at length in order to convey the drama of what may seem on the surface a simple and minor change. Other technological advances make localized differences. Changes in the way we record and transmit information, by contrast, have systemic effects. They transform human possibilities and the way we structure our common life. There were three such revolutions in the past: writing, the alphabet, and the invention of printing. We are living through the fourth, the birth of instantaneous global communication. We do not yet know, and will not for centuries, what its cumulative effects will be. Will it spell the end, or at least the decline, of the nation state? Will it lead to new forms of community and collaborative action? Will it hasten the demise of local languages in favour of the dominant tongue of the Internet, American-English? Will it bring about a fundamental reorientation of human consciousness, from a space-bound to a more time-centred modality? One thing is certain: the changes will go deep and they will be, among other things, 'spiritual'. Writing gave birth to civilization. The alphabet gave rise to monotheism. Printing made the Reformation possible. Precisely because religion tracks the deepest connections between self, other, and the universe, it is sensitive to transformations of this kind. New communication technologies make possible new modes of relationship, new social, economic, and political structures, and thus new ways of understanding the human situation under God.

9.4 CREATIVITY: THE IMPERATIVE OF EDUCATION

The most obvious application of the Jewish experience relates, therefore, to *creativity*. In ancient times, wealth and power lay in the ownership of persons, in the form of slaves, armies, and a workforce. In the feudal era they lay in the ownership of land. In the industrial age they were ownership of capital and the means of production. In the information age they lie in access to and deployment of intellectual capital, the ability to master information and turn it to innovative ends—what Joseph Nye calls 'soft' power (Nye 2002). The labour content of manufactured goods continues to fall. Huge profits go to those who have ideas. To an ever-increasing degree, multinational enterprises (MNEs) are outsourcing production and peripheral services and becoming, instead, owners of concepts: brands, logos, images, and designs (Klein 2001). In such an age, immense advantage accrues to those with intellectual and creative skills. Education, not merely basic but extended, becomes a necessity, even a fundamental human right. Investment in education is the most important way in which a society offers its children a future.

This is a biblical insight. By making mankind in His image, the creative God endowed humanity with creativity, giving us the mandate to 'fill the earth and subdue it' and inviting us to become, in the rabbinic phrase, 'God's partners in the work of creation'. Specifically—following through the possibilities raised by the invention of the alphabet—Judaism made education a primary religious duty. Time and again throughout the Pentateuch, Moses emphasizes the importance of education: 'And when your children ask you...then tell them...' 'On that day you shall tell your child...' (Exodus 12: 26; 13: 8). And most famously, 'Teach [these commandments] diligently to your children, speaking of them when you sit at home and when you walk on the road, when you lie down and when you rise up' (Deuteronomy 6: 7). In one of the formative acts of Judaism Ezra, returning to Israel from Babylon, assembled the people at one of the gates of Jerusalem and reinstated the teaching of the Law in a vast ceremony of adult education: 'They read from the Book of the Law of God, making it clear and giving the meaning so that the people could understand what was being read' (Nehemiah 8: 8). Ezra became a new archetype: the teacher as hero. From then on, Judaism steadily evolved the institutions—schools, houses of study, and the synagogue as a house not only of prayer but also of public reading and explanation of the Torah—that were to sustain it after the fall of the Second Temple and the global dispersion of Jewry. As H. G. Wells points out, 'the Jewish religion, because it was a literature-sustained religion, led to the first efforts to provide elementary education for *all* the children in the community' (Wells n.d.: vol. 1, 176).

From a Jewish perspective, therefore, the first imperative of the new information technology is to make available to every child the universe of knowledge opened up by access to the Internet and CD-ROMs. As with the invention of the alphabet and printing, so with the personal computer and the Internet: what makes them so significant an enhancement of human possibilities is their contribution to the *democratization of knowledge*, and thus ultimately of dignity and power (Friedman 2000). Much talk about globalization focuses on politics and economics: global governance and the international economy. Important though these are, much depends on the degree to which populations are positioned to take advantage of new opportunities which, in turn, depends on the extent and depth of investment in education. Indeed, so rapidly are techniques and technologies changing that the concept of a period of education—childhood to young adult—may have to be revised in favour of lifelong learning, itself a classic value of the Judaic tradition.

Education is still far too unevenly distributed. A hundred million children worldwide do not go to school. There are twenty-three countries—mostly in Africa, but they include Afghanistan, Bangladesh, Nepal, Pakistan, and Haiti—in which half or more of the adult population are illiterate. In thirty-five countries—including Algeria, Egypt, Guatemala, India, Laos, Morocco, Nigeria, and Saudi Arabia—half or more women cannot read or write. Compared to North America, Latin America suffers a 50 per cent higher poverty rate and a 70 per cent higher high school dropout rate. Within the United States itself, Hispanics are significantly poorer and less well educated than other groups (Harrison and Huntington 2000: xviii–xix). There is a high correlation between education and economic achievement: it has been estimated that every additional year of schooling in a poor country adds between 10 and 20 per cent to a child's eventual income.

The first and most potent global intervention, therefore, is to ensure that every child has access to information, knowledge, and skills. The model here is the Bolsa-Escola scheme in Brazil that provides subsidies to poor families provided that their children attend school regularly. School participation in Brazil has risen, as a result, to 97 per cent of the child population (Soros 2002: 37, 84; Clinton 2001). Few things could do more to enhance human dignity and few are less contentious. That is because, even in the short term, knowledge is not a zero-sum good. The more of my power I share, the less I have; the more of my wealth I share, the less I have; but my knowledge is not reduced when I give it to others. To the contrary, it was precisely the pooling of knowledge, made possible by the invention of printing, the birth of learned societies, and the spread of scholarly periodicals, that led to the exponential growth of science in the modern West. Knowledge grows by being shared.

9.5 CO-OPERATION: CIVIL SOCIETY AND ITS INSTITUTIONS

One of the dominant metaphors of modernity has been the idea of competition as the driving force of progress. In *The Leviathan* Hobbes spoke of the 'generall inclination of all mankind', namely 'a perpetuall and restlesse desire of Power after power, that ceaseth onely in Death' (Hobbes 1991: 70). Adam Smith showed how economic competition and the pursuit of self-interest could lead, through trade and the division of labour, to the economic advance of all. Charles Darwin, in *The Origin of Species*, argued that it was the struggle for survival in the face of finite resources—natural selection—that explained evolution. Social Darwinians, among them Herbert Spencer, argued that the same law of survival applied to societies and cultures. The significance of governments and markets in the modern world is that they are mediated arenas of competition.

More recently, however, a whole series of disciplines has converged from different starting points on another insight. Economists and sociologists like James Coleman, Robert Putnam and Francis Fukuyama speak of *social capital*.[7] Sociobiologists such as Robert Axelrod, Anatol Rapoport, and Martin Nowack, tracking the growth and decline of species through computer simulations of the 'iterated prisoners' dilemma, talk of *reciprocal altruism*. Political theorists, under the banner of 'communitarianism' or 'civil society', have begun to pay renewed attention to Edmund Burke's 'little platoons', Alexis de Tocqueville's 'habits of association' or Peter Berger's 'mediating structures'. What all these developments have in common is a new awareness of the significance, not of competition but of co-operation.[8] In any long-term competitive situation, victory (or survival) goes not to the strongest (best-adapted, most adroit) individual but to the group that has the most developed and extensive structures of collaboration. A football team (or primate species, or political party, or society) may be full of individual virtuosi but it will fail unless its members can act effectively together as a team.

This has been one of the transformative insights of the past twenty years. For several centuries, Western political thought has been dominated by two entities: the state and the market. The state is us in our collective capacity as a nation. The market is us in our individual capacity as choosers and consumers. Between them, they were thought to exhaust the political domain. Thinkers of the right preferred the market; those of the left favoured the state. What we and others have argued is that this is an impoverished view of our social ecology. It omits 'third sector'[9] institutions like the family, the community, voluntary organizations, neighbourhood groups, and religious congregations which have in common that they are larger than the individual but smaller than the state. Their significance, and it is immense, is that they are where we learn the habits of co-operation, whether we describe it as reciprocal altruism or social capital or trust. Families and communities are not arenas of competition. To use the vocabulary I developed in *The Politics of Hope*, they are places where relationships are *covenantal*, not contractual. They are based not on transactions of power or exchange, but on love, loyalty, faithfulness, mutuality, and a sense of shared belonging. They are less about the 'I' than about the 'We' in which my 'I' becomes articulate, as a child of this family, that history, this place, that set of ideals.

It was Joseph Schumpeter, in *Capitalism, Socialism and Democracy*, who pointed out that market based-capitalism contains the seeds of its own destruction. It 'creates a critical frame of mind which, after having destroyed the moral authority of so many other institutions, in the end turns against its own' (Schumpeter 1947: 143). The combined power of the state and the market causes third sector institutions to atrophy. Marriage and the family become fragile. Communities disintegrate. Attendance at places of worship declines. Voluntary groups become more fragmented and ephemeral. We prefer, in Robert Putnam's phrase, to go 'bowling alone'. The result is that it becomes 'very difficult for any individual to find any stable communal support, very difficult for any community to count on the responsible participation of its individual members'. This, argues Michael Walzer, 'works against commitment to the larger democratic union and also against the solidarity of all cultural groups that constitute our multi-culturalism' (Walzer 1992: 11–12).

The Judaic emphasis on third sector institutions hardly needs spelling out. For two millennia, without a home, sovereignty, or power, Jews and Judaism survived and flourished on the basis of three foundations: the family, the synagogue, and the school. The synagogue itself was not merely a house of prayer. Its name in Hebrew was the *bet knesset*, 'the home of the community'. It became, in post-biblical times, a kind of mini-welfare state where funds were collected and distributed to the poor. It housed societies for visiting the sick, caring for the needy, and burying the dead. It functioned as a courtroom to which all had access and could air their claims (Sacks 1995). The history of diaspora Jewish life is an extended case study in the existence of a civil society without the instrumentalities of a state.

To be sure, the problem does not arise in the same way throughout the world. In some societies, most notably the liberal democracies of the West, individualism may have gone too far. In others—those that have not yet, or only recently, become democratized—it may not have gone far enough. Excessive centralization inhibits the growth of civil associations, just as excessive commercialization erodes them (Soros 2000). The proper balance is precarious and hard to maintain. Yet the encouragement of civil society is an essential feature of the successful transition from totalitarian societies and centralized economies to democratic capitalism. Without stable association with others over extended periods of time, we fail to acquire the habits of co-operation which form the basis of trust on which the economics and politics of a free society depend. Self-interest alone does not generate it; indeed self-interest without trust yields outcomes that are individually and collectively destructive. The market, in other words, depends on virtues not produced by the market, just as the state depends on virtues not produced by the state.[10] No economic incentive can make families stay together, or neighbours help one another, or parents spend more time with their children. No government can make us solicitous, law-abiding, honest, public-spirited, or reliable. These things depend on third sector institutions, which (as Alexis de Tocqueville saw so clearly in his *Democracy in America*) has been one of the classic tasks of religious groups in liberal democracies.

9.6 COMPASSION: THE CONCEPT OF TZEDAKAH

One of the defining texts of Judaism is the biblical statement in which God articulates the mission with which Abraham and his descendants are to be charged:

Shall I hide from Abraham what I am about to do? Abraham will surely become a great and powerful nation, and all nations of the earth will be blessed through him. For I have chosen him so that he will direct his children and his household after him to keep the way of the Lord by doing what is right [*tzedakah*] and just [*mishpat*], so that the Lord will bring about for Abraham what He has promised him. (Genesis 18:17–19)

The key words, *tzedakah* and *mishpat*, signify two kinds of justice. *Mishpat* means retributive justice or the rule of law. A free society must be governed by law, impartially administered, through which the guilty are punished, the innocent acquitted, and human rights secured. *Tzedakah*, by contrast, refers to distributive justice, a less procedural and more substantive idea.

It is difficult to translate *tzedakah* because it combines in a single concept two notions normally opposed to one another, namely charity and justice. Suppose, for example, that I give someone £100. Either he is entitled to it, or he is not. If he is, then my act is a form of justice. If he is not, it is an act of charity. In English (as with the Latin terms *caritas* and *iustitia*) a gesture of charity cannot be an act of justice, nor can an act of justice be described as charity. *Tzedakah* is therefore an unusual term, and one particularly deserving of attention.

It flows from the theology of Judaism, in which there is a difference between possession and ownership. Ultimately, all things are owned by God, creator of the world. What we possess, we do not own—we merely hold it in trust for God. The clearest example is the provision in Leviticus: 'The land must not be sold permanently because the land is Mine; you are merely strangers and temporary residents in relation to Me' (Leviticus 25: 23). One of the conditions of trusteeship is that we share part of what we have with others in need. What is regarded as charity in other legal systems is, in Judaism, a strict requirement of the law and can, if necessary, be enforced by the courts.

What *tzedakah* signifies, therefore, is what is often called 'social justice', meaning that no one should be without the basic requirements of existence, and that those who have more than they need must share some of that surplus with those who have less. The view articulated in the Hebrew Bible has close affinities with Amartya Sen's concept of 'development as freedom' meaning that freedom is not simply the absence of coercion but also the removal of barriers to the exercise of human dignity: 'poverty as well as tyranny, poor economic opportunities as well as systematic social deprivation, neglect of public facilities as well as intolerance or overactivity of repressive states' (Sen 1999: 3).

The society with which the Israelites were charged with creating was one that would stand at the opposite extreme to what they experienced in Egypt: poverty, persecution, and enslavement. Their release from bondage was only the first stage on the journey to freedom. The second—their covenant with God—involved collective responsibility to ensure that no one would lack the means to live a dignified existence. Thus portions of the harvest, vineyards, and fields were to be set aside for the poor. So too were tithes in certain years, and the produce of the seventh, 'sabbatical' year. No one could be made to work on the seventh day, so that for one day each week all economic and political hierarchies were suspended. A free society cannot be built on *mishpat*, the rule of law, alone. It requires also *tzedakah*, a just distribution of resources. What is clear—indeed taken for granted by the Bible—*is that an equitable distribution will not emerge naturally from the free working of the market alone.*

Tzedakah is a concept for our time. The retreat from a welfare state and the financial deregulation and monetarist policies set in motion by Reagonomics and Thatcherism have led to increased inequalities in both the United States and Britain. In America in the past twenty years 97 per cent of the increase in income has gone to the top 20 per cent of families, while the bottom fifth have seen a 44 per cent reduction in earnings. By 1996 Britain had the highest proportion in Europe of children living in poverty, with 300,000 of them worse off in absolute terms than they were twenty years before (Hertz 2001: 38–61).

The 'digital divide' has heightened inequalities between countries also. The average North American consumes five times more than a Mexican, ten times more than a Chinese, thirty times more than an Indian. One quarter of those who die each year do so from AIDS, tuberculosis, malaria or diseases related to diarrhoea, most of them children without access to clean water. In eighteen countries, all African, life expectancy is less than fifty years; in Sierra Leone it is a mere 37 years. Infant mortality rates are higher than one in ten in 35 countries, mostly in Africa but including Bangladesh, Bolivia, Haiti, Laos, Nepal, Pakistan, and Yemen (Harrison and Huntington 2000: xviii). Huge power and wealth now accrues to multinational enterprises. Of the hundred largest economies in the world, only 49 are nation states; 51 are corporations. Meanwhile, third world workers producing the goods the multinationals sell do so often under Dickensian conditions involving child labour, unsanitary factories, and less-than-subsistence wages. As George Soros notes, 'Markets are good at creating wealth but are not designed to take care of other social needs' (Soros 2002: 5).

One of the most profound insights of *tzedakah* legislation is its emphasis on human dignity and independence. Millennia ago, Jewish law wrestled with the fact that domestic welfare, like foreign aid, can aggravate the very problem it is intended to solve. Welfare creates dependency and thus reinforces, rather than breaks, the cycle of deprivation. *Tzedakah* therefore, though it includes direct material assistance (food, clothing, shelter, and medical aid), emphasizes the kind of aid that creates independence, as in Moses Maimonides' famous ruling:

The highest degree, exceeded by none, is that of the person who assists a poor person by providing him with a gift or a loan or by accepting him into a business partnership or by helping him find employment—in a word by putting him where he can dispense with other people's aid. With reference to such aid it is said, 'You shall strengthen him, be he a stranger or a settler, he shall live with you' (Leviticus 25: 35), which means strengthen him in such a manner that his falling into want is prevented. (Maimonides, *Mishneh Torah*, Gifts to the Poor 10: 7)

The supreme form of *tzedakah* is therefore one that allows the individual to become independent of other people's aid.

The Bible is acutely aware that the workings of the free market can create, over time, inequalities so great as to amount to dependency and which can only be removed by periodic redistribution. Hence the sabbatical year in which those who had sold themselves into slavery through poverty were released, and all debts cancelled. In the jubilee year, ancestral land returned to its original owners. The idea was from time to time to restore a level playing field and give those who had been forced to sell either their labour or their holdings of land the chance to begin again. It was this biblical legislation that lay behind the successful campaign, Jubilee 2000, to provide international debt relief to developing countries and underlies Chancellor of the Exchequer Gordon Brown's proposal for a 'modern Marshall Plan' for the developing world (Brown 2002).[11]

Globalization, writes Zygmunt Bauman, 'divides as much as it unites... What appears as globalization for some means localization for others; signalling a new freedom for some, upon many others it descends as an uninvited and cruel fate' (Bauman 1998: 2). There can be no doubt that some of the economic surplus of the advanced economies of the world should be invested in developing countries to help eradicate extreme poverty and hunger, ensure universal education, combat treatable disease, reduce infant mortality, improve work conditions, and reconstruct failing economies. As with *tzedakah*, the aim should be to restore dignity and independence to nations as well as individuals. Whether this is done in the name of compassion, social justice, or human solidarity it has now become a compelling imperative. The globalization of communications, trade, and culture globalizes human responsibility likewise. The freedom of the few must not be purchased at the price of the enslavement of the many to poverty, ignorance, and disease.

9.7 CONSERVATION: ENVIRONMENTAL SUSTAINABILITY

The record of human intervention in the natural order is marked by devastation on a massive scale. Within a few thousand years of the first human inhabitants of America, most of the large mammal species, among them mammoths, mastodons, tapirs, camels, horses, and bears, had become extinct. The same pattern can be traced almost everywhere human beings have set foot, but the process has become hugely accelerated by industrialization, pollution, and the destruction of rain forests. Today, 1,666 of the 9,000 bird species are endangered or at imminent risk of extinction. It has been estimated that, if present trends continue, half of the world's total of thirty million animal and plant species will become extinct in the course of the next century. If we do not change our patterns of production and consumption, we face the real possibility of environmental catastrophe (Diamond 1992).

Yet again, the Bible offers a compelling insight. Behind the sabbatical and jubilee years and the Sabbath day itself is a principle today called 'sustainability'. What these laws represent is the idea that there are limits to human exploitation of the environment which, if not observed, lead to the exhaustion of the land, or of other natural resources, or of people themselves. The Sabbath set a boundary to human striving. One day in seven, there could be no exploitation of nature, no work, no buying or spending. Slaves could rest as free human beings. Even domestic animals were relieved of labour. During the sabbatical and jubilee years the land itself could not be worked. It too was entitled to rest. Other biblical laws, such as the prohibition against sowing a field with mixed seeds, or mixing meat and milk, or wearing clothes of mingled linen and flax, were designed to inculcate a sense of the integrity of nature. Legislation governing the conduct of war forbade needless destruction of fruit-bearing trees, a principle expanded in rabbinic law to cover the entire range of wasteful consumption and environmental pollution.

At the heart of the biblical vision is a tension between the mandate of Genesis 1, to 'fill the earth and subdue it', and that of Genesis 2 in which man is placed in the Garden 'to serve and protect' it. The Hebrew verb 'to protect' has a specific legal connotation, meaning the responsibility of a guardian into whose hands something has been placed for safekeeping. He must preserve it intact and, if possible, enhanced. The human covenant therefore signifies that we are, collectively, the guardians of the natural universe for the sake of future generations. As an ancient rabbinic comment puts it, when God finished creating the universe he said to the first humans: 'See the world I have made—and I have given it into your hands. Be careful, therefore, that you do not ruin my world, for if you do, there will be no one to restore what you have destroyed' (Midrash *Kohelet Rabbah* 7: 20).

The sense of limits is one of the hardest for a civilization to sustain. Each in turn has been captivated by the idea that it alone was immune to the laws of growth and decline, that it could consume resources indefinitely, pursuing present advantage without thought of future depletion. Few have committed this error more consciously than the age we call 'modernity', with its belief that rationality, science, and technology would create open-ended progress toward unlimited abundance. In the words of Christopher Lasch, 'Progressive optimism rests, at bottom, on a denial of the natural limits on human power and freedom, and it cannot survive for very long in a world in which an awareness of those limits has become inescapable' (Lasch 1991: 530). Many of the world's great faiths contain teachings of great wisdom on environmental ethics.[12] We need to recover their sense of limits if we are to preserve the sustainability and diversity of life itself.

9.8 CO-EXISTENCE: THE DIGNITY OF DIFFERENCE

Since 11 September 2001, it has become clear that one of the greatest dangers of the twenty-first century is the existence of tensions and resentments—religious and cultural as well as economic and political—that can lead to devastating acts of terror. This is not war in the conventional sense, between nation states. It has to do with what Thomas Friedman calls 'Super-empowered individuals' (Friedman 2000: 14) or groups with access to weapons of mass destruction (chemical, biological, and eventually nuclear), able to organize themselves non-territorially through the new communications technologies and to cause huge destruction and disruption. These groups understand the capacity of the Internet to abolish spatial boundaries, and the power of television to maximize visual impact. They also know that the hyper-connectivity of the contemporary world is its vulnerability.

This raises large issues, some practical, others deeper and more long-term. The practical questions of security and surveillance have to do with the time lag between new technologies and the development of defensive strategies against their misuse. The deeper question is about the shape of the 'new global order' or disorder. In the early 1990s this was the subject of an important debate between what Francis Fukuyama foresaw as the 'end of history' and Samuel Huntington's quite different scenario of a 'clash of civilizations' (Fukuyama 1992; Huntington 1996). Fukuyama's argument was that economics was superseding politics. The Cold War had ended and the Soviet Union collapsed without a shot being fired, because the command economy of communism could not compete with the market economies of the West. Pressure of rising material expectations would eventually force nations into the disciplines of the global market, which would in turn lead to open societies. Democratic capitalism was the destination at which all states would eventually arrive. Huntington thought otherwise. Modernization did not entail Westernization. The politics of ideology might be over, but the politics of identity was taking its place. The rifts between the great civilizations were as deep as ever. The culture of the West was not about to conquer the world. The tower of Babel would yet again run up against the confusion of languages.

In retrospect, the most prophetic analysis was given by Benjamin Barber in his 1992 article and subsequent book, *Jihad versus McWorld* (Barber 1992, 2001). Globalization, he argued, had both centripetal and centrifugal tendencies. On the one hand, economic, cultural, and ecological forces were binding us ever more closely together (McWorld). On the other, the end of the Cold War was giving rise to 'a retribalization of large swathes of humankind by war and bloodshed' (Jihad). His sombre conclusion was that 'The planet is falling precipitately apart and coming reluctantly together at the very same moment.'

There are no easy answers to this dilemma but there is an instructive precedent. Judaism is that rarest of phenomena: a particularist monotheism. The God of Abraham, according to the Hebrew Bible, is the God of all humanity, but the faith of Abraham is not the faith of all humanity. So strange is this idea that it was not taken on by the two daughter monotheisms to which Judaism gave rise, Christianity and Islam. These faiths are both universalist monotheisms, holding that since there is only one God, there is only one true religion, one path to salvation, to which ideally all mankind will be converted. Judaism believes otherwise: that there are many ways to serve God and that one does not have to be Jewish to do so. 'The righteous of the nations of the world [i.e. non-Jews] have a share in the world to come' (*Tosefta, Sanhedrin* 13).

Mankind has spoken to God in many languages, through many faiths. No language need threaten the others; none should supersede the other. Religious truth is not solely ontological (a matter of what is) but covenantal (a relationship between a specific group and God). Ontologies conflict, covenants do not. To use a biblical metaphor: God is a parent who loves His many children, each for what they uniquely are. The miracle of creation is that unity in heaven is worshipped through diversity on earth. To attempt to eliminate diversity (by conversion, missionary activity, or holy war) is to fail to understand the integrity—the *dignity*—of difference. Hence the great command in the Bible is 'Love the stranger', the person who is not like yourself. Fundamentalism—the attempt to impose a single truth on a plural world—is religiously misconceived. The spiritual challenge is to recognize God's image in one who is not in my image.

This is an extremely difficult set of ideas, yet it may now be the only way to do justice to the human condition. According to the Hebrew Bible, God makes two covenants, one (in the days of Noah after the Flood) with all humanity, the other with Abraham, and later his descendents at Mount Sinai. Judaism therefore embodies a dual ethic, one a universal code applying to everyone, the other a particular way of life demanded of the heirs of those who followed Moses into the wilderness. There was a time when most people were surrounded by others who shared their history and faith. It was plausible in those days to believe that one's own path to God was the only path there was. Today that belief is unsustainable, practically if not intellectually. Our lives and fate are interwoven with others who believe, act, think, and feel in ways different from ours. We therefore have to make space for difference (the Abrahamic covenant) while affirming our shared humanity (the Noahide covenant).

There have been five universalist cultures in the history of the West—cultures that imposed their way of life on others through conquest, conversion, or the 'soft' power of ideas. They were the empires of ancient Greece and Rome, medieval Christianity and Islam, and the European Enlightenment. Globalization is the sixth, the first to be driven not by power or ideology but by the neutral, impersonal forces of the market. Each in its time was perceived as deeply threatening to those whose local cultures and traditional identities were at risk, and they fought back with whatever weapons were at hand. That, post-11 September 2001, is what we must avoid in the future.

There are three options facing the West: to impose its values on others, to let market forces do likewise, or actively to respect the dignity of difference, and grant cultural diversity the same protection as biodiversity. The third is the only choice likely to succeed, indeed the only one, in our opinion, that *ought* to succeed. The logical consequence of fundamentalism—that the world would be richer (more perfect, more complete) if all faiths (cultures, traditions) disappeared except ours—is offensive and absurd. It has however been believed by most people at most times. We therefore face a major intellectual, ethical, and religious challenge, to move from conversion to coexistence, from truth to truths, and to an active respect for difference.

9.9 TOWARDS A GLOBAL COVENANT

The wisdom of the world's religions may seem at best irrelevant, at worst dangerous, to a world driven by economic forces. In the West, especially Western Europe, society has become secularized. In the Middle East and parts of Asia it has witnessed a growth of fundamentalism that threatens economic development and political freedom alike. Whatever therefore the prospects for the future, religion seems part of the problem rather than part of the solution.

This view, in our opinion, is a mistaken one, though it is a mistake with a distinguished pedigree. The two most influential works of Western modernity—Hobbes' *Leviathan* and Adam Smith's *The Wealth of Nations*—were predicated on the idea of man the maximizing animal. Politically this led to the social contract; economically to the division of labour and the free market. Mankind, however, is not merely a maximizing animal. We are also, uniquely, the meaning-seeking animal. We seek to understand our place in the universe. We want to know where we have come from, where we are going to, and of what narrative we are a part. We form families, communities, and societies. We tell stories, some of which have the status of sacred texts. We perform rituals that dramatize the structure of reality. We have languages, cultures, moralities, and faiths. These things are essential to our sense of continuity with the past and responsibility to the future. Without them it is doubtful whether we would have reasons for action at all beyond the most minimal drives for survival.

Part of the process we call modernity—most obviously associated with the European Enlightenment—was to call into question the salience of almost everything associated with the word 'religion.' *Écrasez l'infâme*, said Voltaire, and others, less provocatively, agreed. The new paradigm was science which rested its conclusions not on weightless clouds of revelation and prophetic insight but on testable hypotheses, experiments and refutations. Technology would help us master nature. Constitutional monarchy, followed by representative democracy, would control power. Economics would maximize wealth. Together they would generate the linear advance that went by the new name of 'progress.'

That was a noble aspiration and much of it remains valid today. But mankind is now older, sadder, and wiser. Reason did not dispel prejudice. Technology, whether in the form of weapons of mass destruction, over-exploitation of natural resources, pollution of the atmosphere, or genetic manipulation, threatens the sustainability of nature itself. Representative democracy remains the best form of government yet discovered, but nation states seem increasingly unable to control global phenomena from the less acceptable activities of multinational enterprises to ecological devastation; and we have not yet evolved adequate forms of global governance. Market capitalism has increased wealth beyond the imagination of previous generations, but cannot, in and of itself, distribute it equally or even equitably. These are problems that cannot be solved within the terms set by modernity, for the simple reason that they are not procedural, but rather valuational or, to use the simple word, moral. There is no way of bypassing difficult moral choices by way of a scientific decision-procedure that states: 'Maximize X.' We first have to decide which X we wish to maximize, and how to weigh X against Y when the pursuit of one damages the fulfilment of the other. The human project is inescapably a moral project.

Economic superpowers, seemingly invincible in their time, have a relatively short life span: Venice in the sixteenth century, The Netherlands in the seventeenth, France in the eighteenth, Britain in the nineteenth, and the United States in the twentieth. The great religions, by contrast, survive. Islam is 1,500 years old,

Christianity 2,000, and Judaism 4,000. Why this should be so is open to debate. Our own view is that civilizations survive not by strength but by how they respond to the weak; not by wealth but by the care they show for the poor; not by power but by their concern for the powerless. The ironic yet utterly humane lesson of history is that what renders a culture invulnerable is the compassion it shows to the vulnerable. The ultimate value we should be concerned to maximize is human dignity—the dignity of all human beings, equally, as children of the creative, redeeming God.

Is this a 'religious' insight? Yes and no. There have been secular humanists who have affirmed it; there have been religious zealots who have denied it. What matters most is not why we hold it, but that we hold it. Global capitalism heralds the prospect of a vast amelioration of the human condition. Equally it threatens inequalities that will eventually become unsustainable and cultural vandalism that will become unbearable. Man was not made for the service of economies; economies were made to serve mankind; and men and women were made—so we believe—to serve one another, not just themselves. We may not survive while others drown; we may not feast while others starve; we are not free when others are in servitude; we are not well when billions languish in disease and premature death.

Our global situation today is like the condition of European nations during the great wars of religion of the sixteenth and seventeenth centuries in the wake of the Reformation. Then, as now, there were many societies riven by conflict. The question arose: how can people of violently conflicting beliefs live peaceably together? Out of that crisis came the idea—variously framed by Hobbes, Locke, and Rousseau—of a social contract by which individuals agreed to cede certain private powers to a central authority charged with the maintenance of order and pursuit of the common good.

We are not yet in sight of a global contract whereby nation states agree to sacrifice part of their sovereignty to create a form of world governance. That is a distant prospect. Biblical theology, however, suggests an alternative, namely a global *covenant*. Covenants are more general, moral, and foundational than contracts. Ancient Israel initiated its social contract when, at the request of the people, Samuel anointed Saul as king, creating Israel's first national government. It received its social covenant several centuries earlier in the revelation at Mount Sinai. The relation between covenant and contract is akin to that between the American Declaration of Independence (1776) and its Constitution (1789). The latter specifies the constitutional structure of the state, the former the moral principles of the society on which it is founded. *What we need now is not a contract bringing into being a global political structure, but rather a covenant framing our shared vision for the future of humanity.*

One idea links the first chapter of Genesis to the Declaration of Independence, namely that 'all men are created equal'. Philip Selznick's articulation of this idea seems to me compelling: 'Moral equality', he writes, 'is the postulate that all persons have the same intrinsic worth. They are unequal in talents, in contributions to social life, and in valid claims to rewards and resources. But everyone who is a person is presumptively entitled to recognition of that personhood.' Accordingly, each is entitled to 'the basic conditions that make life possible, tolerable and hopeful'—to what they need to sustain 'their dignity and integrity as persons' (Selznick 1994: 483–5). That is at least a starting point for a global covenant in which the nations of the world collectively express their commitment not only to human rights but also to human responsibilities, and not merely a political, but also an economic, environmental, moral, and cultural conception of the common good, constructed on the twin foundations of shared humanity and respect for diversity. Our last best hope is to recall the classic statement of John Donne and the more ancient narrative of Noah after the Flood and hear, in the midst of our hyper-modernity, an old-new call to a global covenant of collective human dignity and responsibility.

NOTES

1. For a detailed examination of the role of international commerce, and particularly that of the early trading companies, see Moore and Lewis (1999).
2. On this, see e.g. David Landes (1998) and Peter Jay (2001). See also Chapter 2 of this volume.
3. For an account of biblical and post-biblical Judaism, see Sacks (2001).
4. The story of the origin and early development of the alphabet has most recently been told in Man (2001).
5. See Voegelin (1956); and also Deepak Lal's interpretation of 'cosmological' in Chapter 2 of the present volume.
6. *Troilus and Cressida*, Act 1, scene 3.
7. John Dunning, in a recent paper, considers the importance of *relational capital* as a competitive advantage (Dunning 2002). More broadly, in another contribution, he explores the notion of alliance capitalism (Dunning 1997).
8. I have told this story in Sacks (2000: 233–44).
9. Sometimes referred to as 'civil society' institutions.
10. I have explored this view, and debated it with Norman Barry, in Sacks (1999).
11. See also his contribution to this volume (Chapter 14).
12. See e.g. the series of books on World Religions and Ecology: M. Batchelor and K. Brown (eds.), *Buddhism and Ecology*; E. Breuilly and M. Palmer (eds.), *Christianity and Ecology*; R Prime (ed.), *Hinduism and Ecology*; F. Khalid and J. O'Brien (eds.), *Buddhism and Ecology*; A. Rose (ed.), *Judaism and Ecology* (London: Cassell, 1992).

REFERENCES

Barber, Benjamin (1992), 'Jihad vs. McWorld', *Atlantic Monthly*, (March).
—— (2001), *Jihad vs McWorld* (New York: Ballantine).
Bauman, Zygmunt (1998), *Globalization: The Human Consequences* (Cambridge: Polity).
Brown, Gordon (2002), *Tackling Poverty: A Global New Deal* (London: HM Treasury).
Clinton, Bill (2001), 'The Struggle for the Soul of the Twenty-First Century' (London: BBC Dimbleby Lecture, 14 December 2001).
Diamond, Jared (1992), *The Third Chimpanzee* (New York: Harper Perennial).
Diringer, David (1962), *Writing* (London: Thames & Hudson).

Donne, John (1930), *Complete Poetry and Selected Prose* (London: Nonesuch).

Dunning, J. H. (1997), *Alliance Capitalism and Global Business* (London and New York: Routledge).

——(2002), 'Relational Capital, Networks and International Business Activity.' In F. Contractor and P. Lorange (eds.), *Cooperative Strategies and Alliances* (Oxford: Elsevier Science), 569–93.

Friedman, Thomas (2000), *The Lexus and the Olive Tree* (London: HarperCollins).

Fukuyama, Francis (1992), *The End of History and the Last Man* (London: Hamilton).

——(1999), *The Great Disruption* (London: Profile).

Gottwald, Norman K. (1980), *The Tribes of Yahweh* (London: SCM Press).

Harrison, Lawrence, and Huntington, Samuel (eds.) (2000), *Culture Matters* (New York: Basic Books).

Hertz, Noreena (2001), *The Silent Takeover* (London: William Heinemann).

Hobbes, Thomas (1991), *Leviathan*, (Cambridge: Cambridge University Press).

Huntington, Samuel (1996), *The Clash of Civilizations and the Remaking of World Order* (New York: Simon & Schuster).

Jay, Peter (2001), *Road to Riches* (London: Phoenix).

Klein, Naomi (2001), *No Logo* (London: Flamingo).

Landes, David (1998), *The Wealth and Poverty of Nations* (London: Little, Brown & Co.).

Lasch, Christopher (1991), *The True and Only Heaven* (New York: W. W. Norton).

Maimonides, Moses, *Mishneh Torah, Gifts to the Poor*, 10: 7.

Man, John (2001), *Alpha Beta: How Our Alphabet Shaped the Western World* (London: Headline).

Midrash Kohelet Rabbah, 7: 20.

Moore K., and Lewis D., (1999), *Birth of the Multinational* (Copenhagen: Copenhagen Business Press).

Nye, Joseph S. (2002), *The Paradox of American Power* (New York: Oxford University Press).

Ong, Walter J. (1988), *Orality and Literacy* (London: Routledge).

Sacks, Jonathan (1995), *Community of Faith* (London: Peter Halban).

——(1999), *Morals and Markets* (London: Institute of Economic Affairs).

——(2000), *The Politics of Hope*, 2nd edn. (London: Vintage).

——(2001), *Radical Then, Radical Now* (London: HarperCollins).

Schumpeter, Joseph (1947), *Capitalism, Socialism and Democracy* (London: George Allen & Unwin).

Selznick, Philip (1994), *The Moral Commonwealth* (Berkeley, California: University of California Press).

Sen, Amartya (1999), *Development as Freedom* (Oxford: Oxford University Press).

Soros, George (2000), *Open Society: Reforming Global Capitalism* (London: Little, Brown & Co.).

——(2002), *On Globalization* (Oxford: Public Affairs).

Voegelin, Eric (1956), *Order and History*, vol. 1: *Israel and Revelation* (Missouri: University of Missouri Press).

Walzer, Michael (1992), *Citizenship and Civil Society* (Rutgers, NJ: New Jersey Committee for the Humanities Series on the Culture of Community), 13 Oct. 1992, part 1, 11–12.

Wells, H.G. (n.d.), *The Study of History* (London: George Newnes).

Whitehead, Alfred North (1942), *Adventures of Ideas* (Harmondsworth: Penguin).

10

The Challenge of Global Capitalism: The Perspective of Eastern Religions

DAVID R. LOY

10.1 INTRODUCTION

At first sight, the goals set for this chapter as outlined in John Dunning's introductory chapter would seem impossible to meet. This is for two reasons. The first is that there is no such thing as 'Eastern religions'. Southern, Central and Eastern Asia encompass a variety of quite different cultural traditions, many of which are as much philosophical as religious. (The distinction between religion and philosophy is Western.) Secondly, none of them, so far as I know, has anything to say about the challenge of capitalism, global or otherwise, which means there is no perspective for me to represent.

The logical implication would seem to be . . . well, to give up and stop right here! Yet the globalization of market capitalism presents us with an issue so important that it seems wiser to avail ourselves of every possible resource that might help us to understand it. Moreover, the viewpoints and insights provided by Asian religio-philosophical traditions may be especially valuable, since they approach the issues involved from non-Western perspectives not already implicated in the development of capitalism (cf. Max Weber's Protestant entrepreneurs). It may then help us to notice presuppositions otherwise taken for granted.

The magnitude of our topic, therefore, overrules the more prudential response. And although the various Asian traditions have not commented on capitalism, their teachings do include many statements about poverty, wealth-creation, and other economic themes. The implications of these claims for globalizing capitalism can be developed.

Nevertheless, that does not resolve the other basic problem: which Eastern religions are to be discussed? In fact, modern scholars do not much care for the term 'Eastern religions', which puts into the same pot some very different ingredients that do not usually mix well. In particular, the Indian-influenced traditions of South Asia are strikingly different from the Chinese-influenced traditions of East Asia. Indeed, in many ways Indian culture is more similar to that of the West (which shares some of its 'Indo-European' roots) than to Chinese culture.

One tradition, however, has been uniquely successful on both sides of the Himalaya. Buddhism is the one Indian religious and philosophical system that, over time, has spread not only over South and South-East Asia (although eventually almost disappearing from its homeland), but has also thrived in Central and East Asia. Naturally, Buddhism changed considerably as it did so, yet it has proved especially attractive because it emphasizes a core of essential truths about the human condition that appeals to people in a variety of cultures.

In sum, Buddhism is probably the best representative of something that does not quite exist, *viz.* the archetypal Eastern religion. It therefore provides us with the focus that this chapter needs, and what follows will emphasize the economic implications of Buddhist teachings, although there will also be some reference to other Asian traditions. To create the necessary context for discussing capitalism, I begin with a short summary of (mostly) Buddhist views on poverty and wealth creation, followed by a discussion of Buddhist economics. The remaining sections draw out the implications of those teachings for the form and content of global capitalism.

10.2 WEALTH AND POVERTY

Shakyamuni Buddha (*c.* 563–483 BC), the founder of Buddhism, is believed to have renounced a privileged life of pleasure and leisure for the arduous life of a forest dweller. However, his ascetic practices did not produce the enlightenment he sought. He went on to discover a 'middle way' that does not simply split the difference between sense-enjoyment and sense-denial. It focuses on calming and understanding the mind, for such insight can liberate us from our usual preoccupation with trying to become happy by satisfying our cravings. The goal is not to eradicate all desires, but to experience them in a non-attached way, so we are not controlled by them.

To achieve this, Buddhism does not depend upon a theistic revelation in the way that the Abrahamic religions—Judaism, Christianity, and Islam—do. The Buddha is not an omnipotent God who can save us; instead, he reveals the path that we, ourselves, must walk in order to save ourselves. Contrary to the stereotype of Buddhism as a world-denying religion, the Buddhist goal does not advocate transcending this world in order to experience some other one. Rather, it is better understood as attaining a wisdom that realizes the true nature of this world, including the true nature of oneself.[1]

These concerns are reflected in the Buddhist attitude toward wealth and poverty. In the words of Sizemore and Swearer (1990: 2), 'a non-attached orientation toward life does not require a flat renunciation of all material possessions. Rather, it specifies an attitude to be cultivated and expressed in whatever material condition one finds oneself. To be non-attached is to possess and use material things but not to be possessed or used by them.' In short, the main issue is not how poor or wealthy we are, but how we respond to our situation. The wisdom that develops naturally from non-attachment is knowing how to be content with what we have, for 'the greatest wealth is contentment' (*Dhammapada*, verse 204).

This does not mean that Buddhism encourages poverty or denigrates enterprise or wealth. The Buddha emphasized many times that the goal of the Buddhist path is to end our *dukkha* (often translated as 'suffering' but better understood as 'ill-being' or 'unhappiness'). He summarized his teachings into four noble (or ennobling) truths: life is *dukkha*; the cause of *dukkha* is craving (*tanha*); there is an end to *dukkha* (i.e. the goal of *nirvana*); the way to end *dukkha* is to follow an eightfold path that cultivates right understanding, right conduct, and right mental development.[2] None of the four truths implies that material poverty is a desirable state. Rather, poverty is a source of unhappiness in itself, and also makes it more difficult to follow a spiritual path.

Nevertheless, Buddhism does not approve of a life devoted to acquiring wealth. The ultimate goal of liberating insight may be more difficult to pursue if we are destitute, but a life focused on money may be as bad, or worse. Shakyamuni warned repeatedly against that danger: 'Few are those people in the world who, when they obtain superior possessions, do not become intoxicated and negligent, yield to greed for sensual pleasures, and mistreat other beings.'[3] An intense drive to acquire material riches is one of the main causes of our *dukkha*. It involves much anxiety but very little real satisfaction. Instead, the Buddha praised those who renounce all attachment to material things in favour of a life devoted wholeheartedly to the path of liberation, by joining the community (*sangha*) of monks and nuns.

Despite the above, however, Buddhism does not claim that wealth is, in itself, an obstacle to following the spiritual path. The five basic precepts that all Buddhists are expected to follow—to avoid killing, stealing, lying, sexual misconduct, and intoxicating drugs—mention nothing about abstaining from riches or property, although the precepts do imply much about how we should pursue them. The value of riches cannot be compared with the supreme goal of *nirvana*-awakening, yet, properly acquired, wealth has traditionally been seen as a sign of virtue, and, properly used, can be a boon for everyone. This is because wealth creates opportunities to benefit people and to cultivate non-attachment by developing one's generosity. The problem with wealth is not its possession but its abuse. 'Wealth destroys the foolish, though not those who search for the goal' (*Dhammapada*, verse 355). In short, what is blameworthy is to earn wealth improperly, to become attached to it, not to spend it for the well-being of everyone, to squander it foolishly, or use it to cause suffering to others. Right livelihood, the fifth part of the eightfold path, emphasizes that our work should not harm other living beings and specifically prohibits trading in weapons, poisons, intoxicants, or slaves.

That wealth can indicate virtue follows from the Buddhist belief in karma and rebirth. Karma is moral cause-and-effect: what we do to others will be done to us. If karma is an exception-less law of the universe, what happens to us later (in this life or in a future lifetime) is a result of what we have done in the past and are doing now. Wealth is a consequence of one's own previous generosity, and poverty a result of one's own misbehaviour (most likely avarice or seeking wealth in an immoral way). Not all contemporary Buddhists accept that karma is so inexorable, or understand it so literally, but the traditional belief implies (in the long run, at least) complete harmony between a person's morality and his or her prosperity. Karma is the Buddhist *locus* for the Golden Rule at the top of John Dunning's pyramid of virtues (see Chapter 1): strong support for the values of responsible global capitalism, yet also a strong critique of any irresponsible global capitalism that emphasizes self-gain at others' expense.

Although this approach is arguably representative of many other religions in South Asia (and, indeed, elsewhere), their various perspectives cannot be simply conflated. Hinduism, in particular, also accepts karma and reincarnation but traditionally emphasizes four 'goals of life': *kama* (sense gratification), *artha* (prosperity), *dharma* (religious merit, duty), and *moksha* (spiritual liberation). Very early in the development of the Hindu tradition too, the pursuit of *kama* and *artha* was set in an ethical (*dharmic*) context, and they were never understood as something to be sought for their own sake regardless of ethical consequences. These four goals were anchored in the responsibilities of particular castes, each caste having its own set of rules and regulations that upheld the norms of *artha*, *kama*, and *dharma* (*moksha* being pursued mainly by *Brahmins*, the priestly caste). This emphasis on caste obligations based on caste differentiation, which remains a major problem in India today, has also meant caste restraints on economic freedom (e.g. entrepreneurship), which continue to complicate inter-caste relationships and limit economic growth. It also explains why Hinduism has not been very successful in non-caste cultures outside India, and why that tradition may have less to contribute to the debate on the globalization of capitalism.

The situation in East Asia was, and remains, quite different. The most successful indigenous tradition developed out of the teachings of the Chinese sage Confucius (*c.* 551–479 BC). In addition to its dominance in China, Confucianism has been extremely important in the social and political life of Korea and Japan as well. The post-war economic success of the 'Asian tigers'—Japan, South Korea, Taiwan, Hong Kong, and Singapore, all of which have a strong Confucian heritage—suggests that Confucianism may encourage capitalist development in a way similar to the European Protestantism that Weber studied (Weber 1930). This is a controversial issue, but some of the relevant points are clear. Perhaps the most important is that Confucianism does not emphasize an afterlife, nor the pursuit of any salvation that involves abrogating the traditional social responsibilities of this life. It advocates high moral standards—especially diligence, loyalty, reliability, and reciprocity—in economic activities that usually focus first of all on the benefits for one's (normally extended) family. While being politically conservative—emphasizing deference to authority—Confucianism has supported, and continues to support, entrepreneurship and the accumulation of private capital.

The role of Confucianism in East Asian economics can be overemphasized: the traditional diligence and self-reliance of its extended families have other social roots as well. However, the important point is that the Confucianism practised in East Asia (and in many other expatriate Chinese communities) does not display the ambivalence toward wealth creation that is found in Buddhism and many of the other major traditions in South Asia. That is why, although modern capitalism did not originate in East Asia, it has often found fertile ground there.

10.3 BUDDHIST ECONOMICS

Everything we have so far discussed concerns attitudes that we, as individuals, should cultivate or avoid. What kind of economic system do they imply? Buddhism, like Christianity, lacks an intrinsic social theory, which means that we cannot look to traditional Buddhist texts for perspectives on specific economic issues, such as the globalization of capitalism. However, some Buddhist scriptures do have significant social and economic implications. Perhaps the most relevant is the Lion's Roar Sutra (*Cakkavatti-sihanada Sutta*),[4] which shows how poverty can lead to social deterioration.

In this sutra the Buddha tells the story of a monarch in the distant past who initially relied upon the Buddhist teachings, doing as his sage advised: 'Let no crime prevail in your kingdom, and to those who are in need, give property.' Later, however, he began to rule according to his own ideas and did not give property to the needy. As a result, poverty became widespread. Because of poverty, one man took what was not given (i.e. stole) and was arrested. When the king asked him why he stole, the man said he had nothing to live on. So the king gave him enough property to carry on a business and support his family.

Exactly the same thing happened with another poor man, and when other people heard about this they, too, decided to steal so they would be treated in a similar way. This made the king realize that if he continued to give property to thieves, theft would increase. So he decided to get tough on the next one: 'I had better make an end of him, finish him off once for all, and cut his head off.' And he did.

At this point in the story we might expect a parable about the importance of deterring crime, but it turns in the opposite direction. When people heard about the beheading, they thought: 'Now let us get sharp swords made for us, and then we can take from anybody what is not given, we will make an end of them, finish them off once and for all and cut off their heads.' They launched murderous assaults on villages, towns, and cities, and went in for highway-robbery, cutting off their victims' heads. 'Thus, from the not giving of property to the needy, poverty became widespread, from the growth of poverty, the taking of what was not given increased, from the increase of theft, the use of weapons increased, from the increased use of weapons, the taking of life increased.' The long-term result was degradation of life and social collapse.

Despite some fanciful elements, this myth has significant economic implications. Poverty is presented as a root cause of immoral behaviour such as theft and violence. The Buddhist solution to such deprivation does not involve accepting one's 'poverty karma'. The problem began when the king neglected his responsibility to give property to those who needed it. This influential sutra implies that social breakdown cannot be separated from broader questions about the benevolence of the economic order and the corrective role of the state. The solution to poverty-induced crime is not severe punishment but rather helping those in poverty to provide for their basic needs.

What, if anything, does this imply about the moral imperatives of global cap-italism? The sutra encourages economic activity, not the provisions of welfare: the king evidently reforms the first thieves by giving them enough property to become self-supporting. More important, however, is the sutra's emphasis on the role of the state in addressing poverty. The great economic debate that has pre-occupied the West for more than a century—the role of the state versus that of the private sector—is not addressed directly, of course, but the sutra does emphasize the economic responsibility of rulers, and presumably states today, for the welfare of the economically vulnerable.

If we try to translate that emphasis into (for example) contemporary controver-sies about World Bank and IMF structural adjustment plans, which often involve a 'temporary' reduction in the quality of life for those already poor, this sutra may be understood to imply that such interventions may be socially dangerous as well as morally questionable. Buddhism certainly agrees with Dunning's first point in his introductory chapter: *viz.* the economy is not an end in itself. It should be obvious that an economic system exists for the sake of people, not vice-versa. Proponents of globalizing capitalism argue, as they must, that such an economic system ben-efits most people, but it is increasingly difficult to overlook the fact that business interests are usually allowed to trump all others, at least in the 'short term'; and that whether or not globalization does benefit the poor, it benefits the wealthy—those who have capital to invest—much more.

However, notice also what the Lion's Roar Sutra does *not* say. Today we some-times evaluate such situations by talking about the need for 'social justice' and the state's role in 'distributive justice'. This emphasis on social justice, central in the Abrahamic religions, is not found in traditional Buddhism. As the above story indicates, the Buddhist emphasis on karma implies a different way of under-standing and addressing that social problem. The traditional Buddhist solution to poverty is *dana* 'giving' or 'generosity'.

Dana is the most important concept in Buddhist thinking about society and economics, because it is the main way non-attachment is cultivated and demon-strated. Buddhists are called upon to show compassion to those who need help. The doctrine of karma seems quite harsh insofar as it implies that such unfortun-ates are reaping the fruit of their previous deeds, but this is not understood in a punitive way. Although they may be victims of their own previous selfishness, the importance of generosity for those walking the Buddhist path does not allow us the luxury of being indifferent to their situation. We are expected, even spiritually required, to lend assistance. This appeal is not to justice for a victim of circum-stances. Despite the prudential considerations expressed in the sutra—what may happen if we are not generous—it is the morality and spiritual progress of the *giver* that is the main issue. In the language of contemporary ethical theory, this is a 'virtue ethics'.[5] It offers a different perspective that cuts through the usual political opposition between conservative (right) and liberal (left) economic views. According to Buddhism, no one can evade responsibility for his or her own deeds and efforts. At the same time, generosity is not optional: we are obligated to respond compassionately to those in need. In the Lion's Roar Sutra, the king started the social breakdown when he did not fulfil this obligation.

In modern times, however, the social consequences of *dana* in Asian Buddhist countries have usually been limited. The popular emphasis has been on 'making merit' by supporting the *sangha*, i.e. the community of renunciate monks and nuns. The *sangha* is dependent on that support because monks and nuns are not allowed to work for money. Karma too is often understood in a commodified way, as something that can be accumulated by *dana* 'giving'. Since the amount of merit gained is believed to depend not only upon the value of the gift but also upon the worthiness of the recipient, and since members of the Buddhist *sangha* are viewed as the most worthy recipients, one receives more merit from donating food to a well-fed *bhikkhu* (monk) than to a poor and hungry layperson.

I think that this preoccupation with accumulating merit is incompatible with the Buddhist emphasis on non-attachment, for it seems to encourage a 'spiritual materialism', which ultimately is at odds with the highest goal of spiritual liberation. Is it also incompatible with capitalism? Historically, at least, the answer is yes. This merit-making system has encouraged Buddhists not to reinvest excess capital to make more capital, but to invest it in a 'spiritual bank' by donating to monks and temples—a bank which, it is believed, will eventually yield the beneficial returns of good karma and a better rebirth next time around.

However, it is perfectly possible for karma also to be understood in a way more compatible with some basic capitalist values. If we tend to get what we deserve, this encourages us to work diligently and develop other economic virtues such as honesty and reliability. Nevertheless, the traditional Buddhist emphasis on *dana* seems inconsistent with an economic system focused on capital accumulation and investment. Although *dana* cannot substitute for social justice today, the Buddhist viewpoint is that there is no substitute for the social practice of *dana* as a fundamental aspect of any healthy society. When those who have much feel little or no responsibility for those who have nothing, a social crisis is inevitable. This highlights the necessary role of charity and other forms of personal generosity (e.g. tithing).

10.4 A BUDDHIST PERSPECTIVE ON GLOBALIZING CAPITALISM

Although traditional Buddhist teachings do not include a developed economic theory, we have seen that they do have important economic implications. These implications can be further developed to help us understand and respond to the new world order being created by globalizing capitalism.

The first thing to notice is perhaps the most important. As the parable of the unwise king shows, Buddhism does not separate economic (secular) issues from ethical or spiritual ones. The notion that economics is a 'social science'—discovering and applying objective, trans-cultural economic laws—obscures two relevant truths. First, the distributional issue of who gets what, and how they get it, always has moral dimensions, so that issues of production, exchange, and distribution should not be left only to the dictates of the marketplace. If some people receive much more than they need, and many others receive much less than they need, some sort of redistribution is necessary, as the Lion's Roar Sutra seems to recommend. *Dana* is the traditional, if imperfect, Buddhist way of redistributing wealth or income. Today it is obvious that such a traditional response is inadequate, all the more so because economic globalization is aggravating the distribution problem between North and South. If globalizing capitalism can do a better job, what reforms are necessary to help it do so?

The other truth is that every system of production and consumption encourages the development of certain personal and social values and discourages others. Here we would take issue with those who wish to distinguish the values of capitalism itself from those of the individuals and institutions who participate in it. People make the system, but the system also makes people. Capitalism tends to reward those who have certain values, and to penalize those who do not act according to those values. We need to consider not only what values will encourage and support responsible global capitalism, but also what values global capitalism tends to encourage and support. As Phra Payutto, Thailand's most distinguished scholar-monk, has put it:

It may be asked how it is possible for economics to be free of values when, in fact, it is rooted in the human mind. The economic process begins with want, continues with choice, and ends with satisfaction, all of which are functions of the mind. Abstract values are thus the beginning, the middle and the end of economics, and so it is impossible for economics to be value-free. Yet as it stands, many economists avoid any consideration of values, ethics, or mental qualities, despite the fact that these will always have a bearing on economic concerns. (1994: 27)

This clarifies the basic Buddhist approach: individual and social values cannot be de-linked. A crucial issue is whether an economic system is conducive to the ethical and spiritual development of its participants. When we evaluate the characteristics and consequences of global capitalism, therefore, we should consider not only its ecological impact, and how efficiently it produces and distributes goods, but also its effects on human values, and the larger social effects of those values.

In Chapter 1 Dunning emphasizes three values that he identifies as moral imperatives for responsible global capitalism: *creativity, co-operation,* and *compassion.* The order of their presentation does not seem to be accidental; capitalism emphasizes them in that order. But it is perhaps significant that Buddhism, like many other religious traditions, would prefer to reverse the order. The most important virtue in Buddhism is compassion; community is also valued; but the capitalist emphasis on wealth creation and progress has not usually been stressed, because that is not seen as the primary solution to human *dukkha*, which is understood as primarily a *spiritual* problem. On the other side, however, economists argue that economic growth is required for the reduction of our physical *dukkha* (hunger, inadequate healthcare, etc.), for it is doubtful that redistribution of existing wealth could be adequate by itself even if it were politically possible. This suggests more of a role for creativity and entrepreneurship than Buddhism has traditionally emphasized.

Most discussions of responsible global capitalism tend to proceed at a high level of abstraction, but, sooner or later, we need to address the value-roles of particular institutions, such as MNEs and the stock market. Today, for example, probably most people in the developed world are involved in the purchase and sale of equities and bonds, if not directly then indirectly through pension funds. What effect does this have upon the moral values of the marketplace?

An intriguing fact about the stock market is that, with few exceptions, it tends to function as an ethical 'black hole', that dilutes and 'anonymizes' the responsibility for the actual consequences of economic growth. On one side of that hole, investors want increasing returns in the form of dividends and appreciating stock prices. On the other side, that expectation translates into a general, anonymous pressure for profitability and growth, preferably in the short run. However well intended they may otherwise be, CEOs who are unable to meet this demand are liable to lose their jobs. The globalization of market capitalism means that such goals as profitability and growth are becoming increasingly important as engines of world economic activity. All too often, everything else, including the environment, employment, and the quality of life, tends to become subordinated to them.[6]

Who is responsible for this pressure for growth? The system has attained a life of its own. We all participate in this process, as employers, workers, consumers, and investors, but with little or no personal sense of moral responsibility for what happens, because such awareness has been diffused so completely that it disappears in the impersonality of the economic process.

10.5 THE THREE POISONS

Much of the philosophical reflection on economics has focused on whether economic values are rooted in our basic human nature. Those who defend capitalism have often argued that its emphasis on competition and personal gain is grounded in the fact that humans are fundamentally self-centred and self-interested. The point of Adam Smith's 'invisible hand' metaphor is that by pursuing our own individual self-interest we end up promoting the common good. On the other side, critics of capitalism have responded by replying that our human nature is less selfish and more generous, and that the general good is better promoted by emphasizing more co-operative (e.g. social-democratic) policies.

Early Buddhism avoids that debate by taking a different approach. Shakyamuni Buddha emphasized that we all have both wholesome and unwholesome traits (*kusala/akusalamula*). What is important is the practical matter of how to reduce our unwholesome characteristics—including 'afflictive emotions' such as anger, pride, lust, greed, envy, etc.—and how to develop the more wholesome ones (Dalai Lama 1999: 81, 86). This process is symbolized by the lotus flower. Although rooted in the mud and muck at the bottom of a pond, the lotus grows upward to bloom on the surface, a representation of our potential to purify ourselves.

What are our unwholesome characteristics? These—and they have been repeatedly emphasized by other contributors to this volume—are usually summarized into the 'three poisons' or roots of evil: greed, ill-will, and delusion. The Buddhist path involves eliminating these by transforming them into their positive counterparts: *viz.* greed into generosity (*dana*), ill-will into compassion, and delusion into wisdom. If collective economic values cannot be separated from personal moral values, we cannot evade the question: which traits encourage, and are encouraged by, the globalization of capitalism?

10.5.1   Greed/Generosity

Greed is an unpopular word both in corporate boardrooms and in economic theory. Economists' concern to be objective does not allow the moral evaluation of different types of demand. From a Buddhist perspective, however, it is more difficult to ignore that capitalism often promotes and even requires greed in two ways. The engine of the economic process is the continual desire for profit, and in order to keep making that profit consumers must continue wanting to consume more.

These forms of motivation have been extraordinarily successful—depending, of course, on one's definition of success. According to the Worldwatch Institute, more goods and services were consumed in the forty years between 1950 and 1990 (measured in constant dollars) than by all the previous generations in human history (Durning 1992: 38). Significantly, however, this was not simply a matter of meeting latent demand: according to the *United Nations Human Development Report* (*UNHDR*) for 1999, the world spent at least $435 billion the previous year for advertising, not including public relations and marketing.

While this growth has given us opportunities that our grandparents never dreamt of, we have also become more sensitive to its negative consequences, including the staggering ecological impact and the unequal distribution of this new wealth generated by capitalism. Whether or not this global maldistribution is worsening or improving, and how much of that maldistribution is a consequence of globalizing capitalism, are controversial issues. Yet no one can deny that present inequities are certainly great and seem to be worsening—at least between the extreme rich and extreme poor. Also according to the 1999 *UNHDR*, the average African household now consumes 20 per cent less than it did twenty-five years ago. The 20 per cent of people in the richest countries now enjoy 86 per cent of the world's consumption, the poorest 20 per cent only 1.3 per cent—a gap that seems to have increased over the last two decades of the twentieth century.

But these grim facts about 'their' *dukkha* should not keep us from noticing the consequences for 'our own' *dukkha*. From a Buddhist perspective, the fundamental problem with consumerism is the delusion that consuming is the way to become happy. If (as the second noble truth claims) insatiable desires are the source of the dis-ease that we experience in our daily lives, then such consumption, which distracts us and intoxicates us, is not the solution to our unhappiness but one of its main symptoms. That brings us to the final irony of our addiction to consumption: according to the same *UNHDR*, the percentage of Americans who considered themselves 'happy' peaked in 1957, despite the fact that consumption per person has more than doubled since then. Nevertheless, studies of

US households have found that between 1986 and 1994 the amount of money people *think* they need to live happily has doubled. That seems paradoxical, but it is not difficult for Buddhism to explain: once we define ourselves as consumers, we can never have enough, because consumerism can never really give us what we want from it. It is always the *next* thing we buy that will make us happy.

Higher incomes have enabled many people to be more generous, but increased *dana* has not been the main effect because capitalism is based upon a different principle, – that extra capital should be used to generate more capital. Rather than redistributing our wealth, as the Buddhist king in the Lion's Roar Sutra was encouraged to do, we prefer to invest that wealth as a means to accumulate more and spend more. That is true regardless of whether or not we need more— a notion that has become rather quaint, since we now take for granted that one can never have too much money. This way of thinking is uncommon, however, in societies, including many Buddhist ones, where advertising has not yet conditioned people into believing that happiness is something you can purchase. Economists and international development agencies have been slow to realize what anthropologists have long understood, *viz.* that in traditional cultures, income and wealth are not the primary criterion of well-being. Sometimes they are not even a major one, as the anthropologist Delia Paul discovered in Zambia:

One of the things we found in the village which surprised us was people's idea of well-being and how that related to having money. We talked to a family, asking them to rank everybody in the village from the richest to the poorest and asking them why they would rank somebody as being less well off, and someone as poor. And we found that in the analysis money meant very little to the people. The person who was ranked as poorest in the village was a man who was probably the only person who was receiving a salary. (Quoted in Chambers 1997: 179)

His review of the relevant anthropological literature led Robert Chambers to conclude: 'Income, the reductionist criterion of normal economists, has never, in my experience or in the evidence I have been able to review, been given explicit primacy' (Chambers 1997: 178).

In order for capitalism to successfully globalize, such traditional ways of thinking become problematic. To facilitate access to resources and markets, a 'money culture' is necessary that emphasizes income and expenditure. But is it a form of cultural imperialism to assume that we in the 'developed' world who take such a money culture for granted know more about worldly well-being than 'undeveloped' societies do? Our obsession with economic growth seems natural to us because we have forgotten the historicity of many of the 'needs' we now take for granted, and therefore what, for Buddhism, is an essential human attribute if we are to be happy: the importance of self-limitation, which requires some degree of non-attachment from things and therefore from the markets that buy and sell them. Until they are seduced by the globalizing dream of a technological cornucopia, it does not occur to traditionally 'poor' people to become fixated on fantasies about all the things they might have. Their ends are an expression of the means available to them. We project our own values when we assume that they must be unhappy, and that the only way to become happy is to start on the treadmill of a lifestyle increasingly preoccupied with consumption.

All this is expressed better within a traditional Buddhist analogy. The world is full of thorns and sharp stones (and now broken glass too); what should we do about this? One solution is to pave over the entire earth, but a simpler alternative is to wear shoes (Dalai Lama 1999: 58–9). 'Paving the whole planet' seems a good metaphor for our collective economic globalization project. Without the wisdom of self-limitation, we may not be satisfied even when we have used up all the earth's resources. The other solution is for our minds to learn how to 'wear shoes', so that our collective ends become an expression of the renewable means that the biosphere provides.

Why do we assume that lack of money and consumer goods must be *dukkha*? Perhaps that brings us to the heart of the matter. Has material wealth become increasingly important in the 'developed' world because of our eroding faith in any other possibility of salvation? Has increasing our 'standard of living' become so compulsive for so many of us because it serves as a substitute for the sense of security previously provided by traditional religious values?

From that perspective, our evangelical efforts to economically 'develop' other societies, which cherish their own spiritual values and community traditions, may be viewed as a contemporary form of religious imperialism. Does that make the globalization of capitalism a new kind of mission to convert the heathen?

10.5.2   Ill-Will/Compassion

I have emphasized that ending our *dukkha* is the primary challenge that Buddhism addresses; and that the major way that Buddhism addresses it is with compassion. That is because our compassion not only increases the happiness of others who receive it, it also increases our own. 'For if it is correct that those qualities such as love, patience, tolerance, and forgiveness are what happiness consists in, and if it is correct that compassion is both the source and fruit of these qualities, then the more we are compassionate, the more we provide for our own happiness' (Dalai Lama 1999: 127).

In order to determine the ethical value of an action, Tibetan Buddhism considers its utilitarian consequences less important than the individual's *kun long*—his or her 'overall state of heart and mind'. Ethically, wholesome actions arise naturally when our *kun long* is basically compassionate. 'Compassion—which entails ethical conduct—belongs at the heart of all our actions, both individual and social' (Dalai Lama 1999: 30–1, 173). Insofar as the ultimate goal of economic growth is also increasing the sum of human happiness, this key Buddhist insight leads to a crucial question: how much does global capitalism encourage the development of compassion (e.g. by increasing opportunities to help people), and how much does it discourage its development (by emphasizing individual self-interest)?

Conventional economic theory assumes that material resources are limited while our desires are infinitely expandable. Without the norm of self-limitation, this situation becomes a formula for strife. The three poisons do not work independently; greed, ill-will, and delusion interact. This chapter is written in the wake of the collapse of Enron Corporation, the largest bankruptcy in US history, and a controversial one. One of the many reasons for the controversy surrounding it is the way the top management provided golden parachutes for themselves while allowing the pension funds of ordinary employees to become worthless. This may be an extreme example of how greed works against compassion, but regrettably that sort of story is all too familiar, because it regularly recurs.

As we also know, desire frustrated is a major cause—perhaps the major cause—of ill-will. The Buddha warned against negative feelings such as envy (when we have no opportunity to acquire possessions available to others) and avarice (the selfish enjoyment of goods while greedily guarding them from others). A global society in which such psychological tendencies predominate may be materially wealthy but it is spiritually poor. A global society where people do not feel that they benefit from sharing with each other has already begun to break down.

10.5.3 Delusion/Wisdom

For its proponents, the globalization of market capitalism is a victory for 'free trade' over the inefficiency of protectionism and the corruption of special interests. Free trade and capital mobility seem to exemplify the supreme value that we place on economic freedom. They optimise the access to resources and markets. What could be wrong with that?

Approaching the issue from a non-Western perspective, such as Buddhism, suggests that globalizing capitalism is neither natural nor inevitable. It is one historically conditioned way for us to understand and organize our material world, with disadvantages as well as advantages, for it is based upon certain presuppositions about the nature of that world.

The critical stage in the development of market capitalism occurred during the Industrial Revolution, when new technologies led to the 'liberation' of a critical mass of land, labour, and capital, the output of which became understood in a new way, as commodities to be bought and sold. In order for market forces to interact freely and productively, the world had to be converted into extractable resources available for exchange. As Karl Polanyi (1957) has shown, there was nothing inevitable about this commodification. In fact, it was disliked and resisted by many people at the time, and was only successfully implemented because of the strong support of the business community and governments.

For those who had capital to invest, the Industrial Revolution proved to be quite profitable; but that was not the way most people experienced market commodification. The biosphere (which from an ecological perspective could be considered our mother as well as our home) became commodified into a collection of resources to be exploited. Human life became commodified into labour, or work time, also priced according to supply and demand. Family patrimony, the cherished inheritance preserved for one's descendants, became commodified into capital for investment. All three were reduced to *means* which the new economy used to generate more capital for more development for more profit for more capital...

From a religious perspective, an alternative way to describe this process of commodification is that the world and its beings (including humans) became de-sacralized, a process which has continued throughout the past century. Today we see biotechnology doing this to the genetic code of life; soon our awe at the mysteries of reproduction—one of the last bastions of the sacred—will be replaced by the ultimate shopping experience. The 'developed world' is now largely secularized, but elsewhere this social and economic transformation is far from finished. Is that why the International Monetary Fund and the World Trade Organization have become so important? A less sanguine way of viewing their role is that they exist to ensure that nothing stands in the way of converting the rest of the earth—the 'undeveloped world', to use our revealing term for it—into resources and markets.

This commodified understanding presupposes a sharp duality between humans and the rest of the earth. Value is created by our goals and desires; the rest of the world has no meaning or value except insofar as it serves human purposes. However natural this dualistic understanding now seems to us, Buddhist teachings question it, for it is one of our more problematical delusions, at the heart of our *dukkha*.

There are different accounts of what Buddha experienced when he became enlightened, but they all agree that he realized the non-dual interdependence of things. The world is not a collection of things but a web of interacting processes. Nothing has any reality of its own apart from that web, because everything, including us, is dependent on everything else. As the Dalai Lama puts it (1999: 36), '[w]hen we consider the matter, we start to see that we cannot finally separate out any phenomena from the context of other phenomena.' The Vietnamese Zen master (and poet) Thich Nhat Hanh has expressed this more concretely (1988: 3–5):

If you are a poet, you will see clearly that there is a cloud floating in this sheet of paper. Without a cloud, there will be no rain; without rain, the trees cannot grow, and without trees we cannot make paper. The cloud is essential for the paper to exist. If the cloud is not here, the sheet of paper cannot be here either...

If we look into this sheet of paper even more deeply, we can see the sunshine in it. If the sunshine is not there, the tree cannot grow. In fact, nothing can grow. Even we cannot grow without sunshine. And so, we know that the sunshine is also in this sheet of paper. The paper and the sunshine inter-are. And if we continue to look, we can see the logger who cut the tree and brought it to the mill to be transformed into paper. And we see the wheat. We know that the logger cannot exist without his daily bread, and therefore the wheat that became his bread is also in this sheet of paper. And the logger's father and mother are in it too...

He goes on to show that 'As thin as this sheet of paper is, it contains everything in the universe in it.' Such interdependence challenges our usual sense of separation from the world. The Cartesian sense that I am 'in here,' inside my head behind my eyes, and the world is 'out there,' alienates us from the world we are 'in.' The important teaching of *anatman* 'nonself' denies this duality, which Buddhism views as psychologically and historically conditioned. Our sense of a self apart from the world is a delusion—what would now be called a construction— because the sense of 'I' is an effect of interacting physical and mental processes that are interdependent with the rest of the world. This makes each of us a manifestation of the world. The Buddhist path works by helping us to realize our interdependence and non-duality with the rest of the biosphere, and to live in accordance with that. This path is incompatible, therefore, with any economic system that treats the earth only as a commodity, or that works to reinforce our delusive sense of separation from it and from other people.

10.6 UPGRADING MORAL BEHAVIOUR

Does the above critique—our extrapolation of basic Buddhist teachings—imply that global capitalism is incompatible with Eastern religions such as Buddhism? Some may draw that conclusion, but I am not so sure. To say it again: Buddhism does not itself advocate any particular economic system, and neither does it *prima facie* reject any. Historically, Buddhism has been quite pragmatic and flexible regarding such institutions. Furthermore, this would seem to be an area where the Buddhist tradition has something to learn, insofar as its central concern is eliminating *dukkha* and promoting human happiness. Buddhism arose and developed in cultures where technologies were comparatively primitive and unchanging; and where the economic opportunities to improve one's lot were usually very limited. Traditionally, Buddhism has focused on mental *dukkha*— the unhappiness caused by our ways of thinking and feeling—but physical *dukkha* is also *dukkha* that should be addressed. Despite all the problems with modern technologies and economic globalization, Buddhism today needs to acknowledge the opportunities they can offer for promoting individual and social happiness. On the other side, though, we also need the Buddhist insight that economics and technology cannot by themselves resolve our *dukkha*.

The crucial issue remains the relationship between an economic system and the individual and social values it promotes: in other words, how responsible global capitalism is or can become. Professor Dunning emphasizes the importance of governments in their supervisory and regulatory role, which is indeed necessary, yet that also highlights the worrisome tendency of some capitalist institutions, especially powerful corporations, to subvert such regulation. The US electoral process is an egregious example, but there are many others. However, the fact that this subversion is now so obvious also suggests the possibility of a solution, at least in democratic societies.

In this fashion, I come to Professor Dunning's two ways of upgrading the moral behaviour of global capitalism: the *top-down*, including laws and regulations such as safety nets for those adversely affected by globalization; and the *bottom-up* approach, possibly including such grass-roots efforts as consumer and stockholder movements. If we want to improve the quality of global capitalism, both directions must be addressed. This chapter concludes with some reflections on what that might involve from a Buddhist perspective.

If it is agreed that responsible global capitalism is not an end in itself but a means toward a better life and a healthier society, it becomes difficult to avoid the conclusion that today we need more democratic supervision of international markets, which need to become more transparent in their operations. If it is also true that societies do not exist for the sake of markets but *vice-versa*, it is also true that during the last two hundred years the tail has often wagged the dog. Many, perhaps most people, have had to adapt to economic changes that were forced upon them by undemocratic (or only nominally democratic) rulers. If global capitalism is to become truly more inclusive and socially responsible, today such forced transformations must be recognized as unacceptable. The issue becomes: how can more democratic decision making be encouraged?

Top-down. Perhaps the most pressing immediate issue is the public supervision of corporations, especially global ones responsible for an increasing share of the world's economic product. I think that the first concern should be to reduce their influence on public institutions, especially to protect the electoral process from the effects of their 'contributions', and to address the role of corporate lobbyists. A second stage could require the boards of large corporations to include employee and environmentalist representatives, to ensure that profit is not the only factor considered in decision making. In the end, I suspect it will be necessary to redefine the nature of corporations by means of their social umbilical cords: that is, by rewriting their corporate charters to ensure that corporations exist to promote the public good, and not *vice-versa*.[7] One possibility is to reinstitute the penalty of institutional death—revoking charters—for corporations that repeatedly engage in illegal activities, or otherwise seriously violate the conditions of their charters.

We should not underestimate the difficulty of doing these things, but it is doubtful whether global capitalism can ever become truly responsible without such measures.

Bottom-up. A religious approach provides a different perspective on what the real bottom is. To start at the bottom is to begin with people's basic values, including religious commitments.

In his introductory chapter Professor Dunning offers the revealed teachings of the monotheistic faiths as one possible source for moral values influencing business practices. Here there is an interesting contrast with Buddhism. Buddhist values, like other Buddhist teachings, are not revealed to us but discovered by those who follow the Buddhist path. Shakyamuni Buddha is not a God; through his own efforts he discovered the *dharma*, and by following in his footsteps we can discover those same truths for ourselves. Buddhist precepts are not moral laws that someone or something else obligates us to follow. Rather, the incentive is that if we live according to them, our karma will improve and our lives will naturally become more happy. This does not require anyone to identify himself or herself as a Buddhist, but it does require our own effort to transform ourselves.

This may be in accord with a general spiritual shift in contemporary societies, where fewer people are inclined to identify themselves with religious institutions, yet more people say they are interested in the spiritual dimension of their lives. That can be dismissed as another example of our more self-centred individualism, but I believe it is much more than that. Other complementary movements, such as downshifting and voluntary simplicity, suggest a change of mood in some parts of the more affluent nations. It is difficult to determine how widespread this is—corporate media, dependent on advertising revenues, i.e. promoting consumerism, have little incentive to spotlight it—but if this grows into a genuine social movement, it might become the most important example of a bottom-up route to upgrading our collective moral behaviour, by first upgrading our collective spiritual consciousness.

I emphasize this because from a Buddhist viewpoint, and perhaps from any truly religious viewpoint, the most problematic aspect of capitalism today is its tendency to function as a religious surrogate, a 'religion of the market' (Loy 1999). If religion teaches us what is really important about the world, and therefore how to live in it, today the most important religion for an increasing number of people all over the world is consumerism. Overproduction has long since shifted the focus from manufacturing goods to manufacturing demand, in one of the more trenchant examples of how capitalism has remoulded society in order to solve its own problems.

How might an 'upgraded' spiritual consciousness express itself economically? I see an expanded role for religious (or religious-inspired) voluntary associations such as churches, charities, and pressure groups, which can employ their own economic power as well as the oxygen of publicity to influence the values and direction of global capitalist development. There is also the possibility of concerted efforts by major religious leaders, perhaps even coming to serve the same role in the moral sphere that the 'Group of 8' now perform in the economic sphere (Dunning, Chapter 1, p. 33). Such inter-religious co-operation still faces many obstacles, but it is increasingly becoming another important aspect of globalization.

Since governments are also deeply implicated in the new 'religion of the market'—measuring their success by such indices as the GNP or growth in GNP—grass-roots efforts are also indispensable for influencing the political process. One way to start might be with a movement to restrict the role of advertising, on the grounds that today much of it has become as bad for our psychological and spiritual health as tobacco is for our physical health.

Such a grass-roots transformation in consciousness would doubtless empower many such economic reforms, which would either help to make global capitalism more socially responsible, or, if failing in that, would work to replace it with something else more responsible to our spiritual concerns.

NOTES

I am grateful to Jon Watts, Santikaro Bhikkhu, Ian Whicher, and John Dunning for their comments on earlier drafts of this chapter.

1. As it spread and adapted to different cultures, Buddhism has changed so much that it is difficult to generalize about its teachings. My focus in this chapter is on the teachings of Shakyamuni as preserved in the Theravada Buddhism of South and South-East Asia. The Pali sutras, which are believed to record his original teachings, provide a foundation generally accepted by all Buddhist traditions. The Nikayas cited in my text are an important part of those teachings. The *Dhammapada* is a very popular collection of Buddhist aphorisms taken from the Pali canon. For general introductions to Buddhist teachings, see Rahula (1962), Conze (1980), Thich Nhat Hanh (1998), and the Dalai Lama (1998, 1999). For Buddhist ethics, see Harvey (2000). For Buddhist economics, see Schumacher (1975), Payutto (1994), and Sizemore and Swearer (1990).

2. The present Dalai Lama has suggested (1999: 28, 49) that binding ethical principles can be derived from the starting point that we all desire happiness and want to avoid suffering: an ethical act is one that does not harm others' experience or expectation of happiness.

3. *Samyutta-Nikaya* III, *Kosalasamyutta* 167–8, in *The Connected Discourses*, 169.

4. *Digha-Nikaya* III, 65 ff., in *The Long Discourses*, 396–405.

5. See e.g. MacIntyre (1988).

6. But for a rather different perspective of the social responsibility of business see Robert Davies (Ch. 13) in this volume.

7. Again, this has been taken up by other contributors to this volume, notably by Hans Küng and Robert Davies.

REFERENCES

Chambers, Robert (1997), *Whose Reality Counts?* (London: Intermediate Technology), with the wittiest endnotes I have ever read.

Connected Discourses of the Buddha, The: A New Translation of the Samyutta Nikaya (2000), trans. Bhikkhu Bodhi (Boston: Wisdom Publications).

Conze, Edward (1980), *A Short History of Buddhism* (London: Allen & Unwin).

Dalai Lama, The (1998), *The Art of Happiness* (New York: Putnam).

—— (1999), *Ethics for the New Millennium* (New York: Riverhead Books).

Dhammapada, The (1976), (Bombay: Theosophy Company).

Durning, Alan (1992), *How Much is Enough?* (New York: Norton).

Hanh, Thich Nhat (1988), *The Heart of Understanding* (Berkeley, Calif.: Parallax Press).

—— (1998), *The Heart of the Buddha's Teaching* (Berkeley, Calif.: Parallax Press).

Harvey, Peter (2000), *An Introduction to Buddhist Ethics* (Cambridge: Cambridge University Press).

Long Discourses of the Buddha, The: A Translation of the Digha Nikaya (1995), trans. Maurice Walshe (Boston: Wisdom Publications).

Loy, David R. (1999), 'The Religion of the Market'. In Harold Coward and Dan Maguire (eds.), *Visions of a New Earth: Religious Perspectives on Population, Consumption and Ecology* (Albany: State University of New York Press).

MacIntyre, Alastair (1988), *Whose Justice? Which Rationality?* (South Bend, Ind.: University of Notre Dame Press).

Payutto, P. A. (1994), *Buddhist Economics: A Middle Way for the Market Place,* trans. Dhammavijaya and Bruce Evans, 2nd edn. (Bangkok: Buddhadhamma Foundation).

Polanyi, Karl (1957), *The Great Transformation* (Boston: Beacon).

Rahula, Walpola (1962), *What the Buddha Taught* (New York: Grove Press).

Sizemore, Russell F., and Donald K. Swearer, eds. (1990), *Ethics, Wealth and Salvation: A Study in Buddhist Social Ethics* (Columbia, SC: University of South Carolina).

Schumacher, E. F. (1975). *Small is Beautiful: Economics as if People Mattered* (New York: Perennial Books).

United Nations Human Development Report (UNHDR) (1999) *http://www.undp.org/hdro/overview.pdf*

Weber, Max (1930), *The Protestant Ethic and the Spirit of Capitalism* (London: Allen & Unwin).

PART III

11

A Universal Culture of Human Rights and Freedom's Habits: Caritapolis

MICHAEL NOVAK

11.1 INTRODUCTION

When Rome was overrun by Goths under Alaric in AD 410—men pulled in ropes toward captivity, women raped, statues overturned, walls torn down, buildings gutted, treasures carted off—desolate Romans in the provinces blamed the Christians. None of this would have happened, they said, if Rome had remained faithful to the pagan gods of ancient Rome. In rebuttal, the most learned Latinist of his day, a Catholic bishop in Northern Africa, Augustine, felt obligated to develop—over a sixteen-year period—an account of how God works among men that would end these accusations and chart a new future for the earth. The Roman empire of the time had fashioned the nearest thing to a 'global empire' the world had yet seen, extending westwards, eastwards, and especially northwards much farther than Alexander's empire several centuries before. The fruit of Augustine's labours was *The City of God*, an imposing tome of 22 long chapters ('books').[1] It bears reading still today, for it sheds much light upon our contemporary situation; at the end of this chapter we shall return to it.

The premise of the present chapter is that something new has again arisen in our midst—the first outlines of a truly global, planetary civilization, pulled willy-nilly by prevailing winds. These winds blow in shifting and uneven patterns, but they do seem to drive all nations towards some sort of universal culture of human rights and some form of international economic dynamism. Nations may not be becoming *identical* (far from it), but they are at least developing 'family resemblances'. Analogous pressures bear upon all, from certain prevailing directions. These pressures are today called 'globalization'. What are they?

11.2 THREE DIMENSIONS OF GLOBALISM

In its depths, globalism has at least three dimensions: political, cultural, and economic.

11.2.1 Political

Political expressions of globalization are multiplying, beginning with the World Wars of the twentieth century. In the 1920s, Stalin, Mussolini, and Hitler burst upon the world stage, shouting that dictatorship is the most efficient form of government in fulfilling the general will and in lifting up the poor. But the world learned bitter and unforgettable lessons from the age of dictatorship. As John Paul II points out in his 1991 *Centesimus Annus*, democracy has many faults but no system yet invented better protects the human rights of minorities and individuals, both from single tyrants and from the tyranny of the majority. Thus, nearly everywhere around the world, dictatorship is being rejected, and peoples are striving to develop the political parties and coalitions that lead to government based on the consent of the governed and under the rule of law. 'The rule of law' means a law that looks upon all as equals, and on none with special favour.[2]

After the Second World War, the Universal Declaration of Human Rights broadcast a condemnation of certain evils (genocide, torture, etc.) to all nations, and awakened virtually all peoples.[3] Outside the United Nations building in New York City stands a statue of Francesco de Vitoria (1486–1546), the great Christian thinker from Spain who is regarded as 'the father of international law.' Like international law, Christianity sees all the world's people as one. All have been given a vocation to 'build up the kingdom of God' on earth, a kingdom never finished, but before the last day always partial, incomplete, and flawed.

The struggle to devise systems of positive law that guide, teach, and shape peoples in ways worthy of the destiny their Creator intended for them entails a long struggle of trial and error, against human resistance and rebellion, and in the face of human ignorance, errant passion, and wilful blindness. The struggle for an international rule of law is a long historical adventure.

A further political expression of globalization is the simultaneous movement against the hegemony of the nation state from 'above' and from 'below'. In Europe, for example, individual states are yielding some of their sovereignty and prerogatives to the European Community. They are forming new realities larger than the nation state. Simultaneously, many nation states are under pressure to grant new autonomy to internal regions within their own domain. Thus, the former United Kingdom is today ceding more and more autonomy to Scotland and Wales: Lombardia is pressuring the Italian central state for greater recognition and autonomy; and in France, Germany, and elsewhere constituent regions of nation states seek ampler room for local self-government.

This double movement towards larger units 'above' and smaller units 'below', even though it arises from many mixed motives, including unworthy ones, is anticipated by the principle of subsidiarity: some problems are best solved at smaller and more local levels, while others require larger, cross-cultural entities.[4] The practical tendency of contemporary thought favours the most concrete and immediate level consistent with practical wisdom; the 'universal', utopian tendency favours more extensive organizations and institutions, even on a global scale.

11.2.2   Economic

Before 1989, few thinkers predicted the sudden collapse of socialism as an economic system. Until that time, many still saw socialism as the wave of the future, and others were arguing for a 'third way' between socialism and existing capitalist societies. The collapse of socialism as an economic idea eliminated the socialist alternative, and cast doubt on a main pillar of 'the third way'.[5] For one thing, welfare states have promised greater awards to future retirees than they have any prospect of paying, since their populations are rapidly aging, and younger workers grow ever scarcer. Both because of abortion and because of a lessened willingness of young couples to have large families, many nations have been experiencing a severe 'birth dearth', the opposite of a population explosion—a severe population contraction.[6] Thinkers around the world who once depended upon socialist ideas—or at least on the ideas of social democracy and the welfare state—are only now awakening to this portending financial crisis.

A second implicit assumption of the welfare state—namely, that the central state will be relatively protected from the world economy, and able, by itself, to dictate its own course—is also no longer secure. Like gale-force winds, the international forces of invention and discovery, global trade, open market exchange, free capital flows, and labour mobility across borders rush right through the individual welfare states. The tidy and self-enclosed social systems of these nation states, locked into the forms of social welfare developed in the early twentieth century, are under sudden and intense stress. Such stress might well provide a favourable new opportunity for the renewal of civilization, if it leads to new ways of thinking, and new social institutions.

Some of the global pressures from outside may be illustrated by the following facts. In 1965, gross world product (GWP) was 1.7 trillion dollars; by 1999, it had leapt to 30.2 trillion dollars. In part, this tremendous increase in the wealth of the world was due to new inventions and discoveries, and to millions of new small businesses put into operation by poor peoples who had never had the chance to become entrepreneurs in the past. In part, though, this immense growth in wealth is also due to an even larger increase in world trade. Between 1965 and 1996, world trade from one country to another skyrocketed from 186 billion dollars to 6.37 *trillion* dollars.[7]

The *kind* of goods exported by the less developed countries also changed dramatically. In 1965, 85 per cent of the total exports of such countries were in the form of primary commodities. By 1998, 79 per cent of their export had shifted to manufactured goods, only 21 per cent still in commodities. A great deal of the new manufacturing in the world is now taking place in countries in which, just a few decades ago, there was practically no manufacturing. This has been a great boon to the poor of those countries. While still only a relatively small percentage of their populations today works in manufacturing industries, these few are now drawing income and benefits far superior to any that their families knew in the past. They are also learning new skills and aptitudes.

In the last thirty years, moreover, just as gross world product exploded, world trade exploded, and so also did foreign direct investment, which leapt to 400 billion dollars in 1997, fourteen times the level in real terms of two decades earlier.[8] The daily turnover in foreign exchange markets increased from around 20 billion dollars in the 1970s to 1.5 trillion dollars in 1998. International bank lending grew from 265 billion dollars in 1975 to 4 trillion dollars in 1994.[9]

These indicators shed light on why we find ourselves living in a very different world from that of just thirty years ago. The world today is far richer, more interconnected, and more dynamic. Each nation is more interdependent with other nations than it was then. Some find this new global interdependence frightening, and claim to prefer the security of isolation. Yet the interdependence of one country with another better exemplifies the solidarity of all human beings than did their earlier isolation from each other. As certain fathers of the church in the Near East pointed out in the third and fourth centuries of the Christian era, international commerce gives practical expression to the need which the different nations have of one another—this one producing wine, that one wool, the other one grain, and still another olive oil—and in this way testify to the fundamental unity of the human race.

On the other hand, these relatively sudden transformations have exacted heavy costs. Local industries, for many generations protected from the larger world, now face the stiff winds of competition from other peoples who can manufacture the same goods more cheaply, more efficiently, and sometimes with higher quality. Dozens of sources of strain and friction have been brought about by the emergence of the global economy from the global wars that wracked the twentieth century. Not the least of these is the lack of a hospitable philosophy of globalization. Most ideologies of our time (fascism, socialism, third worldism, etc.) have been hostile to the new sources of economic dynamism, and have long repressed the forces of individual creativity, initiative, imagination, and markets that make possible the open entry of the poor and the marginalized into the 'circle of development'. Most advanced thinkers, whether for traditionalist or for socialist reasons, have been radically anti-capitalist. Thus, they find themselves ill-prepared for present sources of dynamism, invention, and growth.

11.2.3   Cultural

Globalization means that we experience today an unprecedented network of contacts between peoples and cultures. Television images from one part of the world now reach families in another part of the world almost simultaneously. All can be watching the same images at the same time, or at least as the waking day turns around the globe. Between 1980 and 1998, the number of television sets per 1,000 people worldwide nearly doubled, from 121 to 247; and the number keeps growing.[10] Sitting in our own homes or offices, we watch weather reports on television describing temperatures and changes of climate in a long list of other cities on every continent around the world. Ideas of human rights and democracy also spread rapidly around the world, as do images of suffering and injustice. So also, alas, do images of seduction, hedonism, and rebellion against the good and the true.

Again, more people than ever before are traveling today from one country to another. Traffic by airplane today has become so cheap and convenient that the crowds who come to London, Rome, Paris (and other great cities) are no longer merely aristocrats or the learned, as in earlier times, but from among the far more humble. On a more permanent level, many families today have members who are living in other countries in far parts of the world—even our families have become planetary.

But that is not all. Multiple lines of international commerce and trade are weaving a single circle of exchange. More and more people today spontaneously begin their thinking by trying to imagine the needs and wants of people on the far side of the planet. Thus the American writer Thomas Friedman describes a Jordanian political journalist who tells him with satisfaction that CNN has just begun to include Amman in its reports on the day's temperatures and weather forecasts; for him Jordan now exists in a way it had not before; it counts for something in the eyes of others. And shortly thereafter an Israeli businessman explained to Friedman that he and his associates no longer think first about local economic conditions, and what they will produce for those, and then about some possibilities for export. Rather, they now find themselves thinking about the whole planet and about what they might be able to export, and then they think about how to produce it. We have become different sorts of persons, the man explained; we think of ourselves in a new way—a planetary way.[11]

Consider a few other indicators:

- Travellers from one country to another doubled between 1980 and 1996, from 260 million to almost 600 million travellers per year. This is equivalent to one-tenth of the world's population every year.
- Between 1990 and 1996, the time spent on international telephone calls more than doubled from 33 billion minutes to 70 billion minutes.
- In constant 1990 prices, the cost of a three-minute telephone call from New York to London fell from $245 in 1930 to almost $50 in 1960, to $3 in 1990, to 35 cents in 1999.[12]

Profound changes are occurring in the ocean depths of cultures, as well. In Indonesia and Burma and Burundi and Ghana and in all corners of the world, one hears more and more people appealing to the same universal ideas: human dignity, the right to personal economic initiative, liberation from poverty. As one writer from Africa has written:

> In the days when governments were the only source of information for the ordinary citizens, the government could, through propaganda and censorship, get citizens to believe that conditions in their countries were not much worse than those obtaining in other places.... With the improvement in the global communication system, large proportions of the populations of Africa have come to know much more than their governments would have wished them to know. In this way they have learnt much more about the achievements and failures of different forms of government and economic systems in other parts of the world and the standard of life in countries with different political and constitutional systems. They have also become aware of the growing interest of the international community in democratic governance and sound economic management, and the international support for democracy and human rights in the continent of Africa and elsewhere. This development has not only undermined the previously successful propaganda of governments, but has also given very potent incentives and encouragement to those who fight for democracy in these countries. In the past these persons were often discouraged by the fact that there was not much support at home for their efforts or much interest in their struggle internationally. (Mensah 1999)

Certain ideals for society and the individual appear to have universal force, and are now inspiring people everywhere. If, in fact, the nations of the world ever come to a universal culture of respect for human rights, it will be a world that is much closer to respecting the dignity of the individual person, and in that way at least demonstrating solidarity among all peoples. In important aspects, the entire world is now living through a common cultural drama, the attempt to build societies worthy of such ideals as individual dignity and universal solidarity.

11.3 THE CRISIS IN MORAL ECOLOGY

Liberty, political and economic, depends upon a supportive *moral ecology*. The American founding father James Madison once observed that a people incapable of governing their passions in their private lives could hardly be capable of practising self-government in their public lives. Human beings are capable of reflection and deliberate choice, yes, but it takes some training and work over a lifetime to develop the habits of temperance, equanimity, courage, sobriety, and the other virtues that enable them to make cool and collected judgements and to keep their course steady under heavy fire. The practice of liberty is protected by a bodyguard of sound habits. As the great American hymn puts it: '*Confirm thy soul in self-control / Thy liberty in law.*' For human beings as individuals, liberty is a form of self-control or self-government, placing as many actions as possible under the domain of sober reflection and deliberate choice. However, most people are capable of self-government only when the surrounding society supports them in that difficult task, shaming them when they stray too far, and encouraging them with noble examples and daily inducements of praise.

11.3.1   The Great Global Transformation, 1900–2000

It is doubtful that the world ever went through so great a transformation in one single century as it did during the twentieth century. This was the century whose first half was wracked by two world wars that cumulatively swept more lives away in violence (more than 200 million) than had in some earlier centuries constituted the entire world population. However, this was also the century in which the immense tide of invention and discovery that sprang from the development of a new type of economy (the capitalist economy), and because of the consequential new levels of healthcare and physical plenty, the population of the world leapt from 1.6 billion in 1900 to 6 billion in 2000. In significant measure, this increase in population was due to the fact that children, once born, were living far longer lives by the end of the century than at the beginning; average life expectancy around the world shot up from about 47 to 65. It jumped from 44 to 80 in one of the nations most developed in this respect, Japan, and from 31 to 44 in one of the least developed, Ethiopia. [13] From the time of Christ until about the year 1820, the world's population grew at a relatively miniscule rate, rising from 231 million to 268 million in the year 1000, to just over one billion in 1820. From then on it began a rise so steep and sudden that it shot almost straight up, rising to 6 billion in 1998.[14]

Some other fascinating indicators of the Great Transformation are as follows: the number of automobiles sold worldwide in 1900 was 4,000; in 1998, 54 million. In 1900, average hours of work per week in Britain were 52, but dropped to 36 by 1998. [15] In 1950 (the first year the UN compiled such data), the average infant mortality rate was 157 deaths per 1,000 live births; by 2000, this had been lowered to 60. (In India, for instance, from 190 to 73.)[16]

11.3.2   What is Moral Ecology?

What is moral ecology? It is the sum of all those conditions—ideas, narratives, institutions, associations, symbol systems, prevailing opinions and practices, and local dispensers of shame and praise—that teach us the habits necessary for human flourishing and support us in their practice. Our families, neighbourhoods, schools, churches, associations, and other institutions that affect our daily lives, especially in our younger years, establish the 'climate' in which we are reared. An honest, truthful, and straightforward culture makes it much easier for us to mature as moral beings, to develop sound habits and good characters, and to conduct ourselves with candour, honesty, and truthfulness. Growing up in a culture that is devious, corrupt, and hostile to truthfulness makes such development not only difficult but also far less frequent. But in addition to these immediate institutions, the ecology in which we live out our moral lives is also either polluted or invigorated by the narratives, symbols, images, ideas, solicitations and songs exhaled by such modern broadcast media as television, radio, cinema, and other instruments into the minds and souls of modern societies.

Professor Allen D. Hertzke is one of the first to have offered a sustained presentation of moral ecology as a testable intellectual concept, in an article called

'The Theory of Moral Ecology.'[17] He shows its parallels to, but also differences from, the concept of biological ecology. His approach is to employ the concept of 'threshold' to designate that point at which the relative frequency of some moral acts within a limited 'ecosystem' causes deterioration or 'degradation' of the context of many other human actions. Such deterioration, in turn, makes sound decisions by other agents far more difficult to sustain, and inflicts heavy costs (such as necessary defensive actions) on yet others. He notes that there are both left-wing and conservative uses of 'moral ecology', so that the concept itself is ideologically neutral. Moreover, there are forms of degradation to a given moral ecological system about which all can agree.[18]

When human beings can expect others to deal with them honestly and in non-threatening ways, they do not have to take defensive precautions. Everyday transactions support a high degree of openness and amiability. It is quite otherwise when sudden acts of violence begin to appear, such cases of robbery or burglary, a higher incidence of rape, increasing threats of extortion, growing contempt for the effectiveness of systems of justice, and the pervasive practice of cynicism and deception. Widespread painting of graffiti on public buildings with total impunity, the breaking of windows, the vandalization of public telephones and restrooms, public urination in the streets, the scattering of garbage—all these are signs of individual freedom and a lawless impulse run amok. There are also signs of profoundly violent and anomic passions ready to erupt at any time in spasms of destruction. Frequencies of such behaviours can be measured, and hypotheses about their significance tested. So also can hypotheses about their causes and preconditions.

On the more positive side of the ledger, such ideals as the 'free society,' for instance, have their own proper narratives, a history laden with heroic and symbolic figures, seminal ideas, special disciplines and asceticisms, and visions of the good life, which drive us onward and inspire us. All this, too, is part of moral ecology.

11.3.3   The Crisis of Moral Ecology

A free society is constituted by three interdependent, independent systems. It is constituted by a *democratic republic* in its political life, based upon the consent of the people, the division of powers, and the rule of law; an *inventive economy* in its economic life, based on personal initiative, personal property, and open markets; and a *culture of self-government* in its moral–cultural life, based upon the widespread practice of the virtues required of a free people: self-mastery, respect for others, law-abidingness, public-spiritedness, and the like. All three of these systems must be functioning in some measure of mutual balance, each checked and modified by the other two.

A healthy economic system is indispensable, if the love and respect of the people, especially the least fortunate, for the system is to be maintained. But the good order of the political system is more fundamental, since, without the rule of law, a proper economy swiftly degenerates into mutual destruction. Most fundamental of all is the culture of self-government, for citizens who cannot govern their passions in their private lives cannot be relied on to practise self-government in their public lives, either. In our time, since the secrets of a sound economy and a sound polity are fairly well understood, *the single most severe point of crisis* lies in our uncertain understanding of the moral ecology of the culture proper to freedom, on both the national and the global scale.

In Eastern Europe after 1989, for example, the cries 'freedom' and 'democracy' were on everyone's lips. But after two or three years of open elections, while economies had not yet begun to improve, people learned that free elections are not enough. Unless the economy is growing, and the life of those at the bottom is showing at least some tangible improvement, people will not love or respect democracy. Then, once people had also learned that passing laws permitting free markets, private property, and the financial improvement of one's own condition did not of themselves produce wealth, they learned another lesson. Economic prosperity does not arise from passing new laws. With intellect and will, citizens must breathe life into the bones of the law. Economic prosperity depends on the *subjective* commitment of millions of individuals to a new way of life: they must look around, see what needs to be done, and take the initiative to do it themselves; they must work, invest, take risks, solve day-to-day difficulties, and bring new realities into being. That is, they must practise *economic creativity*. They must learn to work well with others—with workmates, customers, suppliers, and all those on whom their success depends. In other words, they must learn a new morality. They must put in place a new moral atmosphere, with new habits, practices, and expectations.

To live well in a free society is morally far more demanding than to live in a socialist or traditionalist society. One must reach deep into oneself to find new moral resources. One must summon up initiative. One must take prudent risks and be prepared to lose everything, in order to create something new that did not exist before. Only thus is new wealth produced. To be a self-governing people in a free society is morally more demanding than to live in subjection under a communist state or in a traditional dictatorial society.

The mastering of the virtues required by a vital democracy, like those required by a free economy, also demands significant personal effort and institutional support. Some have called the requisite political virtues, generically, 'civic republicanism', but the name for them is not so important as daily practice. Among them are such habits as civility, personal responsibility, co-operativeness, a spirit of compromise (through which everyone, faced with as few 'zero-sum' choices as possible, gains a little), and the habit of 'loyal opposition' rather than mutual ill-will. We would be well served by a written guide to all required good habits, political, economic, and cultural, such as Aristotle provided Athens in the *Nicomachean Ethics*. At present, we do not have one.

Analytically, in all three of its constituent systems, the free society is driven by the *open, unrestricted drive to question,* to inquire, to better understand. The free society, then, is also 'the open society,' as Karl Popper named it.[19] It is driven by two different questions: (1) questions for understanding ('What is it?') and (2) questions about the preponderance of evidence ('Is that so?'). Questions of the first type seek insight; questions of the second type seek a grip on reality. The free society craves and needs both for its prospering and survival.

The crisis of moral ecology occurs today because prevailing ideologies and practices demonstrate that *inadequate self-knowledge* eats at the heart of the free society. Three examples: too many theories about *economics* stress the centrality of the 'self-interest' and 'the bottom line,' as expressed in predominantly material, even narrowly monetary, terms; too many theories about *politics* pretend to a realism based upon 'power' and 'interest'; too many theories about *culture* select relativism, subjectivism, or licence as foundational principles, such as, Freedom means 'Do as you wish' and 'Construct reality as you choose'.

But all these forms of self-knowledge suffer from premature closure. They cut off inquiry before all-important questions have been asked. The fact that a company has a healthy bottom line does not obviate further questions as to whether its business activities are honest and just. The fact that a nation has particular interests and the power to secure them does not still all questions about the justice or decency of its actions. The fact that an individual (or a culture) chooses a particular construction of reality raises further questions: is that construction illusory? Self-mutilating? Destructive of others?

The ongoing emergence of a single world, under pressure from prevailing political, economic, and cultural winds, now confronts us with the need to think through an adequate *human ecology*. What are the common (perhaps not yet fully imagined) narratives, symbols, ideas, habits that are emerging from global human experience, and that in the future have the capacity to lead us toward a flourishing world culture? Ideally, such a culture will not be homogeneous, but diverse. All parts of it will prosper, no parts left behind in the immemorial misery of the pre-scientific, pre-capitalist, pre-democratic past. The human rights and human potential of all will be respected, institutionally and culturally.

These are large questions, and the outline of a plan of action will require the common labour of many minds. As a small contribution toward that large work, this chapter offers a modest point of departure.

11.4 THE FOUR CARDINAL VIRTUES OF HUMAN ECOLOGY

Consider for a moment four vices that would poison any hope of a global ecology of amity, let alone of free co-operation among peoples and nations.

Were any people or nation to proceed with *arrogance*, as if they were all-seeing and all-knowing, others would be repulsed and driven into stern resistance. Were any people or nation to begin *suppressing questions, inquiry, the gathering of evidence*, others would rebel. Were any people or nation to *enslave, demean, or use others as mere means*, it would win the contempt of onlookers and the fierce resentment of those so demeaned. Were any people or nation to *treat other peoples highhandedly, doing to them what it would not tolerate being done to itself*, other peoples would look on with disgust. No doubt there are other vices destructive of an amicable world order. Let us begin with these, and turn them into their opposite virtues. From these vices, we may derive four cardinal virtues—hinge virtues—on which at least a rudimentarily sound moral ecology for the human race might turn. I call them (but the names are not nearly so significant as the realities) cultural *humility*; respect for the regulative ideal of *truth*; the *dignity of the individual*; and human *solidarity*.

11.4.1 Cultural Humility

A proper sense of one's own fallibility, past sins, limits, and characteristic faults does not require the embrace of cultural relativism. In order to see one's own faults and limits, and those of one's culture, it is not necessary to hold that all cultures are equal. The reality of the world is so large and the universe of being so immense that it is foolish to imagine that all of it can be grasped and comprehended by any finite body. Moreover, every culture is implicated in certain specific historical sins, omissions, even horrific deeds. Every culture has characteristic blind spots. Every culture suffers from the illusions that false pride engenders. Every culture overestimates its strengths and underestimates the depth and reach of its weaknesses. Every culture is led by self-love to pay far too little attention to the cultures, needs, and achievements of its neighbours. Every culture looks with humorous disdain on the mannerisms, tastes, and proclivities of cultures different from its own; comedians of one culture mock idiosyncrasies of others.

All these characteristic faults are reasons for leaders and individuals in one culture to lean over backwards in trying to be fair to people of other cultures, recognizing that they may well be mistaken in their initial perceptions and judgements. They need to warn themselves about the potential distortions introduced into their perceptions by their own self-love, self-preoccupation, and habitual inattention to others.

On the other hand, it is obviously true that some cultures have more rapidly achieved economic growth than others. It is also true that some better practise religious liberty, freedom of the press, and the rule of law. Neither political nor economic development has proceeded at the same pace in all nations. Nonetheless, without embracing cultural relativism and without bad faith, one may recognize the limits, sins, and characteristic blind spots of one's own culture, even while remaining grateful for its worthy achievements. No one culture represents the dazzling fullness of the whole human race.

Humility means being aware that no one possesses the truth, but that all of us stand under the judgement of truth. In my truth, there is some error, and in the error of others (in those of my adversary, for instance) there is bound to be some truth. In short, the humble man knows that he needs the help of others to see events and circumstances truly, and so he watches carefully to detect what his enemies may be seeing that he doesn't. Aware of his own past errors of judgement, mistakes, and misperceptions, as well as of the potential distortions introduced by his own passions and urgent interests, and recognizing from past experience his own limits, he shows his adversaries and weaker allies a serious and genuine respect.

11.4.2   Truth

It was one of the great discoveries of the peoples of Eastern Europe, living under
the oppressive daily presence of engines of what came to be called THE LIE, that
many of them learned to *refuse under any condition to co-operate with THE LIE.*
Perhaps it was not clear to them what 'the truth' might be; but they had become
quite adept at recognizing the lie.[20] Lying took place even in the reporting of
weather predictions; when there was to be a great communist parade or festival,
such predictions were invariably favourable. In addition, under torment or torture, those in prison such as Shcharansky and Mihajlov often reported that they
learned an important lesson.[21] As long as they were faithful to their own sense of
truth, they retained a power which their jailers could not take from them. As long
as they were determined not to be complicit in the lie, they felt an integrity of
soul, and a certain inner, virtually indomitable power. Of course, their liberty
could be taken from them by mind-altering drugs or even by certain tortures
beyond their power to retain consciousness and to endure. But up to those levels,
they became painfully aware of the sheer moral power of their own inner
determination not to lie.

This awful experience may have been a backward way of coming to the concept of truth, but it was altogether appropriate. Such men and women came to
think of 'truth' not as a proposition imposed upon them, but rather as a kind of
inner light and imperative to fidelity. In this light, maintaining fidelity to truth as
opposed to lying and falsification is exceedingly important for a civilized society. It
is a necessary condition for a free society. For if there is no such regulative ideal,
then human relations do not fall under the authority of truth and evidence, but
only of authoritarian will and power. If there is no truth, then there can be no just
claims against tyranny, and no evidence of violation of rights, one way or the other.
Appeal to truth is an indispensable condition for the practice of liberty. The old
adage, 'The truth shall make ye free', was lived out in the experience of many dissi-
dents behind the Iron Curtain. In fact, in the concentration camps and torture
chambers, fidelity to truth was sometimes the only form of liberty to be enjoyed.

Those in the West who play with the idea that relativism is crucial for liberty
are playing with fire, since regimes built solely on the principle of lying, without
any possibility of appeal to evidence and fair judgement, dwell under the sign of
stark naked power. Under that sign, thugs move into positions of leadership, and
the finer spirits concerned about such niceties as evidence and argument are
driven first to the periphery and eventually to prison. Against them, one cannot
shout, 'Injustice!' For to that they reply, 'Says who?' And one cannot say, 'Those
charges are false!' For there is no longer any such thing as 'true' or 'false'. It is now
power, power alone, which speaks.

Truth as a regulative ideal is, in this sense, a crucial concept for a civilized
society. It is the necessary concept, if people are to have respect for one another's
fairness in reasoning and judgement, and to submit opposing judgments to
the light of evidence. Only such a concept makes conversation in the light of

evidence possible. Civilized persons converse; they reason with one another; they argue. Barbarians club one another. Barbarians live under the sign of naked and unadorned power. The free live inside the gates within which evidence is respected.

11.4.3 The Dignity of the Individual Person

What, after all, is human dignity? The English word dignity is rooted in the Latin *dignus*, 'worthy of esteem and honour, due a certain respect, of weighty importance'. In ordinary discourse, we use *dignity* only in reference to human persons. (But, of course, in the Bible it is also used of other special persons or 'spiritual substances', that is, beings capable of insight and choice such as God, angels, and demons.) Both Aristotle and Plato held that most humans are by nature slavish and suitable only to be slaves, lacking natures worthy of freedom and proper to free men. The Greeks did not use the term *dignity* for all human beings, only a few. By contrast, Christianity insisted that every single human is loved by the Creator, made in His image, and destined for eternal friendship and communion. Following Judaism, Christianity made human dignity a concept of universal application. 'Inasmuch as ye have done it unto one of the least of these my brethren, ye have done it unto me' (Matt. 25: 40). Christianity made it a matter of self-condemnation to use another human as a means to an end. Each human being is to be shown the dignity bestowed on him by God because each is loved by God as a friend. Each has God as 'a father.' Obviously, many students of economics are neither Christians nor even believers in God. They, therefore, do not look at the world in this way. Nonetheless, as a matter of intellectual history, it is of some utility to discover the origin of concepts, and to observe how its secularized equivalent takes shape.

As every tree in the world is an individual with its unique location in space and time, and with a shape all its own, so it is with every member of every species of plant and animal. To speak of the individual in this sense is to speak of what can be physically located, observed, seen, and touched. In this context, the common good would be either the sum of the goods of each individual member or 'the greatest good of the greatest number'. A purely materialistic conception of the individual is compatible with a high valuation on each individual. But it is also compatible with the view that the whole is greater than any part and ought to take precedence over any part. It is this latter view that George Orwell satirized in *Animal Farm*. In this view, the human being in the social body is like the steer in the herd, the bee in the hive, the ant in the colony, an individual whose good is subordinated to the good of the species.

A *person* is more than an individual. As the concept of *individual* looks to what is material, so the concept of person looks to intellect and will: the capacities of insight and judgement, on the one hand, and of choice and decision, on the other. A person is an individual able to inquire and to choose, and, therefore, both free and responsible. For Aquinas, the person is in this sense made in the image of the Creator and endowed with inalienable responsibilities. The good of such a person, who participates in activities of insight and choice (God's own form of life), is to be united with God, without intermediary, face-to-face in full light and love. The ultimate common good of persons is to be united with God's understanding and loving, the same activities of insight and choice coursing through and energizing all.

Analogously, on earth and in time, the common good of persons is to live in as close an approximation of unity in insight and love as sinful human beings might attain. Since this requires respect for the inalienable freedom and responsibility of each, and since human beings are imperfect at best and always flawed in character, it is by no means easy at any one historical moment either to ascertain the common good or to attain it. In order to solve both these problems, even approximately, persons need institutions suitable to the task.

But what sorts of institutions are likely to raise the probabilities of success in identifying and achieving the common good in history? These must be invented and tested by the hazards of history. They are not given in advance. Human beings proceed toward the common good more in darkness than in light.

Two fundamental organizational errors are ruled out, however, by an accurate judgement about the requirements of the human person *qua* person. The specific vitalities of the person spring from capacities for insight and choice (inquiry and love). From these derive principles of liberty and responsibility, in which human dignity is rooted. The human person is *dignus*, worthy of respect, sacred even, because he or she lives from the activities proper to God. To violate these is to denigrate the Almighty. On the one hand, then, it is an error to define individualism without reference to God and without reference to those other persons who share in God's life. A self-enclosed, self-centred individualism rests upon a misapprehension of the capacities of the human person, in whose light each person is judged by God, by other persons, and by conscience itself (whose light is God's activity in the soul). The person is a sign of God in history or (to speak more accurately) participates in God's own most proper activities, insight and choice. The person is *theophanous*: a. shining-through of god's life in history, created by God for union with God. This is the impulse in history, guided by Providence, and discerned by the authors of the US Declaration of Independence, when they spoke of human persons as 'endowed by their Creator with inalienable rights,' and strove to invent institutions worthy of human dignity.

On one side, then, a self-enclosed individualism falsifies the capacities of the human person. On the other side, so does any vision of the common good as a mere sum of individual goods (or the greatest good of the greatest number). Even if it were true (in some dreadful utilitarian calculus) that a hundred persons would experience more pleasure from torturing one person than that person would experience pain, such an action would be an abomination. The person is never subordinate to the common good in an instrumental way. Persons are not means but ends, because of the God in Whom they live and Who lives in them, and because of their nature as rational beings capable of reflection and choice. The common good of a society of persons consists in treating each of them as an end, never as a means. To arrange the institutions of human society in such a way that this happens without fail is by no means easy.

The human race has so far only approximated the achievement of such institutions. Over most of the planet's present surface, including most of the world's peoples, persons are still conceived of as means to the ends of the state. Their personal liberty is not respected. Every form of collectivism, in which each member is treated as a means to the good of the state, violates the dignity of the human person.

Among the figures of the Enlightenment, Immanuel Kant (1724–1804) is probably the one who most clearly spoke to the concept of human dignity. He did so in the light of a categorical imperative that he discerned in the rational being, and he made famous this formulation of the principle of human dignity: '*Act so that you treat humanity, whether in your own person or in that of another, always as an end and never as a means only.*' This is not, of course, a description of the way in which humans always (or even mostly) treat other human beings. It is, in the Kantian scheme, a prescription, an imperative, a duty. (In other schemes, it might appear as an aspiration, a good to be pursued, an ideal for which to strive.)

Still, it is not difficult to see in Kant's formulation a repetition in non-biblical language of the essential teaching of Judaism and Christianity: '*Thou shalt love thy neighbour as thyself*' (Lev. 19: 18). '*And this commandment have we from him, That he who loveth God love his brother also*' (1 John 4: 21). This interpretation of Kant seems correct for two reasons: First, the ancient philosophers of Greece and Rome, before the contact of those regions with Christianity, did not reach this principle. Second, one must note the quiet but strong culture of German pietism in which Kant grew to maturity.

From the point of view of modern history, of course, it seems absurd to say that humans are not means but only ends. In the twentieth century, more than a hundred million persons in Europe alone died by violence, often in a way they could not have foreseen even in their worst nightmares. In our century, history has been a butcher's bench, and the words 'human dignity' have often sounded empty.

11.4.4   Solidarity

When Leo XIII described in *Rerum Novarum* (1891) the tumultuous changes then churning through the formerly agrarian and feudal world of pre-modern Europe, he saw the need for a new sort of virtue (a reliable habit of soul) among Christian peoples, lay people especially, and he wavered between calling it *justice* or *charity, social justice* or *social charity*.[22] By the time of *Centesimus Annus* (1991), one hundred years later, John Paul II had brought that nascent intuition into focus in the one term *solidarity*. By this term, he did not mean the great Polish labour union which contributed so much to bringing down Communism—although no doubt the worldwide fame of the term *Solidarnosc* added helpful connotations to what he intended—but rather the special virtue of social charity that makes each individual aware of belonging to the whole human race, of being brother or sister to all others, of living in *communio* with all other humans in God.

Solidarity is another way of saying globalization, while singling out the dimension of communal interiority and personal responsibility. Solidarity is not an impersonal habit of losing one's self in groupthink, disappearing into a collectivity. Solidarity points simultaneously to the personal responsibility and initiative of the human subject and to communion with others. It is exactly the reverse of what socialists meant by collectivization. Solidarity awakens, and does not lull, individual conscience. Solidarity evokes responsibility and enlarges personal vision and connects the self to all others.[23]

In these days of globalization, even as described in merely economic terms, it is almost impossible for any intelligent human being to imagine the self as an unencumbered, detached, solitary individual, unlinked to others. Interdependence so forces itself upon the world's consciousness, in fact, that most attempts to define globalization fail. There are at least five standard definitions of globalization, each one inadequate standing by itself:

- Globalization is not merely a dramatic drop in transportation and communication *costs*.
- Globalization is not only the shrinkage of a formerly vast realm of distant and remote nations into one small 'village,' linked in instantaneous *communications*.
- Nor is it merely the centripetal energies of a single global *market* interconnected by Internet and satellite and cellular phone and television.
- Globalization is not the mere geometric increase of 'foreign direct investment' and cross-border *trade*.
- Although of course globalization today is all these things,[24] globalization also has an *interior dimension*. External economic globalization has changed the way individuals experience themselves and the way they think. (See Section 11.1.3, above.)

All these are steps toward the interior realities of solidarity. Are human beings not planetary creatures, one another's brothers and sisters, members of one same body, every part serving every other part?[25] These are the best of times for those committed to solidarity, and pinching times for those committed to a view of themselves as solitary individuals—pinching like shoes that do not fit.

It may be useful to remark at this point that the imperative for globalization began with the commission to all Christians, 'Go preach the gospels to all nations,' which turned Christianity away from being the religion of one tribe or one people only, and commanded it to see the whole human race as one people of God. Whatever its historical genesis, this global viewpoint is now the natural ecology of the human race as a whole.

11.5 OTHER VIRTUES

To hold that free societies can emerge on earth even in nations whose citizens do not practise the habits necessary for political, economic, and cultural liberty, would be reckless. For the free society is not really free if it does not depend upon the freely taken actions of it citizens. But where suspicion, cynicism, greed, ambition, irresponsibility, shoddy workmanship, deliberate deception, and other unacceptable habits have been allowed to thrive, goals such as the rule of law, respect for the dignity and human rights of others, and public-spirited amity are all but unrealizable, and practices of corruption thrive. Much of daily living is taken up with defensive tactics, as every party tries to protect itself against the depredations of others.

11.5.1 Political Virtues

Democratic institutions call for certain required democratic habits, that is, settled dispositions, inclinations, and modes of acting that others can rely upon. In the same way, a dynamic and inventive economy also depends on certain specific habits, inclinations, and dispositions of character, including a high degree of social trust,[26] and faith in the integrity and transparency of patterns of economic transactions. When people lose confidence in the integrity of the money supply, for example, as the German people did during massive inflation in the Weimar Republic of the 1920s, money is reduced to being barely worth the paper it is printed on. What gives money value is faith—faith in the integrity of the system, and in the resoluteness of the promise to pay the bearer something reasonably close to the expenditures of labour and effort it cost them to acquire it.[27] When this faith collapses, social disaster results. A democracy's fiduciary responsibility to protect the value of money is of high moral importance.

11.5.2 Economic Virtues

In speaking of the economic habits of the free society, we should probably stress economic *initiative* and *creativity*. In the free society, citizens must be self-starters; they must show imagination, develop the habits of enterprise and invention, and bring into being groups and services that did not exist in their environment before. Without initiative and creativity, economic life is in either stasis or decline. The dynamic force moving economies forward toward prosperity is within the human mind, heart, and will, shaped by sound habits of initiative, risk-taking, creative imagination, and a practical talent for turning dreams into realities.

It goes without saying that habits of trustworthiness, courtesy, reliability, and co-operativeness are also the mark of successful business activities, generating bonds of trust and loyalty among co-workers in the same firm, and between the firm and its suppliers, customers, and pensioners. Acts of disloyalty in any of these directions can bring down firms.

Business is a crucial field of moral activity. Great good can be done through it, but also significant evil.

11.5.3 Cultural Virtues

Obviously, bad habits such as law-breaking, cutting corners, cheating, lack of self-control, backbiting, envy, and personal greed at the unfair expense of others deeply wound a culture and injure its general sense of community and common purpose. Instead of focusing their energies on new future achievements, citizens in such republics are bound to waste many efforts in defensiveness and self-protection.

Such mechanisms penalize the entire society. Considering the large number of sound habits necessary in the political, economic, and cultural spheres of the free society, it is obvious that the free society must also become an unusually virtuous society, nourishing in all spheres a large number of sound and reliable habits. Where the culture is morally lax, the flag of liberty also sags. The frequency with which social vices appear determines the level of police and other regulatory supervision, not only raising social costs, but also marking a descent into tyranny. The more virtuous the habits of its citizenry, the freer a society can be. When for every million citizens there are one million inner policemen (called 'consciences'), the number of police in the street can be few. When consciences are not reliable, the number of policemen in the street must necessarily grow.

11.6 THE ROLE OF MAJOR INSTITUTIONS

11.6.1 State

Aristotle long ago remarked that the ethos of a nation is deeply affected by the architectonic of its polity. When a nation undergoes occupation by a foreign army, for example, some formerly reliable citizens begin to co-operate with the enemy, perhaps for the rewards that such co-operation promises, perhaps out of fear. Especially when the foreign occupation has a criminal character, it becomes exceedingly difficult for ordinary citizens to maintain their customary honesty and sound moral habits. Cynicism is forced upon them; they must defend themselves on all sides, and feel great pressure to narrow their sphere of moral action to life in the family and among trusted friends. Just as the architectonic of a polity can corrupt or even destroy the moral ethos of a nation, so also it can nourish good habits and sound ethical practices. It does so where laws are good and reasonable, clear and reliable, and citizens can count on their just administration. Then the sphere of personal liberty open to the good habits of citizens expands, and the ordinary workings of good habits tend to produce good outcomes in both political life and economic life. Good laws and good habits generate a sort of 'beneficent circle', just as bad laws and bad habits generate a 'vicious circle'.

Nowadays, modern means of communication give government officials an important moral voice. By the legislation of good laws, by the just administration of laws, and by the public promotion of noble examples from the past, governments can do quite a lot to create the sort of political architectonic favourable to a sound human ecology. It is a grievous error for a government either wholly to neglect or to thoroughly dominate the moral ethos of the people. No democracy can long survive the moral decadence of its people, for the abdication of self-control is an invitation to tyranny.

11.6.2 Voluntary Associations

It should be obvious, however, that the major role in the cultural formation of the habits necessary to a sound human ecology are much more thoughtfully, successfully, and intensively practised by associations closer than the state to the actual features of daily life: first of all, the home and the family, but secondly, the neighbourhood associations, schools, fraternal societies, and social groups of all sorts (Red Cross, Boy Scouts, Girl Scouts, Knights of Columbus, Hadassah, Masonic Lodges, Sunday schools, church socials, and many more). All these play important roles. Since the Second World War, great crises in politics and economics seem to have gripped everyone's attention, while moral questions were often shunted aside as 'old-fashioned.' Moral capital stored up from previous generations is swiftly dissipated, however, and the decline of family life and ordinary moral habits has been steep. A reaction is underway, and (in the opinion of Nobel-Prize-winning historian Robert Fogel) even 'A Fourth Great Awakening'.[28]

An increasingly important player in the world of voluntary associations is the philanthropic foundation. The great number of family fortunes spawned by the long economic boom since the Second World War is now resulting in the most massive intergenerational transfer of wealth in world history, as the founding generation disposes of them to their heirs. Much of this wealth—in the US, an estimated \$20 to 30 billion—is likely to be poured into philanthropic foundations, new and old, and into other charitable works. How this money will be spent is of great moment to civilization. Indeed, as more and more nations grow in wealth, the tradition of private philanthropy looms ever larger as a potential source of cultural, moral, intellectual, and artistic renewal throughout the planet.

11.6.3   Supra-National Religious Bodies

A third major institutional force is the world's religious bodies. Since the conventional idiom of most scholarly analysis is astringently secular, there are probably no major institutions in the world less commented upon and less studied than religious institutions. It may or may not be true that the great proportion of the world's journalists are not very religious, do not assign religion much importance in world affairs, even do not care enough about religion to study it intensively. It is true that many of them have long and complacently accepted the 'secularization thesis', according to which the world is inexorably and inevitably becoming more and more secular. Perhaps that is why the great explosion of religious energy that has characterized the waning years of the twentieth century and the opening years of the twenty-first has been so startling to Western elites.

By far the largest proportion of the six billion persons upon this planet are religious believers, and only a relatively small proportion are atheists or agnostics. According to various sources, there are two billion Christians in the world, with these numbers growing very rapidly in the third world, while declining in Western Europe. There are just over a billion Muslims, a large majority of them in Asia, whose numbers are also growing rapidly. There are 700 million Hindus, a smaller number of Buddhists, and hundreds of millions of other believers of various sorts.[29]

Thus it happens that significantly more than half of the world's population draws most of its signals about moral behaviour from religious sources, rather than philosophical. This is not the place for a thorough investigation of the potential contributions of the world's major religious bodies to human ecology. Yet it would be an unwise observer who thought that religion will not play a prominent role in the formation of human culture during the course of the twenty-first century.

11.6.4 Business Corporations

Business corporations themselves are important sources of moral teaching. Through their own internal 'cultures' and, in many cases, formal 'codes of behaviour', business corporations embody important moral habits. They are often schools in learning cross-cultural co-operation, habits of teamwork and self-discipline, prudence, modesty, and peaceful methods of persuasion. Long ago, well before the current age of globalization, John Stuart Mill wrote in his often-reprinted *Principles of Political Economy*:

The economical advantages of commerce are surpassed in importance by those of its effects, which are intellectual and moral. It is hardly possible to overrate the value, in the present low state of human improvement, of placing human beings in contact with persons dissimilar to themselves, and with modes of thought and action unlike those with which they are familiar. Commerce is now, what war once was, the principal source of this contact...There is no nation which does not need to borrow from others, not merely particular arts or practices, but essential points of character in which its own type is inferior. (Calomiris 2002: 21)

Anyone with experience in corporations around the world—Coca-Cola, for instance, or Phillips, or Barclays—knows the ring of truth in such words. Many with long experience in corporate life speak gratefully about the horizon-expanding opportunities their work has brought them. Nonetheless, it is no doubt true that for too long business schools tended to emphasize the more 'scientific' and 'value-neutral' aspects of economics, rather than the spiritual and moral dimensions of the business vocation. They affected a certain tough-minded 'realism' by emphasizing 'the bottom line,' while neglecting the human dimensions of business reality. At the end of day, any man or woman examining personal conscience can look back on much good done and, alas, at times, on having witnessed (hopefully not in his own firm) certain evil or dishonest or even cruel acts done in the name of business. The vocation of business is noble, precisely because it contains within itself capacities for great good or great evil.[30]

Evil actions on the part of businessmen have an even greater power to wreak harm than activities in some other fields, because a flagrant wrong can do harm not only in itself, but also in stoking public cynicism concerning the free society. The quiet good that can be done by the intelligent deployment of sound business habits, including keen cultural sensitivities, is likewise of high importance in raising cultural standards all around the world. Not least, it often brings acute instruction in tolerance and cross-cultural understanding, through respect for the talents of co-workers from many different cultures.

11.7 FAITH AND REASON

It would be foolish to ignore the predominant role of religious faith in forming the moral conscience of a substantial majority of the world's citizens. Such terms as 'the decline of belief' and a 'secular age' may roughly enough describe some elites but do not apply to most peoples of the world.

In trying to reach a global moral vision, furthermore, it is not necessary to discover common principles on which everyone can agree, 'some lowest common denominator'. Universal principles need not be univocal. Different traditions may for good reason have somewhat different means of expressing common ideals, yet there may well be 'family resemblances' among these statements. It is not necessary to find a single formulation that does full justice to all virtues. For practical co-operation in moral conduct, 'family resemblances' may be quite sufficient.

In counting up the great religious bodies of the world, the universe of discourse is fairly small. Virtually all of the world's major religious bodies have significant insight to contribute to our understanding of the 'cardinal virtues'—cultural humility, respect for the regulative ideal of truth, respect for individual dignity, and solidarity. To a rather remarkable degree, moreover, these diverse traditions point in a similar or correlative moral direction.

For this reason, it seems quite feasible to encourage all the world's religious bodies to apply their energies to thinking through a global moral vision in fraternal dialogue with other bodies. Each tradition might be encouraged to show towards other traditions a welcoming spirit. For good dialogue to take place, it is not necessary that all become homogeneous, or even merely syncretistic. Maintaining a clear awareness of one's own differences in the context of civility and fraternity makes for richer dialogue.

It goes without saying, too, that those on whose consciences religion has no personal purchase should address the same questions of a global moral ecology with every resource that reason can bring to bear. For 'reason' itself is understood diversely in different traditions; it is itself an analogous, not a univocal, concept. Reason is important to religious people too, it must also be remembered, who do not surrender their capacities for the intelligent and inquiring use of reason by virtue of adding to it the intellectual habit of faith.

The partisans of the free society, marked by a universal respect for human rights, are not too many but too few. In the nineteenth century liberals too quickly declared themselves the foes of religion—the 'enlightened' against those still living in darkness—while religious people in self-defence closed their minds to many of the sensible, practical points that liberals were making. We should not make those mistakes in the new century. The contributions of all persons of goodwill are sorely needed.

11.8 CARITAPOLIS

In *The City of God*, St Augustine differentiates between two different cities, the Earthly City (the one with which we have been primarily concerned in this chapter) and the Invisible City, the City made up of those who love God and who experience God's love within them. This City, whose invisible filament of divine love encircles the world, this quite vital, but typically invisible dimension of human life, Augustine thought, operates at times like a bearer of warmth and light to the Earthly City, drawing it onwards to be better than itself, so that it might be moved by a law of amity, respect and co-operation higher than its own.

During the past century, the formerly separated peoples of the world have grown greatly in number and in physical expansion, until the whole planet now seems abuzz with activity. All peoples are coming into frequent contact with one another. All are *interpenetrated* by new media of communication such as television, the Internet, and the cell phone.[31] We have become aware of one another's concrete reality as never before in history. People in one part of the world can see with their own eyes how people in other parts of the world live. They hear ideas formerly unheard, and discern currents of passion and emotion of which they were formerly unaware.

St Augustine observed that the Earthly City was everywhere a world in conflict, racked by injustice, and scarred by some truly unacceptable practices such as slavery and torture, which he saw no possibility at that time of removing from the world. But nowadays, the move to eliminate slavery and torture, like the move to respect individual and social rights, has gained moral power around the world. Even if these movements have not been everywhere successful, they have transformed a significant number of societies. Simply to survive, other courses of action now are thrust upon the human race that were before hardly imaginable.

Whereas St Augustine suggested that the best we could do in the Earthly City was to reach a tentative balance of power, a balance of fear, today necessity imposes upon us a universal relation more vitally interconnected than that. It will not be enough today for citizens not to fear each other, although I am far from denying that fear plays an important role in human affairs even today. It will not be enough merely to 'tolerate' each other. Slowly but surely, it is becoming necessary to respect one another, to pay one another the honour of taking each other seriously. This is at least an approximation of the friendship with one another which remains, as it were, a gravitational pull.

The founder of my native state, Pennsylvania, conceived the idea of establishing a new commonwealth based upon friendship. His name was William Penn (1644–1718) and he had been imprisoned in England for belonging to a dissident church, the Society of Friends (Quakers). Penn often pointed out that, in offering His friendship to human beings, God founded this world upon the principle of freedom, which is the air and the aliment of friendship: Without freedom, no friendship. The Pennsylvania model of religious liberty, for instance, having brought reasonable social harmony, became the closest model for the US Constitution of 1787. A later example: when firemen and policemen in the Twin Towers in New York City gave their lives for their fellows on 11 September 2001, they showed the greatest of all loves. That a polity needs to be founded to some degree on friendship, therefore, has some basis in existing fact.

Many hostilities today are rooted in caricatures and false information about one another. Campaigns of hatred and vilification are reported to be taking place in schools and houses of worship, in newspapers and on television stations. Given the power of contemporary weapons systems and the vulnerabilities of modern urban life, creative individuals and institutions will need to strive mightily to overcome envies, hatreds, and hostilities that set people against people.

Caritapolis is the City of Communion, that is, participation in the love of God that the Christian gospel announces.[32] It is not solely a City of human communion, one human with another, but of humans also with God; love shared among all. If there is one Creator of all human beings, His love for humans (in Judaism, Christianity, and Islam at least) is the magnet toward which creatures are pulled, the Origin to which they return, the Measure by which their own poor efforts are judged.

Nowadays, world relations based on fear of one another, resentment, envy, or lack of respect would be, even if long merely smouldering, ultimately explosive. In a complex world civilization such as ours, with so much potential for disaster, working toward a set of relations that command mutual respect is the only prudent course. The realism demanded by Augustine (and often seconded by Reinhold Niebuhr[33]) remains obligatory. In the meantime every step taken towards a global vision, in which all human beings receive the honour due them by their nature, advances the shabbier, much battered, but still stumbling forwards Earthly City a step closer toward a faint approximation of that 'shining city on a hill', *Caritapolis.*

NOTES

1. St Augustine (1958).
2. 'The Church values the democratic system inasmuch as it ensures the participation of citizens in making political choices, guarantees to the governed the possibility both of electing and holding accountable those who govern them, and of replacing them through peaceful means when appropriate. Thus she cannot encourage the formation of narrow ruling groups which usurp the power of the State for individual interests or for ideological ends. Authentic democracy is possible only in a State ruled by law, and on the basis of a correct conception of the human person. It requires that the necessary conditions be present for the advancement both of the individual through education and formation in true ideals, and of the "subjectivity" of society through the creation of structures of participation and shared responsibility' (John Paul II 1991: 46).
3. Glendon (2001).
4. 'Long before the encyclical *Quadragesimo Anno* proclaimed the principle of subsidiarity as 'the most important principle of social philosophy,' Abraham Lincoln had formulated it thus for practical use: "The legitimate object of government is to do for a community of people whatever they need to have done but cannot do at all, or cannot so well do for themselves in their separate and individual capacities. In all that people can individually do as well for themselves, governments ought not to interfere."' (Oswald Nell-Breuning 'Social Movements: Subsidiarity', in Rahner(1968), 6: 115.).

5. For criticism of the author's views by Anthony Giddens, John Lloyd, and Paul Ormerod, and his reply, see Novak (1998*a*).
6. Wattenberg (1987).
7. Curzon Price (1999).
8. UNCTAD, *World Investment Report* (various years). Also, World Bank (2001) reports $619 billion in worldwide foreign direct investment for the year 1998.
9. World Bank (2001).
10. Ibid.
11. Friedman (1999).
12. Jolly (1999).
13. *World Population Prospects* (2001).
14. Maddison (2001).
15. Figures published by *Time*, 13 April 1998 at http://www.time.com/time/time100/timewarp/timewarp.html Accessed 13 February 2002.
16. *World Population Prospects* (2001).
17. Hertzke (1988), in his 'Abstract', proposes: 'The theory of moral ecology synthesizes a vast empirical literature . . . into a parsimonious nomological formulation. The philosophical and policy implications of moral ecology, in turn, highlight a poignant Tocquevillian dilemma: How can liberal societies, which leave individuals and companies largely free in the moral arena, shield themselves from cumulative moral depredation?'
18. My own work on moral ecology antedates Hertzke's (1988) essay, as he observes in his notes. While I found his treatment helpful, in what follows I continue my own line of reflection in my own way.
19. Popper (1971) and Pezzimenti (1997).
20. Novak (1995).
21. Shcharansky (1998) and Mihajlov (1977).
22. Leo XIII (1891).
23. 'It is above all a question of *interdependence*, sensed as a *system determining* relationships in the contemporary world, in its economic, cultural, political and religious elements, and accepted as a *moral category*. When interdependence becomes recognized in this way, the correlative response as a moral and social attitude, as a "virtue," is *solidarity*. This then is not a feeling of vague compassion or shallow distress at the misfortunes of so many people, both near and far. On the contrary, it is a *firm and persevering determination* to commit oneself to the *common good*; that is to say to the good of all and of each individual, because we are responsible for all. . . . The exercise of solidarity *within each society* is valid when its members recognize one another as persons' (John Paul II, 1987).
24. Jolly (1999).
25. 'What we nowadays call the principle of solidarity . . . is clearly seen to be one of the fundamental principles of the Christian view of social and political organization. This principle is frequently stated by Pope Leo XIII, who uses the term "friendship," a concept already found in Greek philosophy. Pope Pius XI refers to it with the equally meaningful term "social charity." Pope Paul VI, expanding the concept to cover the many modern aspects of the social question, speaks of "civilization of love."' (John Paul II, 1991: 10). 'Moreover, it is becoming clearer how a person's work is naturally interrelated with the work of others. More than ever, work is *work with others* and *work for others*: it is a matter of doing something for someone else. Work becomes

ever more fruitful and productive to the extent that people become more knowledgeable of the productive potentialities of the earth and more profoundly cognizant of the needs of those for whom their work is done.' (Ibid. 32).

'Even in recent years it was thought that the poorest countries would develop by isolating themselves from the world market and by depending only on their own resources. Recent experience has shown that countries which did this have suffered stagnation and recession, while the countries which experienced development were those which succeeded in taking part in the general interrelated economic activities at the international level. It seems therefore that the chief problem is that of gaining fair access to the international market, based not on the unilateral principle of the exploitation of the natural resources of these countries but on the proper use of human resources' (Ibid. 33).

26. Fukuyama (1996).

27. 'Money today is mostly an account, a set of computer numbers always rapidly changing with entries and withdrawals (and occasionally a computer error or a mistaken manual entry by a computer clerk). Money has become more of an intellectual artifact than a physical thing. Moreover, to an extraordinarily high degree, its current value is based on spiritual attitudes such as faith and trust. Burst these like a pin prick in a bubble and the value of money can collapse very quickly. Consult the Asian crisis of early 1998, or the collapse of the Russian ruble.

'These two examples, Asia and Russia, indicate that more is involved in the value of money held on accounts these days than purely economic factors. In Asia, the lack of truly democratic accountability, the lack of transparency, the phenomenon of one-party rule and the rewarding by political authorities of relatives and cronies, and severe problems of transition upon the death of dictators, and other chiefly political factors undermined confidence in economic transactions. Too many unseen hands manipulate economic factors beneath the table. Imputed valuations collapsed.

'In Russia, the repression of all religious and moral inspirations during seventy long years of Communist Party rule deeply injured the moral ethos of the nation, and the failure of the political system after 1991 to establish the rule of law; to suppress violence, extortion, murder, and gangsterism; and to tie the value of money to real and universally dispersed assets, gravely wounded trust in normal economic life' (Novak 1999).

28. Fogel (2000).

29. Brunner (2001), synthesizes the information found in the *Encyclopedia Britannica, 1999*. See also, 'Major Religions of the World Ranked by Number of Adherents' (2001).

30. Novak (1998*b* and 1996).

31. 'And where is the mobile-phone market growing most rapidly? In the developing world, in places like Afghanistan, where such technology has meant the difference between being connected to the world and being cut off.... Bangladesh, whose person-to-phone ratio was 275-to-1, has had over 300 villages outfitted with phones. "For Bangladeshi farmers," Micklethwaite and Wooldridge write, "the phones provide liberation from middlemen. Rather than having to accept a broker's price, Bangladeshi farmers... find out the fair value of their rice and vegetables and avoid getting gouged in the process"' (Lot 2002).

32. *Caritas* is a specific type of love; not a sentimental love (as in the Latin word *affectus*); nor the generic attraction of the opposite sexes for one another (*amor*); nor the love

by which one chooses one other to whom to commit oneself (*dilectio*); nor even requited *dilectio*, human friendship (*amicitia*); but the suffering love (*caritas*) characteristic of the Persons of the Trinity for One Another, exhibited for humans to see in the life and death of Christ. For a fuller treatment, see chapter 10 of Novak, Brailsford, and Heesters (2000).

33. See e.g. Niebuhr (1964).

REFERENCES

Augustine (1958), *City of God* (New York: Image Books).

Brunner, B. (ed.), (2001), *Time Almanac 2002* (Boston: Family Education Company), 433.

Calomiris, C. (2002), *A Globalist Manifesto for Public Policy* (London: The Institute of Economic Affairs), 21.

Curzon Price, V. (1999), 'La globalisation et la pensée liberale', unpublished lecture for the Summer University of Aix-en-Provence.

Fogel, R. W. (2000), *The Fourth Great Awakening and the Future of Egalitarianism* (Chicago: University of Chicago Press).

Friedman, T. L. (1999), *The Lexus and the Olive Tree: Understanding Globalization* (New York: Farrar, Straus, and Giroux), 8–9.

Fukuyama, F. (1996), *Trust: The Social Virtues and the Creation of Prosperity* (New York: Free Press).

Glendon, M. A. (2001), *A World Made New: Eleanor Roosevelt and the Universal Declaration of Human Rights* (New York: Random House).

Hertzke, A. D. (1988), 'The Theory of Moral Ecology', *The Review of Politics* (Fall), 629–59.

John Paul II (1987), *Sollicitudo Rei Socialis*, English: *The Social Concern of the Church* (Vatican City: Libreria Editrice Vaticana), Section 38.

——(1991), *Centesimus Annus*, English: *One Hundred Years* (Vatican City: Libreria Editrice Vaticana), Sections 10, 32, 33.

Jolly, R. (principal co-ordinator) and Ross-Larson, B. (ed.) (1999), *Globalization with a Human Face: Human Development Report, 1999* (New York: United Nations Development Programme).

Leo XIII (1891), *Rerum Novarum*, English: *On the Condition of Working Classes* (Boston: Daughters of St. Paul), Sections 11, 16, 17, 19, 27, 45.

Lot, J. (2002), 'Is Globalization Christian? Why the WTO protestors had it wrong', *Christianity Today* (Jan./Feb.); online version accessed 14 Feb. 2002, http://www.christianitytoday.com/bc/2002/001/12.32.html.

Maddison, A. (2001), *The World Economy: A Millennial Perspective* (Paris: Organization for Economic Co-operation and Development), 28.

'Major Religions of the World Ranked by Number of Adherents' (2001), (www.adherents.com), updated 16 Aug. 2001, accessed 13 Feb. 2002.

Mensah, T.A. (1999), 'International and Governmental Structures and their Relation to Democracy.' In H. Zacher (ed.), *Democracy: Some Acute Questions*, Proceedings of the Fourth Plenary Session of the Pontifical Academy of Social Sciences, 22–25 April 1998 (Vatican City: Pontificia Academia Scientiarum Socialium, 1999), 354–5.

Mihajlov, M. *Underground Notes* (London: Routledge & Kegan Paul, Ltd.), 105–24.

Niebuhr, R. (1964), *Nature and Destiny of Man* (New York: Charles Scribner's & Sons), vol. 2, 272–4.

Novak, M. (1995), *Awakening from Nihilism: The 1994 Templeton Prize Awarded to Michael Novak* (Washington, DC: Crisis Books), 43–55.

—— (1996), *Business as a Calling* (New York: The Free Press).

—— (1998*a*), *Is There a Third Way?* (London: The IEA Health and Welfare Unit).

—— (1998*b*), 'The International Vocation of American Business', The Hansen-Wessner Memorial Lecture (Chicago: The ServiceMaster Company).

—— (1999), ' "In God We Trust" ovvero il denaro e la sua morale.' In *Nuntium* 12–20; repr. in 'God and Money', *Catholic Dossier* (May/June 1999): 14–18.

Novak, M., Brailsford, W., and Heesters, C. (eds.) (2000), *The Free Society Reader* (Lanham, Md.: Lexington Books).

Pezzimenti, R. (1997), *The Open Society and its Friends, with letters from Isaiah Berlin and the late Karl R. Popper* (Leominster/Rome: Gracewing/Millennium Romae), 173–8, 182–4.

Popper, K. R. (1971), *Open Society and Its Enemies* (Princeton: Princeton University Press), 2 vols.

Rahner, K. (ed.) (1968), *Sacramentum Mundi: An Encyclopedia of Theology*, 6 vols. (New York: Herder & Herder), 6: 115.

Shcharansky, A. (1998), *Fear No Evil: The Classic Memoir of One Man's Triumph over a Police State* (New York: Public Affairs).

Wattenberg, B. J. (1987), *The Birth Dearth: What Happens When People in Free Countries Don't Have Enough Babies?* (New York: Ballantine Books).

World Bank (2001), *World Development Report 2000/2001*, (Oxford: Oxford University Press). Available at http://www.worldbank.org/poverty/wdrpoverty/index.htm; Accessed 8 Feb. 2002; 12:10 p.m.

World Population Prospects: 2000 Revision, vol. 1, *Comprehensive Tables* (United Nations Publication, 2001).

12

On The Political Relevance of Global Civil Society

RICHARD FALK

12.1 ENGAGING THE PROJECT

The pursuit of a responsible global capitalism, the unifying theme of this volume, needs to be understood, above all, as both a political project and an evolving process. By this is meant that there must be given some attention to what political scientists call the problem of agency, the actors, and social forces that are committed to the desired course of change. Such a view is sceptical about reliance on patterns of voluntary adjustment, whether as a result of moral sentiments, the benevolence of those in the private sector whose behaviour is under critical scrutiny, or as a pragmatic response to social pressures. Ideas do matter, and voluntary adjustments can be significant under certain circumstances, but the history of social change confirms the view that very little of lasting significance occurs without threats posed to the established order by those advocates of change sufficiently engaged to mount a struggle, take risks, make sacrifices, and in the end, generate incentives for elites to strike bargains of accommodation. Crudely put, the humanization of industrial capitalism since the mid-nineteenth century must be understood predominantly as an outcome of struggle, centring upon the emergence in civil society of a robust labour movement increasingly influenced by radical thought, especially by the Marxist critique of capitalist exploitation combined with revolutionary optimism about the socialist future of humanity.

When the forces seeking change become 'dangerous classes' then elites move beyond gestures of compromise to seek negotiated settlements that aim to institutionalize a regulatory regime that is reflective of a new societal consensus giving rise to an equilibrium between civil society and the private business sector. The great triumph of capitalism was its willingness to give ground in relation to successive phases of this challenge during the latter part of the nineteenth and until last decade of the twentieth century. In so doing, it gradually incorporated into its operations a sufficient degree of moral sensitivity to overcome the challenges posed by Marxist ideas and labour radicalism, a challenge made also geopolitically formidable after the First World War. The Russian Revolution, followed by Soviet ideological and diplomatic pressures, the Great Depression of the 1930s, and the rise of an anti-capitalist fascist alternative in Europe, mounted a second round of pressures for moral adaptation. Unless the political leaders could address the material, social, and psychological needs of their citizens, capitalism would be discredited to the point where it would fall victim to extremisms of left and right. Again moral adjustments were mainly achieved as a result of pressures, both from within and without, and a sense in the private sector, that unless social reforms were accepted, the capitalist system could not survive, and especially could not be combined with political liberalism, which here meant moderation of governmental authority as assured by the rule of law reinforced by constitutionalism. Economists, especially Keynes, gave intellectual respectability to a new, and more socially responsible capitalism, that pledged full employment, and accorded organized labour an important seat at the tables of government and policy formation.

But the long period of the Cold War, with its priorities of national security, the changing nature of capitalist enterprise, and the public dislike of the governmental bureaucracy that administered the huge programmes of social democracy, created a climate of opinion that over time became anti-government and anti-labour. Such a climate gave rise in the 1980s to the Thatcher/Reagan reorientation of capitalism around a more economistic approach that weakened the weight of moral factors, especially the compassionate elements of welfare capitalism, and substituted in their place an increased reliance on efficiency and the profit motive. When the Cold War wound down, inducing the collapse of the Soviet Union, the ideological endorsement of neo-liberalism by the governments and rapidly constituted business elites of the successor states was immediate and abrupt. The Chinese embrace of capitalism, coupled with its spectacular rate of economic growth, provided further testimony that the way to go was through reliance on capital-guided market factors. Also influential was the impressive records of sustained economic growth by Japan and the emerging markets, especially in Asia. This ideological consensus was further promoted by the growing influence of international financial institutions, the efforts of the World Economic Forum at its annual meetings at Davos, and the actions taken at the Group of Seven annual economic summits of industrial countries. Moreover, it was being increasingly accepted even by left-leaning political leaders in the third world. In this 'end of history' atmosphere, it seemed as if the global future belonged to this interplay of banks and corporations, helped along by the dominance of neo-liberal ideas as promoted by leading governments, by the Internet, and by the waning national and global influence of labour.

It is not surprising that, in such a political environment, global capitalism abandoned its moral pretensions, and reverted to its virtually unregulated form of the early industrial revolution. There no longer existed, domestically or internationally, a credible socialist alternative, and it was socialism with its explicit focus on human well-being that all along gave capitalists the practical incentive to achieve moral credibility in the eyes of the public, even at the cost of narrowing profit margins. But if there is no socialist alternative, these incentives disappear, and efficiency and profitability arguments fill the air far more persuasively. The United States Government was (and remains) the most ardent champion of the neo-liberal attention to markets, privatization, and the logic of competitiveness, by increasingly shaping its global diplomatic leadership role around the promotion of what it labelled as 'market-oriented constitutionalism', a phrase echoed in the final declarations of the World Economic (G-7) Summits.

In the face of these developments, there are abundant reasons to be concerned about the overall effects of economic globalization. In the 1980s and early 1990s, the income gaps between rich and poor within and between societies were widening at an exponential rate, while poverty afflicted half of the world's population that was earning less than $2 per day, not to mention the hundreds of millions without safe drinking water, health facilities, and educational opportunities. Whole regions, especially sub-Saharan Africa and the Caribbean/Central America, were virtually excluded from the benefits of global economic growth. There were resentments associated with the way in which the IMF and World Bank seemed to be following the lead of Wall Street and Davos, without regard to their social effects or moral implications, especially in relation to the more economically disadvantaged countries and the poor generally. It became clear that these global managers of fiscal discipline were often precluding third world governments from devoting scarce resources to social priorities and rapid development.

Despite these signs of distress there was little adverse reaction to globalization until the two shocks of the late 1990s. First, the Asian Economic Crisis, which started in 1997 with volatile currency markets and banking scandals in South Asia, not only cancelled overnight the gains of the poorest half of the population in countries such as Indonesia, Thailand, and Malaysia, but burst the bubble of globalization. These regional adversities, in a variety of forms, soon spread to Japan, Russia, Turkey, and elsewhere in succeeding years. Second, there was the dramatic birth of the anti-globalization movement at Seattle during the WTO ministerial meetings at the end of 1999, which generated a series of demonstrations around the world whenever and wherever the policymakers of globalization gathered. The movement reached its climax at Genoa, where turbulent and large Genoa anti-globalization manifestations took place, which were timed to coincide with the meetings of the G-7 (now G-8, with the inclusion of Russia).

As with earlier efforts of capitalism to achieve wider societal acceptance, these developments posed new threats to the global capitalist order: functional threats associated with the absence of appropriate regulation and normative threats arising from the spreading grassroots perception of globalization as both immoral and anti-democratic. More to the point, these challenges helped to shape a double political project: first, the transformation of globalization by civil society; and, second, the legitimation of globalization by business elites and their allies in government. The problem of agency was far from solved, but, at the very least, the combination of chaotic markets and massive street protests shook the champions of globalization out of their mood of complacency. At the same time it convinced the core elements of the anti-globalization movement that they were making progress and were onto something big and worthwhile. This interplay between demands for reform from civil society and accommodation and response by global business world marked a new point of departure for world politics in that it was no longer merely a sequel to the Cold War, but rather represented the beginning of contestation in an era of economic globalization.

The common ground was the need for *normative* (moral, legal, and regulative) adjustment in the actual and perceived workings of the world economy, so that economic growth was seen as contributing a greater share of the returns on investment and trade revenue to *public goods* (domestically, regionally, and globally); and by so doing, to insulate fragile economies from sharp declines. As with the backlash against the abuses of early industrial capitalism almost two centuries ago, it became clear that unbridled market forces lead to corruption, exploitation, and zones of severe deprivation. The humanizing of capitalism is not a self-generating force, but must be achieved by the constant exertion of pressure. These include both challenges from those that allege victimization and responses by those that control economic policy.

Such an evolving set of circumstances was seriously dislocated by the events of 11 September, and its aftermath, especially the military campaign in Afghanistan. All at once, the United States was at war—not in a conventional sense of a struggle carried on against another state, but in the form of an undertaking to crush terrorism on a worldwide basis. Such a war, new in the annals of warfare, knows no boundaries of time or space, and its perpetrators—on both sides—pick their targets without any show of deference to the territorial rights of sovereign states. With the United States as the chief target of the al Qaeda network, as well as the leader of the response, the preoccupations of the moment have shifted away from transnational economic issues, back in the direction of traditional strategic geopolitics with its focus of global security and the war/peace agenda. The world economy persists, evolves, and its positive and negative effects are felt in a variety of settings, but at this point it is no longer the focal point of political and media attention. Indeed, it is now unclear whether we are experiencing a temporary diversion in the emergent era of globalization or we are at the early stages of a second Cold War fought along civilizational lines.

The transnational forces of civil society are also in the process of regrouping. To some extent, their attention has also shifted in the direction of war/peace issues and the adoption of priorities associated with the resistance to what is seen as American empire-building. True, the World Social Forum (modeled as a counterpart to the World Economic Forum) in 2002 held successful meetings in Porto Allegro, Brazil, but the momentum for global economic reform and regulation seems to have slowed to a virtual halt. There are some minor counter-trends that could in time, alter this assessment, such as the acknowledgement that mass impoverishment may act as breeding grounds for terrorists, leading to some attention being devoted to economically deprived states by the United States and other governments. It is probable that the African tour devoted to poverty reduction and foreign economic assistance of US Treasury Secretary Paul O'Neill and U2 singing star Bono in the Spring of 2002 could not have happened without the goad of 11 September. Nevertheless, it will take time to redirect the energies of global capitalists and their critics on how to bring moral considerations and fairness back into the standard operating procedures of the globalizing world economy.

12.2 THE POLITICS OF LANGUAGE

The emphasis of this chapter is upon social forces and moral pressures that are responding in politically significant ways to the patterns of behaviour associated with the current phase of global capitalism. As a consequence, it seems preferable to frame such activity by reference to 'global civil society' rather than to 'transnational civil society'. Even so, the word 'society' is definitely problematic at this stage of global social and political evolution, due to the increasing porosity of natural boundaries and the persisting weakness of social bonds transcending nation, race, and gender. Such a difficulty exists whether the reference is to 'transnational civil society' or to 'global civil society'. But the transnational referent tends to root the identity of the actors in the subsoil of national consciousness, and in so doing, tends to neglect the degree to which the orientation is not one of crossing borders, but of inhabiting and constructing a polity appropriate for the globalizing social order. Such a nascent global polity is already partly extant, yet remains mostly emergent (Wapner 1996).

A similar issue arises with respect to the selection of appropriate terminology to rely upon when identifying the actors. It seems convenient to retain the term non-governmental organizations (NGOs) to designate those actors associated with global civil society, because it is accurate and convenient, widely used, and thus easily recognizable. But it is also somewhat misleading in relation to the fundamental hypothesis of a diminishing ordering capability by the sovereign state and states system. To contrast the actors and action of global civil society with the governments of states, as is done by calling them NGOs, is to confer a derivative and subordinate status, and to imply the persistence of a superordinate Westphalian world of sovereign states as the principal constituents of the contemporary world order. Until recently, this hierarchical dualism was justifiable because the pre-eminence of the state was an empirical reality, and the absence of any other significant international actors capable of autonomous action.

To overcome the difficulty of relying upon this somewhat anarchistic statist rhetoric, James Rosenau has proposed an alternative terminology to that of NGOs by calling such entities 'sovereignty free actors' (Rosenau 1990). Besides being obscure, such a substitute terminology is still operating in a Westphalian shadowland in which actor identities are exclusively derived from sovereign actors, namely, states. A comparable problem exists if the reference is to 'transnational social forces', although the sense of 'transnational' is more flexible and autonomous than 'sovereignty free'. Another possibility was proposed some years ago by Marc Nerfin (Nerfin 1986), in the form of a framework that recognized the social reality of 'the third system' (the first system being that of states, the second of market forces), from which issued forth civil initiatives of motivated citizens supportive of the global public good.

There is by now a wide and growing literature on 'global civil society,' especially as related to environmental politics on a global level (Wapner 1996; Lipschutz 1996; *Global Civil Society Yearbook* 2001). For our purposes, global civil society refers to the field of action and thought occupied by individual and collective citizen initiatives of a voluntary, non-profit character both within states and transnationally. These initiatives proceed from a global orientation, and are responses, in part at least, to certain globalizing tendencies that are perceived to be partially or totally adverse. At present, most of the global provocation is associated directly or indirectly with market forces and the discipline of regional and global capital. As will be made clear, such a critical stance towards economic globalization does not entail an overall repudiation, but it does seek to identify the ways in which its adverse effects correct social injustices, and reconcile the management of the world economy with aspirations for global democracy.

To further focus our inquiry, I also propose to rely upon a distinction that I have used previously, although always with some misgivings: that is, between global market forces identified as *globalization-from-above* and a set of oppositional responses of transnational social activism and global civil society that are identified as *globalization-from-below* (Falk 1993, 1995). This distinction may seem unduly polarizing and hierarchical, and to construct a dualistic world of good and evil. My intention is neither hierarchical nor moralistic, and there is no illusion that the social forces emanating from global civil society are inherently benevolent, while those from the corporate/statist collaboration are necessarily malevolent. Far from it. One of the contentions of the chapter is that there are dangerous chauvinistic and extremist societal energies being released by one series of ultra-nationalist responses to *globalization-from-above* that are threatening the achievements of the modern secular world that had been based on the normative side of the evolution of an anarchic society of states in the cumulative direction of humane governance (Bull 1977). It is no less important to acknowledge that there are strong positive effects and potentialities arising from the various aspects of *globalization-from-above* (Hirst and Thompson 1996; Held and McGrew 1999). At the same time, the historic role of *globalization-from-below* is to challenge, resist, and transform the negative features of *globalization-from-above*, both by providing alternative ideological and political space to that currently occupied by market-oriented and statist outlooks and by offering opposition to the excesses and distortions that can be properly attributed to globalization in its current phase. That is, *globalization-from-below* is not dogmatically opposed to *globalization-from-above*, but addresses itself to the avoidance of its adverse effects, and to providing an overall counterweight to the essentially unchecked influence currently exerted by business and finance on the process of decision at the level of the state and beyond.

In the context of seeking responsible global capitalism, I believe that it is global civil society, as embodied in the idea of *globalization-from-below* that offers such a vision, and provides the most credible—indeed, possibly the only significant answer to the challenge of agency. These social forces remain weak and divided, but compared to considering socialist political parties and organized labour as alternative agents of change and reform, it is *globalization-from-below* that alone seems capable of raising doubts in a politically relevant manner about the various irresponsibilities of dominant operating modes of global capitalism. Of course, to raise doubts is not to solve the agency problem, but it is a foundation upon which to build further, especially by gaining support from such largely superseded oppositional forces of the industrial phase of global capitalism, and even from states that feel hostile, or at least ambivalent, about the drift of the world economy. So, at this point, the most useful designation for the new wave of opposition to post-Cold War global capitalism is probably best understood as '*globalization-from-below and allies*'.

12.3   RESPONDING TO ECONOMIC GLOBALIZATION

There have been varied failed responses to economic globalization, conceived of as the capitalist portion of the world economy. Without entering into an assessment of these failures, it is worth noticing that the efforts of both Soviet-style socialism and Maoism, especially during the period of the Cultural Revolution in China, to avoid the perceived deforming effects of global capitalism, were dramatic and drastic, and ended in disaster. By contrast, despite the difficulties, the subsequent embrace of the market by China under the rubric of 'modernization', and even by Russia (and the former members of the Soviet empire), in the form of the capitalist path have been generally successful. The same is true for many third world countries that have forged a middle path between socialism and capitalism, and in doing so have relied on the state as a major player in the economy, particularly with respect to market facilitating support services, public utilities, and energy. For most of these countries, as well, the change from a defensive hostility toward the world market to a position of enthusiastic accommodation has been generally treated by domestic elites as a blessing.

In the last two decades, the learning experience at the level of the state has been largely one of submission to the discipline of global capitalism as it pertains to the specific conditions of each country. Fashionable ideas of 'de-linking' and 'self-reliance' are in a shambles, as is perhaps best illustrated by the inability of North Korea, the greatest of all champions of a stand alone anti-capitalist economics, to feed its population. In contrast, its capitalist rival sibling, South Korea, has often been observed scaling the peaks of affluence, as well as moving ahead with democratization. Looked at differently, it is the geopolitical managers of the world economy who use such policies of exclusion and denial as a punishment for supposedly deviant and hostile states seeking to legitimize such a coercive diplomacy under the rubric of 'sanctions', a policy often widely criticized in this period because of its cruel effects on the civilian population of the target society. Even Castro's Cuba, for so long an impressive holdout, is relying on standard capitalist approaches to attract foreign direct investment, and open its economy to market forces. Fukuyama's notorious insistence on the end of history is superficially correct, at least for now, if understood as limited in its application to the global triumph of capitalism, and not extended to cultural and political life (Fukuyama 1992; Clark 1997).

Another response to the hegemonic influence global capitalism has taken the negative form of extreme backlash politics. Such a response looks for inspiration either backwards towards some pre-modern traditional framework deemed viable and virtuous (as with religious extremists of varying identity, or of indigenous peoples), or forwards by ultra-territorialists who want to construct an economic and political system around the archaic model of protectionism, keeping capital at home and excluding foreigners to the extent possible. These responses, aside from those of indigenous peoples, have a rightist flavour because of their intense affirmation of a religious or nationalist community that is at war with the evil 'other' or the infidel, being identified as secularist or outsider, and more graphically, as Western, Christian, Crusader, American. The most menacing form of such backlash politics is now associated with the al Qaida efforts to launch an inter-civilizational war on 11 September. To the extent that these movements have gained control of states, as in Iran since the Islamic Revolution, or even threatened to do so, as in Algeria since 1992, the results have been dismal: economic deterioration, political repression, widespread civil strife, exclusion from world markets. Even more serious, however, is its recourse to mega-terrorism that has unleashed a global war against terrorism being conducted under US leadership on a broad basis that poses its own dangers (Falk 2002).

Specific causes of these backlash phenomena are related to the perceived political and economic failures of global capitalism, and its secularist and materialist outlook as an example of post-colonial Western or American hegemony. However, the correctives proposed have yet to exhibit a capacity to generate an alternative that is capable of either successful economic performance or able to win genuine democratic consent from relevant political communities. At the same time, at least prior to 11 September, the anti-globalization movement was coming of age. One aspect of its growing maturity was its tighter internal discipline and intellectual coherence. Another was its entry into dialogue in prime-time arenas of global capitalism such as the World Economic Forum and the World Bank; and, perhaps most impressive of all, its capacity to work in collaboration with governments to promote global reforms.

The predominance of an insufficiently regulated and morally irresponsible phase of global capitalism has also induced a series of attempts by civil society to mitigate the adverse effects of economic globalization. The most effective of these responses have been issue-oriented, often involving local campaigns against a specific project. One of the early attempts to enter the domain of transformative politics more generally was made by the emergence of green parties at the national level throughout Europe during the 1980s. Significantly, this green movement worked *within* the framework of sovereign states rather than at the transnational level. Green activism has often exhibited tactical brilliance and media savvy in its moves to expose some of the dysfunctionality of national and

global capitalist behaviour, especially the disregard of environmental harm arising from a rush to profits. The early political success of the green movement was
less a result of its capacity to mobilize large numbers in support of its causes and
programmes, and more to the extent to which it put the environmental challenge
high on the policy agenda of states and the international community. But the
green movement's attempt to generalize its identity to provide an alternative
leadership for the entire society—and particularly for its younger members—
across the full range of governance, or to transnationalize its activities to foster
global reform met with frustration and internal controversy that fractured green
unity, most vividly in Germany, but elsewhere as well. Those that argued for a
new radicalism beyond established political parties within a green framework
were dismissed as utopian dreamers, while those who opted for influence within
the existing framework were often scorned as victims of co-optation, derided as
opportunists, or written off as gradualists. The green movement and its political
parties have persisted in Europe, but mainly as one more voice in civil society.

Occasionally as in Germany they have played prominent roles in government
forming a coalition with Social Democrats, but, in general, they are no longer
widely perceived as a vehicle for an alternative world-view to that provided by
global capitalism; nor are they possessed of a sufficiently loyal and united constituency to pose a threat to mainstream economic or political thought. Because
of its initial creative focus on the environmental agenda, both conservatives and
progressives on political economy issues were both drawn to green politics, giving the perspective of its originality, but at the cost of being unable to broaden
its appeal to major constituencies whose policy priorities were other than the
environment. In particular, greens were unable to develop a coherent position on
global capitalism as their ranks were split between socialists and free marketers,
which both inhibited their cause and made it difficult for the green movement to
be an effective contributor to anti-globalization politics.

Local grassroots politics has been another type of response directed at the sit-
ing of a nuclear power reactor or large dam, mobilizing residents of the area facing displacement and loss of traditional livelihood, and sometimes involving
others from the society and beyond, who identify with the poor, the displaced, and
with nature. These struggles have had some notable successes. But these are reactions to symptomatic disorders associated with the choice of developmental short-
cuts, either motivated by glory-seeking national leaders, by greedy investors, by
international financial institutions thinking mainly of aggregate economic growth,
and most often some combination of these factors. Such local forms of resistance
can be effective, and over the years, have led the World Bank, and more generally
the investment community, to be more sensitive to the human, environmental, and
health effects of large-scale development projects. As a consequence, the whole
process of conceiving large-scale developmental projects has evolved to the point
that it does fulfil many of the mandates of a responsible global capitalism, although
continual public vigilance is needed to monitor specific undertakings, as the temptation to cut corners at the expense of the environment and local essentially

disenfranchised poor people is always a live possibility, as indeed is the willingness to be guided by experts far from the scene of societal and ecological disruption (Roy 2001). The World Commission on Dams brought together stakeholders of dams, development, and capitalism to forge a policy consensus, reflecting both the growing influence of global civil society perspective, as well as its own non-confrontational evolution (Dubash et al. 2002).

Closely related to the above issues have been a variety of activist attempts by elements of global civil society to protect the global commons against the more predatory dimensions of globalization (Shiva 1987; Rich 1994; Keck and Sikkuk 1998). Here Greenpeace has had a pioneering and distinguished record of activist successes. For instance, by exhibiting an imaginative and courageous willingness to challenge entrenched military and commercial forces by direct action it has had a dramatic impact on public consciousness, and has helped to reshape market behaviour in the process. Examples include its campaigns to outlaw commercial whaling, to oppose the plan of Shell Oil to dispose of the oil rig Brent Spar in the North Sea, to mobilize global support for a fifty year moratorium on mineral development in Antarctica, and, perhaps most significantly of all—though focused on the behaviour of governments rather than market forces—its resistance for many years to nuclear testing in the Pacific (Prins and Sellwood 1998). Rachel Carson's lyrical environmentalism and Jacques Cousteau's extraordinarily intense dedication to saving the oceans suggest the extent to which even single, gifted individuals can exert powerful counter-tendencies to the most destructive sides of an insufficiently regulated market or of governments that put military activities ahead of all other concerns. But these efforts, although plugging some of the holes in the dikes, are not based on a coherent critique or alternative ideology. As a consequence, they can only operate at the level of the symptom and in particular situations, while neglecting the disorders embedded in the dynamics of globalization. There is no effort to build a movement that focuses a large portion of its energies on monitoring or reshaping the outlook and operational ethos of global capitalism.

Some other global civil society initiatives, especially in the 1970s, promoted awareness of the cumulative dangers associated with further unregulated economic growth in a setting of a continuing expansion in world population. One of the earliest such initiatives was that promoted by the Club of Rome, a transnational association of individuals prominent in business, science, and society that led to the famous study *The Limits to Growth* (Meadows 1972). The study relied upon a rather elaborate, yet, in the end, misleading, computer program, which purported to measure the interplay of trends in population growth, pollution, resource scarcity, and food supply. It concluded that industrialization as then being practised on a global scale was not sustainable, but was tending toward imminent catastrophe for the entire world. Around the same time, a group of distinguished scientists from various countries working with the British journal, *The Ecologist*, issued their own warning, but with a redeeming vision, under the title *Blueprint for Survival* (Goldsmith 1972). These alarms stimulated a debate and led to some temporary adjustments, but the resilience of the world capitalist system at the time was such that no fundamental changes occurred, and the warning issued as signals soon faded into background. Neither a sense of alternative nor a movement of protest and opposition took hold. There existed no organized transnational social forces back in the 1970s. The Cold War was still dominating political consciousness, and the most that was achieved was the birth of a global environmental protection movement that enlisted the support to varying degrees of many governments. Socialism was still a formidable force; there was no disposition to indict capitalism, because of its wider geopolitical role, principally the economic containment of the Soviet Union; and the minimal international consensus that existed, was devoted to such issues as reducing fertility rates in poor third world countries, resource conservation, and seeking more regulatory authority at the global level (Falk 1972).

The World Order Models Project (WOMP), which started its work in the late 1960s, is illustrative of a somewhat more far-reaching and comprehensive effort to challenge the existing world order and find alternatives, through the medium of diagnosis and prescription by a transnational group of independent academicians. The efforts of this group have been confined to the margins of academic reflection on world conditions. Also, until recently, the policy focus and animating preoccupation has been centred on war, and only recently has it been broadened to include environmental danger. Although WOMP has produce overall assessments of the world situation, its background and the interests of its participants made its work less sensitive to the distinctive challenges and contributions of economic globalization than to the dangers to global security associated with the nuclear arms race, and the general problems of overcoming mass poverty in third world countries through rapid and sustainable economic development (Mendlovitz 1975). As such, the emphasis of WOMP on war and war-making sovereign states did not come to terms with either the durability of the state, or the need to avoid its instrumentalization by global market forces. These efforts failed to address systematically the issue of reforming global capitalism. WOMP also failed to appreciate that the principal world order danger is no longer the unconditional security claims of the sovereign state, but rather the inability of the state to protect its own citizenry, especially those who are most vulnerable, in relation to the economic and social downsides of global market forces. This refocusing of concern that took hold of the political imagination in the 1990s, that is, after the Cold War, has itself been temporarily eclipsed by the renewed priority accorded to the security role of the state in the aftermath of 11 September.

A better connected and more recent effort to address overall global issues was attempted by the Commission on Global Governance—an initiative inspired by Willy Brandt and the earlier work of the Brandt Commissions on North/South relations, as expressed in its main report, *Our Neighborhood* (Global Governance, 1995). This venture, claiming authority and credibility on the basis of the eminence of its membership drawn from the leading ranks of society—including past and present government ministers—seemed too farsighted for existing power structures and yet too timid to engage the imagination of the more activist and militant actors in civil society. The Commission's report failed to arouse any widespread or sustained interest despite the comprehensiveness and thoughtfulness of its proposals. As an intellectual tool, it was also disappointing. It failed, for example, to clarify the challenge of globalization that existed in the early 1990s. It ignored the then especially troublesome character of Bretton Woods approaches to world economic policy, and it exempted the operations of global capitalism from critical scrutiny. As a result, the Commission's efforts to anchor an argument for global reform around an argument for 'global governance' seemed more likely to consolidate *globalization-from-above* than to promote a creative equilibrium based on struggle that was beginning to be associated with the still disparate activities grouped beneath the rubric of *globalization-from-below*.

In part, the timing of the Commission's efforts was unfortunate, as they had begun their work in the aftermath of the Gulf War when attention and hopes were centred on the future of the United Nations, and had finished at a time when the UN was being criticized harshly, if somewhat unfairly, for its attempts to resolve conflicts and protect the populations in Somalia, Bosnia, and Rwanda in the period between 1992 and 1994. But this did not excuse the failure of the Commission to address clearly and explicitly the adverse consequence of globalization, a focus that would have put such a commission on a collision course with the then reigning adherents of the neoliberal economistic world picture. Given the claims of 'eminence' and 'independent funding' that characterized the Commission, it is not to be expected that it would be willing or able to address the structural and ideological deficiencies attributable to the prevailing world order framework. This inevitably meant that, despite the best efforts of its membership to make a contribution to global policy making, the actual impact of its work and report was to confirm a sense of pessimism about finding an alternative world picture to that provided by the existing neoliberal prism on global capitalism, which in the context of this chapter—indeed of this volume as a whole—was tantamount to giving up on the search for a responsible global capitalism.

What is being argued, then, is that the various challenges arising from global capitalism in its post-industrial phase have not, as yet, engendered a sufficient response in two respects. First, there is an absence of an ideological alternative to what is offered by the various renditions of neoliberalism, and which could provide the social forces associated with *globalization-from-below* with a common analytical framework, political language, and programme. Second, there is need for a clear expression of a critique of *globalization-from-above* that seeks to meet the basic challenges associated with poverty, social marginalization, and environmental decay, while preserving the economic benefits derived from capitalism in its present form. The political imperatives of *globalization-from-below* are thus at once *both* drastic and reformist. While accepting the global capitalist framing of economic choice, they believe that ethical and ecological factors should be brought to bear more systematically. In short, they favour an abandonment of neoliberalism in the search for a more socially and politically regulated framework for this latest phase of global capitalism.

It is crucial to realize that the world order outcomes arising from the impact of economic globalization is far from settled, and in no sense predetermined. The forces of *globalization-from-above* have taken control of globalization and are pushing it in an economistic direction that is influencing the state to adopt a set of attitudes and policies: that is, privatization, free trade, fiscal austerity, competitiveness, and above all, growth. But there are other options and policy objectives, such as 'sustainable development', 'global welfare', and 'cybernetic libertarianism'. The further evolution of global capitalism is likely to reflect increasingly the play of these diverse perspectives and priorities. The perspectives and priorities of *globalization-from-above* are being challenged in various ways, but activist resistance has been mainly piecemeal and critical. Important, also, is the effort directed at the mobilization of the now disparate forces of *globalization-from-below* in the direction of greater solidity and political weight, and to revive discussions about how to achieve a responsible global capitalism in the new setting of world affairs that has pushed economic policy concerns once again into the background. Preoccupations with global security arise not only from the mega-terrorist threats of the post-September 11 atmosphere, but also from the threats of catastrophic regional wars fought with weaponry of mass destruction, as illustrated by the India/Pakistan confrontation in 2002 over Kashmir. It is my conviction that such a mobilization is most likely to occur beneath the banner of a reformed democracy, which becomes more and more responsive to the basic aspirations of peoples everywhere to participate in the processes that are shaping their lives, and with growing attention given to security factors, non-material values, including the control of crime and the resolution of political grievances (the roots of terrorism) that exist around the world. In effect, the next phase of the anti-globalization movement, as it regains its focus in the first decade of the twenty-first century will almost certainly become more concerned with the 'political' aspects of a socially acceptable and humane political economy for this era of globalization. In the 1990s the preoccupation of global civil society mirrored the economistic musings of those who were fashioning neoliberal global designs at Davos, the board rooms of world corporations and banks, and brainstorming sessions held at the World Bank and the IMF.

The purpose of the next section of this chapter is to clarify what is meant by 'democracy' and 'politics' in relation to the analysis of world economy given the confusing relevance of the global war on terrorism.

12.4 TOWARDS RESPONSIBLE GLOBAL CAPITALISM: A PLEA FOR NORMATIVE DEMOCRACY

It will not be possible to attain a responsible global capitalism unless there is a more transparent and supportive form of global governance than currently exists; and this will not be achieved without a continuous and robust pressure exerted by global civil society. For this reason, I place great emphasis and invest my hopes in efforts to overcome the current global democratic deficit. As earlier indicated, this quest would have been simpler and more attainable without the disruptive effects of 11 September, the ensuing war on global terror, and the menace of large-scale regional warfare. Whether or not these disruptions are of temporary duration is difficult to assess at present; but however long, the importance of democratizing global governance structures remains a political imperative that is linked directly to the presence or absence of a responsible global capitalism.

To introduce the idea of 'normative democracy' is to offer a proposal for a unifying ideology that is capable of both mobilizing and unifying the disparate social forces that constitute global civil society, and providing the political energy necessary to advance the quest for a greater moral responsiveness within the wide orbit of global market activities. Our specification of normative democracy is influenced strongly by David Held's work on democratic theory and practice, particularly his formulations of 'cosmopolitan democracy' (Held 1995). However, it offers a slightly different terminology so as to emphasize the agency role of global civil society with its range of engagements that go from the local and grassroots to the most encompassing arenas of decision (Held 1995; Archibugi and Held 1995). Normative democracy also draws upon Walden Bello's call for 'substantive democracy', set forth as a more progressive movement alternative to the more limited embrace of 'constitutional democracy'(Bello 1997). I prefer the concept of normative to that of substantive democracy because it highlights ethical and legal norms, and in so doing, reconnects politics with moral purpose and values. It also underscores the moral emptiness of neoliberalism, consumerism, and most forms of secularism. There is a practical reason too: to create alternatives to the current appeal of religious extremists as the sole politically relevant source of ethical response to the inequities and materialism of contemporary global capitalism. At the same time, it is important to recognize the indispensable role of moral purpose and spiritual concerns in the renewal of progressive politics (Falk 2001).

Contrary to widespread claims in the West, there is no empirical basis for the argument that the economic performance of a country is necessarily tied to constitutional democracy and human rights. Several countries in the Asia/Pacific region, most significantly China, have combined an outstanding macroeconomic record with a harsh authoritarian rule. *Globalization-from-above* is not an assured vehicle for the achievement of Western-style constitutional democracy, including the protection of individual and group rights. But democracy, as such, is the essence of a meaningful form of political action on the part of global civil society, especially to the extent that such action, even when radical in its goals, refrains from and repudiates violent means. In this respect, there is an emergent, as yet implicit, convergence of ends and means on the part of several distinct tendencies in civil society: these include issue-oriented movements; non-violent democracy movements; and governments that minimize their links to geopolitical structures. This convergence presents several intriguing opportunities for coalition-building, and a greater ideological coherence among the various institutions and interest groups seeking to achieve a responsible global capitalism. Against this background, normative democracy seems like an attractive umbrella for theorizing, not dogmatically, but to exhibit affinities.

Normative democracy adopts a comprehensive view of the fundamental ideas associated with the secular modern state. Security is conceived as extending to environmental protection and to the defence of economic viability (*Turkish Daily News*, 29 July 1997; but see Soros 2002). Human rights are conceived as encompassing the social and economic rights of individuals, and such collective rights as the right to development, the right to peace, the right of self-determination. Democracy is conceived as extending beyond constitutional and free periodic elections to include an array of other assurances that governance is oriented toward human well-being and ecological sustainability, and that citizens have access to the various arenas of decision making.

The elements of normative democracy can be enumerated, but their content and behavioural applications will require amplification and adaptation in varied specific settings. This enumeration reflects the dominant orientations and outlook of the political actors that make up the constructivist category of a substantive profile of normative democracy. It is not an enumeration that is a wish list, but rather is descriptive and explanatory of an embedded consensus with respect to political reform. The elements of such a consensus include the following ingredients:

1. *Consent of citizenry*: some periodic indication that the permanent population of the relevant community is represented by the institutions of governance, which confer legitimacy through the expression of consent. Elections are the established modalities for territorial communities to confer legitimacy on government, but referenda and rights of petition and recall may be more appropriate for other types of political community, especially those of regional or global scope. Direct democracy may be most meaningful for the governance of local political activity.
2. *Rule of law*: all modes of governance should be subject to the discipline of the law as a way of imposing effective limits on authority and of assuring some form of checks and balances as between legislative, executive, judicial, and administrative processes. Also, there is need for sensitivity to the normative claims of civil initiatives associated with codes of conduct, conference declarations, societal institutions (for instance, Permanent Peoples Tribunal in Rome).
3. *Human rights*: taking account of differing cultural, economic, and political settings and priorities, the establishment of mechanisms for the impartial and effective implementation of human rights by global, regional, state, and transnational civil sources of authority. Human rights are conceived by reference to the elements of human dignity. They encompass economic, social, and cultural rights, as well as civil and political rights, with a concern for both individual and collective conceptions of rights, emphasizing tolerance toward difference and fundamental community sentiments.

4. *Participation*: effective and meaningful modes of participation in the political life of the society, centered upon the processes of government, but extending to all forms of social governance, including the workplace and home. Participation may be direct or indirect, that is, representational, but it enables the expression of views and influence upon the processes of decision making on the basis of an ideal of equality of access. Creativity is needed to find methods other than elections by which to ensure progress toward full participation.

5. *Accountability*: this implies suitable mechanisms for challenging the exercise of authority by those occupying official positions at the level of the state, but also with respect to the functioning of the market and of international institutions. The establishment of an international criminal court in 2002 provides one mechanism for assuring accountability by those in powerful positions that have been traditionally treated as exempt from the Rule of Law.

6. *Public goods*: a restored social agenda that corrects the growing imbalance, varying in seriousness from country to country, between private and public goods. Such an imbalance exists with respect to the relief of poverty, and the improvement of health, education, housing, and basic human needs, but also in relation to support for environmental protection, regulation of economic globalization, innovative cultural activity, infrastructural development for governance at the regional and global levels. In these regards, a gradual depoliticalization of funding, either by reliance on a use or transaction tax imposed on financial flows, global air travel, or some form of reliable and equitable means to fund public goods of local, national, regional, and global scope, is worth serious consideration.

7. *Transparency*: an openness with respect to knowledge and information that builds trust between the institutions of governance and the citizenry at various levels of social interaction. In effect, establishing the right to information as an aspect of constitutionalism, including a strong bias against public sector secrecy and covert operations, and criminalizes government lies such as the sort recently revealed in connection with CIA lying about alleged 'UFO sightings' so as protect the secrecy of US Air Force spy missions. Internationally, transparency is particularly important with respect to military expenditures and arms transfers. The priority given to counter-terrorist activities of the government, provide a sweeping rationalization for governmental secrecy, especially in the wake of 11 September anxieties.

8. *Non-violence*: underpinning *globalization-from-below* and the promotion of substantive democracy is a conditional commitment to non-violent politics and conflict resolution. Such a commitment does not nullify rights of self-defence as protected in international law, strictly and narrowly construed. Nor does it necessarily invalidate limited recourse to violence by oppressed peoples. However, this ethos of non-violence clearly imposes on governments an obligation to renounce weaponry of mass destruction and to negotiate actively phased disarmament arrangements. It also demands commitments dedicated to demilitarizing approaches to peace and security at all levels of

social interaction, including peace and security at the level of city and neighbourhood.

12.5 GLOBALIZATION-FROM-BELOW AND THE STATE: A DECISIVE BATTLE

Without entering into detailed discussion, it seems that different versions of neoliberal ideology have exerted a defining influence upon the orientation of political elites governing sovereign states. Of course, there are many variations reflecting conditions and personalities in each particular state and region, but the generalization holds without important exception (Sakamoto 1994; Falk 1997). Even China, despite adherence to its ideology of state socialism, has implemented by state decree, and with impressive results, an extreme market-oriented approach to economic policy. This suggests that the state can remain authoritarian in relation to its citizenry without necessarily jeopardizing its economic performance—and indeed advancing its competitiveness—so long as it adheres, more or less, to the discipline of global capitalism. In these respects, neoliberalism as a *global* ideology is purely economistic in character, and does not imply a commitment to democratic governance in even the minimal sense of periodic fair elections. Order and stability plus a high degree of receptivity to foreign investment and trade are all that is currently *necessary* to be a global economic player, as evidenced by China's admission to the World Trade Organization in 2001. Of course, where geopolitics intrudes, exclusions without an economic rationale may take place, as, for example, when the United States takes the lead in sanctioning a wide variety of governments it deems hostile to its interests. Sometimes, as with the case of Cuba, the exclusion is mainly justified by reference to deficiencies of human rights, but such an argument is mounted so selectively as to appear arbitrary.

Globalization-from-below, in addition to a multitude of local struggles, is also a vehicle for the transnational promotion of substantive democracy, an ideological counterweight to neoliberalism, and as a partial programme for a responsible global capitalism. It provides an alternative, or series of convergent alternatives, that has not yet been posited as a coherent body of theory and practice, but nevertheless offers the tacit common ground of an emergent global civil society. Normative democracy, unlike backlash politics or the coercive diplomacy of sanctions that closes off borders and hardens identities, seeks to promote a politics of reconciliation that maintains much of the openness and dynamism associated with *globalization-from-above*, but counters its pressures to privatize and marketize the production of public goods.

In effect, the quest of normative democracy is to establish a social equilibrium that takes full account of the realities of globalization in its various aspects. Such a process cannot succeed on a country-by-country basis as the rollback of welfare in Scandinavia suggests, but must proceed within regional and global settings. The state remains the instrument of policy and decision making that most affects the lives of peoples, and the primary link to regional and global institutions. In the last two decades the state has been instrumentalized to a considerable degree by the ideology and influences associated with *globalization-from-above*. This has resulted in declining support for public goods despite a period of strong sustained economic growth. It has also produced a polarization of the distribution of the wealth created, leading to incredible wealth for the winners and acute suffering for the losers. An immediate goal of those disparate social forces that constitute *globalization-from-below* is to reinstrumentalize the state to the extent that it redefines its role as mediating between the logic of capitalism and the priorities of its peoples, including their short-term and longer-term goals. Of course, this support for a strong state is associated with its social capabilities and responsibilities, and not with the sort of security prerogatives that have indeed let the state to again take command over the course of global policy formation.

Evidence of this instrumentalization of the state on behalf of the claims of global civil society is present in relation to global conferences on broad policy issues that had been organized under UN auspices. Transnational citizens' campaigns for global reform were beginning to make an impact on the public consciousness and behavioural standards in the 1990s. These UN conferences increasingly attracted an array of social forces associated with global civil society, and gave rise to a variety of coalitions and oppositions between state, markets, and militant citizens that were organized to promote substantive goals (e.g. human rights, environmental protection, economic equity, and development). At the same time they also became arenas of political participation that were operating beyond the confines of state control, and were regarded as provocative and threatening by the established order, which consisted of a coalition between market forces and geopolitical leaders. One effect is to withdraw support for such UN activities, pushing the organization to the sidelines on global policy issues as part of a process of augmenting geopolitical control over its agenda and orientation. Such a reaction represents a setback for *globalization-from-below*, but it also shows that the social forces that are associated with the promotion of normative democracy can be formidable adversaries.

Such a process of reinstrumentalization could also influence the future role and identity of regional and global mechanisms of governance, especially as these may add to the regulatory mandates directed towards market forces and the normative mandates with respect to the protection of the global commons, the promotion of demilitarization, and the overall support for public goods. However, presently in the foreground are preoccupations with mega-terrorist threats to security, especially in the United States and its close allies, as well as the global campaign that has been directed at combating terrorism generally, and intertwined with the diplomatic emphasis on regional war prevention.

12.6 CONCLUSIONS

In this chapter I have argued that the positive prospects for global civil society depend very much on two interrelated developments: (i) achieving consensus on 'normative democracy' as the foundation of coherent theory and practice, and (ii) waging a struggle for the outlook and orientation of institutions of governance with respect to the framing of global economic policy. The state remains the critical focus of this latter struggle, although it is not, even now, a matter of intrinsic opposition between its role as an instrument of *globalization-from-above* and that of social movements as an instrument of *globalization-from-below*. In many specific settings, coalitions between states and social movements are emerging, as is evident in relation to many questions of the environment, economic development, and human rights. It may even come to pass that transnational corporations and banks adopt a longer term view of their own interests by seeking to influence the policy content of *globalization-from-above*, and by so doing, to heal relations with their critics and improve their image as constructive global citizens with the preferences of global civil society.

The popularity of codes of conduct and other voluntary programmes are suggestive of an eagerness on the part of the managers of global capitalism to improve their image as ethically sensitive and humanly constructive players in the world economy (Broad 2002). It is also helpful to remember that such an unanticipated convergence of previously opposed social forces led to the sort of consensus that produced 'social democracy' and 'the welfare state' at the level of the state over the course of the nineteenth and twentieth centuries. There is no evident reason to preclude such comparable convergences on regional and global levels as a way of resolving some of the tensions being caused by the manner in which globalization is *currently* being enacted.

Even 11 September gives rise to some moves in these directions, as well as its major diversionary impact. The 2002 odd couple journey of U-2 singer Bono touring Africa with the US Secretary of the Treasury, Paul O'Neill, on the theme of enhancing the role of foreign economic assistance and reducing the debt burden could not have occurred without the growing realization that 'failed states' are dangerous to the rich and powerful. Such a climate of awareness may yet push global capitalism to seek legitimacy by affirming a stakeholder ethos that includes the poor, workers, future generations, and environmental protection. As described by Hans Küng in Chapter 6 and Robert Davies in Chapter 13, the UN Secretary General has been encouraging such a voluntary process of engagement on the part of the business sector, by creating within the UN System of a 'global compact' that formalizes in a public way corporate commitments to these goals, which certainly moves away from the spirit and substance of neoliberal and irresponsible global capitalism. Whether such initiatives are more than gestures will depend on whether the vigilance of global civil society assumes a potent form.

NOTE

Portions of this chapter were drawn from a previous article published in *Oxford Development Studies* (Falk 1998).

REFERENCES
Archibugi, D., and Held, D. (eds.) (1995), *Cosmopolitan Democracy: An Agenda for a New World Order* (Cambridge: Polity Press).

Bello, W. (1997), 'Alternate Security Systems in the Asia-Pacific', Bangkok Conference of Focus Asia, 27–30 March.

Broad, R. (2002), *Global Backlash: Citizen Initiatives for a Just World Economy* (Lanham, Md.: Rowman & Littlefield).

Bull, H. (1977), *The Anarchical Society: A Study of Order in World Politics* (New York: Columbia University Press).

Clark, I. (1997), *Globalization and Fragmentation: International Relations in the Twentieth Century* (Oxford: Oxford University Press).

Dubash, N. K., Dupar, M., Kothari, S., and Lissu, T. (2001), *A Watershed in Global Governance? An Independent Assessment of the World Commission on Dams* (Lokayan, India: World Resources Institute).

Falk, R. (1972), *This Endangered Planet: Proposals and Prospects for Human Survival* (New York: Random House).

—— (1993), 'The Making of Global Citizenship'. In J. Brecher, J. B. Childs, and J. Cutler (eds.), *Global Visions: Beyond the New World Order* (Boston, Mass.: South End Press).

—— (1995), *On Humane Global Governance: Toward a New Global Politics* (Cambridge: Polity Press).

—— (1997), 'State of Siege: will globalization win out?' *International Affairs* 73: 123–36.

—— (1998), 'Global Civil Society: Perspectives, Initiatives, and Movements', *Oxford Development Studies* 26(1): 99–110.

—— (2001), *Religion and Humane Global Governance* (New York: Palgrave).

—— (2002), *Winning (and Losing) the War Against Global Terror* (Northampton, Mass.: Interlink).

Fukuyama, F. (1992), *The End of History and the Last Man* (New York: Free Press).

Global Civil Society Yearbook (2001) (Oxford: Oxford University Press).

Global Governance, Commission on (1995) (Oxford: Oxford University Press).

Goldsmith, E., et al. (1972), *Blueprint for Survival* (Boston, Mass.: Houghton Mifflin).

Held, D. (1995), *Democracy and the Global Order: From the Modern State to Cosmopolitan Governance* (Cambridge: Cambridge University Press, 1995).

—— and McGrew, A., et al. (1999), *Global Transformations* (Cambridge: Polity Press).

Hirst, P., and Thompson, G. (1996), *Globalization in Question* (Cambridge: Polity Press), 1–17, 170–94.

Keck, M., and Sikkink, K. (1998), *Activists Beyond Borders: Advocacy Networks Beyond Borders* (Ithaca, NY: Cornell University Press).

Lipschutz, R. D. (1996), *Global Civil Society and Global Environmental Governance* (Albany, NY: State University of New York).

Meadows, D., and Associates (1972), *The Limits to Growth* (New York: Free Press).

Mendlovitz, S. H. (1975), *On the Creation of a Just World Order* (New York: Free Press).

Nerfin, M. (1986), 'Neither Prince nor Merchant: Citizen—an Introduction to the Third System', *IFDA Dossier* 56: 3–29.

Prins, G., and Sellwood, E. (1998), 'Global Security Problems and the Challenge to Democratic Process,' in D. Archibugi, D. Held, and M. Kohler (eds.), *Re-imagining Political Community: Studies in Cosmopolitan Democracy* (Cambridge: Polity Press), 252–72.

Rich, B. (1994), *Mortgaging the Earth: The World Bank, Environmental Impoverishment, and the Crisis of Development* (Boston, Mass.: Beacon Press).

Rosenau, J. N. (1990), *Turbulence in World Politics: A Theory of Change and Continuity* (Princeton: Princeton University Press).

Roy, A. (2001), *Power Politics* (Boston, Mass.: South End Press).

Shiva, V. (1987), 'People's Ecology: The Chipko Movement.' In R. B. J. Walker and Mendlovitz (eds.), *Towards a Just World Peace: Perspectives from Social Movements* (London: Butterworths), 253–70.

Soros, G. (2002), *On Globalization* (Oxford: Public Affairs).

Wapner, P. (1996), 'The Social Construction of Global Governance,' paper presented at Annual Meeting, American Political Science Association, 28–31 Aug. 1996.

13

The Business Community: Social Responsibility and Corporate Values

ROBERT DAVIES

13.1 INTRODUCTION: WHY WAIT FOR THE BARBARIANS AT THE GATE?

The process of globalization over the past decade has created unprecedented opportunities for global companies in trade, investment, services, and production. The fact that the rapid pace of growth of economic opportunity has not corresponded with the growth of leadership in business ethics and a sense of corporate responsibility has potentially threatening consequences for the reputation of free market economies and businesses. Public concern is accelerated by a wider use of electronic communications that is changing the nature of politics as much as that of business operations. The leadership of a few progressive companies, the rise in consciousness of corporate responsibility as an essential feature to sustain global capitalism, and emerging evidence of partnership initiatives which hold the key to equitable development, are all encouraging pointers towards progress.

This chapter looks at the development of corporate social responsibility and corporate values in the context of rapid and uneven globalization. It challenges the idea there is any such thing as 'values-free' business, and affirms that all business and business leaders—for good or ill—are engaged in processes which underpin values in human behaviour. Business cannot divorce itself from its economic and social context, taking the privileged protection of corporate laws, yet not expecting to meet social expectations. Businesses operate in communities that are deeply divided by inequalities in wealth, health, knowledge, influence, and life chances. Globalization, more than anything, has brought the business world head to head with poverty and economic exclusion. The electronic media and cheaper mass access to advanced information and communications technology have shrunk the world, and changed permanently the nature of politics and activism with revolutionary consequences for both government and business.

Business has the capability of bringing creative and sustainable solutions to many of the ills facing the world such as ill health, illiteracy, and unemployment, and to reinforce freedoms and choice, if it engages in the challenges which will contribute to its long-term sustainability and profitability. The challenge for those engaged in promoting corporate social responsibility is not just to make a compelling business case, as important as that is, but to elevate business values and integrity. It is to spread awareness that one cannot cherry-pick globalization and reap the rewards of open markets without responding to the forces that will ultimately undermine free markets. It is to recognize that responding to the challenges of diversity and transparency is at the heart of successful internationalization of business. It is to dare to appeal to business leaders, in an imperfect world, for values based leadership, decency and integrity, and an absolute commitment to attack corruption as the essential bedrock of business activity with a human face.

In a globalizing world, business leaders will need to be more pro-active and progressive. They cannot rely on their business and trade associations that are so often held back by the slowest ship in the convoy, national interests, legalistic defence of rights and lack of vision. The consequences of business and business leaders failing in this challenge will be growing and corrosive public and media cynicism, declining values and respect for property at work, negative activism and efforts to regulate business by international institutions lacking competence and capacity. If business leaders do not appear to exercise positive steward-ship and honesty—why should employees, customers, and communities?

I have been influenced by several writings on the subjects of business ethics and corporate social responsibility over many years. But much of my thinking is directly influenced by being a player in the corporate social responsibility arena through the most exciting and changing of times. Not least the period from late 1999 to 2002 when globalization, corporate governance, voluntary regulation, corruption, and business ethics faced unprecedented challenges due to protests, consumer agitation, scandals, and a questioning media.

Managing in a world of opportunity and conflict seemed so much more complex following the 11 September terrorist attacks in the US which reminded us all how geo-political issues could threaten security in new ways which business must heed. Companies and business leaders who thought they were global, realized, often with a sense of inner confusion, that they may not, in fact, under-stand the forces unleashed in the world in which they were expanding their economic influence.

For those interested in the development of social responsibility and corporate values, the thirteen years from 1989 to 2002 have been a period of unprecedented change. The period started with the collapse of state communism and the central command economies around the world, where some 90 per cent of the world's population suffered the economic decay and gradual collapse of state planned economies. It ended with over 90 per cent of the world's population in market orientated economies facing a range of unprecedented opportunities. The same period was defined by crises in the form of corporate governance scandals in the US and elsewhere, the discrediting of self-regulation among accounting profes-sions, widespread corruption in transition economies, and insecurity from liquidity crisis, and some of the harsher effects of globalization in unprotected economies.

At the heart of these dramatic changes has been a reminder that ethics do not live naturally with either free markets or command economies. There has been a vivid demonstration that regulated markets in even the most experienced capitalist economies are tough to set up and run, and that the cost of getting it wrong is corrosive public cynicism of business and hostility towards its leaders. There is not a great deal of evidence that the lessons have been learned or that governments have the capacity or desire to regulate for corporate responsibility, even if opportunistic politicians have the ingenuity to make political capital out of the problems.

Although the challenges of corporate governance will do little but increase, there does not appear to be a groundswell in mood amongst business leaders to take a high profile on the need for its significant reform, or a movement of those who feel that the machine is broken and needs fixing, or that business leaders will go further to self-regulate. A vacuum will be left to those who choose to fill it, such as campaigning financial journalists, pensions and investment activists, NGOs, or others. One measure of the slide into unremarkable cynicism and abuse towards CEOs is how the essentially pro-business UK *Sunday Times Business News* publishes an annual 'Executive Pay Survey' of FTSE 100 CEO pay cross-linked to shareholder value, and it describes it as its 'fat-cat table' (*Sunday Times*, 7 July 2002). What is clearer is that the capacity has now grown for E-enabled interest groups and super E-empowered activists to step into the leadership vacuum, where neither politicians nor business leaders can easily tread, and demand decent and transparent behaviour.

It has become starkly clear that the end of this period has seen a defining moment for the rules of capitalist corporate governance. However, its implications are uncertain. Will drastic action follow, or will we default to satisfaction and complacency when the stock markets rebound after the 2001/2002 plunge in value? At a peak of the bad news in June 2002, when a further set of corporate scandals rocked the US and Wall Street stock prices, President George W. Bush, in one of his weekly radio addresses, was provoked to take a stern view. He said that those guilty of corporate fraud should be sent to jail for the sake of US capitalism as 'a few bad actors can tarnish our entire free enterprise system' and added 'corporate America has got to understand there is a higher calling than trying to fudge the numbers, trying to slip a billion here and a billion here and hope nobody notices' (weekly radio address, 28 June 2002).

13.2 THE EMERGING SOCIAL RESPONSIBILITY MOVEMENT

The history of corporate social responsibility since the Industrial Revolution reveals that shocks and scandals—whether disasters, impropriety, law suites, revelations, denial of capital, threats and the sanction of regulation—have often, if regrettably, achieved more progress in raising ethical behaviour than has moral suasion. Most companies and their leaders only respond when the Barbarians arrive at their gate.

It is not that there are not ethically strong, progressive, and incorruptible business leaders who pursue enterprise and values with energy and vision. There are, of course, countless enterprises that are exemplars of business morality, and contribute dynamically to the betterment of society and community, often where ownership and control has been less separated. I have been deeply privileged to work with some of the best and most visionary in our business organizations. But while the many 'bad actors' or indifferent business leaders and managers ignore the importance of these issues, the leadership of the best will be tarnished by the acid of the worst. The underpinning of modern business and the capital raising process demands confidence, trust, and reputation. Its legal protections and privileges, from patent law and fiscal benefits to limited liability, demand a contract with society—a license to operate.

Corporate responsibility is a pact for the mutual benefit between society that needs business for economic and social development, and business that needs a supportive business environment. It is also a pact between capital and management in modern companies, which has been as shaken up by some recent scandals where management disregarded the bond of transparency with shareholders. All too often, professional managers and their advisers have been tempted to see the resources of public companies as their own property without the sense of stewardship that owner-managers once had. The balance can only be struck by combining professionalism with transparency.

The old state communist societies, such as in the former Soviet Union and its satellite states, and China, with their massive and uncompetitive state owned enterprises, put social welfare as the central objective of business. It proved wholly unsustainable as a model that failed to recognize market signals, and faced equal dislocation when the pact was broken, and there was plundering of assets by their managers. When the pact breaks such as in the corporate governance crisis, recriminations and hostility arise which threaten and undermine the development of society. It is also as true in rich industrialized nations as transition economies and developing countries that may struggle under the burdens of corruption.

The past decade has equally been a period when corporate social responsibility and the pressures for good corporate governance have never become greater; and many leading companies and business leaders have aspired to new models of business-aligned corporate social responsibility in their core business practices and community relations. A set of pioneering companies are demonstrating that ethics need not be in conflict with competitiveness, that it can, if managed effectively and transparently, contribute to positive reputation, and that you can win support from the investment community as well as from customers and employees.

New actors have emerged in the form of cross-border business led organizations such as the International Business Leaders Forum and World Business Council for Sustainable Development, and many at a national level to forge collaboration in good practices. Inter-governmental organizations such as the OECD, the United Nations through its UN Global Compact, and the World Bank have become a force to emphasize the value of corporate citizenship. The Socially Responsible Investment (SRI) movement has gained critical mass in Europe and America. Activist NGOs have engaged in campaigns for corporate social responsibility as well as those against the downsides of globalization. The media have taken a more critical, better informed, and analytical stand on social responsibility issues. (See Nelson 2002.)

The critical challenges for business at this watershed are in restating and supporting a 'values based approach' to their governance and relations with all stakeholders. This is an approach that puts values at the heart of business that wins and maintains credibility and motivation of all stakeholders in all markets, will provide the foundations, both for long-term profitability and for a useful contribution to societal goals.

Corporate social responsibility tends to mean different things in different business settings and times. As a concept, it emerged first in the 1960s among internationalizing companies from America and those involved in former colonial states in Africa and Asia. US corporations such as IBM, and Xerox in its earlier day, with marketing companies throughout the world, developed concepts of stakeholder relations to justify their positions as overseas companies engaged in new markets. It also evolved as a response to the American civil rights movement in the 1960s and 1970s and claims for economic justice in the troubled US cities and later in the conflicts in UK inner cities.

Those multinational enterprises engaged in commodities and natural resource developments, evolved the concept in the face of sustained threats to post-colonial investors, nationalization and an increasingly negative environment for business. Some, in any case, had a long tradition of good business standards and active, if paternalistic, community support. The pressure was on companies to justify their presence, and the little interest taken in business at that time by the UN system was essentially negative in its approach to multinational enterprises, some of whom had been accused of engaging in 'political interference'. Some of the first social impact studies appeared at this time, focusing on economic, social, and human development contributions and far less on environment which had not yet emerged as a significant concern.

In the main, corporate social responsibility was seen as a defensive shield at times when business and its property were under threat. It emerged in a similar form at the time of intensive anti-apartheid campaigning against South African investment in the 1970s, with calls for disinvestment and an onus on demonstrating the contribution(s) that could be made by a continued presence.

Throughout these years, corporate responsibility, sometimes used interchangeably with 'corporate citizenship', was often equated with corporate philanthropy as there were a large measure of community support and charitable donations involved in action, whether in the regeneration of US cities, the building of schools and health centres or the funding of scholarships. To this day, US corporate and foundation behaviour, conditioned to major roles as a donor in US society, sees corporate responsibility mainly as a philanthropic strategy, whereas a European model is emerging with far greater emphasis on non-philanthropic activity. Japanese major company behaviour has often followed the American model, even though it gives significant emphasis to its supply chain contributions.

Although corporate social responsibility (CSR) is developing rapidly as a field of study, these dynamic new movements are relatively under-researched. My observations on the emerging challenges for leadership and corporate citizenship are based on my personal experience of running an international non-profit organization—The Prince of Wales International Business Leaders Forum (IBLF). This is an organization which engages in dialogue with leaders of international business from Europe, Asia, America, and the Middle East; and for, the past twelve years, has attempted to encourage the implementation of corporate citizenship as management practice in over fifty countries.

The IBLF is a centre for international leadership in responsible business practice, and also a centre for innovation in cross-sector partnership. Over the period of the Forum's existence, it has been an incubator for innovative partnership initiatives ranging from enterprise in former communist states, corporate governance standards, ICT in education and human rights to preventative health initiatives—all focusing on the social aspects of business. It is, in itself, one of the actors in the emerging CSR movement.

What is corporate social responsibility and what is driving it ? Put simply, it is the framework for the role of business in society. It is the set of standards of behaviour to which a company subscribes in order to make its impact on society positive and productive. The production and selling of goods and services, business ethics, environmental practices, recruitment and employment conditions, approach to human rights, and investment in the community are examples of such an impact.

There is then 'Corporate Community Investment' which, alongside mechanisms for developing and measuring business standards, is a vital tool of corporate social responsibility. It involves a practical set of programmes and processes which enable companies to bring the skills and time of their employees to areas of community need, along with other resources such as donated goods and services, matched giving, and use of premises. This is an important means by which companies can reach, as well as engage, employees—but is one element of corporate citizenship and secondary to its core business activities.

A Strategy One/Edelman attitude survey of elites in Europe and the US in 2002 recognized these distinctions. On average 64 per cent of elites felt corporate responsibility was about ethics, whereas only 12 per cent defined it as corporate philanthropy and around 20 per cent said it was both.

Business engages in corporate social responsibility in four spheres of influence. The first is at the workplace, which is directly under the control of the company. It does so in terms of standards, quality, procedures, emissions, and management of waste. The second is in the marketplace through distribution, marketing and consumer standards, supply chains, and business relationships. The third is in communities affected by production and distribution. The fourth is in the realm of public policy where business can bring its influence openly on institutions, public sector regulators, and the social infrastructure such as education and transport systems.

In an initiative taken by the World Economic Forum with the IBLF and published as a report (2002) the dimensions of corporate citizenship were outlined as:

- good corporate governance and ethics,
- responsibility for people,
- responsibility for environmental impacts, and
- the broader contribution to development.

In our experience corporate responsibility emerges in response to one or a combination of five forces. First, there is the push of *top-down* compliance such as reporting requirements or government regulations which introduce a compulsory approach on top of which good companies will tend to innovate. Many business standards in the industrialized OECD countries were once voluntary and have now become compulsory. Examples include health and safety regulations, minimum wages and working hours.

The second force is the working of markets where customers, employees, or capital markets exert some form of preference, pressure or signal. Until relatively recently market signals were few and far between, and social preferences, unlike price and brand preferences, were slow to emerge and of little quantified significance. Some dramatic changes have occurred due to the ability of alternative opinion formers to exert disproportionate influence through the use of electronic communication, and the shifting patterns of influence on social issues.

Thirdly, there is 'reputation pull'—where companies are motivated to behave well to promote and safeguard their reputation, or ability to attract investment. At a time when poor standards are quickly discovered by the electronic media and activists, and good practices contribute to good business reputation, this force has become particularly strong.

Fourthly, there is ethics, either in the form of the institutionalized values of business founders and leaders, codes of practice, or individual judgements. These have also become more important as issues of bribery and corruption have taken a higher profile and regulations within OECD countries have toughened sanctions, and gained further momentum following the 11 September terrorist attacks in the US which resulted in a clampdown on money laundering and an emphasis on 'know your customer' financial practices.

Fifthly, there is the impact of shock and crisis, where there is a scandal, revelation, disaster, or loud and embarrassing protest. The accusations of 'sleaze and corporate greed' that underlie some of the scandals of 2002 have many hallmarks of shock, and there may be unforeseen consequences from regulators, institutional investors, shareholder groups, and activists. These factors mutate into issues of corporate risk—either legal risk or what is emerging as 'moral risk'. Legal risk entails the adverse consequences for the company or its officers arising from non-compliance with the law, and may extend into environmental liabilities, asbestos risks, class actions on diversity, and so forth. Moral risk is more reputational, but can exert intense demands on management attention and damage goodwill even though legal action may not be involved—as will often be the case in relation to complicity in human rights abuses, questionable marketing practices, and aggrieved communities.

13.3   CORPORATE RESPONSIBILITY AND CROSS-BORDER BUSINESS CULTURES

As a practitioner, I have always been concerned about the 'imperious' tendencies of promoting corporate responsibility in an international setting. Is this 'political correctness' on a grand scale, or even protectionism in the use of a tactic to keep newly industrializing cultures out of the 'club'? All too often those in the CSR 'industry' appear quick to criticize companies when they lack the management trimmings of corporate responsibility posts, policies, budgets, and programmes.

The international nature of the operations of business in trade, investment, and production brings a more complex dimension to business ethics and corporate responsibility in both the cultural aspect of doing business in environments with different norms and values, and in diversity of employees and stakeholders. While, until recently, some companies would argue that they should 'respect' local values even if these are more tolerant of low standards and corruption, the prevailing ethos of the leading multinational enterprises and international institutions including the OECD and UN is that standards should be universal. This is not without dilemmas in operating in different cultures, not least where preference is given to relationships along family, tribal, ethnic, and community lines.

There is increasingly a feeling among some more progressive business leaders, which I strongly share, that the key to this is diversity and respect for diversity. This means recognition of and respect for ethnic and gender diversity, and ensuring that it is reflected in employment and all business relationships, including efforts to ensure that management and governance structures better reflect the composition of the world and communities in which a company does business. It also implies commitment to trust that transcends culture and nationality. It means willingness to collaborate outside ones own national business 'clique', whereas there is a counter-force which appears to press managers to stick with their own culture and nationality and familiar business organization and practices.

Through this approach, which will result in a more diverse base of employee and business relationships, the cultural dimension can be understood, integrated, and celebrated, and the debate on values and ethics broadened without compromising commitment to a universal standard. These companies will be far more successful at international business by having a mind-set that is aligned to the international nature of their economic performance.

There are some companies such as Unilever and Schlumberger, that have achieved some success, but many companies fail in this respect, and their confusion and dilemmas on questions of values and culture will remain with them as they do business in a multinational and multicultural context. For example, many companies and managers operating in Muslim countries and with Muslim employees, found themselves at a serious loss to understand many of the issues raised between Islam and the West in the wake of the 11 September terrorist attacks. This may not have been so difficult and confusing had there been a greater commitment to diversity and a better integration of understanding of cross-cultural issues in the company at all levels.

Business culture and definitions of corporate responsibility must always take account of the local context. In many parts of Asia the role of enterprises has long had a social objective—not least in the times of state communism—which is now subject to change and traumatic restructuring. In most parts of Asia, bonds of family and friendship in economic relations generally count for far more than in the developed Western world where the professionalization of business, the separation of ownership, and control and impact of mobility have diminished the significance of bonds of friendship and community. Similarly, courtesy and respect for age, wisdom, leadership, neighbours, and customs throughout Asia are still striking in comparison to those in the West.

It may therefore be seen as curious as to why business practices in Asia are coming under such close scrutiny from investors, business partners, consumers, the media, and the public in the industrialized West. Asian leaders sometimes see some 'double standards' being preached by Western lawyers from places whose own industrial revolutions and heritage of practices, including questionable business standards, were dominant for more than a century.

Companies that address diversity, transparency, and commitment to universal standards in human relations, health, safety, and the environment will be in a stronger position to manage the cultural dimension of corporate responsibility in our globalizing world.

13.4 NEW DRIVERS OF CORPORATE RESPONSIBILITY

The corporate responsibility movement at the current time is emerging as several drivers impact upon these five forces I have identified *viz.* compliance, reputation, market signals, ethics, and the impact of shocks. In my view there are five critical drivers at present for corporate responsibility responses from the business community.

13.4.1 Changing Patterns of Public Trust

Public distrust of corporations and institutions is now at high levels around the world and pre-dated the scandals of 2002. Many of the campaigns against bad corporate behaviour are run by NGOs. In another Strategy One survey for Edelman Global Communications of 'global elites' in the US, Europe, and Asia conducted in June 2000, interviewees were asked who could best be trusted on key issues such as environment, human rights, and health. Consistently, between 50 per cent and 60 per cent trusted NGOs on these issues, compared with under 10 per cent trusting corporations, around 15 per cent trusting governments and around 10 per cent trusting the media. As NGOs are often those voicing concerns about corporate behaviour, it indicates a significant distrust of corporations by opinion leaders.

An update on the survey in July 2002 following the various corporate scandals in the US showed a deteriorating position in terms of trust in business. Elites in Europe and the USA seemed to expect business to deploy questionable ethics: to quote the StrategyOne/Edelman survey 'elites assume shady corporate behaviour behind closed doors'. Over two-thirds of elites perceived the integrity and behaviour of CEOs as being a serious problem, and less than a third had confidence that business could resolve these problems. Trust in professional firms, including accountants, lawyers, and consultants appears to have hit an all time low in Europe and America—with less than a third of the elites trusting these advisers.

A global public attitude survey on 'Corporate Social Responsibility' conducted by Environics International of Canada in association with the IBLF and the Conference Board of the USA in 1999 polled 25,000 people in twenty-three countries on six continents in the Americas, Europe, Africa, and Asia. Its findings indicated that public expectations of the social responsibilities of large companies were both high and universal. Seventy-nine per cent of respondents felt that large companies should be held 'completely responsible' for protecting the health and safety of workers, 73 per cent for protecting the environment and 72 per cent for avoiding child labour. In all countries a majority of people felt that companies should set higher ethical standards and should help build a better society for all, or should operate somewhere between this and strictly making a profit. In the home countries of the major multinational enterprises (US, Britain, Japan, and Germany) two-thirds of the sample put ethical behaviour ahead of profits and employment. In North America, 67 per cent of the sample had considered, or had actually taken (51 per cent), punitive action against companies not seen as socially responsible in the past year with 53 per cent (and 39 per cent) being the figures for Europe, and 38 per cent (and 14 per cent) being the figures for Asia.

There is clear evidence of shifting public attitudes on a global scale and in the media against short-term irresponsible behaviour of companies, and in particular transnational companies and those with high profile brands. Companies are increasingly concerned with the reputational impact of campaigns on employees, the recruitment market, and customers.

Business processes are now perceived by the public as an element of the product or service and the quality mix, and customers require reassurance that harm is not being done. The integration of the supply chain into this process now means that both producers of consumer goods, particularly those with high profile brands, and retailers are developing systems of assurance extensively throughout their value chain, which cannot be avoided. This element of market drivers reached critical mass in our experience at least two or three years ago.

13.4.2   The Corporate Governance Crisis

A range of crises in very recent years have had an impact on corporate behaviour, often due to the globalization of investment and quotations of non-American companies on US securities exchanges. CEO pay has also been a persistent question in recent years with open arguments between activist shareholders and corporate boards on whether such remuneration has been out of line with profits, and whether stock-options, as a major form of payment, have rewarded deal making and short-termism over shareholder value and more solid performance.

For companies listed in the US, reputational pressures are far greater on issues such as discrimination, diversity, and past allegations of corporate abuse which open companies to class action risks. Corporations from Switzerland and Germany have been tarnished and conceded millions in compensation for wartime behaviour in 'Holocaust' bank and insurance accounts, 'Nazi gold', and 'slave labour'.

The discovery that the banking system underpinned financial transfers by terrorists involved in the 11 September attacks initiated long overdue action to clamp down on money laundering, and demanded stronger 'know-your-customer' approaches by financial services. The same events also enabled more rapid progress to be made on the introduction of legislation across OECD countries to outlaw corporate payments for bribery from 2001.

The trail of corporate scandals in 2002 has added momentum to the corporate governance crisis, by reminding everyone that the cancer is as much in the rich advanced world as elsewhere, and unprecedented in its scale of deceit. The UK had tightened disclosure rules following a series of corporate governance scandals and frauds in the 1980s and 1990s including those involving Polly Peck, BCCI, Maxwell, and Barings Bank. In Japan, a whole series of cover-ups of corporate debt and bad loans have characterized the banks, housing institutions, and many major corporations for almost half a decade since the 1990s.

The series of US scandals commenced at the start of 2002 with Enron hiding losses in off balance sheet companies that overstated its profits by $600 m. WorldCom overstated its profits by as much as $3.8bn. After Global Crossing filed for Chapter 11 bankruptcy, it was discovered that they could effectively book revenues when in many cases no money at all changed hands. Adelphia Communications, America's sixth largest cable television operator, faced regulatory and criminal investigations into its accounting. The CEO of the Tyco conglomerate was charged with avoiding $1 m. in New York State sales taxes on purchases of artwork on borrowed funds worth $13 m. The US Securities Exchange Commission SEC filed a civil suit against photocopy giant Xerox for misstating four years' worth of profits, resulting in an overstatement of close to $3bn. Xerox negotiated a settlement with the SEC with regard to the suit and agreed to pay a $10 m. fine and restate four years' worth of trading statements, while neither admitting, nor denying, any wrongdoing. The penalty was the largest ever imposed by the SEC against a publicly traded firm for its accounting misdeeds.

In this atmosphere of corporate distrust, the role of investment banks has also faced increased scrutiny. Analysts were suspected of advising investors to buy stocks they secretly thought were worthless. The rationale for this 'false advice' was that they might then be able to secure highly lucrative investment banking and advisory business from the companies concerned. Merrill Lynch reached a settlement with the New York Attorney General who imposed a $100 m. fine but demanded no admission of guilt.

Confidence in financial reporting was further shaken around the world when the auditors Arthur Andersen reacted to the early Enron disclosures by destroying Enron documents; and in June 2002 the company was found guilty in an obstruction of justice case. These events were to have a major effect on corporate reporting and risk assessment.

It would not be an exaggeration to say that, in addition to any 'ethical shock' and 'political fallout' as suggested by the US President's explicit complaint about rotten apples and intolerable behaviour, there has been a shock of earthquake proportions through Western corporations by the latest scandals. The implications are unclear—but most surely the rigour of corporate reporting and audit will increase. Self-regulation will be severely questioned by regulators, politicians and public. Reputations and trust are severely tarnished by the behaviour of the few. Cynicism about the motivations of business leaders, greed and excess, are widespread.

At a time when many workers, investors and pension owners are reeling from the downgrading of their stock, the post-bubble recession and job insecurity, there had seldom been a time when there was greater hunger for values. Many major companies have initiated reviews of their ethics and governance codes. Willingness to talk openly and confront bribery and corruption has increased. The 'shock theory' of the ratchet-like advancement of corporate governance standards has gained credibility.

13.4.3   The Changing Nature of Activist Politics

Another side of the equation is the increased influence of activist politics across the world and the supercharged capacity of E-enabled activist groups to campaign with massive reach and minimal cost against companies. At a time when mainstream party politics has become increasingly sterile and boring in the West, and the public have become progressively more disillusioned, the trust levels achieved by NGOs have soared ahead of all institutions. This, of course, raises questions of ethics and accountability of these institutions—and some of these have been touched on by Richard Falk in the previous chapter—but it seems to be a fact of life with which business must live.

In the meantime activism—particularly engaging companies with brand names—and its apparent greater responsiveness than many governments, has become the best and easiest political game in town. It can engage young people directly, on their own terms, and with their own preferred technology. With perceived NGO campaign victories in areas such as third world debt, access to medicines in South Africa, halting of all nuclear materials movement in Germany, and the global landmine ban, confidence in what can be achieved in the new politics is riding high. The immense capital embedded in brands has been found to have an Achilles heel its in vulnerability to reputational attack.

The very means being used by companies and financial institutions to integrate financial processes and accelerate globalization—the miracle tools of the

Internet, wireless SMS messaging, and low cost digital technology—are being used with equal speed and effect in the ideas and mobilization market, whether in campaigns to boycott US goods in Saudi Arabia, mobilize UK fuel price protestors, or US sports-shoe boycotts. It was no surprise to my staff on the streets of the Philippines capital Manila in 2000 that the massive 'people's demonstrations' that overthrew the then President were mobilized and co-ordinated using the cheap SMS paging and messaging systems. This is merely the tip of the E-enabled icebergs that stand in the shipping lanes to defy corrupt governments and complacent companies.

13.4.4   The Impact of Anti-Globalization Movements and Global Institutions

Next I turn to consider the perceived inequities and downsides of globalization and international sustainable development challenges that have also fuelled the anti-globalization movement. While early protests against the World Trade Organization (WTO), World Bank and multinational enterprises met with official scepticism and denial, there were changes in the official ethos accepting the shortcoming of globalization. It was sufficient for many to recognize that there has been a 'moral victory' in highlighting concern even if there are vociferous disagreements as to whether the nature or the fact of globalization is at fault. Many more thoughtful critics of globalization have focused on the inequitable nature of trade regulations and formidable barriers to fair trade placed in the way of poor countries, as well as the impact of economic inequalities within countries. The business community is seen, like it or not, as having a key role to play either in 'doing no harm' or in being a positive partner in development.

The UN Secretary General Kofi Annan summarized the position seen from the perspective of the United Nations:

In today's world, the private sector is the dominant engine of growth; the principal creator of value and wealth; the source of the largest financial, technological, and managerial resources. If the private sector does not deliver economic and economic opportunity—equitably and sustainably—around the world, then peace will remain fragile and social justice a distant dream. This is why I call today for a new partnership amongst governments, the private sector and the international community. (United Nations 2000)

The World Bank President James Wolfensohn, in his fourth annual meeting speech entitled 'Coalitions for Change' put partnerships for development at the heart of the agenda for a sound development framework:

Globalization can be more than the unleashed forces of the global market. It can also be the unleashing of our combined effort and expertise to reach global solutions. We need to build coalitions for change. Coalitions with the private sector which will bring investment, create jobs, promote the transfer of technology and skills, and foster social responsibility. Coalitions with civil society and communities to mobilise the kind of grass roots support we have seen behind the debt campaign and to extend it to health, to education for all, to participation, and to poverty reduction. Coalitions with governments to assist them in taking charge of their own development agendas with the participation of their citizens. Coalitions with each other to put an end to the turf battles, the wastage, and the duplication. Coalitions with the religions, with trade unions, and with foundations to benefit our common work. Coalitions of commitment to the seven United Nations pledges on sustainable development; gender; education; infant and child mortality; maternal mortality; reproductive health; and the environment. (Wolfensohn 1999)

The perceived failures of globalization across a world which in 1989 embarked on a mass transition to market economies, the visible evidence of the growing gap between rich and poor both within countries and between countries, and the constantly increasing environmental pressures, are all heightening the pressures on business. The widespread operation of companies and their supply chains in countries with weak and often dysfunctional governments, and where standards, if and where they exist, cannot be enforced effectively or fairly, has added demands on companies that they engage directly in improving labour standards and enforcing human rights. With over fifty countries at risk of conflict, managing challenges in these countries and regions has become a more critical issue. Some good which may have come from the appalling tragedy of the events of 11 September was the rising of the profile of the evil of corruption through the need rapidly to tackle issues of money laundering and bribery.

Many of the examples are well known where there has been significant reputational damage to companies exposed to these risks. The IBLF published, with Amnesty International, 'The Geography of Risk' (2002) which analysed the challenges in countries and industry sectors. A questioning and globally networked media have made company operations and impacts all too transparent. There are massive challenges for companies in tackling health and human development issues.

One of the fundamental problems of addressing ethics and corporate responsibility in an international setting is the existence of many governments that lack the capacity for proper market regulation, let alone the many states which are weak, corrupt, and in a few cases 'failed states' such as Afghanistan and parts of countries engaged in internal conflict and civil war. Companies engaged in such locations—often natural resources companies who have little choice in where to invest—have a compelling reason to engage in collective efforts to promote an enabling environment for corporate citizenship.

13.4.5   Socially Responsible Investment Gains Critical Mass

A further driver has been the critical mass reached in the past two years by the socially responsible investment (SRI) movement which is now a significant influence in asset management. Public companies in Europe and America are now facing systematic institutional investor questions in these areas and increasingly sophisticated if imperfect tools and measures, led by SRI investors and fund managers with significant asset portfolios in the multi billions of dollars. Shareholder activism has thus shifted from the marginal to the mainstream.

In the past five years, supply chains and the emergence of SRI in European and American markets gathered momentum as a driving force. SRI now has widespread and growing concern in the US and Europe (UK, Germany, Netherlands, and Nordic Countries). In 1999, one dollar in every eight under professional management in the US was invested in an SRI fund—a total of $2,160bn., up from more than 80 per cent from $1,185bn. in 1997. In the UK, the top five SRI funds manage over £400bn. Morley Fund Management, the £105bn. investment arm of CGNU, Britain's largest life assurer, now compiles a list of companies which are committed to advancing social and environmental issues. It has developed a 'sustainability matrix' and has specialist sustainability funds with £150 m. under management.

SRI is far less developed in Asia, but could take off if European and US growth rates, underpinned by the global drivers that are now at work, are experienced: Japan has 10 options worth US$1bn. and Australia is developing fast with an A$10bn. market in just two years. In Hong Kong, Taiwan, and Singapore there are small starts with specialist funds. Asian companies now appear in the Dow Jones Sustainability Index—Japan (32), Australia (11), also in Hong Kong and Malaysia, but screening is currently considered weak in that companies are included with poor corporate governance track records. Pressures on corporate governance, ethics, and anti-corruption are escalating in the region, if slow to secure implementation in many countries, and will also drive transparency and reporting.

Looking at how SRI has suddenly become a mainstream driver in Europe, there are four critical trends that underpin and will increase investor activism in Europe. First, UK pension regulations have been changed to give pension trustees for the first time rights to question ethical investment policies and changes in 'stakeholder pensions' leave investors the power to make individual investment decisions. Secondly, insurers now demand social risk analysis. Thirdly, institutions are giving higher profile to these issues—the Paris Bourse requires sustainability reports from 2002, and the European Union has brought out a Green Paper followed by a White Paper addressing the issue and European companies are keen to avoid regulatory action on reporting. Finally, the media, including Dow Jones, have added momentum to reporting on corporate social responsibility and SRI—mainly through the Dow Jones Sustainability Index and the *Financial Times* FTSE4Good launched in July 2000.

Alongside these developments have been the emergence of frameworks and standards for measurement and reporting—which add to the momentum and the ability to develop benchmarking and reporting. These are identified and evaluated in several publications, notably ILO (1997/2000), UN (2000), OECD (2000), EU Commission (2000), and World Economic Forum/IBLF (2002).

13.5 VALUES AND CORPORATE POLICIES—HOW DO COMPANIES RESPOND TO THESE ISSUES ?

Managements of forward-looking companies are responding on a number of levels to these reputational and operational challenges. Although this has become more mainstream, it is not yet widespread amongst international companies, and the good practices should still be considered at the vanguard. Companies, particularly those with public profiles and brand names, are increasingly taking these issues seriously and review practices.

CEOs and Boards are accepting accountability for leadership and responding to rising expectations of universal standards. They are adopting explicit policies for corporate citizenship and integrating these with corporate governance. They are recognizing the important employee audience and promoting employee engagement in social issues and community programmes and ensuring effective employee feedback. External issues are being managed as potential business risks to reputation particularly in the areas of environment, health, and human rights. The supply chain and business partners are seen as legitimate areas of influence for CSR standards, and many companies question their suppliers on these issues which results in massive reach into the small and medium-size company sector around the world.

Policies for corporate social responsibility are being removed from the philanthropy or CSR department 'silo'. There is increasing emphasis on defining benefits and seeking competitive advantage from action. There has been an increase in social audit and social reporting which appears set to increase as a result of other drivers from the investment community, media, and business partners.

As the leading companies have responded to this rapidly over the past four or five years, a ripple effect is emerging of 'leadership companies' in reporting, accountability, social investment, and supply chain specifications. It is now becoming totally standard for suppliers in developing regions such as Southern Europe, Asia, and Latin America to be questioned by downstream customers on their social standards.

Just as there are new risks from emerging social challenges to business, there are competitive opportunities in managing these for good reputational result. The key is to align profitable business strategies and core practices with the effective management of social issues. The sheer brilliance of business when turned to business processes can, with the same visionary leadership, be broadened to these emerging areas of the quality mix.

There is little evidence that meeting business standards in countries with weak governments adds to costs to make production non-viable, even if it adds complexity to management and may, in fact, lead to reduced access to supply chains. Engagement in solving social issues can add to employee and customer motivation and deliver a reputational premium. Many companies are recognizing this and attention is beginning to turn more to the questions of *how* and the management processes that underpin this.

13.6 CURRENT CHALLENGES TO WIDESPREAD DEVELOPMENT OF CORPORATE SOCIAL RESPONSIBILITY AND VALUES

Over the past few years in starting-up and running organizations and projects around the world to promote corporate responsibility in action I have often asked myself why this approach to business is not deeper, wider, and more rapid. If the drivers are at work on these issues, and stakeholders demonstrate approval of businesses and business leaders who show a lead as corporate citizens, and if there is a sound business case, why is it that this is not more widespread? Why do good business leaders sometimes let harm happen? Why wait until the Barbarians are at the gate?

Among OECD governments and many leading companies and institutions, there is a groundswell of recognition that corporate social responsibility is required as a business ethic. But there are many who doubt whether relying on the voluntary principal will produce the result. There are feelings among many concerned about this that there will be too many free-riders, and all too many who subscribe to the principles, and sign up on the numerous declarations now available, but will only do the minimum for a quick 'PR effect'. The tension is ever constant amongst the stakeholders around the UN Global Compact, the doubters within NGOs who are advocating partnerships, and middle-of-the-road politicians who see corporate responsibility as a middle route to industrial social harmony. The current climate of distrust of business and business leaders motives viewed in mid-2002 just adds momentum to this drift.

It is widely recognized that the voluntary principal is the only valid formula in places where social infrastructure and business frameworks are weak—such as in many emerging and developing economies who simply cannot regulate effectively. It is recognized that enthusiasm and enterprise produces more creative results than box-ticking and minimum compliance. There are those who feel passionately that the answer is to legislate for transparency and then let activists and stakeholders drive the change and compliance in the pursuit of 'win-win' initiatives which contribute to profitability and sustainability—and there is much in this more market orientated model.

Lack of understanding of issues of corporate responsibility and internationalization, which are seldom addressed in formal business education or management development, result in a *laissez-faire* attitude to it in management practice. The involvement of top managers in high profile sponsored social events—the 'charity event' syndrome—sometimes results in the categorization of serious corporate citizenship action as 'social agenda'. Top managers are sometimes simply ignorant of the issues.

There are examples of companies now integrating understanding of corporate responsibility into management development as well as management appraisal. BP, Standard Chartered Bank, Nestlé, and Shell are some of the best known of these. The IBLF 'Insight' programme and the joint 'ENGAGE' programme between IBLF and Business in the Community in the UK deliver a vital experiential learning approach to management and employee development through discovery and community engagement.

The professionalization of corporate social responsibility in the hands of the new 'CSR-Professionals' is not without its risks. It can result in a programme-driven approach focused on projects undertaken in a corporate 'silo', or as corporate philanthropy initiatives. At the end of the day, there is no substitute for driving corporate responsibility through the bloodstream of general managers. Corporate responsibility must be addressed by leaders as a mainstream management and business issue, with incentives in place, and *not* as a project—through core business practices rather than philanthropy. In implementing this within business processes the communications agenda must be addressed—leadership entails reviewing how and how far policies and results are to be communicated and reported.

All engaged in the promotion of corporate responsibility need to avoid becoming lost in a jungle of political correctness that insists on perfect practices in a profoundly imperfect world. We should see corporate responsibility as a journey where continuous progress should be expected and made towards sustainability goals, and engaging stakeholders in dialogue. It would also be refreshing to see demands for accountability and transparency be made with equal consistency across all sectors including public sector and such critics of business as NGOs. It should not be reserved just for private enterprise that, it can be argued, tests itself against consumer preference constantly as well as the growing rigour of audit.

Partnership is a critical mode for business to engage in the broader societal issues to ensure legitimacy, effectiveness, and sustainability, which requires development of leadership skills which can be applied to partnership working and collaboration. Companies that pursue collaboration and networking in their business models with suppliers, business partners, and institutions in their home countries and internationally, yet want to 'do their own thing' in corporate social responsibility, to maintain control and assert national and bilateral interests, will not make an impact. It will demonstrate that they take it less seriously than their core business.

Some companies lack the trigger due to less proximity to consumer markets, or lack of pressure from regulators, investors or in their supply chain, or lack of operations in countries and communities where social challenges are significant. However, the number immune from pressures is decreasing as public awareness increases and benefits of values-driven leadership become clearer. There are dangers in suggesting there is such a thing as a single 'business case' for corporate responsibility as it varies with type of company, exposure, sector, market, and location. One size simply does not fit all, any more than what is good for Anglo-Saxon companies is good for others where relationships with governments, civil society, and business organizations are different.

Diversity and acceptance of the need to embrace within business and its management, the people and cultures of those places where it does business, will provide essential foundations for corporate citizenship. Not addressing this challenge will prevent a company from acting with corporate responsibility.

In my experience, the main hurdles tend to lie in the vision and leadership style of top business executives. You simply cannot delegate leadership in values and you can expect from managers what reflects your own style. Those who see their role as above all this, who take a narrow or short-term view and who are motivated more by self-interest, or even greed, are less likely to engage in long-term visionary practice.

The demands from analysts and others for constant stock appreciation and quarterly returns can perpetuate short-termism. Successful results and competitive performance are necessary for survival, but the obsession with a narrow concept of short-term economic value will always get in the way of progress in sustainability. We could all heed the words of Albert Einstein who said '*not everything that can be counted counts, and not everything that counts can be counted*'.

REFERENCES

Environics International, International Business Leaders Forum and the Conference Board of USA (1999), *The Millennium Poll on Corporate Social Responsibility* (Toronto: Environics International Ltd.).

European Commission (Green Paper 2001, White Paper 2002), *Promoting a European Framework for Corporate Social Responsibility* (Brussels: European Commission).

International Labor Organization (1997/2000), *Tripartite Declaration of Principles Concerning Multinational Enterprises & Social Policy* (Geneva: ILO).

Nelson, Jane (2002), *Building Partnerships*, United Nations/International Business Leaders Forum, June 2002 (New York: United Nations). Available at http://www.un.org/Pubs/whatsnew/e02088.htm or http://www.csrforum.org/csr/csrwebassist.nsf/content/f1d2a3a415.html

Organization for Economic Co-operation and Development (2000), *Guidelines for Multinational Enterprises* (Paris: OECD).

Strategy One/Edelman (2000), Opinion leader survey privately published for clients.

—— (2002), Opinion leader survey privately published for clients.

United Nations (1974), *The Impact of Multinational Corporations on Development and International Relations* (New York: UN).

—— (2000), *The Global Compact*. Speech by Kofi Annan, UN General Secretary, at the launch at the UN New York, 26 July 2000. (New York: UN).

US–UK Voluntary Principles on Security and Human Rights (December 2000) www.iblf.org/humanrights See 'Business and Human Rights: A Geography of Corporate Risk', IBLF, January 2002.

Wolfensohn J. (1999), address to World Bank Annual Meeting www.worldbank.org

World Economic Forum/International Business Leaders Forum (2002), *Global Corporate Citizenship: The Leadership Challenge for CEOs and Boards* (Geneva: WEF).

14

Governments and Supranational Agencies: A New Consensus?

GORDON BROWN

14.1 INTRODUCTION

Since the tragic events of September 11th, there is growing agreement that the international community—both national governments and international organizations—must work together to tackle the problems and challenges associated with the globalization of the world economy. None of these is more pressing than to address the causes of poverty and help alleviate the suffering often associated with it. For the developed world has not only come to realize that tackling these problems are central to their long-term national security and peace, but that to do so is a moral imperative, an economic necessity and a social duty.

In the years after 1945, visionaries in the US and elsewhere looked ahead to a new world and built—in their day and for their times—a new world order. In a breathtaking leap of faith into a new era, the international community created not just a new set of international institutions—the International Monetary Fund, the World Bank and the United Nations—and a whole set of new rules for a new international economy, but gave expression to a new public purpose based on high ideals. A generation of leaders of the major economies of the world, which had known the greatest of depressions and the greatest of wars, knew also that just as peace could not be preserved in isolation, prosperity could not be maximized in isolation. What they did for their day and generation was so dramatic that Dean Acheson spoke of that period as akin to being present at the creation (Acheson 1969).

These actions defined a new public purpose characterized by high ideals. It was about more than exchange rates, the mechanics of financial arrangements, or even new institutions. As the US Secretary of the Treasury said at the very start of the opening session of the Bretton Woods Conference—which was to create the architecture for much of post-war international commerce until 1971:[1]

prosperity has no fixed limits, it is not a finite substance to be diminished by division. On the contrary the more of it that other nations enjoy the more each nation will have for itself.... prosperity like peace is indivisible. We cannot afford to have it scattered here or there amongst the fortunate or enjoy it at the expense of others.[2]

In short, prosperity, to be sustained, had to be shared. Practicality and morality were presumed to go hand in hand. George Marshall reaffirmed this in his own historic speech at Harvard. We must fight against 'hunger, poverty, desperation and chaos', he insisted, to secure 'the revival of a working economy in the world [that would] permit the emergence of political and social conditions in which free institutions can exist'.[3]

So the post-war arrangements were founded on the belief that international and publicly sponsored action on a new and wider stage could advance a new and worldwide public purpose of high ideals rooted in social justice. This purpose would seek to achieve both prosperity for all by each co-operating with every other, and the establishment of new international rules of the game that involved a commitment to high levels of growth and employment. In short, the job of every economy was to create jobs for all.

The architects of the new international economic order resolved that the failed policies of *laissez-faire* which resulted in vast inequities and recurring depression from the 1870s to the 1930s would not be repeated. During these years, untrammeled, unregulated market forces had brought great instability and even greater injustice. In the post-war era, it was believed that governments had to work collectively if they were to achieve either social justice or economic stability.

The initiatives and institutions of that era were specifically shaped to the conditions of the time. These were characterized by a world economy of protected national markets, limited capital flows, and fixed exchange rates. And for nearly thirty years the system worked. For the hundreds of millions who enjoyed unparalleled prosperity, Bretton Woods took us a long way. But with hundreds of millions still in poverty in the 1970s—when the first golden age of post-Second World War capitalism came to an end—the hopes and dreams of its architects still had a long way to go.

In this first historic phase of post-war international economic management, nation states spoke unto nation states, with an unprecedented degree of co-operation between separated and still largely insulated economies. The international rules of the game then largely consisted of open current accounts, fixed exchange rates and closed capital accounts, and of collective support when countries ran into balance of payments problems.

But over the next generation that new world, too, became old as the existing order of nation states and collective international action was increasingly bypassed by the growth and eventually the sheer force of international financial flows, successively ending dollar convertibility into gold, the fixed exchange rate system, and post-war Keynesian certainties, and bringing in its wake an outbreak of inflation and then stagflation that spread across the Western world.

The 1980s saw a new consensus emerge, essentially an attempt to return to a *laissez-faire* economic agenda. It focused not on what governments should do, but on what governments should not do and emphasized private pursuits almost to the exclusion of public purpose. Enlightened self-interest gave way to sheer self-interest. Instead of rising to the challenge of applying the high ideals of the post-war world to a new world, and instead of aiming for high levels of employment and prosperity for all, sights were lowered, the vision was narrowed.

The new right consensus focused almost entirely on monetary policy designed to reduce inflation and on ensuring minimal government.

Of course it was, and is, right to say that inflation is costly and, once out of control, it is even more costly to reverse. Macroeconomic stability, based on low inflation and sound fiscal policies, is an absolute precondition of economic success. Indeed, in today's globalizing economy, there is a new premium on economic stability. A nation state relying on investment flows from round the world—and also vulnerable to them—now knows that retribution for getting things wrong is swift and terrible.

To be fair too, the new right wing consensus also understood the importance of liberalizing economies from excessive regulation and bad government. But it easily confused means with ends and said, in effect, that inflation alone, not jobs and growth also, were the principle concerns of government. And it promulgated the notion that all government was bad, that government can't make a difference—at least a positive one—in jobs and growth, and that global markets have to be left entirely to market dogmas, which left little place for the public pursuit of high ideals. The assumption that by liberalizing, deregulating, privatizing, and simply getting prices right growth and employment would inevitably follow proved inadequate to meet the emerging challenges of globalization in, for example, South-East Asia where public investment played a catalytic role in securing growth. And this new right consensus could not endure: by the 1990s it was clear that it did not make sense for a world of open not closed markets and of global not national capital flows.

14.2 THE NEED FOR A NEW GLOBAL CONSENSUS

So now we need a new paradigm which recognizes our increased global interdependence, and rejuvenates the earlier notion that an acceptable and sustainable international regime requires a moral underpinning. Some critics identify the issue as whether we should have globalization or not. But, in fact, we believe the issue is whether we manage globalization well or badly, fairly or unfairly. And we have a choice.

Just as in any national economy economic integration can bring stability or instability, prosperity or stagnation, the inclusion of people or their exclusion, so too in the global economy. Managed badly, globalization could leave—indeed has left—whole economies and millions of people in the developing world marginalized, and can be accompanied by a widening gap in the distribution of income within some countries (Dollar and Collier 2001). But managed wisely, globalization can and will lift millions out of poverty, and become the high road to a just and inclusive global economy.

Some are suspicious of the idea of this growing interdependence, but the opening up of the economic world allows us not just to break down old economic barriers that have hampered the diffusion of prosperity but to break through old ideological barriers that have prevented the development of strong, cohesive societies. What we believe to be crucial is that, whatever our concerns about the sheer scale of the challenge of globalization, we must not retreat into the outdated protectionism and isolationism, just as we must not recycle the old laissez-faire doctrine that says there is nothing that can be done.

In the last fifty years no country has lifted itself out of poverty without participating in the global economy. This being so, it is our belief that the richer nations of the world can best help their poorer counterparts not by opting out or by cutting co-operation across the world but by strengthening that co-operation, modernizing international rules, and reforming the institutions of economic co-operation to meet the new challenges.

So what is the way forward? While there are extreme views that cannot—and never should—be accommodated, the last few years have seen increasing agreement about the next steps. Thirty years ago, twenty years ago, perhaps even ten years ago, the divisions between pro- and anti-globalization campaigners would have been so fundamental that no meeting of minds would have been possible. But today, in the first years of the new millennium, many people who are wrongly labelled 'anti-globalization campaigners' would also acknowledge:

- the importance of markets;
- the pivotal role of private capital; and
- that while the unfettered power of any vested interest anywhere is unacceptable, private companies and private—not just public—investments are crucial to making global economic development work in the interests of the excluded.

In short, we need a middle way between government doing everything and government doing nothing. In the 1930s, Franklin Roosevelt found a new way for a national economy—securing the benefits of the market while taming its excesses. Can we find a new way for the challenge we now confront on the global stage?

The issue is not one of either markets or government, but how markets and government can best work together—a kind of 'alliance capitalism' (Dunning 1997). And the way forward for the new global economy is not to retreat from globalization—into either protectionism or old national controls or a failed laissez-faire. It is to ensure global markets can work in the public interest. And transparency in policy making is one way to develop the informed and educated markets we need.

Our aim must be to create and sustain an international financial system for the twenty-first century that recognizes the new realities—open not sheltered economies, international not national capital markets, global not local competition. It must be one that captures the full benefits of global markets and capital flows, minimizes the risk of disruption, maximizes opportunity for all, and lifts up the most vulnerable—in short, the restoration in the international economy of public purpose and high ideals. Our predecessors did this for the post-war world of distinct national economies drawing closer together; now we must do it for the post-national economy, where economically no nation is an island. In a world where the new frontier is no frontiers, we must rediscover the public purpose and high ideals of 1945 through a new deal for global prosperity (HM Treasury 2002).

A strategy for prosperity requires us to both combine policies for economic success and social justice and tackle the causes of poverty. In September 2000, at a UN Millennium Summit, it was agreed by those present, which represented not just governments of countries but international organizations and non-governmental organizations, to sign up to the historic shared task of setting and meeting eight millennium development goals, including:

- that by 2015, instead of 110 million denied primary education, every child has the chance of schooling;
- that by 2015, instead of 7 million avoidable deaths each year, child mortality is reduced by two-thirds; and
- that instead of 1 billion living in absolute poverty, poverty is halved by 2015 on the way to its ultimate removal (UN 2001).[4]

But to will these historic and shared ends it is necessary for the international community to work together to will the means. For this to be done, a new approach is needed to poverty relief and development that both refocuses development aid—treating it as investment for the future—and better integrates the poorer nations into the global economy.

This new deal must be grounded in the moral and social as well as the economic imperatives of the new global economic system. This in turn must be based on the fundamental proposition that there must be both new opportunities for, and new responsibilities accepted by, developed and developing countries alike. It should seek to build the economic foundations for a virtuous circle of debt relief, poverty reduction, and sustainable development and to ensure that the world's poor can earn a fair share in the benefits of global prosperity.

America's post-Second World War achievement, in what we now call the Marshall Plan, should be our inspiration in this post-Cold War world—not just for the reconstruction of Afghanistan but for the entire developing world. The plan proposed by the US Secretary of State George Marshall and instituted in 1948 transferred 1 per cent of national income every year, for four years, from America to Europe (in total the equivalent in today's prices of $75 billion). This was not as an act of charity but a frank recognition that to achieve prosperity would require new public purpose and international co-operation on a massive scale. The post-war generation of leaders saw the moral, social, political, and economic imperatives of a comprehensive plan that went beyond temporary palliatives to wholesale economic and social reconstruction and transformation. They sought a world order that had, as its ambition, opportunity and prosperity not just for some, but for all.

Today's global new deal is being constructed in new times but is based on the same enduring values. As with its predecessors, it recognizes that national safety, social justice, and global reconstruction are inextricably linked, and that a new global social and economic order must be grounded in both rights and responsibilities accepted by all. And, like our predecessors, we must call on the poorest countries themselves to rise to the challenge.

We suggest that there are four building blocks of this global new deal. The first is an improvement in the terms on which the poorest countries participate in the global economy and actively increasing their capacity to do so. This requires a new and clearly identified set of rules of the game in codes and standards that all countries—rich and poor—can sign up to. The second building block is the adoption by the international business community of high corporate standards for engagement as reliable and consistent partners in the development process. This we believe is necessary to back up a code of corporate standards with support for the creation, in developing countries, of investment fora between public and private sectors. The third building block is the moving forward and consolidation of the great progress made at Doha at the last World Trade Organization (WTO) meeting by the swift adoption of an improved trade regime essential for developing countries' participation on fair terms in the world economy.

Stability, investment, and trade are the main long-term drivers of global prosperity, but not all will benefit without a fourth building block, namely a substantial transfer of additional resources from the richest to the poorest countries in the form of investment for development. Here the focus should not be on aid to compensate the poor for their poverty, but on investment that builds new capacity to compete and addresses the long-term causes of poverty.

So by each meeting our obligations to each other, all countries, rich and poor, can share in the benefits of this new global economy. For the richest countries this means new responsibilities—including opening up markets, reforming international institutions and transferring resources to developing countries to help reduce poverty—but also new opportunities from increased trade and a globalization that works in the public interest. For the poorest countries, the new responsibilities include the pursuance of transparent, corruption-free policies for stability and the attraction of private investment—which, in turn, will offer new opportunities through access to increased trade and investment, supported by a transfer of resources from rich to poor.

Let us now briefly discuss each of these building blocks in turn.

14.2.1   Rules of the Game for the Global Economy

The first building block is to improve the terms on which the poorest countries participate in the global economy and actively increasing their capacity to do so. In a world of ever more rapid financial flows, developing countries who need financial assistance can be, at the same time, particularly vulnerable to the judgments and instabilities of global markets (World Bank 2002*b*). Business behaviour clearly shows that firms are most likely to invest in environments which are stable, and least likely to stay in environments which are, or become, unstable (UNCTAD 1998). And we also know that in unstable economies, poverty rises. So for every country, rich or poor, macroeconomic stability is not an option, but an essential precondition of economic success and the fight against poverty.

It is in the interests of stability, and of preventing crises in developing and emerging market countries, that a new rules-based system is being sought;

and that such a system should incorporate a reformed system of economic government under which each country adopts agreed codes and standards for fiscal and monetary policy and for corporate governance. Clear and transparent procedures in economic decisions—for example, presenting a full factual picture of the country's debt position and the health of the financial sectors—and a willingness to be monitored for them are also an imperative of the new global economy. These would improve stability, deter corruption, provide to markets a flow of specific country-by-country information that would engender greater investor confidence, and reduce the problem of contagion. Operating such codes can also support countries along the way to liberalization of their capital markets—and, in so doing, offer them a route map to avoid destabilizing and speculative inflows.

The adoption of codes and standards is not, as some globalization protestors have argued, a modern version of imperialism. It is a route to fairness, a means by which the public interest triumphs over a crude *laissez-faire* which would penalize all countries for the mistakes of some. It is an important means by which we reduce the likelihood of crises and secure growth and prosperity. And just as we believe that—over time—the implementation of codes and standards should be a condition for IMF and World Bank support, so too we would aver that the international community should offer direct assistance and transitional help to support the early implementation of such codes.

Our capacity to prevent crises is enhanced not just by the operation of codes and standards but also by rigorous surveillance and effective international early warning procedures. Over recent years we have seen greater openness in publishing Article IV assessments and their press notices, and have established the Article IV process at the centre of monitoring of codes and standards. The new architecture must involve an enhanced role and authority for the IMF monitoring and reporting on the operation of codes and standards, with the IMF's surveillance and monitoring functions independent of the intergovernmental decisions about financial support for crisis resolution. The independent evaluation office has been established to provide an independent assessment of the IMF's work, but we must do more to improve the accountability of the IMF and ensure developing countries play a more effective role in the governance and policy making of international institutions.

Where governments discharge their responsibilities for transparency and subject themselves to surveillance, the case for commensurately increased responsibilities by the private sector is strengthened. Such responsibilities should include a willingness to participate in an ongoing dialogue with their host countries to identify problems early and develop co-operative solutions for restoring stability. Moreover, where crises do occur, better crisis resolution procedures should involve private creditors, with improved arrangements for the use of standstills and more effective international bankruptcy procedures.

So with codes and standards as the foundation, and more effective systems for surveillance built upon them, there is a real opportunity now to move onto a new paradigm where systems are in place that diminish the likelihood of crises, provide earlier awareness as difficulties arise and allow more measured orderly responses when crises have to be resolved.

14.2.2 Investment

But stability is only the precondition for growth and development. To ensure that such growth and development are socially acceptable and sustainable, rich and poor countries must work together not just to put in place stable economic foundations, but to promote and raise domestic and foreign investment, and find better ways for public and private sectors to work together in raising investment levels.

In the last decade, foreign direct investment (FDI) flows across national boundaries—including to, and between, developing countries—increased fivefold from $235 billion in 1990 to $1,150 billion in 2000 (UN 2001). And there is much evidence to suggest that such investment can be, and indeed has been, an important driver for growth and development generating higher productivity, employment and wealth, and transferring knowledge, skills, and technology (De Mello 1997; Borensztein et al. 1998; Balasubramanyam et al. 1996; Blomstrom and Persson 1983).

But the poorest and least developed countries suffer a double handicap. FDI is too low, with investment per head in developing countries just $35 compared with $805 in the higher income countries. In sub-Saharan Africa FDI is even lower at $12 per person (World Bank 2002a). In addition, domestically generated savings and investment are low with the savings that do exist often leaving the country (Collier, Hoeffler, and Pattillo 1999).

To encourage greater investment, developing countries must work to establish a more favourable business environment. Already the poverty reduction strategies which replaced the old structural adjustment policies have correctly highlighted the importance of investment in infrastructure, sound legal processes that deter corruption and the creation of an educated and healthy workforce.[5] Recent macroeconomic and micro-management reforms in Mozambique, for example, have brought a tenfold increase in foreign direct investment since 1994 (World Development Indicators 2001).

As good practice emerges, the lessons learned from country-by-country experiences of development can be applied region-by-region. One way forward may be for joint investment fora which bring public and private sectors together, to examine the current barriers to investment, and discuss, in the light of regional conditions, how developing countries can secure higher levels of business investment and take the first steps in the international marketplace through intra-regional trade.

One concern of those who campaign against globalization is that developing countries competing for FDI are drawn into a 'race to the bottom'—a downward spiral of poor labour, environmental, and regulatory standards (Hertz 2001; Klein 2001). It is important that companies and governments recognize the distinction between a strong market achieved by competition and a distorted market achieved by anti-competitive behaviour. And where multi-national enterprises (MNEs) are unaccountable across borders—and sometimes appear more powerful than the developing countries in which they operate—companies and governments must do more to restore the right balance, be socially responsible, increase stakeholder awareness and achieve cross-border corporate accountability.

There are already agreed international standards of best practice for MNEs drawn up by the OECD—to which thirty-three countries have already signed up (OECD 2001)—and we must continue to examine how these are being implemented. At the same time, the demand from consumers and shareholders for the best socially responsible business practices to be implemented is growing. Robert Davies has taken up some of these issues in the previous chapter in this volume.

Building on these corporate standards, on that of the Global Compact—introduced by Kofi Annan in 1999—and on the Global Reporting Initiative—through which 100 companies already report their activities—we believe that MNEs should assess and make public to all communities in which they operate information on their economic and social impact in developing countries.[6]

14.2.3　Trade

The third building block is progress on trade liberalization. In the last forty years those developing countries which have managed to be more open and trade more in the world economy have seen faster growth rates than those which have remained closed. From the 1970s to the late 1990s, developing countries that were able to pursue growth through trade grew at least twice as fast as those who kept their tariffs high and their doors closed to imports and competition (Dollar and Kray 2001). We must ensure that all countries have the opportunity to reap these benefits.

It has been estimated that full trade liberalization could lift at least 300 million people out of poverty by 2015. Even diminishing protection by 50 per cent in agriculture and in industrial goods and services would increase the world's yearly income by nearly $400 billion: a boost to growth of 1.4 per cent. All countries and regions stand to benefit, with developing countries gaining an estimated $150 billion a year and higher than average increases in GDP growth (Nagarajan 1999).

This is why we believe the WTO agreement in Doha to launch a new trade round with a development agenda—a package of commitments to progress in areas that will lead to major gains for developing countries and the poorest people in these countries—is so important. We further believe that, in the next phase of negotiations, it is necessary to take forward the agreements to open up trade in agriculture, build the capacity of developing countries to participate more effectively in the negotiations, and open up greater access to medicines.

Indeed, all developed countries should follow the EU's lead in offering free access to all but military products from the least developed countries. It has been estimated that if the US, Canada, and Japan alone carried out this undertaking, it would raise the exports of the poorest 49 countries by 11 per cent (IMF/World Bank 2001).

14.2.4 Financing Development

There cannot be a solution to the urgent problems of the poverty that developing countries face—and to the need for public investment as a partner with private investment—without a fourth reform: a substantial increase in development aid to nations most in need and willing to focus on the fight against poverty. By insisting on dissociating aid from the award of contracts, it has been estimated that gains to anti-poverty programmes can be as high as 20 per cent (Jepma 1994). More effective in-country use of aid can secure further resources for anti poverty work; and better collaboration among donors—pooling of budgets, monitoring of their use to achieve economies of scale and hence greater cost effectiveness and targeting of aid—can also enhance the efficiency of aid in diminishing poverty. Together, better allocation, co-ordination and untying by donors could make current aid up to 50 per cent more efficient (HM Treasury/DFID 2002). Most of all, it is important that developed nations move from providing short-term aid just to compensate for poverty to a higher and more sustainable purpose, and that of aid as long-term investment to tackle the causes of poverty by promoting growth.

At the same time, the recipient countries must be prepared to show that the funds they receive are properly and effectively used. They must develop their institutional infrastructure, end corruption, meet their obligations to pursue stability and create the conditions for new investment, realize their commitment to community ownership of their poverty reduction strategies and ensure that resources go effectively and efficiently to fighting poverty including education and health.

In return, developed countries must be prepared to make a special effort to match their commitment to the 2015 Millennium Development Goals with the resources necessary to achieve them. Increased development assistance is essential to match gains from liberalizing trade, raising private investment, and entrenching stability.

Opinion is converging around this idea of a global new deal. In the run-up to the UN Financing for Development Conference at Monterrey, Mexico in March 2002, the European Union agreed to increase the proportion of Europe's wealth going to development assistance from an average of 0.32 per cent to 0.39 per cent, thus generating $7 billion a year more in aid for health, education, and poverty reduction by 2006. At the same time, President George W. Bush announced a substantial increase in resources for development, committing to an additional $10 billion between 2004 and 2006, and an additional $5 billion a year thereafter—a 50 per cent increase in US aid levels.

But we must go further. The Zedillo report recently estimated that the cost of meeting the Millennium Development Goals would be $50 billion a year, including $20 billion for anti-poverty programmes and nearly $10 billion for education (UN 2001). In recent months, proposals have been made for new and innovative ways to meet this funding gap: examples include the Tobin tax, arms tax, an airline fuel tax, IMF special drawing rights. The European Commission is examining the Tobin tax and the UK Government is open to investigating these ideas.

Another proposal which the author has advocated in recent speeches, involves richer countries making a long-term commitment of increased resources for development for, say, thirty years, channelled through an International Development Finance Facility. This Facility would lock in a clear and binding commitment over the longer term for donors. At the same time it would be able to borrow money secured against these commitments in international capital markets in the years to 2015 to meet our target for extra funds. In this way, it has been estimated that $50 billion more could be available each year to the poorest countries in their fight against poverty (HM Treasury 2002). Access to the Trust Fund's resources should mean access to new investment that increases the capacity and long-term potential growth rate of the poorest countries. And for their part, countries must be required to demonstrate clearly that resources are being properly and effectively used. In short, in today's world, every international initiative relies ultimately on approval by national governments and their peoples. And it comes down, in the end, to the duties national governments—especially the richest national governments—recognize and are prepared to discharge.

14.3 CONCLUSIONS

In an increasingly interdependent world, all can benefit if each meets agreed economic, social, and moral obligations for change. First, there is an obligation on the part of developing countries to end corruption, put in place stable economic policies, to invite investment, to meet their commitment to community ownership of their poverty reduction strategies, and to ensure resources go to fighting poverty including education and health.

Second, there is an obligation on the part of the business community to engage with the development challenge and not walk away, including participating in investment forums and playing their part in preventing and resolving economic crises. Third, there is an obligation on the world community as a whole—international institutions—to reform systems to ensure greater transparency and openness, to open up trade and opportunities for faster development, and to focus on priorities that meet the international development targets.

Fourth, there is an obligation on the richest countries to make a substantial and decisive transfer of resources to the poorest—not aid that entrenches dependency but investment that empowers development. For if the international community is to move with the urgency that the scale of today's suffering demands, national governments must each be bold and acknowledge the obligations of the richest parts of the developed world to poorest and least developed parts of the same world.

Finally, there is an obligation on individuals themselves to engage and to hold government and international organizations to account for progress towards the millennium development goals. The four building blocks outlined above can only be achieved if individuals are sympathetic to the actions undertaken by governments and international organizations in pursuit of them. Of course, governments and international organizations themselves play a part in influencing the moral values of individuals and encouraging them to be global citizens, for example through education, regulation, incentives such as tax relief on charitable giving, and generally publicizing the message that all of us are members of the same global community, bound in one vast network of mutuality across all the lines that might otherwise divide citizens of different countries. Unless all participants in the global economy—supranational entities, national governments, firms, civil society, and individuals themselves—fully embrace this message, there is a real danger that the very real benefits of global capitalism as they are now emerging will be swallowed up in political turmoil and social unrest.

The challenge we face, both as individuals and as part of a global village, is immense. But the answer is not to retreat from globalization. Instead we must advance social justice on a global scale, to the benefit of all—and we must do so with more global co-operation not less, and with stronger, not weaker, international institutions. This global new deal can ensure that the world's poor can share fairly in the benefits of prosperity throughout the world and is grounded in the belief that not only do we have inescapable obligations beyond our front doors and garden gates, responsibilities beyond the city wall and duties beyond our national boundaries, but that this generation has it in its power—if it so chooses—to finally free the world from want.

NOTES

This chapter is based on speeches given by the author at the New York Federal Reserve on 16 November 2001 and the National Press Club, Washington, DC, on 17 December 2001.

1. Described e.g. in Winters (1991).
2. H. Morgenthau, opening address at Bretton Woods conference (1944).
3. G. Marshall, address at Harvard University (1947).
4. The Millennium Development Goals were agreed by international organizations and countries participating in the UN Millennium Summit in September 2000. More information can be found in the report by the United Nations Secretary-General, *Road Map towards the Implementation of the United Nations Millennium Declaration*, September 2001.
5. In September 1999, the World Bank Group and the IMF determined that nationally owned participatory poverty reduction strategies should provide the basis of all their concessional lending and debt relief under the enhanced Heavily Indebted Poor Countries (HIPC) Initiative. Poverty Reduction Strategy Papers (PRSPs) are developed by individual countries and submitted to the Bank and Fund Boards. The PRSPs' aims are: to strengthen country ownership of poverty reduction strategies; to broaden the representation of civil society—particularly the poor themselves—in the design of such strategies; to improve co-ordination among development partners; and to focus the analytical, advisory, and financial resources of the international community on achieving results in reducing poverty.

6. The Global Reporting Initiative was established in late 1997 with the mission of developing globally applicable guidelines for reporting on the economic, environmental, and social performance for corporations and, in the longer term, for any business, governmental, or non-governmental organization. The Global Compact, introduced in 1999, aims to encourage and promote good corporate practices in the areas of human rights, labour, and the environment. Participation in the Global Compact makes it incumbent upon businesses to issue a clear statement of support for the Global Compact and its principles and report annually on progress made or lessons learned in implementing the principles. Participants are also encouraged to undertake activities that support broad UN goals such as poverty eradication. (See also Chapter 6 of this volume.)

REFERENCES

Acheson, D. (1969), *Present at the Creation* (New York: W. W. Norton).

Balasubramanyam, V. N., Salisu, M., and Sapsford, D. (1996), 'Foreign Direct Investment and Growth in EP and IS countries', *Economic Journal* 106: 92–105.

Blomstrom, M., and Persson, H. (1983), 'Foreign Investment and Spillover Efficiency in an Underdeveloped Economy: Evidence from the Mexican Manufacturing Industry', *World Development* 14: 493–501.

Borensztein, E., De Gregorio, J., and Lee, J. (1998), 'How Does Foreign Direct Investment Affect Economic Growth?', *Journal of International Economics* 45: 115–35.

Collier, P., Hoeffler, A., and Pattillo, C. (1999), *Flight Capital as a Portfolio Choice* (Washington, DC: World Bank).

De Mello, L. R., Jr. (1997), 'Foreign Direct Investment in Developing Countries and Growth: A Selective Survey', *Journal of Development Studies* 34: 1–34.

Dollar, D. and Collier, P. (2001), *Globalisation, Growth and Poverty: Building an Inclusive World Economy* (Washington, DC: World Bank).

—— and Kray, A. (2001), *Trade, Growth and Poverty* (Washington, DC: World Bank).

Dunning, J. H. (1997), *Alliance Capitalism and Global Business* (London and New York: Routledge).

Hertz, N. (2001), *The Silent Takeover* (London: William Heinemann).

HM Treasury (2002), *Tackling Poverty: A Global New Deal* (London: HM Treasury).

HM Treasury & Department for International Development (2002), *The Case for Aid for the Poorest Countries* (London: HM Treasury).

HMSO (2000), *Eliminating World Poverty: Making Globalisation Work for the Poor*, White Paper on International Development (London: HMSO).

IMF/World Bank (2001), *Market Access for Developing Countries' Exports* (Washington, DC: IMF/World Bank).

Jepma Catrinus, J. (1994), *International Policy Co-ordination and Untying of Aid* (OECD Development Centre Studies).

Klein, Naomi (2000), *No Logo* (London: Flamingo).

Nigel Nagarajan (1999), 'The Millennium Round: An Economic Appraisal', *European Commission Economic Paper 139* (Brussels: European Commission).

OECD (2001), *OECD Guidelines for Multinational Enterprises—Global Instruments for Corporate Responsibility—Annual Report 2001* (Paris, OECD).

UNCTAD (1998), *World Investment Report—Trends and Determinants* (New York and Geneva: UN).

—— (2001), *World Investment Report—Promoting Linkages* (New York and Geneva: UN).

United Nations Secretary General (2001), *Road Map towards the Implementation of the United Nations Millennium Development Goals* (New York and Geneva: UN).

Winters, L. A. (1992), *International Economics*, 4th edn. (London and New York: Routledge).

—— (2001), *World Bank Development Indicators* (Washington, DC: World Bank).

——(2002*a*), *Impact of Recent Events on Low- and Middle-Income Countries: Response of the World Bank Group* (Washington, DC: World Bank).

—— (2002*b*), *Building Institutions for Markets* (New York: Oxford University Press).

Zedillo, E. et al. (2001), *Report of the High Level Panel on Financing for Development* (New York and Geneva: UN).

15

Global Social Justice: The Moral Responsibilities of the Rich to the Poor

SHIRLEY WILLIAMS

15.1 INTRODUCTION

Globalization has become a fashionable term, indispensable to academics trying to attract attention or politicians trying to sound thoughtful. It is a term used to describe a number of contemporary phenomena: the closely associated and converging technological transformations of telecommunications, the Internet, and television; the revolution in transport represented by supersonic flight, space travel, and high-speed trains; the advances in the life sciences and in machine intelligence among others. If I had to describe globalization in one word, I would resort to a variant on E. M. Forster's plea in *A Passage to India*, 'Only connect' (Forster 1924). I would call it interconnectedness.

Globalization reaches beyond scientific and technological progress to changes in tastes and attitudes. Consumers are becoming eclectic, ranging among the exotic cuisines, clothes, and cultural artefacts now available to them, providing they have the means to indulge their tastes. The treasure house is global—a veritable Ali Baba's cave.

'The means to indulge their tastes', fast efficient transport and global communications have enabled consumers to choose from a huge range of products, and in the world's richer countries these consumers include, for products like food, clothes, and films, a majority of the population. That is the big difference from the nineteenth-century global market fashioned by free trade and the gold standard. That market was global too, and there were few barriers to its operation. But most of the products it offered were accessible only to the relatively wealthy.

Today, the Indian and Chinese restaurants in every middle-size European city cater to a large sector of the population. So do the supermarkets, ignoring seasons by their network of deliveries from everywhere, beans from Kenya, wine from Chile, grapes from South Africa. While taste for cultural products remains more circumscribed because of language and custom, here too music, dance, and film reveal the global influences on them.

As Ralf Dahrendorf (2000) has observed, an identifiable and rather homogeneous global elite has emerged. It is composed of individuals in occupations that largely disregard national boundaries—occupations like banking, financial services, international law, multinational business. These men and women attend a limited and prestigious group of Universities, if not as undergraduates then as graduates, e.g. Harvard, MIT, Stanford, the University of California, London, the Sorbonne, Oxford, and Cambridge, to mention the most obvious ones. They wear similar clothes and shoes. They are computer-literate, and travel with their laptops. They often know each other. They swap notes on the same four and five star hotels, use the same airlines, and share similar enlightened secular views. They value their freedom, and at the same time regard risk as 'chance and opportunity, not a threat to security' (Dahrendorf 2000). They are influenced by the received wisdom of the powerful, in particular the so-called Washington (neoliberal) consensus.

The global elite is complemented by 'global celebs', professional footballers, golfers, pop singers and instrumentalists, models and film stars, whose pictures and images are projected world-wide, and who enjoy celebrity, albeit short-lived, everywhere they go. These are the setters of fashion, and their choices and styles dictate what cohorts of young men and women wear, talk about, and emulate.

Like the globe-trotting intellectual elite, these celebrities are closer to one another than they are to their fellow citizens. In the developing countries, many of those fellow citizens are caught up in globalization because they watch television or listen to transistor radios, but their daily lives are still bounded by local markets and local customs.

Those very constraints, determining the predictable nature of local lives, natural disasters apart, offer a kind of simple security. Many traditional societies have their own moral codes and their own safety nets, based on the strength of the extended family, respect for the old, and shared responsibility for children.

Globalization, by opening up new markets which tempt communities to abandon subsistence agriculture for exportable cash crops, and by creating job opportunities in distant cities and countries, may increase the individual's material well-being, but rarely enhance his or her security. Rural communities may be weakened by the loss of their men to migrant labour. When global markets fail, these communities are painfully vulnerable. Migrant labourers are usually the first to be sacked. But for some, the more enterprising and better educated, globalization offers opportunities that simply did not exist before.

15.2 THE NEED FOR INSTITUTIONAL CHANGE

Institutional changes usually lag behind technological and scientific changes. They may come through the need to remove traditional obstacles to progress, or through fear of the consequences of unregulated scientific and technological change. What matters is the interaction of globalization with existing institutions and power structures. Globalization, like the seas or the weather, is morally neutral and can be harnessed to different ends. How it is used depends upon that interaction. 'The issue', according to Gordon Brown in Chapter 14 of this book, 'is whether we manage globalization well or badly, fairly or unfairly.' The management of globalization has a moral dimension governments often fail to appreciate.

Economists may argue that globalization is a force for good, defined as economic growth. It encourages competition, removes obstacles to trade, stimulates productivity, makes economies more efficient. It is therefore good news for the poor.

But there is a huge flaw in this argument. A pure form of globalization would apply to all the factors of production, capital, land, and labour alike. But of course that doesn't happen. All too frequently, the social and political institutions of the developed rich countries impose limits on their participation in the global economy when it comes to labour. Men and women from the developing parts of the globe are not allowed to move around to maximize their rewards. Nothing is more regulated than the movement of peoples. So the factor of production that the poor have in abundance, namely labour, is controlled, while the factors of production the rich have in abundance, capital and technology, are free to go wherever the returns are highest. Furthermore, attempts to regulate and control the movement of capital are treated by financial markets as reactionary, or even heretical.

Speaking at the United Nations International Conference on Financing for Development, in Monterrey, Mexico on 22 March 2002, the US President, George W. Bush, addressed the importance of human resources. 'The true source of economic progress is the creativity of human beings,' the President declared. 'Nations' most vital resources are found in the minds and skills and enterprise of their citizens.' Formally qualified and skilled men and women are not, however, to be found in abundance in developing countries.

The rich countries are now skimming the labour markets of the world for what they most want—people skilled at the intermediate level of technical and vocational qualifications. The promising computer industries of southern India, Malaysia, and Thailand are being raided by Silicon Valley and Silicon Glen for software engineers and computer programmers, stripping them of their most talented people. Public services in the United States and Britain are, in part, staffed by nurses from the West Indies, doctors from India, and teachers from South Africa, which represents a substantial reverse flow of skilled capital. No one considers whether these poor countries should at least be compensated for the investment they have made in educating and training these people. But the distorted working of a global market regulated for the benefit of the 'haves' rather than the 'have-nots' is not the fault of globalization per se, but of the power structures that direct it.

Adam Smith, in *The Wealth of Nations*, described the benevolent working of an invisible hand, which out of the multiplicity of individual, self-interested choices drew an outcome which maximized the wealth and happiness of the whole community. But Smith lived in eighteenth-century Edinburgh, a well-ordered and enlightened society governed by a shared Presbyterian ethic of honesty, hard work and decent ambition, a society in which the rule of law and obedience to it were well-established.

Furthermore, it was a well-informed community, in which people knew one another and there were not extreme discrepancies of wealth and power. There is no perfect market, but Adam Smith's Edinburgh must have come as close to it as human societies can.

In most markets in practice, asymmetries of power among the participants distort competition. Powerful producers may dominate a market, to the extent of determining prices, as the OPEC oligopoly regularly does. Powerful consumers or buyers can impose terms on producers, as supermarkets do. Lack of information or inadequate information is a substantial factor in distorting markets, and, in many countries, information about certain products is deliberately limited or controlled.

Controlled information, in turn, breeds corruption. Contracts are awarded, not to the most competitive company, but to the one which knows the person awarding the contracts. In some countries, dominated by a limited ruling class or a network of rich families, everything depends not on what you know, but on whom you know.

Transnational corporations well understand that. Among them, there is a gentleman's agreement that in some countries, bribery accompanies business, and there is no point in getting fussed about it.

15.2.1 The Indonesian Example

Let me take two examples of countries whose institutions were inadequately prepared for, and, in consequence, were swamped by, globalization. Indonesia, the world's fourth largest country, seemed well equipped to benefit from globalization. It had a large and fairly well-educated population. It was controlled by a strong government and an even stronger military. It had bountiful natural resources, no threatening neighbours and a distribution of income more equitable than that of most developing countries. Its record in the 1980s and early 1990s was one of rapid growth, rising exports, improving opportunities for young people and an impressive inward movement of foreign capital. Many less well-off Indonesians benefited from the boom elsewhere in South-East Asia, particularly in Malaysia, working in construction and other trades and sending large remittances home.

But Indonesia's financial institutions, notably its banking sector, were too small, inexperienced and unsophisticated to cope with the inflow of capital that followed the liberalization of capital markets, a policy unthinkingly demanded by the international financial institutions and the US Treasury (Stiglitz 2000). Fuelled by the prospect of substantial profits from the East Asian boom, large amounts of speculative capital flowed into the region. The Indonesian banking system proved unable to cope. Some of the weaker banks collapsed.

The IMF, called in to deal with the crisis, insisted on strict monetary and fiscal contraction, despite the absence of high inflation. This policy inevitably led to high interest rates, widespread bankruptcies, and massive unemployment. As part of the policy of fiscal retrenchment, the IMF insisted on the elimination of subsidies for basic foods and fuel. Millions of families were driven into poverty. Foreign investors, including large Western banks, worried about political turmoil, took their money out in droves.

Indonesia, then, was left with a population whose expectations had been inflamed by the South-East Asian boom, and were now dashed by the sudden fall from global grace. As unemployment soared, many Indonesians returned to their villages in the outer islands from the cities, to find their communities occupied by Javanese encouraged to leave the densely populated main island. They found themselves competing for straitened resources. Indonesia's political stability today remains at best uncertain. There have been serious outbreaks of communal and religious violence, notably in Maluku, Kalimantan, and Irian Jaya.

15.2.2   The Russian Example

My second example is Russia. In the immediate aftermath of the collapse of the Soviet Union, Western economic experts emerged with a familiar mantra: liberalization of prices, privatization, and free trade. The trouble was that the former Soviet Union had none of the laws that in Western countries regulate these policies, nor the necessary commercial infrastructure. There was no legal basis for private property, no competition or bankruptcy laws, no independent courts and, once communist rule collapsed, effectively no rule of law.

Their former managers, leaving behind loss-making hulks and unproductive jobs too often stripped all the assets of state-owned companies. New private businesses had no means of recovering debts owed to them, other than by threats or the use of force. In the fight for survival within a drastically declining domestic economy, many businesses and many people went to the wall, especially the old and the rural population. A mafia type of culture emerged as the morality of the new market place. Among its institutional victims were the public services, education and health. Formerly, Soviet citizens had at least enjoyed a modicum of security, a basic but universal health service and a good school system. Now both began to disintegrate.

Western governments, in their short-sighted expediency, had rejected the idea put forward by Grigor Yavlinsky, a prominent Russian politician dedicated to bringing democracy to his country, and Graham Allison, Dean of the John F. Kennedy School at Harvard University of a Marshall Plan for Russia. They, together with others like Kenneth Arrow, the Nobel prize-winning economist, wanted to see a long-term and gradual transition to a free market economy, in which the retention of safety nets and the training of a new generation of civil servants and business leaders would be funded by Western donors (Allison and Yavlinsky 1991).

The proposal was for a new kind of partnership, in which the institutional infrastructure of a market economy, the essential legal and regulatory frameworks, would be constructed *before* market forces were fully unleashed. In the same spirit, the BBC commissioned an ambitious series of broadcasts throughout Russia, under the title 'The Marshall Plan of the Mind', intended to teach people about markets, and to encourage young men and women to learn how to engage with this new business world.

But the moment passed. As described by Joe Stiglitz, then the chief economist of the World Bank, in Chapter 4 of this volume, the macro-economists who believed in imposing their neoliberal doctrines were not persuaded of the need for institutional underpinning of the new market economy. Their arguments prevailed among the decision-makers at the US Treasury and the IMF. The market reforms went ahead on their own.

Politically, the United States and her allies propped up a corrupt and discredited government under President Yeltsin. His administration was, in practice, run by a group of oligarchs who used his authority to make them extremely rich. It was to be years before the institutions needed to establish accountability, transparency and the rule of law began to be put in place. Even now, Russia is more an autocracy than a democracy. President Putin has sweeping decree powers, and uses them to curb the media and exercise direct control over the regions of his vast country.

The market reforms were far from successful, at least initially. Russia is much poorer today than it was in 1990. In the eight years from 1990 to 1998, Russian GNP per head is estimated to have fallen in real terms by an average of 7.2 per cent a year (World Bank 2002), though there was a modest recovery after 1999. Nearly half the population now lives below the poverty line. It is not surprising that many Russians yearn for the old communist regime, despite its terrible record of oppression.

15.3   A MORE HOLISTIC APPROACH TO DEVELOPMENT

Recognition of the interdependence of economic, social, and political reform is only slowly dawning on the international institutions charged with promoting development. 'Good governance' is now seen as a *sine qua non* of the effective use of aid and foreign direct investment alike. As shown, *inter alia*, by recent World Development Reports of the World Bank, these institutions are also now aware that 'good governance' in weak countries requires both the governments concerned and their interlocutors from the developed countries to abide by decent moral standards of public life. In this context, the OECD has drawn up a code of conduct for multinational corporations intended to stop bribery in business conducted with developing nations (OECD 2000). Offers of development aid are increasingly conditional on the practice of good governance by the receiving nation.

This new awareness of social and political factors in development is very welcome, but is still only at an early stage. A few illustrations, in addition to those mentioned by other contributors to this volume (notably Gordon Brown, Hans Küng and Joe Stiglitz), may help to indicate what is going on. Immensely valuable work is being done by the Council of Europe, for example, to train lawyers and judges in human rights, especially in the transition countries of Europe and the former Soviet Union. The Commonwealth Secretariat has arranged training, for instance in policing, by experienced professionals from one Commonwealth country to assist other member states. American Universities run many courses for senior civil servants, politicians, and the military, in particular from the transition countries, to understand their role in democratic societies. The most intensive work of all has been in countries that are candidates to join the European Union, where detailed work on the 'acquis', the body of law and regulation that has to be accepted in total by members, has been undertaken by government officials. But what is provided still falls far short of what is needed.

The rich world's power structure still supports a fundamentally unjust system of global governance. The main institutions of that global governance are the World Bank, the IMF and the World Trade Organization (WTO). The first two reflect the financial and economic power of the United States and the developed Western nations, the so-called G7. In the end, what matters most is the attitude of the US Treasury.

The WTO, while more international in its membership and focus, is, in practice, dominated by the United States and the European Union. True, there are independent panels to resolve trade disputes, but poor countries cannot afford the expensive legal advice and expert consultants needed to draw up their cases. Consequently, even when the case is strong, they tend to lose out.

The last so-called 'trade round', the Uruguay round, reduced tariffs across the board, but left in place substantial protection for textiles and agricultural products in the rich countries, the very areas in which developing countries have a comparative advantage. While talking pieties about the need to reduce world poverty, the European Union has been extraordinarily dilatory in reforming the Common Agricultural Policy, under which European farm exports continue to be subsidized. The alternative of 'stewardship contracts', in which farmers are subsidized to manage and sustain the rural environment, is still only a minor programme.

Soon after delivering similar pieties at the Monterrey conference in Mexico in March 2002, the US President George W. Bush, approved a Farm bill passed by Congress that increased domestic agricultural subsidies by 80 per cent.[1] Among the products to be subsidized more generously are wheat and soya beans, two of the most important exports of Latin America. And this at a time when Argentina is reeling under the effects of a major economic crisis. Truly some Western governments would not shame Machiavelli with the quality of their hypocrisy.

15.4 EXPLOITING DEVELOPING COUNTRIES

International institutions apart, Western governments have been reluctant to move against the plundering of the resources of the third world, and indeed have profited from it. Africa has been plagued by warlords and guerrilla groups trying to seize control of gold fields, diamond mines, and oil. Prolonged and destructive wars have been fought over them. Western governments and corporations have colluded in two ways—by purchasing goods obtained illegally, and by permitting trade in the arms needed to conduct these wars.

The trade in illicit diamonds, often smuggled across unguarded frontiers, is slowly being brought under control by identifying the origin of the gems. Thus legally obtained diamonds from, say, Sierra Leone or Angola, are marked with their country of origin. The diamond trade can play a significant part in stamping out the sale of diamonds by guerrilla groups or by neighbouring governments engaged in smuggling. Parliaments and civil societies alike could usefully hold firms engaged in the diamond trade to account for the sources from which the diamonds come.

This is a good example of the way in which rich and poor countries need to work together if there is to be soundly based development. Botswana is one of the few African countries that has ploughed revenues from the sale of diamonds back into developing its own country. It has invested heavily in schools and health clinics. Until it was hit recently by the AIDS epidemic, its economy had grown by an average of 10 per cent a year between 1980 and 1990, one of the fastest rates in the world, and from 1990 to 1999 it still managed a very respectable average of 4.3 per cent (Europa, 2001).

It must of course be acknowledged that developing countries are all too often the victims of their own rulers as well as being the victims of guerrilla groups or cowboy companies. The examples are legion—Suharto in Indonesia, Mobutu in Zaire (now the Democratic Republic of the Congo), Mugabe in Zimbabwe, Abacha in Nigeria, to name but four. These rulers have sucked resources out of the countries they led, and translated them into their own personal accounts, tucked away in various financial havens. The story of development in badly governed and corrupt countries is all too often the story of the dispossession of their inhabitants.

Western governments, some of whose banks have handled these laundered funds, have been slow to act. Until recently, the Swiss banks insisted on total secrecy. Consequently many dubiously acquired funds were concealed there. But the Swiss authorities have now taken strong action to curb the inflow of such funds. Their banks are sent a warning notice to look out for and report unusual deposits that may be money laundered from the public funds of developing countries. Furthermore, the Swiss authorities have taken active steps to recover such funds. In the case of Nigeria, over a billion dollars have now been returned. Other Western Governments, including that of the United Kingdom, have been reluctant to take action. It has taken concern about the financing of terrorism to compel them to do so and even that stops short of active efforts to track down and recover looted state funds.

If good governance is to be encouraged and supported, as in the case of diamonds, a partnership between developed and developing countries is essential, acting together to prevent such forms of exploitation.

Another example of the need for partnership is the arms trade. As I have pointed out already, the devastating wars of Africa, which have prevented economic and social development in much of that continent, are fought with arms often supplied by Western countries in order to exploit resources then sold to Western countries. It is a lethal trade. On humanitarian grounds if no other, not only must the markets in illegal products be stopped, the arms that fuel the civil wars must be stopped as well.

There has been great reluctance to stop the flow of small arms into Africa, though the European Union initiative, *Everything But Arms*[2] may help. Suppliers that refuse to respect the criteria limiting arms exports to legitimate defence should be blacklisted by Western governments and no further arms should be purchased from them.

As Joe Stiglitz emphasizes in Chapter 4, there is need for a new approach to development; and one which recognizes that economic development is intertwined with political and social transformation. Such an approach should encompass the reconfiguration of traditional institutions without destroying social cohesion. To be successful it also requires the committed co-operation of Western governments and companies as well. Gordon Brown unveils such a plan in his chapter in this volume. *Inter alia*, this would include increased aid, flexible debt relief, transparency in negotiations and in accounting, and codes of conduct for governments and transnational companies alike.

At Monterrey, and subsequently in his speech to the German Bundestag in May 2002, George W. Bush announced an increase in US core development assistance of 50 per cent over the next three years, indicating that aid must be linked to political and legal, as well as economic reforms. The President also spoke about the benefits of free trade, though neither he nor Mr Brown spelled out the obligations of the rich countries to make free trade genuinely reciprocal.

The most imaginative aspect of the original Marshall Plan—designed to help the recovery of Western Europe after the last World War—was not so much to provide aid from the rich to the poor as the co-operative framework within which that aid was administered. This was not a Plan in which the donor dictated the terms, as the IMF and the World Bank have in practice dictated the terms of the structural adjustment programmes and the anti-poverty strategies. The recipient countries monitored one another, for each had an interest in ensuring the funds were well spent. Each recipient country contributed what it could in counterpart aid—sometimes in kind. Each felt involved and committed to the success of the Plan as a whole.

The American administration of that time was keen to encourage European co-operation. Hence it called for each national reconstruction plan to be drawn up within the context of an integrated European plan. Its aspirations were not fully realized. The prerequisites of co-operation were institutionalized in the Organization for European Economic Co-operation (the OEEC). The countries of Western Europe deliberated, argued, and pored over one another's plans (based on the need for dollar imports, the cost met largely from Marshall Aid funds). This intensive multilateral process proved highly effective. Donor and recipients alike were actively and critically engaged in making the best possible use of the available funds (Milward 1984).

The Marshall Plan did not simply emanate from the free market system. It was a deliberate act of policy, driven by recognition of the United States' long-term interests in a strong and united Europe. But there was also a moral dimension, a generosity of spirit and a vision of a continent at last at peace with itself.

The wealthy world today has a similar long-term interest in addressing the huge inequities that deface the world. The selfish interest is obvious. To put it starkly, the poor will not quietly die. Television presents them every day with images of unbelievable prosperity, food, water, shelter, cars, and jobs. Many will take to their boots or their boats to find a better life. The 'wretched of the earth' are already on the move. Unless the rich world faces up to its responsibility to bring about a fairer distribution of the world's wealth, there will be many more moving.

Only two things can stop them—lack of opportunities in their own countries, or a fortress Europe, fortress North America policy that will deteriorate into the use of brutal force. We can see the intimations of that already. A rich world that pulls up the drawbridges from all but the global elite will sooner or later engender a terrorist response. To that, military force can provide no lasting answer. We have no weapons to deal with suicidal would-be martyrs. There has to be a better way.

There is a moral dimension too. It is quite simply morally unacceptable for the inhabitants of the rich world to use up such a large proportion of the world's limited resources of energy, water, and land, and to lead such a wasteful and expensive way of life when so many have almost nothing—one billion people living on less than a dollar a day.

Democratic governments need the support of their citizens to embark on radical changes of policy. In this, they are greatly helped by the non-governmental organizations that bring together committed individuals. There are many effective NGOs concerned with the plight of the poor. In the US, as a recent article in Newsweek pointed out, donations by foundations and private individuals to developing countries exceed government aid several times over.

It was the inspiration of the churches and some private individuals that began the Jubilee 2000 movement to lift the burden of debt from some of the poorest countries in the world. The moral conscience of society is very much alive. Active campaigners are questioning corporations about their environmental responsibilities, and about the consequences of protecting patents, especially for essential medicines. In consequence, pharmaceutical companies have allowed some of their products to be made available at cost in developing countries.

Globalization brings with it not only fateful moral choices. It also offers an opportunity for a network of governments, NGOs, firms and individuals to be formed that will one day construct a new model of a socially just global economy. It is an opportunity which we neglect at our peril.

NOTES

1. US Farm Bill, approved by the Senate, 8 March 2002, and signed by President Bush 13 May 2002. The bill raised subsidies by up to 80 per cent a year.
2. 'Everything but Arms' was a European initiative. It took the form of an amendment to the European Union's generalized scheme of preferences (GSP) (Council Regulation (EC) No. 416/2001 published in the official journal No. L.50 of 1 March 2001).

REFERENCES

Allison. A. and Yavlinsky, G. (1991), *Window of Opportunity. The Grand Bargain for Democracy in the Soviet Union* (London: Pantheon).

Bush, G. W. (2002), Speech at the UN International Conference on Financing for Development. Monterrey, Mexico 22 March.

Dahrendorf, R. (2000), 'Politics and Society.' Millennium Lecture given at the University of Reading. February.

Europa (2001), *Europa Year Book 2001* (Brussels: Europa).

Forster, E. M. (1924), *A Passage to India* (London: Edward Arnold).

HMSO (2000), *Elementary World Poverty: Making Globalisation work for the Poor* (London: HMSO Cmd. 5006).

HM Treasury (2002), *Tackling Poverty: A Global New Deal* (London: HM Treasury).

Milward, A. S. (1984), *The Reconstruction of Western Europe 1945–51* (London: Methuen).

Newsweek (2002), 'Charities that Hate to Just Give', *Newsweek*, 4 April.

OECD (2000), *The OECD Guidelines for Multinational Enterprises* (Paris: OECD).

Stiglitz. J. (2000), 'What I Learned from the World Economic Crisis', *New Republic*, 17 April.

World Bank (2002), *Building Institutions for Markets* (Oxford: Oxford University Press).

16

Conclusions: In Search of a Global Moral Architecture

JOHN H. DUNNING

16.1 INTRODUCTION

The purpose of this concluding chapter is to draw together some of the concerns thoughts and opinions of the contributors to this volume. The three basic questions each was asked to address—from his or her particular perspective—were: (1) How far, and in what respects, does the current stage of global (or globalizing) capitalism (GC) fall short of its social acceptability and long-term sustainability? (2) To what extent can its deficiencies be attributed to a dearth, or misuse, of moral capital, or an inadequacy of incentive or control mechanisms to minimize moral failure? (3) What might be done to upgrade the moral attitudes and behaviour of individuals and the ethical mores of the institutions of GC—and of the system itself—without sacrificing its many economic and social benefits, and, most noticeably, the freedom of choice and lifestyles it offers its participants.

In perusing through the past fifteen chapters, the reader cannot fail to be impressed by the broad consensus among the authors on these issues. At the same time, there were several important differences of perspective and emphasis as to the underlying causes for the sub-optimal performance of GC; the extent to which upgrading the ethical foundations of its institutions may help to reduce these failures; and whether there are any universally acceptable 'rules of the game' and enforcement characteristics (North 1990) that could be applied to this task.

In trying to summarize these points of agreement and difference, I divide this chapter into three main sections corresponding to the three questions posed. In doing so, I should remind the reader again that my task has not been to consider alternatives to global capitalism, as an economic system—however commendable such a quest might be. Rather it has been to consider ways in which its structure, content and effects may be made more user friendly, more democratic and more inclusive. In particular, I have been interested in identifying whether the idea of a universal or global ethic to ensure a more responsible global capitalism (RGC) has any merit in it. Or, even if it is accepted as a laudable objective, is it likely to have any practical effect in a world in which so much political, ideological, and cultural diversity exists? Finally, what role might the attitudes and patterns of behaviour urged by the leading religious persuasions and philosophies of the world play in this task?

16.2 THE CHALLENGES AND OPPORTUNITIES OF GC

There was a general agreement among the contributors that RGC, as a unifying, integrated system of cross-border economic governance, does not exist today—and probably will not exist (even assuming this to be a desirable goal) in the foreseeable future. What has evolved—and particularly so over the past two decades—is, first, a geographical spread of the endemic characteristics of capitalism, to such an extent that upwards of four-fifths of the world's population live under some form (i.e. their own particular variety) of capitalism (Hall and Soskice 2001); and second, an increasing number of linkages which are binding these 'family resemblances'[1] together into a cohesive network of cross-border activities, or what Alan Hamlin in Chapter 3 refers to as 'almost globalization'. Such linkages may be economic (e.g. trade and foreign investment) technological, political, or cultural.

Neither is there any debate that the present state of GC (to use a shorthand expression to describe what is happening) is below its optimum—in that it is not fully achieving its objectives or functioning in a way that is acceptable to all, or even the majority, of its participants. While most contributors readily acknowledge its many advantages—not only as a wealth creating system[2] but as a facilitator of the geographical spread of 'good' technology, ideas, and customs, all, to a greater or lesser extent, were concerned about some of its less welcome consequences. These tended to be grouped into four categories:

1. The goals and values it endorses, and the attitudes and behaviour it fosters.
2. The methods by which wealth is created.
3. The asymmetry of economic power and the large disparities in the distribution of resources, capabilities, and income it engenders.
4. The commodification of markets and homogeneity of consumption and life-styles.[3]

Many examples of the downsides relating to these categories, at both an individual firm and societal level, have been set out in previous chapters. In this connection, some authors were careful to distinguish between the sub-optimal moral and ethical actions deliberately taken by the institutions of GC, and those which insufficiently take into account their likely moral or ethical outcomes.

Whatever the legitimacy of these views, it may be questioned how far they can solely, or even mainly, be attributed to the geographical spread of capitalist regimes. For alongside and bound up with the globalization of markets have occurred dramatic and far reaching technological changes, the liberalization of markets and the emergence of new players on the world economic scene. It is these events, as much as globalization per se, which have heralded in a new era in the capitalist system—which is more complex, more uncertain, and more volatile than those iterations which preceded it.

From the viewpoint of the theme of our volume, the three distinctive features of the present stage of capitalism which we have identified are (*a*) the critical importance of knowledge as the main wealth creating asset of firms and society, (*b*) the growing role of inter-firm co-operative alliances, and networks of alliances, as organizational modalities for such wealth creation,[4] and (*c*) the geographical widening of the radius of economic activity, with all its demands on individual and social relationships, including, as Michael Novak puts it in Chapter 11, those to do with 'an appreciation of the dignity of cross cultural differences'.

It is the overwhelming consensus of the authors in this volume that these changes in the content and impact of GC are requiring not only a reconfiguration and upgrading of the resources and capabilities of its constituent institutions, and that of societal rules and enforcement procedures, but also of the kind of the 'C'-type moral virtues spelled out by John Dunning, Jonathan Sacks, and Khurshid Ahmad.[5] With increasing standards of living in most parts of the world, the choice of how best to allocate scarce resources widens; and, as it does, it increasingly involves value laden issues, and takes on a moral dimension which cannot be ignored or swept aside.

As the substance of this volume has shown, the moral challenges of twenty-first-century capitalism—not least its global dimension—are addressed to each of its constituent institutions *viz.* the market, national or regional governments, supranational entities, and civil society. Questions relating to the fairness, democratic legitimacy, and social inclusiveness of GC and its impact on human dignity demand attention at both a micro and a macro level. Each institution has its own responsibilities—the extent and content of which may well depend on the particular form of capitalism in operation.[6] The debate on how far the rules of the game of GC are to be held accountable for the moral failures associated with economic transactions, and whether these reside in the attitudes and behaviour of persons independently of the rules, is one of the more hotly debated topics addressed by several authors, to which we shall give more attention later in this chapter.

In short then, the globalization of economic activity is part of the emergence of a knowledge-intensive, alliance-based capitalism, which is not only leading to a new range of economic benefits and costs, but is demanding more attention be given to the co-ordinating properties of relationships—at the level of both individual and societal transactions and collective economic activity. However, the widening geographic scope and specialization of many types of cross-border commercial activity is bringing its own moral obligations. These primarily arise as a result of a new awareness of inter-country cultural (and other) differences, which, in the short run at least, tend to raise the transaction costs of co-ordinating or harmonizing the appropriate incentive structures and enforcement instruments for the management of both market and non-market transactions.[7]

16.3 THE MORAL DIMENSION

16.3.1 Morality Matters

The contributors to this volume were unanimous in the view that the content and impact of RGC strongly reflected the moral ecology and ethical infrastructure underpinning its constituent institutions; and that this view was independent of whether one took a specifically religious view of its source, or its determinants; or indeed, whether one believed that the moral basis, scope, and evaluation of its institutions as set out by Alan Hamlin in Chapter 3, were endogenous or exogenous to those institutions.

At the same time, it was stressed that the significance and content of the values of individuals, and the ethics of commercial and political institutions was substantially context specific over both time and space. Most notably, it reflected both the changing features of capitalism, and its constituent institutions, and the existing moral ecology related to these features (Preston 1979; Scruton 1998).[8] In the words of Michael Novak, 'Each age of capitalism depends on a moral culture which nurtures the virtues and values by which its existence depends' (Novak 1982: 56). It was, however, generally agreed that the attributes of contemporary capitalism—as summarized in Section 16.2 of this chapter—demanded a re-evaluation and reprioritization of the moral standards of all kinds of transactions; and of the formal and informal enforcement mechanisms regulating or fostering these standards. In this respect, several authors—notably Alan Hamlin—asserted that, because they allowed only limited freedom of choice to the participating agents, past institutional systems economized on virtue—in the sense that they were dominated by narrowly focused incentives and assumed individuals to be motivated solely by their self-interest.

16.3.2 Moral Failures

It was widely acknowledged that the moral architecture of the current state of GC left much to be desired; indeed Michael Novak believed that it was 'in crisis'. In his reproduction of John Dunning's 'circle of failures' of GC, Hans Küng in Chapter 6 identified some of the components of moral or ethical failure, and how these might lead to a sub-optimal allocation of resources and capabilities, and an unacceptable pattern of behaviour of market and non-market institutions. In turn, such behaviour was likely to raise the transactional and production costs of economic activity; and in consequence lessen the potential benefits of GC.

Another way of viewing the problem is to identify the deficiencies in the behavioural infrastructure underpinning the stock of wealth creating resources and capabilities, and how these are deployed. Though it is difficult directly to separate the moral and ethical ingredients of social capital, it is relatively easy to identify, and indeed to evaluate, some of the latter's features (e.g. by use of crime, marital breakdown, and similar data), and to assess their changing significance over time (Fukuyama 1996, 1999).

Each of the contributors presented their own inventory of moral values and virtues—including those unique to RGC—and argued that, for the most part, the current canon of such values and virtues fell short of what was needed.[9] However, while there was a broad consensus on the content of these, there was less agreement on (*a*) the *relative* significance of each, (*b*) their practical interpretation, (*c*) the trade off between virtues when the practice of one *might* mean a sacrifice of others (e.g. compassion cf. justice, fairness cf. creativity, individual freedom cf. social responsibility) and (*d*) the appropriate enforcement mechanism for upgrading them. As regards (*c*), the conjugate principle, enunciated by A. L. Lowell in 1932 that 'nearly every principle has its converse which is equally sound depending on the circumstances in which it is applied' is no less relevant today.[10] As regards (*d*) this is likely to vary according to the particular virtues being considered. The most effective modality for inducing more compassion and generosity is likely to be very different from that of reducing criminal behaviour or upgrading social justice.

16.3.3 Universal and Context Specific Moral Virtues

While the majority of contributors acclaimed the idea of a global or universal moral code put forward by Hans Küng in Chapter 6, or a 'pervasive unity in the higher values' suggested by Jack Behrman in Chapter 5, there was some scepticism as to the extent to which these could be put into practice. Indeed, Hans Küng himself believed that, to be effective, the words expressing such an ethic 'had to be filled in meaning' (p. 148), or, at least, their practical application had to be embedded within a specific cultural context. It was also accepted that no constellation of rules, virtues, and practices adopted by an individual or society should be forcibly imposed upon another; although, by influence and example, one culture might well be persuaded to embrace at least part of the moral ecology of another.

Several authors emphasized the need to accept a global ethic in governing the behaviour of market and non-market actors, in order to to minimize the transaction costs of some cross-border activities, e.g. trade, fdi, technology transfer, and internet communications. Nevertheless, many of the lesser virtues necessary to the efficient workings and acceptability of GC—and particularly those to do with extra-market transactions—were likely to be strongly context specific. Here it is interesting to draw a parallel between the complementarity of the globalization and localization of the operational strategies of MNEs and their counterpart in the moral and ethical domain. The 'glocalization' of morals looks to formulate universal guidelines of behaviour, while respecting the richness of cultural pluralism and the dignity of difference between nations.

Such an approach is favoured by several authors in this volume, and by such scholars as Donaldson (1996) and Friedman (1999). Indeed, included in his listing of the cardinal virtues underpinning RGC, Michael Novak, in Chapter 11, highlights the need for cultural humility. He, like other contributors writing from their own particular perspectives, was not seeking a single—as opposed to an 'open'—society, advocated by Karl Popper;[11] and certainly not a uniformity of all values but rather 'a family of resemblances'. Again, in the words of Alan Hamlin 'All that is required for a single integrated society is a rough sort of convergence to a set of norms and political cultures that are sufficiently shared and sufficiently deeply embedded to sustain common institutions' (Chapter 3, p. 73)

Khurshid Ahmad takes up this point by suggesting that any acceptable vision of a future global society should hinge on the concept of 'reasonable pluralism', which itself demands, in the words of the philosopher John Rawls (1999) a 'diversity among reasonable people with their different cultures and traditions of thought, both religious and non-religious' (Rawls 1999: 11).

Whatever the views of the contributors on the role of universal v. contextual values, and the relevance of John Dunning's pyramid of virtues (described in Chapter 1), there was a general agreement that the advent of twenty-first-century capitalism demanded a more holistic and integrated approach to its wealth creating and distributive activities, and the need for both market and non-market institutions to revamp their moral ecologies. As to the former, there was a need to consider moral and ethical issues as part of the economic, social, and cultural approach to making GC more acceptable; to look at both the religious and non-religious aspects of morality; to view the role of each of the institutions in global society as complementary to each other; and to consider the ways in which formal and informal rules and enforcement mechanisms might best be addressed.

As to the particular moral attributes which merit special attention, several authors identified the growth of cross-border co-operative ventures as requiring those of trust, honesty, and forbearance, commitment (as well as technical competence); and that of operating in a global village, with huge differences between the haves and have-nots, those of compassion, tolerance, generosity of spirit and human decency—as well as the economic uplifters of aid, trade, and fdi. Such examples—and these are just a few given in the book—affect all strata of society, and, together with a holistic approach by the drivers of improved GC, will, over time, almost certainly lead to a virtuous circle of upgrading moral values, and to a convergence—at least of the fundamental or core values—described by several authors in this volume.

As well as accepting the benefits of cultural pluralism, several contributors pleaded for a more realistic appreciation of the value of subsidiarity in institutional decision taking. Jack Behrman and Joseph Stiglitz in particular, advanced the case for a greater local participation in the deployment of imported cultures, ideas, business management, and political markets. Michael Novak argued that cross-border economic integration should be guided by the concept of solidarity, while Jonathan Sacks believed that cross-border relationships, particularly those involving the 'softer' virtues, e.g. compassion and generosity, should be of a co-operative or covenantal form rather than hierarchically managed from a dominant cultural perspective.

Again, in a search for an acceptable moral architecture for a particular society, much can be learned from the ways in which successful international corporations balance the advantages of harmonizing the strategy of their global operations while encouraging their affiliates not only to make an input into this strategy, but, where appropriate, to adapt it to meet the particular (and often changing) needs of their local suppliers and customers, and the policies of host governments.[12]

Over a longer period of time, most contributors agreed that any substantive upgrading of moral capital would require a change in the mindsets and values of individuals, and of the attitudes and actions of the institutions with which they might be involved. In Chapter 5, Jack Behrman identified the seven conditions which in his view, are necessary if such a transformation is to take place. Other contributors, e.g. Robert Davies writing from a business perspective, pinpointed the likely motives for any change of heart. They include a culture shock (such as occurred on 11 September 2001) legislation, codes of conduct, moral suasion, and a greater awareness of the value and responsibility of behaving in a more socially acceptable way. Such a change of heart may be expressed directly, e.g. by the actions of individuals, or groups of individuals, in their capacity as consumers, workers, and shareholders; or by their participation in institutions, e.g. civil society, corporations, and governments.

Richard Falk (in Chapter 12) is a strong advocate of *globalization-from-below* in the form of action taken, by one or other of the constituents of civil society, to influence the future actions, or counteract the (perceived) adverse effects of past actions of MNEs, governments, and supranational agencies. Other contributors believed that, at the end of the day, it is only by a series of agreements and coalitions between the various participants in GC, e.g. governments and firms, NGOs and consumer groups, and supranational entities that social standards can be advanced. All contributors accepted that more information and a greater sense of awareness is needed about the extent to which the outcome of economic action is affected by its moral infrastructure.

At the same time, there was a general consensus that, in the domain of ethics, governments should consider themselves as civil rather than enterprise associations (Falk, Chapter 12). In this respect, they should not act as moral tutors or seek to impose particular behavioural standards, but should both provide a culture in which moral virtues, spontaneously embraced by individuals and families, can flourish; and establish and monitor the appropriate rules, incentives, and enforcement mechanisms for this to be so. This, however, does not mean that governments should not directly take ethically related actions. These might be both to reduce negative virtues (e.g. anti-drug legislation or actions to reduce terrorism) and implement positive virtues. For example, as Gordon Brown demonstrates in Chapter 14, the US initiated Marshall Plan for European recovery in the early post-World War II period had a strong moral content. No less today the Millennium Plan of 2002 and the views expressed by Shirley Williams regarding the responsibility of the rich nations of the world to provide the relief of poverty—whether for reasons of virtuous self-interest (Novak 1991) or 'proper selfishness'[13] or those of pure altruism, require co-ordinated actions by the institutions of RGC at a national and supranational level.

16.3.4 Upgrading Moral Standards

The question next arises; accepting that there are inadequacies in the moral architecture of GC, how can these be overcome—or at least mitigated? Alternatively, how best (if at all) should the moral resources and capabilities of its constituent actors be increased or utilized more effectively? How far, indeed, should they be? For it is a fact that any increase in moral capital (which includes a reduction in the depletion of such capital), or a fall in the transaction costs of moral failure almost certainly involves the use of scarce resources. This being so, it is important to accept that any examination of the consequences of the enhancement of moral virtues or ethical behaviour must be viewed *net* of the next best use of the resources and capabilities expended on it. It is also worth emphasizing that the consequences of such upgrading may take time—and often a long time—to filter through, and may generate a variety of spill-over effects.

Finally, as we have already suggested, when assessing the effects of upgrading any particular moral virtues, the possible deleterious affects on other virtues and on the overall stock of moral capital needs to be considered. Isaiah Berlin, for example, has vigorously argued that systems of moral values can rarely, if ever, be internally consistent. Indeed, in one of his books, he referred to the 'tragic choice' individuals sometimes had to make in balancing or reconciling such virtues as liberty and equality, resistance and prudence, justice and mercy, tolerance and order (Berlin 1991).

But with these provisos in mind, there was unanimity among the contributors that if GC is to become more socially responsible, its moral ingredients do need upgrading. Four points, in particular, stood out from the discussion on this topic.

1. Though there is some merit in distinguishing between an 'individual' versus an 'organizational' approach to upgrading moral conduct—is it individuals or institutions which need to be reformed? Viewing the issue from a dynamic perspective it is clear that the attitudes and behaviour of each interacts with the other. For example in the corporate world, a particular business manager (or group of managers), by his (or their) views, may affect the morality of the investment *et al.* strategies of the companies which employ him (or them).[14] However, over time, a corporate ethic is built up which, in turn, influences the attitudes and behaviour of its labour force. This is why, in Chapter 7, Brian Griffiths, to name just one contributor, cannot accept Friedrich Hayek's assertion (1988) that the capitalist system—which includes the moral ecology of the institutions which underpin it—is autonomously determined, and (by inference) globalization is a natural and spontaneous process independent of any reference to the beliefs or conduct of its constituent individuals (Hayek 1988). David Loy in Chapter 10 takes a different, but related tack. He believes that the institutions of GC should be judged, at least in part, by the effect they have on the values and conduct of individuals. Thus even though the market may be neutral in its intentions, if it encourages such personal dis-virtues as greed, ill-will, envy, and the commodification of extra-market activities, it should be regarded with some concern.

Other contributors, notably Jonathan Sacks and Michael Novak, prefer to put their faith in the voluntary upgrading of the morality of persons. They believe that at the end of the day, morality resides in people; even though 'morals in action' are largely played out by a collection of people making up an organization—which

Jack Behrman prefers to denote as ethics. It is by the upgrading of these values and their incorporation into the decisions of firms, consumers and labour groups, civil society, governments, and supranational agencies that the kind of moral imperfections depicted in the 'circle of failures' set out on p. 146 will be lessened.

2. In their discussion of the modes by which the moral ecology of GC, may be enhanced, many contributors distinguished between the *top-down* and *bottom-up* approach identified by John Dunning in Chapter 1. Khurshid Ahmad believes that, like the debate on the exogeneity or endogeneity of moral virtues, both approaches need to go hand in hand, each reinforcing the other. The balance between the two is again likely to be strongly contextual, varying between (*a*) the kind of moral virtues one wishes to enhance, (*b*) the types of transactions and economic activities embodying these virtues, (*c*) the individuals and/or institutions engaging in these transactions and activities, and (*d*) at a societal level, the characteristics, e.g. stage of development, size, and cultures, of the communities concerned. In the case of traditional and highly religious societies, for example, the upgrading would be more likely to be achieved by informal rules of behaviour and such enforcement mechanisms as reputation, shame, and guilt; whereas in liberal market economies, more emphasis is likely to be given to *top-down* incentives and penalties imposed by governments, including such measures as laws, regulations, and moral suasion imposed by governments to discourage 'bad' and encourage 'good' behaviour.[15]

Depending on the relative importance and prioritization they attached to particular virtues or moral standards, the contributors to this volume veered towards either a *top-down* or *bottom-up* approach. Thus, those expressing the views of more authoritarian religious persuasions e.g. Judaism and Islam, tend to place more faith on rules and regulations designed to empower or coerce their citizens and institutions to be more dutiful and to be more active in promoting social justice; though they also acknowledged the value of more informal incentives and sanctions established by other subsidiary authorities, notably families or local communities. By contrast, the Christian perspective, as enunciated by Jack Behrman, Brian Griffiths, Michael Novak, the Buddhist view as articulated by David Loy, and the non-religious view of other contributors, e.g. Richard Falk, is to place more emphasis on the moral responsibilities of individuals or small groups by relying on informal rules and enforcement mechanisms.

Here is an area calling out for more serious empirical research. We have already averred that GC as it is now evolving is offering more freedom of choice to its participants—and choice involving a higher moral content—than any previous economic system. At the same time, because of the inherent interdependence of economic transactions—be they adversarial or co-operative—it follows that with individualism comes responsibility. Up to a point such responsibility can be coerced—at least to reduce anti-social behaviour e.g. with respect to crime, bribery, drug abuse, terrorism, unacceptable business practices—but, at the end of the day, it is the informal codes governing the attitudes and conduct of particular individuals and firms which must be tackled. As we have already suggested, this requires a change in the mindset of the actors involved, which, itself, can only be brought about by either a renaissance in religious mores, or, as Deepak Lal would argue, a return to the values of traditional societies, but for both to be reconstituted to meet the needs of the twenty-first century. Acting *in loco parentis*, however, non-market institutions, and especially governments and supranational entities, may pursue policies, on behalf of their constituents, which themselves promote social goals. The Marshall Plan of the post-war period and the Millennium Agreement on debt relief to the poorer countries are examples of such policies.

3. What next of the instruments—the mechanisms—for upgrading moral standards? Using a Northian model (North 1990, 1999) one can perceive of a spectrum of the rules of the game affecting individual or institutional behaviour, ranging from a legislative, or command approach (thou shalt *or* shalt not!) through a variety of incentives and sanctions, to formal contracts, guidelines, and codes, to more informal measures based on a compact, covenant, or gentle-man's agreement, and finally to moral suasion and example. The appropriate instruments and enforcement techniques are likely to be strongly contextual—varying *inter alia* according to the virtues or types of behaviour one wishes to encourage, and the existing moral and ethical ecology of individuals, institu-tions, and the countries involved. But most contributors believed that, in the long run at least, the unique features of GC are likely to require a more covenantal approach to upgrading moral values[16]—although, with respect to the activities of societal importance (e.g. the environment, (moral) education, safety, and the redressing of the asymmetry and/or ill effects of economic power), it was thought that states will continue to make use of a range of *top-down* instruments.

4. Finally, to better understand the kinds of issues just identified, several con-tributors turned to consider the sources of moral behaviour—or the absence of same. What are the drivers of moral behaviour? The consensus of opinion among the contributors was that in our contemporary world, there were four such driv-ers *viz.* (*a*) tradition, (*b*) religious faith or philosophy, (*c*) reputation and status, and (*d*) societal (or peer) values, as each was affected by changes in technology, religious belief and economic and political events. Deepak Lal, in Chapter 2, places a great deal of emphasis on the importance of tradition as a factor fash-ioning the ethical mores of pre-industrial societies, and many Far Eastern coun-tries today. By contrast, he suggests, that in Western societies, although there may be a heritage of religious influence, it is the secularisation of individual and soci-etal mores, which seem relevant to promoting economic welfare, that is currently holding sway. Nevertheless the majority of contributors believe that religion, both as a source of values and as an empowering or enforcing instrument of these values, still remains important;[17] and it is to this issue that we now turn.

16.3.5   Religion and Morality

Jonathan Sacks in Chapter 9 refers to 'religion as the axial of civilization'; and as 'the greatest source of wisdom'; and there is little doubt that in the post-industrial era, religious teachings have been one of, if not *the* predominant origin(s) and driver(s) of behavioural mores. This is not to suggest that faith in a supreme deity is, or ever has been, a *necessary* prerequisite to the kind of moral ecology promulgated by that faith—though many of the adherents, particularly those of monotheistic religions, would claim this to be the case—but that the major faiths and philosophies have been the most influential tutors of moral standards. Moreover, each of the religious persuasions highlighted in this volume have been actively proclaiming their codes of conduct for 2000 years or more, over which time most major civilizations have flourished and then floundered or undergone their own creative destruction.

The other, and from our particular perspective, the most unique, feature about the major religious persuasions is that they are globally oriented. 'Go into the world and preach the gospel' was the command of Jesus Christ;[18] and it is no less true of the teachings and philosophies of the other major faiths and philosophies that have spread throughout the planet. In Chapter 11, Michael Novak recalls that by far the largest proportion of the six billion persons on the planet claim allegiance to one or other of the religious persuasions, and seek to live their lives by the moral precepts set out by several contributors to this volume—and particularly by the apologists of Christianity, Islam, Judaism, and Buddhism, in Chapters 7 to 11.

Indeed, I believe that, in many respects, we already have the makings of a global moral architecture to meet the challenges of global capitalism; and far more so than we have any consensus on the appropriate global economic or political governance systems. Though, in the pursuance and advance of particular economic, political, and cultural activities, particular interests of many hundreds of global organizations already exist, there is no overarching order of global governance—and none seems likely to arise in the near future. As we have already suggested, this is as much to do with differences in attitudes and values about such 'goods' as sovereignty, justice, participation, subsidiarity, reputation, and forms of government, as anything to do with the merits of upgrading moral behaviour or ethical standards *per se*! If it is, then, the case that the religious (and for that matter many non-religious) persuasions *do* have a common global morality to offer, surely one should be able to harness the contents of this morality to promote a more socially inclusive and sustainable GC?

Of course, herein lies the rub! To what extent *de facto* do the major religions speak with a single voice? The almost certain answer from the man in the street would be 'very little'. 'Look', he might say, 'at the contemporary religious-related conflicts in the world, e.g. between Christianity and Islam, Islam and Judaism, Hinduism and Islam and so on—not to mention a myriad of disputes and intellectual wranglings of an intra-faith kind.' However, when one examines the avowed tenets of the major religions—as opposed to the pronouncements and actions of many of their adherents (which incidentally embrace many cultural and otherwise diverse traditions)—this is not the case. C. S. Lewis in his book *The Abolition of Man* (1978) recalls that all the great religious leaders and philosophers throughout history have believed in the concept of absolute values and that certain moral attributes are really true and others really false. Moreover, as portrayed by Brian Griffiths, Jonathan Sacks, Khurshid Ahmad, and David Loy in this volume, there is a great deal of agreement about the content of the core or higher moral virtues which must be at the heart of a more responsible GC. *Inter alia*, all the faiths believe that, to better achieve this goal, the institutions of GC need to give much more attention to enhancing the quality of relational capital, and to better recognize that the promotion of economic goals in an ethically acceptable way is in the long-term interests of all.

Admittedly, as we have already pointed out, there are differences in the relative significance attached to particular virtues, of the practical interpretation of these virtues, and how an unwillingness or incapacity to uphold them should be judged or dealt with. There are also differences of opinion about the merits of the particular contents of GC: the Islamic religion, for example, takes a very different view of the role of interest than does that of Judaism or Christianity. In respect of their heritage, each of the religious communities outlaws or discourages the production or consumption of different goods and services by their adherents, while, at the same time, they insist upon certain patterns of behaviour in the workplace or in commercial transactions. These differences, most of which are as much in evidence today as in years past, would suggest that any full convergence in the content or interpretation of the constellation of moral virtues by the various religious entities is unlikely in the foreseeable future. But neither should it necessarily be sought. For as Michael Novak puts it, the 'dignity of such differences is entirely acceptable—indeed beneficial—in a family of resemblances'.

At the same time, each of the contributors emphasized the need for more dialogue and deliberation between all those concerned with the moral ecology of RGC; and that, without compromising their own beliefs, the individual religious faiths should develop and better publicize their common views and visions, more clearly emphasize their spiritual solidarity and practical concerns on every possible occasion, and better demonstrate their shared concerns and humanity. Several contributors condemned any kind of fundamentalism, be it market or religiously, based. Most echoed Robert Fogel's plea for an upgrading of the spiritual dimension to wealth creating activities (Fogel 2000); while others argued for a more holistic approach which, at the very least, tries to establish and promote the lowest common denominator of the various religious values and norms.

16.4   RECIPES FOR ACTION

16.4.1   The Prerequisites for Action

Having evaluated the role upgrading the moral ecology of both individuals and institutions might play in 'making globalization good', several of the contributors to this volume turned their attention to possible ways in which this might be brought about. In reading between the lines of the many thousands of words written, I cannot but conclude that the main challenge facing GC is not that of a lacunae of 'what to do', or even 'what should be done', but how best to motivate the relevant individuals and organizations to take the needed action. One senses that, notwithstanding such events as 11 September 2001 and, more recently, the exposure to a wide range of unacceptable business practices (described by Robert Davies in Chapter 13), there is still little real sense of urgency among governments, corporations, and the man in the street about the need to upgrade global ethical mores. Nor does there appear to be a general awareness of the interconnection between the dysfunction of personal morality and social unrest in various parts of the world, and what is happening in the global market place. Admittedly, international gatherings (such as the Earth Summit held in Johannesburg in August 2002), religious organizations, and some NGOs do their best to bring this to our attention, but, all too often, as various contributors have pointed out in their chapters, the worthiness of their cause is not backed up by the logic of their arguments. Moreover all too frequently, their adversarial stance to globalization is counterproductive to the covenantal approach to reducing its moral and other failures, as advocated by Michael Novak, Khurshid Ahmad, and Jonathan Sacks.

This being so, it is, perhaps, not surprising that several authors felt somewhat cautious in suggesting specific recipes for action. Nevertheless, some interesting suggestions and pointers were offered; and we shall discuss these with particular reference to (*a*) the individuals, organizations, and societies to whom, or which, they were addressed, (*b*) the character and content of the proposed action (whether it is superficial or substantive, general or particular), (*c*) the particular moral or ethical virtue(s) involved, and (*d*) the time frame of the action. Once again, we shall emphasize that the various suggestions must be interpreted in the context of the specific situations facing the target individuals and institutions.

But first, as Jack Behrman reminds us, before any productive action can be taken—whether it be of a *top-down* or *bottom-up* kind, four basic conditions must be met; and, as we have hinted, we believe that more attention needs to be given to increasing awareness and understanding of these conditions. They are:

1. A real dissatisfaction with the present situation; an acknowledgement that there *is* a crisis in the moral ecology of GC as a system and of its constituent parts.
2. A vision (or dream) of how RGC can best be made more economically efficient, socially responsible, and morally acceptable.
3. A recognition of the resources and capabilities available to achieve these goals and how these may be enhanced and deployed in an optimum way.[19]
4. A genuine will and commitment to take the desired action.

To these conditions, we might add one other, *viz*:

5. The availability of the appropriate enforcement instruments, and, where required, the ability and willingness of the implementing organizations to effectively co-operate with each other.

How might an increased awareness of the need for such conditions be created? In his analysis of the development of corporate social responsibilities and corporate values, Robert Davies identifies five triggers or reactions to the ethical challenges to contemporary business.

These are:

1. The push of regulatory compliance e.g. with respect to dubious accounting standards, or other questionable unacceptable business practices.

2. The market signals sent out by the stakeholders in wealth creating activities (e.g. customers, employers, investors, etc.).
3. Reputation or status pull—where companies are motivated to behave well to protect or enhance their reputations, to reduce moral risks and/or advance their dealings with other firms.
4. Societal ethics, in the form of the more critical attitude towards such practices as bribery, corruption, fraud, and irresponsibility.
5. The impact of shock and crisis, where in Mr Davies' words, 'there is scandal revelation, disaster or loud and embarrassing protest'.[20]

Each of these triggers, or some combination of them, can help to reduce moral failure of business transactions and upgrade or prevent the depletion of the relational capital of enterprises.

It can be readily seen that these drivers could be equally applied to the other institutions of GC and to individuals participating as consumers, employees, entrepreneurs, investors, statesmen, bureaucrats, or voluntary workers.

16.4.2 Implementation at an Institutional Level

At a Corporate Level

This has been dealt with at some length by Robert Davies, and by several other authors, notably Hans Küng, Michael Novak, and Brian Griffiths.[21] These writers justify society's demand for a socially responsible corporate leadership as a *quid pro quo* for various forms of privileges e.g. patent protection offered to corporations by society. They believe that encouragement should be given to this task—which they aver is entirely consistent with the main objectives of business[22]—both by the appropriate *top-down* incentive structures and formal rules of national governments, and by self-enforced codes of ethics. Examples of such codes include *The Guidelines to Multinational Enterprises* issued by the OECD (OECD 1999) and the *Global Compact* initiated by the Secretary-General of the UN in 2000, which is geared towards establishing an ethical framework within which both businesses and interest groups can pursue their various goals.

Most certainly, however, the East Asian crisis, the transitional difficulties Russia has experienced in creating a market economy, and the exposure of several major business scandals in the US, have added force both to the demands for more transparency and accountability, and to tighter controls by national governments over unethical business transactions. It has also lent support to the increasing power of consumers, institutional investors, and labour unions in their pressures on corporations to embrace a more value-based approach to their goals and strategies. It has signalled the need for enterprises to widen their concept of social responsibility away from acts of philanthropy to those embedded in a network of partnerships, and geared towards aligning profitable business strategies and practices with the effective management of broader social issues. It is questioning the merits of short-termism in business relationships.[23] In the view of Robert Davies, it is only if and when these challenges are met that the business community will gain the legitimacy and effectiveness necessary for it to play its full, proper role in responsible GC.

Civil Society

Global companies are only too aware that the delegation of some kinds of decision taking to their foreign affiliates—and particularly those which require an appreciation of local demand and supply situations, and business cultures—is becoming increasingly important to their overall competitiveness. So it may well be with respect to any non-market reaction to the global (or regional) spread of capitalism. Social democracy indeed demands participation and ownership at a level as near as possible to those affected by any economic or political decision taking.

This is why, among other reasons, civil society (which includes all kinds of NGOs, as described by John Dunning in Chapter 1) can and has played an important role in promoting a more socially acceptable and participatory GC. In his chapter, David Loy refers to civil society as 'an oxygen of publicity to affect the values of global capitalism' (p. 248). Joseph Stiglitz in Chapter 4 believes that the participation of a healthy civil society and the involvement and commitment by particular interest groups at a local level is an essential pre-requisite to successful economic transformation. Shirley Williams in Chapter 15 points out that several NGOs played an important role in encouraging governments to adopt the Jubilee 2000 programme; while Khurshid Ahmad asserts that a strong network of voluntary associations is an integral part of the Islamic economic scheme of things. At the same time, as Deepak Lal and other commentators (e.g. Robertson 2000) have noted, NGOs, however well intentioned, can also conduct their affairs in a thoroughly undemocratic manner, and, by their tunnel vision, misguided advocacy and aggressive tactics, bring about—or attempt to bring about—a less efficient and/or a less socially acceptable distribution of resources and capabilities than that currently existing.

In his discussion of the political relevance of global civil society in Chapter 14, Richard Falk offers a proposal for a unifying ideology that, in his opinion, is capable of 'both mobilizing and unifying the disparate social forces that constitute global civil society, and providing the political energy necessary to advance the quest for a greater moral responsiveness within the wide orbit of global market activities'. In doing so, he advocates that more attention should be directed to reconfiguring the content of the political agenda by a series of reforms which may lead to the evolution of more consensus-related societies within which GC may be housed. On pp. 294–6 he lists eight elements of such a consensus, all of which, he believes, can be best advanced by a strong *globalization-from-below* thrust which might act as a counter-weight to the economic power of MNEs and the neo-liberal policies of national governments and supranational entities.

While most of the other contributors to this volume would have little difficulty in endorsing these views, I believe they would also assert the need for the constituents of civil society to be subject to the same rules of conduct as those required by other institutions of GC; and for these to be upheld by self-enforcement mechanisms, or regulatory measures of one kind or another.[24] Perhaps most important of all is the need to encourage more constructive dialogue and discussion between the NGOs, business enterprises, and governments as part of a collaborative effort to enhance the quality of GC. In this connection, it is a step forward that some of the leading NGOs are signatories to, and participating in, the *Global Compact* earlier described.

One final feature of that part of civil society which consists of institutions such as the family, the community, and voluntary associations, is that they are not only training grounds for such virtues as commitment, reciprocal altruism, and trust, but are also places where relationships tend to be more covenantal than contractual. An important difference between these two kinds of relationships is, while the former tend to be held together by an *internalized* sense of identity, kinship, and loyalty, the latter are maintained by a set of *externally* imposed incentives and sanctions (Sacks 1997: 63). If, and where we have suggested, such relationships are likely to become more important as globalization progresses, then these institutions of civil society need to be sustained and nurtured.

16.4.3   States and Governments

The role of governments in helping to promote a moral ethos of its constituents, which is geared towards promoting the kind of capitalism they perceive comes closest to the wishes of (the majority) of its citizens cannot be exaggerated.[25] It is just not true that in every respect the sovereignty of national governments is undermined by global capitalism. As Shirley Williams points out in Chapter 15, most human beings do not move about the world in the way that capital and technology does. Apart from a small 'global elite' identified by her, they are location bound; and, because of this, they look to equally location bound national governments to protect their interests.

As in the past, the role of government is twofold. The first is to set the rules of the game and some of the enforcement mechanisms within which economic transactions can take place in an efficient and socially responsible way. The second is by playing a direct role in the resource allocation process, e.g. by providing, or ensuring the provision of, public goods. As regards the first role, it is true that this has been partly circumscribed by the easier cross-border mobility of some resources and capabilities, in the sense that in their policies to attract these resources and capabilities governments have to take account of those of other governments which are similarly motivated. Such policies, as a good deal of research has shown (e.g. Economist Intelligence Unit 2002) must embrace social and ethical mores. Indeed as Herbert Giersch (1996) has observed, economic morality is itself becoming an increasingly sought after asset by firms in their locational choices.

If this is correct, governments, both national and sub-national, need to give more attention to ensuring that their actions do nothing to undermine economic morality (which is a composite of many of the virtues identified in this volume); and, indeed, initiate policies that offer a more favourable ethical ambience to both their own and foreign firms. The contributors of this volume were also in agreement that the state, through its own enforcement mechanisms, can do much to reduce certain socially dysfunctional and unethical forms of commercial behaviour, and thereby help to counteract the negative virtues of its constituents.

More positively, and accepting the qualifications made earlier in this chapter, governments may act to promote the positive 'C' virtues which several contributors have identified as being essential to meeting Jack Behrman's criteria of the acceptability of GC. This they may do in two ways. First, they may create a social and regulatory environment which discourages the practice of negative moral virtues (e.g. criminal behaviour), while facilitating their constituents to seek ways and means to upgrade more positive virtues. To reiterate an earlier point, we might again quote T. H. Green's words written in 1882: 'The State should promote morality by strengthening the moral disposition of the individual, not by subjecting the individual to any kind of moral tutelage.' Virtually all contributors to this volume agreed with this sentiment. Second, and in line with the second task of governments identified on p. 360, they may take direct action themselves on behalf of their constituents. In Chapters 14 and 15 Gordon Brown and Shirley Williams present their views on the responsibility of richer nations to their poorer counterparts; and the actions which governments of these former nations should take to fulfil these responsibilities. Some of these actions undoubtedly arise out of a spirit of compassion or generosity—virtues shared by all religious persuasions. Others are more a matter of 'virtuous self-interest' in that the successful co-operation (or co-partnership), commitment, coexistence, and (the sharing of the acts of) creation—as identified by Khurshid Ahmad and Jonathan Sacks—in North/South commercial dealings, brings with it benefits for all.

In Chapter 13 Richard Falk distinguishes between the democratic state as an *enterprise* and as a *civil* association. He, and several other contributors to this volume, believe that, in the moral domain, the state should act as a *civil* association, In doing so, one of the ways it can best serve the moral citizenry of most of its citizens is to encourage them either individually or as part of civil society to accept (and indeed fight for the principles of) normative democracy he describes so elegantly. Professor Falk asserts quite strongly that RGC is requiring a realignment of the enforcement mechanisms of national governments. In dealing with market failures, he recommends a strengthening of regulatory regimes, but in the case of social or morally related issues—including the protection of the global commons and the encouragement of civic society—he prefers more normative mandates.

16.4.4 Religious Organizations

As we indicated earlier (p. 355), there is widespread agreement among the contributors to this volume that the informal rules of behaviour and enforcement mechanisms (à la Douglass North), set by the various religious persuasions, have played and (notwithstanding the growing secularization of Western society) continue to play an important part in fashioning the moral citizenry of most individuals, and the ethical behaviour of institutions in the global market place.

This it essentially does by its creeds, edicts, holy books, teachings, and moral suasion, each of which is intended to encourage its adherents to conduct themselves in a way consistent with its beliefs and tenets.

It seems logical, then, that any recipe for action to upgrade the moral content of GC should include a spiritual dimension; and the authors of Chapters 7 to 10, writing from a particular religious perspective, together with Jack Behrman, Hans Küng, and Michael Novak, have spelled out a number of specific proposals as to the ingredients of this role.

Earlier in this chapter I made the point that since most religious persuasions both address their beliefs and philosophies to global society, and recruit their adherents from around the planet, they—as represented by their leaders—are in an excellent position to help formulate a 'globalized' moral code and set of ethical practices which meets both the *criteria of acceptability* for GC suggested by Jack Behrman, and those of *normative democracy* set out by Richard Falk.

I believe that the contents of any such code should embody similar principles to those set out in a *Global Civil Ethic* proposed by the *Commission on Global Governance* in 1995,[26] but applied more specifically to the challenges of GC. At the same time it should be more inclusive than that of the *Global Compact* suggested by the Secretary-General of the UN: and should more specifically take more account of the cultural diversity in the interpretation of the higher moral virtues and the content and practice of the lower moral virtues, than does the *Global Ethic* enumerated initially by the *World Council of Religions*—now called the *Council for a Parliament of the World's Religions.*[27]

There are, of course, numerous international inter-faith organizations and educational institutions which regularly network with each other, arrange seminars, conduct dialogues and issue publications on matters of social justice, development, and economic systems.[28] These usually are NGOs which operate on very low budgets. In consequence, I think it is true to say that none has a particularly high profile among the major institutions of GC. However, in the last two or three years, moral issues have been accorded a considerably higher priority on the economic and political agenda. For example, religious leaders are now asked to participate in discussions with senior business leaders and statesmen at the annual meetings of the *World Economic Forum.* A number of high profile individuals, such as the Prince of Wales and the Archbishop of Canterbury in the UK, James Wolfensohn, President of the World Bank in the US, Crown Prince Hassan of Jordan and HH The Dalai Lama are also lending their support to the promotion of inter-faith understanding.

Notwithstanding these developments, several authors strongly believe that the common moral word[29] of the leading religious faiths needs to be better articulated, publicized and more focused. It is also clear from the pronouncements of some religiously oriented research organizations and pressure groups that the unique economic and other characteristics and consequences of GC are not properly or fully understood. Nor are the long-term implications of implementing some of the proposed measures to combat the (perceived) downsides of GC often addressesed out. Too often, well-meaning individuals and institutions are persuaded to pronounce views or take action on the basis of partial or unsubstantiated evidence or half-truths. Only if there is more education geared towards promoting a holistic appreciation of the benefits and costs of GC, and a willingness to accept that there are no easy solutions to increasing the former or reducing the latter without bringing about adverse consequences of the kind described by several contributors to this volume.

One proposal which I put forward in a lecture given in 1998 (Dunning 1998), and which has been endorsed elsewhere in this volume, is for an annual or biannual meeting of a group of the world's religious and spiritual leaders—rather like that of the Group of 8 in the economic domain—to be convened. The brief of the Group would be to identify, promote, and monitor a set of common ground rules and enforcement mechanisms for upgrading the moral ecology of GC; and to provide information about, and undertake research into, the interface between moral and ethical values, cultural diversity, and the content and consequences of GC. An alternative course of action might be for the UN to set up a high level Commission on the Moral and Ethical Implications of Globalization. The Commission might be supported by a Secretariat which would collect information, undertake research and give advice, e.g. via publications, conferences, and media presentations to both religious organizations and the participants in GC. One model for such an entity might be that of the Commission on Transnational Corporations set up by the Economic and Social Council in 1972 (UN 1974).

How much common ground is there between the major religions as to the moral challenges of GC? What are the differences? How fundamental are they? How far can these be resolved or the dignity of those holding them be preserved? What part does—indeed should—religion play today in identifying and prescribing moral virtues and patterns of ethical conduct? Are the challenges of globalization demanding a reappraisal or adaptation of the role of religion as a moral mentor? Can (or should) spiritual precepts and teaching play a more important role in upgrading the quality of co-operative (and particularly) covenantal relationships? What of the interaction between the religious teachings and practice and that of the beliefs and actions of civil society? These are just a few questions which deserve more serious scholarly attention and public scrutiny than they currently receive.

While it is understandable that the practicability or effectiveness of these proposals should be treated with some scepticism, it is worth recording that history provides many examples of an upsurge or reconfiguration in religious beliefs and practices which have helped enhance the moral attitudes and values of individuals, and, through them, the ethical conduct of institutions. Some examples have been set out by John Dunning, Deepak Lal, and Michael Novak. However, it is also to be observed that frequently the influence of religion was most strongly felt in times of political turmoil, or economic crisis, or when religious dogma and customs were themselves under threat. Such events provided a sense of immediacy both to reappraise the value of particular virtues, and their likely impact on the social content and consequences of economic activity. The question of interest is whether we are in such times today.

I would like to make two other final points. The first is that it might be argued that it is not the task of religion to uphold any particular economic system, but rather to promote the kind of values which help individuals to enjoy a healthy, fulfilling, and meaningful life. While several contributors to this volume would appear to be sympathetic to this view, most would also aver that, in the absence of any viable alternative economic system, religious teachings and practice can better enable RGC to attain its goals, and, by improving the moral climate, it can fulfil a useful function.

The second point is that our plea for the upgrading of the moral capital of the institutions of GC no less applies to the various religious faiths. While, as this volume has amply illustrated, the teachings of these persuasions offer a useful template for both individual and societal behaviour, there is little doubt that neither in the past, nor at present, are these teachings put into practice by many of their adherents. Religious belief *per se* is no panacea for immoral or unethical conduct. None of the contributors to this volume, I suspect, would endorse the attitudes and actions of some religious sects, or, indeed, extreme fundamentalists within their own faiths. To more effectively embrace the common virtues identified by Christianity, Judaism, Islam, and Buddhism—the four religions covered in this volume—there is an urgent need for the organizations promulgating these virtues to put their own houses in order, and to better persuade their adherents to conduct themselves in a way their founders would have expected. Unless this is accomplished, then much of the advocacy set out in this volume will be of no avail, and the dire predictions made by Samuel Huntingdon in his *Clash of Civilizations* (Huntingdon 1996) will become a real possibility.

16.4.5   Individuals

Finally, I would offer a brief comment on possible action which might be addressed to individuals. As has already been indicated, individuals act in various capacities in the global economy—as consumers, workers, investors, and as participants in civil society and political markets and the social democratic process—and, at the end of the day, it is the collective wish of individuals which should determine the goals and contents of capitalism and the actions taken to achieve or complement these goals and content.

Already, in several places in this volume, a distinction has been made between the moral ingredients of global capitalism *per se* (as, for example, illustrated in the 'circle of failures' on p. 146), and those which make up the wider moral and ethical ecology of individual societies. Although, conceptually, it is possible to separate the two types of morality, we believe it makes more sense to consider the former as part of the latter; in other words, efforts directed to increasing the general social capital of society will almost certainly lead to an enhancement of the moral virtues underpinning the economic activities of RGC. This is particularly likely to be so in the case of personal attitudes and behaviour. In consequence, the emergence of GC is compelling societies wishing to derive the most benefit from it to reconsider the composition and strength of their moral and ethical armouries *in toto*. Those like truth, integrity, prudence, honesty, reciprocity, mutual forbearance, compassion, for example are not only, or even mainly, the exclusive concern of GC.

It then follows that the encouragement of these virtues should not only be the responsibility of the institutions of RGC. It behoves society, drawing upon the rich heritage of *all* its institutions, to embrace this role. In doing so, incentives and enforcement mechanisms of both a *top-down* and *bottom-up* variety will play their part. They may be geared to meet short-term or long-term goals. They may be oriented towards both global and local ethically related issues. Included in the former are cross-border efforts to reduce drug smuggling, terrorism, international crime, and the abuse of human rights; and, more positively, the encouragement of an ethos of concern for the (global) environment, a sense of responsibility for the well-being of future generations, and a deeper compassion for those afflicted by ill health, poverty, or natural disasters. Included in the latter are support for families, educational institutions, and religious organizations as the main repositories of spiritual values, and some degree of regulatory guidance over the communications media, especially newspapers and television, which may be tempted to cater to the lowest common denominator of moral standards.

Several contributors, notably Jack Behrman, Michael Novak, and Jonathan Sacks touch upon these issues in their chapters, and offer useful pointers of how the moral and social conscience of individuals may be better alerted and energized.

16.5 A CONCLUDING NOTE

How then might one view the future of global capitalism? Drawing together the main points of consensus among the contributors to this volume we conclude, first, that morality *does* matter; second, that any upgrading in moral virtues and ethical behaviour can only be achieved if there is a paradigm shift in the mindset of both individuals and the institutions of GC; third, that there *are* some moral virtues or ethical standards which are universal or near universal, but these need to be interpreted in the light of different cultural mores and the benefits of subsidiarity in decision taking; fourth, that attitudes and behavioural mores taught by the various religious faiths are as relevant for economic and political decision taking as they have ever been, and perhaps even more so; fifth, that any action taken to eradicate or reduce the moral failures and/or enhance the moral capital of GC needs to be addressed to the *system* of GC, to its constitutional institutions *and* to individuals and interest groups who, individually or collectively, may help fashion the behaviour of the institutions and workings of the system in a more socially acceptable manner; sixth, that any such action needs a combination of the *top-down* and *bottom-up* approach, and be planned and implemented in a holistic and integrated way, and one involving all members of the global community; and seventh, that different enforcement mechanisms are needed to upgrade particular behavioural norms, but that, in an alliance-based, knowledge-intensive, global economy, the internalized and covenantal form of co-operation is likely to become a more effective instrument than external sanctions.

Should one, then, be optimistic or pessimistic about the future? I personally am in two minds (not so unusual for an economist!). On the one hand—and I think this has been amply demonstrated in this volume—I do believe we have the knowledge, resources, and capabilities to make GC work in a more inclusive and socially responsible manner while retaining—indeed enhancing—its economic benefits. I also sense that there is a widerspread undercurrent of unease and dis-satisfaction, not only with its sub-optimal economic performance but with its moral ecology; and it may well be that these undercurrents will grow and spread and provide a groundswell for more concern and action.

On the other hand, I have still considerable reservations whether, as commu-nities, interest groups, or individuals, we have a sufficient sense of urgency, vision, or courage of our convictions to effectively deal with the huge problems and challenges of GC. Indeed, overcoming moral apathy—and, even worse, moral appeasement—is a major challenge in its own right. It is here where I believe strong leadership of the 'moral globalization from above' kind has a crit-ical role to play. The ingredients of such a role have been touched upon by sev-eral contributors to this volume. They include—to take just three examples—a more ethically based international monetary system (particularly with reference to stemming the volatility of cross-border capital flows and the creation of a new international bankruptcy framework); a more open—and less preferential—trading system but one which better takes account of the particular capabilities and needs, and of the institutional cultural diversities of the poorer and transi-tion countries;[30] and a genuinely internationally co-ordinated effort to reduce disreputable business practices including misleading or dishonest accounting procedures.

In all these approaches—which, between them, add up to a paradigm shift in our thinking about the design and values of contemporary capitalism—I believe the 'global' moral teachings of the religious faiths as well as those of more local cultural traditions have a vital role to play—and should be now directed to pro-moting both morally based globalization from above and morally based global-ization from below. In pursuance of this task, several contributors have called for the religious faiths to take a more and more prominent, active and conciliatory approach in influencing the attitudes and thinking of those in the higher eche-lons of governance. For at the end of the day, it is they that act as a moral stimu-lant for the individuals and communities which they represent; and it is the ambience they create which affects not just our attitudes to, and behaviour in, the global market place, but the very fabric of day to day individual and social relationships.

Some years ago the Cambridge economist John Eatwell asserted that 'the mar-ket was a good servant of the people but a bad master'. I think that most, if not all, the contributors to this volume would echo this sentiment in respect of each of the institutions of global (or the globalization of) capitalism, and the system itself. Two centuries earlier, the English philosopher Edmund Burke also made the observation that civil liberty could only flourish if individuals 'put moral chains on their appetites' and that this could only be achieved if society placed a high premium on such virtues as self-restraint, duty, benevolence, encouragement, example, and the development of character.

These two statements sum up the challenges of 'making globalisation good' both to those who set the rules of the game and the enforcement procedures which overarch the value systems determining the creation and distribution of wealth; and the individuals and communities who are the participants and beneficiaries of such activities. And as providers of guidelines to both institutions and individuals, this volume has averred that not only do the teachings of religions and the best of non-religious traditions have a vital role to play, but that these religions and traditions have a responsibility to re-energize their own values and virtues, and promulgate their views and visions with fervour, and at every available opportunity.

NOTES

1. To paraphrase Michael Novak's expression in his discussions of the practicability of a universal moral code.
2. For a recent exposition of the beneficial effects of globalization and poverty reduction, see Dollar and Kraay (2001). Paul Krugman, quoted in Friedman (1999), has also expressed the view that it is only by globalization that the economies of poor countries can be upgraded.
3. Noreen Hertz (2001) puts it in a slightly different way. She argues that we should say 'yes to a market economy: no to a market society' (p. 31).
4. See particularly an excellent quote from the President of the World Bank cited by Robert Davies in Chapter 13 (313–4).
5. In Chapter 1, three—*viz.* creativity, co-operation, and compassion—were identified. To these Khurshid Ahmad (in Chapter 9) added commitment, character, competition, and coexistence; while in Chapter 10 Jonathan Sacks emphasized conservation and covenant.
6. Earlier in Chapter 1 we distinguished between two generic forms identified by Hall and Soskice (2001), viz *liberal market economies*, e.g. UK, US, and Canada, and *co-ordinated market economies* (e.g. Germany, Japan, and Sweden).
7. North (1999).
8. Robert Preston, for example, traces the impact of a series of dramatic societal changes since the time of the Reformation and how these have impacted on moral and ethical mores (Preston, 1979). A slightly different approach is taken by Roger Scruton (1998) who examines the consequences of the successive ages of the Enlightenment, Romanticism and Modernism on the content of moral culture and its enforcement mechanisms.
9. Many other scholars have compiled their own list of virtues. See, for example, those of Bennett (1993), Etzioni (1996), Fukuyama (1996, 1999), and Giersch (1996).
10. Isaiah Berlin (1991) also explored this principle in some depth. In doing so, he saw fewer conflicts in any attempts by society to reduce immorality (and negative virtues) than to promote particular moral values (positive virtues).

11. As for example described and further developed by George Soros (1998).

12. For a case study of the way in which one MNE has leveraged culture-specific events in Russia to its own advantage, see Gratchev (2001).

13. The nomenclature used by Charles Handy and described by John Dunning in Chapter 1.

14. Some examples are highlighted by Robert Davies in Chapter 13.

15. Respectively referred to by Ferdinand Tönnies as *gemeinschaft* (community) and *gesselschaft* (society) type enforcement mechanisms (Tönnies 1955). See also Fukuyama (1999: 8–10).

16. David Elazar has described a covenantal relationship as one which 'expresses the idea that people can freely create communities and polities, people and publics, and civil society itself through morally grounded and sustained compacts (whether religious or otherwise in impetus) establishing thereby enduring partners' (Elazar 1989: 19, quoted in Sacks 1991: 63).

17. Some commentators, e.g. James Piscatori (2002), believe that it is becoming more relevant in shaping both the global political and economic agenda; and, in the case of religious fundamentalism, is not always to the benefit of society.

18. Matthew 28: 19.

19. Recognizing, as we have already said, that such a deployment is not costless and that unless there are positive, net benefits of the actions proposed, it is better not to implement such actions.

20. Several examples of each of these triggers are given throughout this volume, and especially by Robert Davies in Chapter 13.

21. See also an excellent study on the *Social Responsibility of Transnational Corporations* (UNCTAD 1999); and one on *Stakeholder Management and Organisational Wealth* (Post, Preston, and Sachs 2002).

22. See especially the riposte of Brian Griffiths to those economists such as David Henderson (2001) who are sceptical of how far one should encourage businesses to be more socially responsible. To our mind, this debate demands a contextual approach and a proper evaluation of the costs and benefits of other than purely profit maximizing objectives on the part of firms.

23. See especially the views of Richard Sennett (1998) who *inter alia* argues that an undue emphasis on a flexible labour market may lead to a loosening of the bonds of trust, loyalty, and mutual commitment.

24. David Robertson (2000), for example, argues the case for a code of conduct for NGOs—and an attempt to better identify the common position of at least the most significant of these involved in negotiations with governments or supranational entities.

25. We, of course, accept there are other reasons for governments to promote the moral ethos of its citizens.

26. The Commission, set up in 1992, was the brain child of the former West German Chancellor Willy Brandt. It consisted of 28 members—largely statesmen and former government ministers—drawn from several parts of the world. Its terms of reference were to analyse the main forces of global change facing the world community, assess the adequacy of global institutional arrangements, and suggest how they should be reformed and strengthened (Commission on Global Governance 1995: 368). Its report included a section on a Global Civic Ethic which highlighted the need for an enhancement of many of the moral virtues identified in this volume.

27. As described by Hans Küng in Chapter 6. For an examination of the role of culture in economic development, see *World Commission on Culture and Development* (1995). Earlier, the *Stockholm Initiative on Global Security and Governance* (1991) had made useful suggestions on taking the debate about development, the environment, and global governance a step further.

28. Among these one might mention the *World Faiths Development Dialogue, The World Congress of Faiths, The United Religious Initiative, The World Conference on Religion and Peace, The International Inter-Faith Centre, The International Global Strategy Group*, and the *World Council of Churches.*

29. An expression used by Raymond Plant (2001) in his plea for more dialogue and involvement by both Christians and other religious persuasions, which he asserts is a 'central human imperative'.

30. But as Jagdish Bhagwati has recently reminded us, the poorer countries have a responsibility to reduce their own tariff barriers, which *inter alia* are often the cause of their unsatisfactory export performance (Bhagwati 2002).

REFERENCES

Bhagwati, J. (2002), 'The Poor's Best Hope', *Economist*, 22 June, 24–6.

Bennett, W. J. (ed.) (1993), *The Book of Virtues: A Treasury of Great Moral Stories* (New York: Simon & Schuster).

Berlin, I. (1991), *The Crooked Timber of Humanity* (London: Fontana).

CEPR (Centre for Economic Policy Research), (2002), *Making Sense of Globalization* (London: CEPR Policy Paper No. 8).

Commission on Global Governance (1995), *Our Global Neighbourhood* (Oxford: Oxford University Press).

Dollar, D., and Kraay, A. (2001), 'Trade, Growth and Poverty', *Finance and Development*, 38 Sept., 16–19.

Donaldson, T. (1996), 'Values in Tension: Ethics away from Home', *Harvard Business Review*, Sept./Oct., 4–62.

Donaldson, R., and Dunfee, T. (1999), *Ties that Bind: A Social Contract Approach to Business Ethics* (Boston: Harvard University Press).

Dunning, J. H. (1994), *Globalisation, Economic Restructuring and Development*, Raul Prebisch Lecture (Geneva; UNCTAD).

Economist Intelligence Unit (2002), *World Investment Prospects 2002* (London: Economist Intelligence Unit).

Elazar, D. (1989), *People and Polity: The Organizational Dynamics of World Jewry* (Detroit: Wayne State University Press).

Etzioni, A. (1996), *The New Golden Rule* (New York: Basic Books).

Fogel, R. (2000), *The Fourth Great Awakening and the Future of Egalitarianism* (Chicago: University of Chicago Press).

Friedman, T. L. (1999), *The Lexus and the Olive Tree* (New York: Random House).

Fukuyama, F. (1996), *Trust* (London: Penguin Books).

—— (1999), *The Great Disruption* (New York: The Free Press).

Giersch, H. (1996), 'Economic Morality as a Competitive Asset.' In A. Hamlin, H. Giersch, and A. Norton (eds.), *Markets, Morals and Community* (St Leonards, Australia: Centre for Independent Studies): 19–42.

Gratchev, M. V. (2001), 'Making the Most of Cultural Differences', *Harvard Business Review*, Oct. 28–30.

Green, T. H. (1882), *Lectures on the Principles of Political Obligation* (London, repr. 1941): 39–40.

Hall, P. A., and Soskice, D. (eds.) (2001), *Varieties of Capitalism* (Oxford: Oxford University Press.

Hayek, F. A. (1988), *The Fatal Conceit: The Errors of Socialism* (London: Routledge).

Henderson, D. (2001), *Misguided Virtue* (London: Institute of Economic Affairs).

Hertz, N. (2001), *The Silent Takeover* (London: William Heineman).

Huntingdon, S. P. (1996), *The Clash of Civilizations* (New York: Simon & Schuster).

Landes, D. (1998), *The Wealth and Poverty of Nations* (New York).

Lewis, C. S. (1978), *The Abolition of Man* (London: Collins).

Lowell, A. L. (1932), *Conflicts of Principle* (Boston: Harvard University Press).

North, D. C. (1999), *Understanding the Process of Economic Change* (London: Institute of Economic Affairs).

Novak, M. (1991), *The Spirit of Democratic Capitalism* (Lanham, Md., and New York: Madison Books).

Past, J. E., Preston, L. E., and Sachs, S. (2002), *Redefining the Corporation* (Stanford, Calif.: Stanford University Press).

Piscatori, J. (2002), *The Role of Religion in Globalisation* (Oxford: Oxford Centre for Islamic Studies (Mimeo)).

Plant, R. (2001), *Politics, Theology and History* (Cambridge: Cambridge Unviersity Press).

Preston, R. H. (1979), *Religion and the Persistence of Capitalism* (Philadelphia: Trinity Press International).

Rawls, J. (1999), *The Law of Peoples* (Cambridge (Mass).: Harvard University Press.)

Robertson, D. (2000), 'Civil Society and the WTO', *The World Economy* 23(9): 1119–34.

Sacks, J. (1997), *The Politics of Hope* (London: Jonathan Cape).

Scruton, R. (1998), *An Intelligent Person's Guide to Modern Culture* (London: Duckworth).

Sennett, R. (1998), *The Corrosion of Character* (New York: W. W. Norton.)

Soros, G. (1998), *The Crisis of Globalization* (London: Little Brown & Company).

Soule, E. (2002), 'Managerial Moral Strategies in Search of a Few Good Principles', *Academy of Management Review* 27(1): 114–24.

Stockholm Initiative on Global Security and Governance (1991), *Common Responsibility in the 1990s* (Stockholm: Prime Minister's Office).

Tönnies, F. (1955), *Community and Association* (London: Routledge & Kegan Paul).

UN (1974), *The Impact of Multinational Corporations on Development and on International Relations* (New York: United Nations).

UNCTAD (1999), *The Social Responsibility of Transnational Corporations* (New York and Geneva: UN).

World Commission on Culture and Development (1995), *Our Creative Diversity* (Paris: UNESCO).

Index